Boswell in Holland, 1763-1764
is the second of 4 volumes in The Yale
Editions of the Private Papers of James
Boswell to be published as McGraw-Hill
Paperbacks. Other titles in this unique
publishing venture include:

Boswell's London Journal, 1762-1763
(McGraw-Hill Paperbacks 06603, $2.45)

Boswell on the Grand Tour
Germany and Switzerland
(McGraw-Hill Paperbacks 50552, $2.45)

Boswell for the Defence, 1769-1774
(McGraw-Hill Paperbacks 70964, $2.65)

Frederick A. Pottle, the editor of this volume,
is Professor of English and Chairman
of the Department at Yale University. He is
also Chairman of the Editorial Committee
for this series.

A MAP OF HOLLAND

at the time of *Boswell's visit, locating many of the places*

mentioned. REDRAWN BY HAROLD K. FAYE FROM A MAP BY

ROBERT DE VAUGONDY IN HIS ATLAS UNIVERSEL, 1757.

NORTH SEA

Haarlem

Amst.

HOLLAND

Leyden

The Hague

Bodegraven

Leidschendam

Montf

Delft

Gouda

Rotterdam

0   10   20   30
English Miles

Hellevoetsluis

Dordrecht

ZEELAND

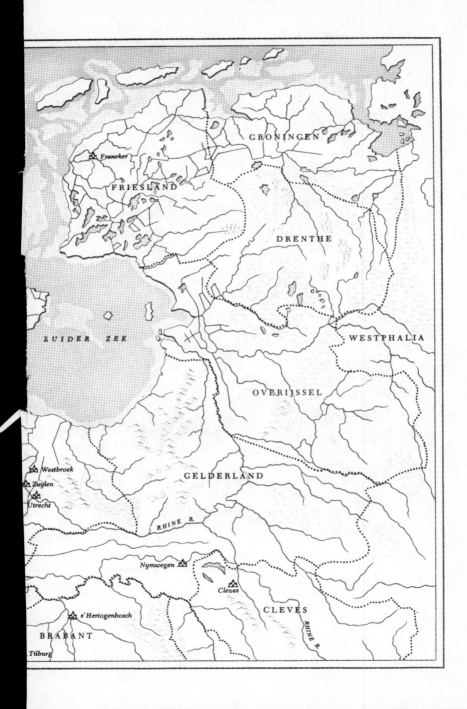

GRONINGEN

⛪ *Franeker*

FRIESLAND

DRENTHE

ZUIDER ZEE

WESTPHALIA

OVERIJSSEL

⛪ *Westbroek*
⛪ *Zuylen*
Utrecht

GELDERLAND

RHINE R.

Nymwegen ⛪

Cleves ⛪

CLEVES

⛪ *s'Hertogenbosch*

BRABANT

RHINE R.

Tilburg

The Tower of the Cathedral and part of the Cathedral Square, Utrecht, as seen from the west, from a wash drawing in ink by J. de Beyer, 1746. Boswell's rooms, which cannot be seen from the artist's vantage point, were at the west end of the Square and facing the Tower.

BOSWELL
IN HOLLAND

1763-1764

INCLUDING HIS CORRESPONDENCE WITH
BELLE DE ZUYLEN (ZÉLIDE)

EDITED BY FREDERICK A. POTTLE

STERLING PROFESSOR OF ENGLISH, YALE UNIVERSITY

McGRAW-HILL BOOK COMPANY, INC.

NEW YORK   LONDON   TORONTO

EDITORIAL COMMITTEE

The Yale Editions of the Private Papers of James Boswell will consist of two independent but parallel series planned and executed for different types of readers. One, the "research" edition, will give a complete text of Boswell's journals, diaries, and memoranda; of his correspondence; and of "The Life of Johnson," from the original manuscript: the whole running to at least thirty volumes. It will preserve the spelling and capitalization of the original documents, and will be provided with extensive scholarly annotation. A corps of expert editors and a permanent office staff are engaged in this comprehensive undertaking, the first volume of which may appear by 1955. The other, the reading or "trade" edition, will select from the total mass of papers those portions that appear likely to interest the general reading public, and will present them in modern spelling and with annotation of a popular cast. The publishers may also issue limited de luxe printings of the trade volumes, with extra illustrations and special editorial matter, but in no case will the trade volumes or the de luxe printings include matter from Boswell's archives that will not also appear in the research edition.

The present volume is the second of the trade edition. The first, "Boswell's London Journal, 1762–1763," was published in 1950.

CONTENTS

LIST OF ILLUSTRATIONS

INTRODUCTION

§I

The editor of a popular or "reading" edition of Boswell's journal is
faced at the start by an inevitable but none the less painful decision: he must harden his heart to the appeal of the subsidiary documents. They are rich and complicated. Besides a fully written
journal for a given period, there may also be a parallel set of memoranda or diary notes, many news-letters by Boswell and many
letters received by him which duplicate or supplement the journal,
and a host of other intimate papers too various to characterize by a
single title. For example, had the *London Journal* of 1762–1763
never been recovered, it would have been possible to construct a
highly readable substitute of at least equal length from Boswell's
daily memoranda and his letters. But no editor with a sense of literary values would *in a reading edition* have relaxed the artful tension of the *London Journal* by thrusting other documents into it,
even though those documents in themselves might make fascinating reading; nor would he print a second parallel volume as a sort
of gigantic commentary on the *London Journal*. In a research edition, an edition intended not to be read but to be studied, a place for
all these papers can and will be found, but in a true reading edition
the most that an editor can do is to present selected snippets from
them in the footnotes; and he must watch himself sternly to see that
he does not overdo even that. And he will feel unhappy about his
exclusions, for these subsidiary papers always contain entertaining
matter and sometimes are more revealing than the journal itself.

In the case of the present volume, an accident otherwise to be
deplored has provided an opportunity for exploiting the other
papers. The *London Journal* ends with the entry for 4 August 1763.
Boswell continued the record in the same ambitious style during

the whole of his stay in Holland, where he went directly from London, but this Dutch journal was lost in his own lifetime. When he left Utrecht in the following June, he packed up many of his papers, including the journal, and left the lot with his friend, the Reverend Robert Brown, to be sent to him in Scotland after his return from his travels. Mr. Brown appears to have entrusted the parcel to a young Army officer, who perhaps carried it as far as London in his cloak-bag. But when the papers arrived at Auchinleck, the seat of the Boswells, the Dutch journal was missing, and earnest appeals for a search which Boswell made to Mr. Brown and others failed to retrieve it. One hesitates, after the casual recovery of a mass of Boswell's letters to Temple in a shop at Boulogne, where they were being used as wrappers for small purchases, to say that any manuscript of Boswell's—especially a large carefully written quarto manuscript of over five hundred pages—is lost beyond recall, but at least Boswell himself finally gave up the Dutch journal and nothing has been heard of it since.

There still remain, however, bales of intimate records for reconstructing his life in Holland. He continued the practice he had begun in London of addressing a memorandum to himself each morning before he put on his clothes, and these memoranda are more trustworthy substitutes for the journal than the London series because he soon fell into the habit of reviewing the events of the preceding day before setting down his counsels for the day ahead. As an exercise in learning French, he wrote a page or two in that language every day. A similar lot of exercises in Dutch has recently been recovered. In order to acquire greater ease and speed in English composition, he also set himself the task of writing daily ten lines of heroic verse. Themes and verses were written rapidly on the first topics that came into his head; and the first topic that came into Boswell's head was likely to be Boswell. He kept a register of letters sent and received, a general expense account, and a special account of sums won and lost at cards. And, finally, a surprisingly large number of the letters which he received and wrote have now come to hand, including several to his confidants, John

Johnston and William Johnson Temple, giving long and detailed reports of his activities.

The volume that follows is for the greater part a substitute for the lost journal, made by fitting together in chronological sequence selections from these miscellaneous papers. As a sequel the reader is then given the entire correspondence between Boswell and the most remarkable person he met in Holland: Isabella van Tuyll (Belle de Zuylen, also known as "Zélide"). This correspondence, which began just as he was leaving Holland and continued intermittently for the next four years, may safely be called one of the oddest series of love letters ever written.[1]

§II

"Substitute" suggests inferiority; and of course there can be no question of the literary superiority of Boswell's fully written journal to his memoranda, his verses, and to most of his letters. But it should be noted that his language exercises, for the very reason that the subject was *not* considered important, sometimes have an ebullience, a gaiety, an inconsequential conversational charm that he never achieved in the formal essays he later wrote; that some of his letters here printed are up to his best standard of writing; and that Belle de Zuylen's are masterpieces of epistolary art. And there are various kinds of superiority. The printing in *Life* and *Reader's Digest* of a history of the Boswell Papers, and the presentation by the B.B.C. of an hour's broadcast on the same subject, indicate the extent of popular interest in what I may venture to call the Boswell saga. And the response to the publication of *Boswell's London Journal, 1762–1763* shows that this interest is not confined to the saga, not excited merely by a detective mystery. Hundreds of thousands of people have testified an inclination to *read* the Boswell Papers. Now, it is quite certain that the present volume gives a much better general impression of what the collection is like than any single journal can; gives the reader as fully as it is possible to give him through the medium of print the feelings the editor himself had in

[1] It has been given its own special Introduction, p. 293.

exploring the papers for the first time. The reader may imagine that he is handling the papers themselves: that I have merely stacked them in chronological order for him, and have given him a pair of spectacles that make the most crabbed hand legible and unfamiliar languages intelligible. If I continue to stand at his elbow, it is only to answer questions.

§III

There is another kind of superiority, too, and it is important. When Dr. Johnson said that it was the biographical part of literature that he loved most, he was not restricting himself to biographies of high literary excellence. He meant that he loved facts about human nature as revealed in almost any kind of intelligible account. If a reader's main interest in the Boswell Papers is biographical revelation, if he wants to know human nature by exploring the mind of James Boswell, he will find the memoranda of this volume more rewarding than any fully written journal. They show Boswell physically and mentally in undress. They are utterly *private* documents: in them Boswell, addressing himself, withholds nothing and exaggerates nothing.

"Pray, pray be *retenu*." "Be quite *retenu*, pious and careful. Amen." "You was a little irregular yesterday, but it was but for one day to see the Utrecht concert. You don't like it, and you're not to go any more." "You did charmingly yesterday. You attended well to everything." "You have struggled, you have conquered." "Be prudent and *retenu*. Never aim at being too *brilliant*. Be rather an amiable, pretty man. Have no affectation. Cure vanity." "Let not Satan tempt you as Cupid." "Write to Temple of *Veuve*. Separate fiery passion. Tip her valet." "Oh, affect not passion and oddity!" "You was so bad as really to think of despairing." "You was direfully melancholy and had the last and most dreadful thoughts. You came home and prayed." "Confused and changed and desperate." "Dreadful." "Gloomy." "Bad." "Very bad. You got up dreary as a dromedary." "You awaked shocked, having dreamt you was condemned to be hanged." "Desperate. This day, *Easter*, rouse. Be

Johnson. You've done no harm. Be *retenu*, &c. *What* am I?" "You
went out to fields, and in view of the tower, drew your sword glittering in the sun, and on your knee swore that if there is a Fatality,
then that was also ordained; but if you had free will, as you believed, you swore and called the Great G— to witness that, although
you're melancholy, you'll stand it . . . "

§IV

"Boswell kept his good resolutions by writing them down, and
redressed his backslidings by copying them out," says Geoffrey
Scott, a witty and not unfair summary of Boswell's life as a whole
but one that should not have been applied to the Utrecht period.
Boswell, who liked to buttress his resolution by times and seasons,
had resolved that he would reform on the day he left England for
Holland. He did. For ten months in Holland he was by heroic effort
modest, studious, frugal, reserved, and chaste. And he almost went
out of his mind.

The miscellaneous papers of the Utrecht period furnish perhaps the best materials extant for a study of Boswell's melancholy.
It was not, as has been carelessly and cruelly assumed, an affectation, an attempt to imitate Johnson. No one who has read the following pages can believe that for a moment. They are of course not
all gloomy. But when they are, they are the record of a soul in torment: groaning, wailing, repining, but also of a soul struggling
and resisting with every resource in its power. The fact is that
Boswell had been subject to fits of depression long before he met
Johnson, from his early boyhood.

He was the kind of neurasthenic who gets no sympathy from
other people because he seems so healthy. His physical machine
was extremely robust and, until he was past middle age, would
stand any amount of punishment. As a matter of fact, he found on
numerous occasions that he could dispel his gloom by sitting up
late or not going to bed at all. What made him at times so desperately unhappy was not the weather, was not lack of exercise, was
not acrimonious juices and lax solids (the diagnosis he obtained

from a Dutch physician), was not idleness, was not drinking, was
not remorse of conscience. It was frustration: frustration of his
overweening ambition by any course of life, whether idle or
methodically industrious, which did not promise to make him a
Great Man *soon;* frustration of his powerful urges to pleasure by
monotony, by unexciting routine. Be good, be prudent, be sober, be
reserved, be industrious, and you will be happy, said his father; and
he copied it down and said it over and over to himself. But suppose
you gave the formula a good hard try and it didn't work? Suppose
you toiled and prayed and hung on by your teeth, and life only got
blacker and blacker until you woke in the morning out of dreams
that you were about to be hanged or that you were actually suffering the agonies of death? Johnson gave short shrift to Boswell's plea
that because he was unhappy when he did his duty he ought to be
granted a dispensation; life, Johnson had long since concluded, was
a state in which much is to be endured and little to be enjoyed. But
knowing that Boswell bore a very heavy burden, he granted him
unfailing charity.

The sudden emergence from gloom, the glorious exaltation
that one sees at the end of the Utrecht period, is as characteristic as
the gloom itself. Boswell never needed a period of convalescence.
Make him somehow a Great Man, send him upon a jaunt in which
he can experience change, excitement, constant agitation, and you
restore him as by a magic infusion. And he will never get so tired
and inelastic that the formula will not work.

§V

The manuscripts from which this book has been compiled are
as follows:

1. Memoranda and Notes for Journal in Holland, 10 August
1763 to 17 June 1764, 157 unpaged octavo leaves, roughly 7 by
4 inches, unbound, nearly all written on both sides. Boswell's
usual procedure is to fill exactly one page per day. In the manuscript as we now have it, there are no entries for 17 April, 30 April,
and 1 May 1764, and none for a number of days at the beginning,

earlier than 15 September 1763; otherwise there is an entry for
every day. Many passages are in French.

2. Journal in Holland, 24 May to 18 June 1764, 32 quarto
pages, numbered by Boswell 537–568, roughly 9 by 7½ inches,
unbound. Some passages are in French. This portion of the Dutch
Journal survives because Boswell wrote it up *after* he left Utrecht.
(See p. 258.)

3. French Themes, 232 quarto pages, roughly 9 by 7 inches,
unbound. Entirely in French. Only a few of these themes are
dated or certainly datable, but since we know that Boswell's
practice was to write one or two pages every day, including
Sunday, it is possible to set up for most of the series a chronology
that cannot be far out of the way.

4. Dutch Themes, 20 quarto pages, roughly 8 by 6½ inches, unbound. The first theme is dated 1 February 1764, and some of the
others are certainly assignable to that month. It is impossible to
tell whether we have all that Boswell wrote or not; the fact that the
last theme is incomplete is not decisive. (See p. 79.) Entirely in
Dutch.

5. Ten-Lines-a-Day Verses. Dated from 25 September 1763 to
16 April 1764 with no gap save for 29 February 1764. (See p. 171.)
34 unpaged quarto leaves, unbound, written on both sides, 9 by 7¼
inches.

6. Upwards of fifty letters sent by Boswell or received by him
between 6 August 1763 and 18 June 1764, and over thirty letters
of later date in, or connected with, the correspondence with Belle
de Zuylen. The letters received by Boswell are of course originals,
as are also the letters from Boswell to Johnston and Boswell to
Temple. (He retrieved his letters to Johnston from Johnston's
executor after Johnston's death; of the letters to Temple he had
asked back all those that he wrote from the Continent, intending
to use them as materials for a book of travels.) One of his letters in
the Zélide correspondence now at Yale is an original, and one
other in that correspondence is printed from an original not at
Yale. (See pp. 307, 342.) The rest are copies made by Boswell.

Many of the letters are in French. There is at Yale a Register of Letters sent and received during the Utrecht period. It is not complete and not entirely accurate, but is often very useful for fixing dates and indicating lost letters.

7. Miscellaneous manuscripts: dialogues at The Hague, addresses made at the Literary Society at Utrecht, expense account, special account of sums won and lost at cards, "portraits" by Belle de Zuylen, &c., &c. These are generally in French.

A relatively small amount of this matter was printed by the late Geoffrey Scott in Colonel Isham's privately printed edition of the Boswell Papers, but the greater part of the contents of this volume now appears for the first time. If completely printed, the documents would fill at least three volumes the size of this. The reader should not suppose that marks of omission indicate a policy of bowdlerization. My object has been, within the covers of a single volume, to present a complete continuous account of Boswell's life in Holland, and also to give a wholly representative selection from the materials, so far as that is reconcilable with a policy of pleasant and fairly rapid reading. My omissions have been made to remove banality and excessive repetition (*some* repetition is essential to the plan), and to focus the narrative by the elimination of minor personages, casual happenings, and trivial obscurities.

The spelling, capitalization, and punctuation have been reduced to accepted modern norms, and abbreviations and contractions have been expanded at will. All quotations in the Introductions and notes, whether from Boswell or other sources, have been standardized in the same fashion.[2] The texts have been broken into

[2] The standard of spelling for all but proper names is *The Concise Oxford Dictionary* (English) and *Kramers' Engels Woordenboek* (Dutch). For Dutch place-names the English edition of Baedeker has been followed. Dutch personal names have been brought into conformity with the standard Dutch biographical dictionaries, except that the English convention of *y* for *ij* and sometimes *ck* for *k* are retained: "Sommelsdyck" rather than "Sommelsdijk." For English and Scots names appeal has been made to *The Dictionary of National Biography*, Mrs. Margaret Stuart's *Scottish Family History*, G. E. Cokayne's *Complete Peerage* and *Complete Baronetage*, Sir James Balfour Paul's *Scots Peerage*, and various other special books of reference.

paragraphs where such breaks make for easier reading. A few clear inadvertencies have been put right without notice. Square brackets indicate words added by the editor where the manuscript shows no defect and where there is no reason to suspect inadvertency on the part of the writer; angular brackets indicate reconstructions by the editor of words lost through defects in the manuscripts (usually holes in letters made by breaking the seal), where the reconstruction is not entirely certain. As in *Boswell's London Journal, 1762–1763,* the notes have been numbered in recurring series of nine, disregarding pages and dates. This device avoids the unattractive typography which results from the use of double reference figures in the text, and eliminates the extensive resetting (every line of text that bears a footnote reference and the first line of every footnote) that is required in linotype composition if the notes must begin a fresh series with each page. Such resetting is expensive, but the stronger objection to it is that it always invites errors.

Documents in foreign languages have generally been given in English translation only. In the case of Boswell's French, this is a clear gain. Though he became fluent in French, he never became really idiomatic or even accurate in that language; and if one substitutes the literal English equivalents, the result is generally good Boswellian English. Belle de Zuylen's writings are a different matter; but one's regret at losing her exquisite French is lessened by the fact that the majority of the versions of her letters here printed are by Geoffrey Scott, and have been thought by exacting critics to be about as accomplished as the originals. The French texts of all but one of her letters to Boswell have been printed and can be found in the second volume of Colonel Isham's privately printed edition of the Boswell Papers; I provide the French text of the one new letter in an appendix to the present volume. To serve as a sample of the whole, I have also given in an appendix the complete French text of one of Boswell's themes written near the end of his stay at Utrecht. The projected research edition of the Boswell Papers (see p. vi) will of course give all these documents in the language in which they were written.

ACKNOWLEDGMENTS

Because of the experimental nature of this volume, I have asked and received an unusual amount of assistance from the other members of the Editorial Committee. The general plan and the mechanics of arrangement were worked out in conference, and all the members later read the completed copy for the printer and helped me reduce it to manageable length. Mr. Liebert provided the artist with the materials for the map, and he and Professor Hilles read the proofs. Our Advisory Committee is so widely scattered that it is not possible to take the advice of all its members in laying out each volume. *Some* members are consulted very actively during the preparation of each volume in the matters in which they possess expert knowledge, and *all* members are requested to review the books as they appear and to give us their counsel concerning general policies to be followed in succeeding ones. Consequently, though it may be assumed that we follow what we believe to be the majority opinion of the Committee, no single member of it can be held in any way responsible for our decisions. Dr. Breuning read the entire book carefully in typescript, furnished us with the charming sketch which appears as our frontispiece, and gave invaluable assistance in explaining local allusions. I also return my grateful acknowledgments to Professor Peyre, Dr. Powell, Mr. Roberts, and Dr. Simpson, all of whom read the proofs and sent me corrections and additions. Professor Peyre has besides put me deeply in his debt by allowing me to refer to his judgment my translations of many passages in the French.

The surviving fragment of Boswell's Dutch Journal, the Inviolable Plan, all but one of the letters between Boswell and Belle de Zuylen, and three others of the letters in this volume were printed by Geoffrey Scott in 1928. The long and difficult manuscript containing the Memoranda in Holland was first transcribed and annotated twenty years ago as a class exercise by Dr. Hale Sturges, then a student in the Yale Graduate School. In the same class, Professor Joseph Foladare reviewed Scott's text of the Dutch

Journal and collected annotation for it. Dr. Charles H. Bennett then reviewed both texts, and made large additions to the annotation of the Memoranda. I have had these unpublished stores to draw upon in preparing the present volume, as well as a spirited translation of the French Themes made for Colonel Isham in 1927 by the late Professor Elizabeth W. Manwaring. To all of them I record my deep obligation. Dr. Bennett has also read the proofs.

To the following I acknowledge indebtedness for help with particular problems which I wish I had room to specify: Professor Jean Boorsch, Professor Franklin Edgerton, Professor Curt von Faber du Faur, Dr. George L. Lam, Dr. C. A. Malcolm, Professor Georges C. May, Professor Edmund T. Silk, Mr. Alastair Smart, and Mrs. Anne W. Van Lonkhuyzen. Finally, I tender my warm thanks to all the members of the office staff of the Yale Editions of the Private Papers of James Boswell during the last year: Paul Brodtkorb, '52, Mrs. Shirley Cochrane, Mrs. Lucyanna Fitzgerald, Mrs. Louise W. Hine, Mrs. Mary Jane Hook, Mrs. Marion S. Pottle, Joseph W. Reed, '54, Dr. Marshall Waingrow, Mrs. Patricia B. Wells, and Thomas M. Woodson, '53. Dr. Waingrow has laboured to insure the accuracy of the text in all its stages, has collected materials for annotation, and is mainly responsible for the index.

F. A. P.

Yale University, New Haven
18 January 1952

*Une personne sensée qui lirait nos lettres ne vous trou-
verait peut-être pas trop raisonnable, mais pour moi,
je ne veux pas gêner mon ami: tout ce que sa singularité
voudra me dire sera bien reçu. L'imagination est si folle
que quand on se permet de dire tout ce qu'elle dicte, il
faut bien dire des folies. Et quel mal à cela? Je n'en vois
aucun.*—BELLE DE ZUYLEN TO BOSWELL, 16 FEBRUARY 1768.

Boswell in Holland, 1763–1764.

SKETCH OF BOSWELL'S LIFE TO AUGUST, 1763. James Boswell was the eldest son of Alexander Boswell, a Scottish judge who took the style Lord Auchinleck from the family estate in Ayrshire. A bashful, studious, puritanical boy up to the age of eighteen, he became suddenly robust and restless, took to frequenting the theatre and mooning after actresses, and then horrified his father by running away to London and making his submission to the Roman Catholic Church. Lord Eglinton, an Ayrshire neighbour of Lord Auchinleck's living in London, salvaged him from Romanism by making him a Deist and a rake, and suggested to him that a good way to obtain perpetual London residence (which was what young Boswell now desired above everything else in the world) would be to secure a commission in His Majesty's Foot Guards. Lord Auchinleck, who wished him to follow the law, flatly refused to purchase him a commission in the Guards, but after two unhappy years of struggling with him, agreed to let him go up to London again to see if he could obtain a commission through influence. Boswell's extended account of this period of residence in London, long believed to have been lost, was discovered by Professor C. Colleer Abbott at Fettercairn House in 1930 and was first published towards the end of 1950.[1] It is a remarkable study of the mind of a young man trying to free himself from parental domination and at the same time struggling to define to himself the implications of an unusual literary gift.

Boswell had gone up to London hoping to transform himself from a raw and romping boy into a high-bred man of pleasure, a

[1] *Boswell's London Journal, 1762–1763*, McGraw-Hill Book Company, Inc. (New York), and William Heinemann, Ltd. (London), 1950.

combination of Addison, Steele, and West Digges, an actor famous
for his impersonation of Macheath in *The Beggar's Opera.* Though
he had the liveliest sense of piety and was strict in attendance at
divine service, he prided himself on his intrigues with actresses and
women of fashion, and in his frequent street affairs was ashamed
rather of the grossness of his debauchery than of its immorality.
But on 16 May 1763 he met Samuel Johnson, whose writings he
had long admired; and though the meeting made no great immediate impression on him, his continuing association with Johnson caused him soon after to develop a bad conscience about these
affairs. He opened his heart to Johnson, was strengthened in his religious faith, and got Johnson to outline a plan of regular study for
him. The quest for a commission having proved futile, as Lord
Auchinleck had predicted it would, he finally gave in to his father
and consented to apply himself to the law. It was agreed that he
should spend one winter in study at Utrecht, and that he should
then be allowed to visit Paris and some of the German courts.

Johnson, who had become very fond of him, made a two-days'
journey with him to Harwich to see him off. "My revered friend,"
says Boswell in *The Life of Johnson,* "walked down with me to the
beach, where we embraced and parted with tenderness, and engaged to correspond by letters. I said, 'I hope, Sir, you will not forget me in my absence.' JOHNSON. 'Nay, Sir, it is more likely you
should forget me than that I should forget you.' As the vessel put
out to sea, I kept my eyes upon him for a considerable time while
he remained rolling his majestic frame in his usual manner; and at
last I perceived him walk back into the town, and he disappeared."
That majestic frame and that revered voice, save for recollection,
were to be absent from Boswell's journal for two years and a half.

The selection of Utrecht as the place for Boswell's legal education had nothing odd or unusual about it. Scots law, a totally different system from the English, makes a great deal of Roman law; and
as the Dutch were the great masters of Roman law, it was usual for
young men preparing for the Scots bar to complete their education
in Holland. Boswell's father and grandfather (also a lawyer) had

studied at Leyden; Utrecht had been selected for Boswell on the advice of Sir David Dalrymple, a common friend to Boswell and his father and a mediator of their differences. Though the main objective was the law, it was hoped that he might also improve himself generally in culture and in manners; and for this purpose Utrecht was thought to offer advantages over Leyden.

Since at least his seventeenth year, Boswell had been subject to recurring fits of intense depression; and he left England with gloomy forebodings. One of the few hopeful features of the situation so far as he was concerned was that he had relatives in Holland. Lord Auchinleck's grandmother, Veronica, Countess of Kincardine, was a Dutch lady of the noble family of Sommelsdyck, and the representative of the family (Lord Auchinleck's second cousin) still lived at The Hague.

From this point on, a selection from the documents themselves may be allowed to tell the story.[2]

MONDAY 1 AUGUST 1763 [London] ... Resolve now study in earnest. Consider you're not to be so much a student as a traveller. Be a liberal student. Learn to be reserved. Keep your melancholy to yourself, and you'll easily conceal your joy.... Prepare like Father.... Mark this and keep in pocket. You are not to consider yourself alone. You have a worthy father whose happiness depends on your behaving so as at least to give no offence, and there is a prudent way to save appearances. Be reserved and calm, and sustain a consistent character. It will please you when high, and when low it will be a sure comfort, though all things seem trifling; and when high again, 'twill delight. So when you return to Auchinleck, you'll have dignity....

TUESDAY 2 AUGUST.... Bring up journal. Be with Johnson at two and dress at three. Give out linens, and pack up, and be

[2] See pp. x, xiv for a detailed description of the various kinds of documents used, and a statement of the editorial method followed.

placid, and get into grave humour for journey, and write out instructions, &c.

[UNDATED MEMORANDUM] Set out for Harwich like Father, grave and comfortable. Be alert all along, yet composed. Speak little, make no intimates. Be in earnest to improve. It is not you alone concerned, but your worthy father. Be reserved in grief, you'll be so in joy. Go abroad with a manly resolution to improve, and correspond with Johnson. Be grateful to him. See to³ attain a fixed and consistent character, to have dignity. Never despair. Remember Johnson's precepts on experience of mankind. Consider there *is* truth. Consider that when you come home with a settled composure you will enjoy life much, without exhausting spirits and setting yourself up as a buffoon or a jolly dog. Study [to be] like Lord Chesterfield, manly. You're your own master quite. . . .

[Receipt for passage to Holland]

Harwich, 6 August 1763

Receive on board the Prince of Wales packet-boat Mr. Boswell. Whole   JAS. : : : : : :⁴

FRIDAY 12 AUGUST [Leyden]⁵ ... Don't smoke any more, because it makes you sick and a foreigner need not do it. . . .

[Events of 6–15 August, Boswell to John Johnston of Grange]⁶

Utrecht, 23 September 1763

MY DEAR JOHNSTON,—I find myself at a loss how to begin this letter. As it is my first to you from a foreign country, I should

---

³ "Take care to."

⁴ The signature (presumably that of the purser) is large, handsome, and illegible. "Whole" probably means that Boswell had a room to himself.

⁵ The memorandum for this day was written entirely in French.

⁶ John Johnston, laird of a small property in Dumfriesshire, a young man of about Boswell's own age, was a "writer" (solicitor or attorney) in Edinburgh. Since their first meeting in 1755 in a class in Greek at the University of Edin-

perhaps break off⁷ with a pompous exordium; but a pompous
exordium will not offer me its services. Perhaps, too, I should begin
with an apology for not writing sooner; but this I imagine you
will own is hardly necessary after you have read this page. I am
now fairly begun, and shall say no more on the subject. I shall
give you my history since I set out from London as well as I can.
I tell you beforehand that it is strange and affecting; so do not
be suddenly shocked.

I set out upon my travels with a kind of gloom upon my mind.
My enthusiastic love of London made me leave it with a heavy
heart. It might not have been the case had I been setting out on
an immediate tour through the gay regions of Italy and France.
But to comply with my father's inclinations I had agreed to pass
my first winter at Utrecht, a Dutch university town of which I
had received the most disagreeable prepossessions. Mr. Samuel
Johnson honoured me with his company to Harwich, where he
saw me embark and set sail from Britain. I was sick and filled with
a crowd of different ideas. But we had a good passage, and landed
on Sunday the 7 of August, at twelve at noon. I shall not be tedious
with particulars, but give you the great lines of my story. I went
to Rotterdam, where I met with Mr. Archibald Stewart (Sir
Michael's youngest son), who is settled a merchant there. I was
not much acquainted with him. But he insisted that I should stay
in his house, where I met with every civility.⁸ Novelties enter-

---

burgh, Boswell and Johnston had been inseparable; indeed, though Boswell
called William Johnson Temple (see below) his most intimate friend, he had,
up to the spring of 1763, seen more of Johnston, and had leaned more heavily
on him. He had written the London journal of 1762–1763 for Johnston's
perusal, forwarding it to him by post in weekly parcels. During his last
month in England he had written him no fewer than sixteen letters. The
present letter to Johnston was written more than a month later than the letter
to Temple which follows it, but has been chosen to open the series because it
gives a fuller account of Boswell's misery during the first ten days of his
residence in Holland than does the letter to Temple.

⁷ "Start," "open": a usage now obsolete.

⁸ Stewart was a young man of Boswell's own age or even younger, his father

tained me for a day or two, and then I went to Leyden and passed some days. I began to turn low-spirited, and set out for Utrecht. I travelled between Leyden and Utrecht nine hours in a sluggish *trek schuit*[9] without any companion, so that I brooded over my own dismal imaginations. I arrived at Utrecht on a Saturday evening. I went to the Nouveau Château d'Anvers.[1] I was shown up to a high bedroom with old furniture, where I had to sit and be fed by myself. At every hour the bells of the great tower[2] played a dreary psalm tune. A deep melancholy seized upon me. I groaned with the idea of living all winter in so shocking a place. I thought myself old and wretched and forlorn. I was worse and worse next day. All the horrid ideas that you can imagine, recurred upon me. I was quite unemployed and had not a soul to speak to but the clerk of the English meeting,[3] who could do me no good. I sunk quite into despair. I thought that at length the time was come that I should grow mad. I actually believed myself so. I went out to the streets, and even in public could not refrain from groaning and weeping bitterly. I said always, "Poor Boswell! is it come to this? Miserable wretch that I am! what shall I do?"— O my friend, pause here a little and figure to yourself what I en-

a Scots baronet (Stewart of Blackhall) and member of the Scots bar. He had acquired an unenviable reputation for raking and extravagance, and had been exiled to redeem himself as a man of business. A gay, cheerful, and generous soul, he gave Boswell help at a time when he needed it desperately.

[9] "The usual way of travelling in ... most parts of the United Provinces ... is in *trek schuits,* or draw-boats, which are large covered boats, not unlike the barges of the livery companies of London, drawn by a horse at the rate of three miles an hour" (Thomas Nugent, *The Grand Tour,* 3d ed., 1778, i. 48).

[1] "The Castle of Antwerp" (Het Kasteel van Antwerpen), a hotel which existed on the same spot until 1950.

[2] The lofty tower of the mediaeval cathedral. The nave had collapsed in the seventeenth century, leaving the tower standing alone. See the frontispiece to this volume.

[3] That is, of the English-speaking (Presbyterian) church. His name was Carron; his father was French and his mother English. Boswell later engaged him as French teacher.

dured. I took general speculative views of things; all seemed full of darkness and woe. Tortured in this manner, I determined to leave Utrecht, and next day returned to Rotterdam in a condition that I shudder to recollect. . . .[4]

[Boswell to William Johnson Temple][5]

Rotterdam, 16 August 1763

MY DEAREST TEMPLE,—Expect not in this letter to hear of anything but the misery of your poor friend. I have been melancholy to the most shocking and most tormenting degree. You know the weakness and gloominess of my mind, and you dreaded that this would be the case. I have been at Leyden; from thence I went to Utrecht, which I found to be a most dismal place. I was there entirely by myself and had nobody to speak to. I lived in an inn. I sunk altogether. My mind was filled with the blackest ideas, and all my powers of reason forsook me. Would you believe it? I ran frantic up and down the streets, crying out, bursting into tears, and groaning from my innermost heart. O good GOD! what have I endured! O my friend, how much was I to be pitied! What could I do? I had no inclination for anything. All things appeared good for nothing, all dreary. I thought I should never recover, and that now the time was come when I should really go mad. I could not wait on Count Nassau.[6] I sent him Sir David Dalrymple's letter, said I was obliged to go to Rotterdam upon business of importance, and did not know if I should return.

[4] Other portions of this letter follow on pp. 10, 18, and 30.
[5] William Johnson Temple, an Englishman from Berwick-on-Tweed, had met Boswell in 1755 in that same Greek class of which John Johnston had been a member. The common passions of Johnston and Boswell were Scottish scenery and antiquities; of Temple and Boswell, literature and religion. Temple had gone to Cambridge to study law and had kept chambers in the Inner Temple, London, where Boswell had seen a good deal of him in the preceding spring and summer. When Temple returned to Cambridge in July, 1763, to qualify for holy orders, Boswell had moved into his chambers.
[6] The chief magistrate (Hoofdschout) of Utrecht.

I set out yesterday at twelve o'clock and came here at night to the house of Mr. Archibald Stewart, the gentleman whom Nicholls[7] spoke of. He is a very fine fellow. Though volatile, he has good sense and generosity. I told him my miserable situation and begged his assistance as the most unfortunate of mortals. He was very kind, took me to his house, talked with me, endeavoured to amuse me, and contrived schemes for me to follow.

I am distracted with a thousand ideas. The pain which this affair will give my worthy father shocks me in the most severe degree. And yet, alas! what can I do? But perhaps I should have endured the utmost torment rather than have left Utrecht. But how can a man endure anything when his mind is quite ruined? My mind is just as if it were in a mortification. O Temple! all my resolutions of attaining a consistent character are blown to the winds. All my hopes of being a man of respect are gone. I would give a thousand worlds to have only mere ease. I look back on the days I passed in the Temple with you as on days of the highest satisfaction. And yet, my friend, I cannot but remember that even then we passed many a weary hour. But was not that owing to ourselves? Was it not because we were idle and allowed time to lie heavy on our hands? Alas, what can I do? I cannot read. My mind is destroyed by dissipation. But is not dissipation better than melancholy? Oh, surely, anything is better than this. My dear friend, I am sensible that my wretchedness cannot be conceived by one whose mind is sound. I am terrified that my father will impute all this to mere idleness and love of pleasure. I am not yet determined what to do. Sometimes I think I should no more yield to this than to any other passion. But, indeed, it forces me to yield. It weighs me down. It crushes my spirit. I am filled with shame on account of my weakness. Shall I not be utterly exposed? Shall I not be utterly contemptible?

[7] Norton Nicholls, common Cambridge friend of W. J. Temple and the poet Thomas Gray; one of Gray's favourite correspondents. Boswell had met him in Temple's company on 13 May.

I would fain return to London and shelter myself in obscurity. Yet I would wish to stay some time abroad. I think I shall go to Brussels. It is a gay agreeable place, and may relieve me. I shall wait upon Count Byron.[8] I shall go to the Academy there. But then, what will my father say? GOD ALMIGHTY pity me and relieve me, for I know not what to think. I sometimes have gleams of ease and imagine myself better, and then I resolve to go back to Utrecht and brave the distemper. But I fear it would be impossible. Could I, who have passed my time in the delicate felicity of London and in real spirited life, support a formal Dutch college? My dear friend! Perhaps you will sympathize more with me than I imagine. Perhaps you will think it was rash in me to agree to go to Utrecht, and that after finding it so severe upon me I do right to go to Brussels. If my father would but think so, what would I give! Perhaps I may go back to Utrecht; perhaps I may go to Leyden. But I think I shall first go to Brussels, and perhaps I may grow well. Is it possible that I can ever be well again? Shall I ever be tolerably happy?

Dempster[9] is at Paris. I have written to him and begged to see him at Brussels. He is humane and knows life well. O my friend! what shall I do? Write to me to the care of Mr. Archibald Stewart, merchant at Rotterdam. Remember me with sincere affection to Bob.[1] If Nicholls be with you, present my compliments to him. Talk of me as far as you think prudent. I would fain hope that

---

[8] Not satisfactorily identified, but probably in some way related to Ernst Johann, Reichsgraf von Biron, Duke of Kurland (1690–1772), favourite of the Empress Anna of Russia and virtual ruler of Russia during her reign. In a letter of 31 July 1763 Temple had referred to Count Byron as his father's most intimate friend; in replying to this letter of Boswell's he said he thought Count Byron was at Vienna.

[9] George Dempster, M.P., Scots lawyer and politician, eight years older than Boswell, had for some time been associated with Boswell in his publishing schemes, and was one of his principal literary companions and cronies.

[1] Temple's younger brother, an Army officer on half-pay. Boswell had shared Temple's chambers in London with him.

my mind may yet strengthen. Adieu, my ever dear friend, and believe me ever yours, with the most sincere regard,

JAMES BOSWELL.

Let not this dreadful affair affect you too much. There is no real harm done. I may grow well soon. I can now feel how my poor brother[2] was afflicted. We cannot hear often from each other. Let us endeavour to think of each other, and wait patiently to see what time will produce. O dear! I am very ill.

[Events of 16–*c.* 30 August, Boswell to Johnston, continued]

Utrecht, 23 September 1763

... Good GOD! what distracted horrors did I now endure! Sometimes I thought of going to Berlin, sometimes to Geneva, sometimes to Paris; but above all of returning to London and my dear calm retreat in the Inner Temple. I recollected that Dempster was in Paris. I wrote to him my situation and begged he would meet me at Brussels. Irresolute and fickle every hour, I was for writing a new letter. Mr. Morgan, a North-American who had just taken his degrees in physic at Edinburgh,[3] was making a tour of Holland. I agreed to go with him. We went to Gouda, Amsterdam, Haarlem, &c. I remembered an advice of yours, and did not go but was taken.[4] We then came round by Utrecht, where we stayed a day or two. But it still appeared so terrible that I could not stay.

[2] John Boswell, a lieutenant in the Army, had suffered the first of a series of attacks of insanity the previous autumn. He was at that time about nineteen years old.

[3] John Morgan, M.D., of Philadelphia, founder of the Medical College of the University of Pennsylvania and its first professor; Physician-in-Chief of the American Army, 1775–1777. In his memorandum of 25 August Boswell calls him *un fat bonhomme* ("a coxcomb"). Morgan's journal of his tour from Rome to London, 6 July–31 October 1764, has been published, but his journal of his tour in Holland appears to have been lost.

[4] Johnston had probably advised him to let other people manage for him when he was depressed.

So we returned to Rotterdam. I was now a little better and began to think that I might put up at Leyden. In the mean time I got a letter from Dempster, who had come from Paris to Brussels, sixty-two leagues[5] in thirty hours, a strong proof of his regard for me and generosity of soul. It was hard to think that he had set out before my letter bidding him write first could reach Paris, and so had missed seeing me. I received a letter from Temple imputing my misery to idleness and beseeching me to act a part worthy of a man. . . .

[Received *c.* 25 August, George Dempster to Boswell]

Grand Miroir, Brussels, Monday 22 August [1763]
MY DEAR BOSWELL,—Judge of my love for you and of the regret I feel for your present situation from this circumstance. I received both yours at Paris on Saturday at two o'clock afternoon. By five I was in my post-chaise, and this morning, Monday, at five o'clock of the morning I arrived here, having made a journey of sixty-two leagues in thirty hours. I can't tell you how great my disappointment is at not finding you according to promise here. It is impossible for me to wait till this brings·you, but next post I'll write you a long letter to set you on your legs again. Adieu, thou mass of sensibility![6]

[Received *c.* 26 August, Dempster to Boswell]

Brussels, Tuesday 23 August 1763
I AM NOW, MY DEAR FRIEND, in the last hour that it is possible for me to wait for you in Brussels, and I find myself so circumscribed with regard to the time of my being in Scotland that I cannot bestow another week in a journey to Amsterdam or Utrecht to meet with you. Amidst all my regret for your distress, I cannot

[5] One hundred and eighty-six miles by the eighteenth-century coach route.
[6] The letter ends without a signature.

help feeling a little satisfaction on the complete accomplishment of my prediction. I told you Oxford was a joke to Utrecht.[7] I told you your worthy friend Sir Davy's sense of gaiety and yours would differ; and pray remember I *foretold* that your fund of patience and affectation was too small to bear living among a set of Dutch professors in tartan nightgowns, long pipes—admirers of Voet and of Vinnius,[8] who set a real value on a library of musty books, who consider mirth as a shame and rampaging as a sin, who neither care how they spend their time or what kind of weather it is, provided their sundials, their barometers, and thermometers indicate properly. Besides, let us add to all this your ignorance of their coins and of their language. The brutality and phlegm of the inhabitants, the tedious method of transportation in track scoots[9]—Sir, you may depend upon it, these are sufficient to turn the head of a marble statue and to affect the serenity of a Lord Auchinleck.

But after all, my dear Boswell, these ills are either exceedingly trifling in themselves or become so by the short time to which you will be exposed to them. Consider them as good Christians do misfortunes, as meant to prepare you for a better life in another country. Consider Holland as the dark watery passage which leads to an enchanted and a brilliant grotto. For such is a French academy; and above all, such will you find Paris on your return when you understand the language. . . .

But Boswell, what is to be done? Can you bear this for a couple of months and then go to a French academy—to Angers, to Metz, to Caen? I am sure you will like that manner of life. In the mean time, I should think you might amuse yourself in acquir-

---

[7] Boswell had made a jaunt to Oxford in the previous April and had been extremely gloomy there. See *Boswell's London Journal, 1762–1763*, 1950, p. 244.
[8] Voet and Vinnius were famous Dutch jurists. "Nightgown" in the eighteenth century meant what would now be called a dressing-gown.
[9] *Trek schuits:* see p. 6. Dempster's spelling indicates how the words were usually pronounced by English travellers. A closer approximation to the Dutch pronunciation of *schuits* is found in the "Brooklyn" pronunciation of the English word *skirts*.

ing the French, keeping a journal and writing your friends, and debauching a Dutch girl.

For Gᴏᴅ sake, keep your disgusts secrets. The Dutch are so happy in their own dulness that I fear they can make but small allowance for your dissatisfaction. As you love your father, your friends—as you love Johnston, Erskine,[1] yourself, and me, don't give too much way to your sensibility. Have recourse to our usual scepticism. Remember how much all pleasures depend on the mind, and then, pray, try to Dutchify your immortal soul. Had I been fortunate enough to have met with you, I would have been its tailor. I would have dressed it in a short jacket and one hundred pair of breeches. I would have taught it silence and smoking. I would have reconciled it to dulness and stinking cheese.

Have you forgot your former objects of ambition? Do you know no country in the universe is better worth seeing to a man that has political views? Examine their industry, their commerce, the effects of frugality, freedom, and good laws. Inquire with regard to their methods of levying taxes, in which they surpass all Europe, since they neither restrain commerce nor oppress the poor. Observe the mixture of the monarchical and republican form of their government. Inquire which of these principles does, consider which of 'em ought to predominate.—But for heaven sake, no more sallies into the street. Rather come over to London and return to your former apartments in the Temple. You have done too much to satisfy your father. No mortal can blame you for returning to that place which you find fittest from[2] preserving a *mens sana in corpore sano.* Adieu. Pray write to me immediately at London, where, however, I shall only remain a very few days.[3]

[1] The Honourable Andrew Erskine, younger son of the fifth Earl of Kellie, a lieutenant in the Army, had been closely associated in mirth and rampaging with Boswell and Dempster since the spring of 1761. He and Boswell had published a volume of their own letters to each other in the previous April. See *Boswell's London Journal, 1762–1763.*

[2] One would expect *for,* but the manuscript is clear and sense can be made with *from:* "that place which you find fittest from its having preserved ... "

[3] The letter was sent unsigned.

[Received *c.* 30 August, Temple to Boswell]

Trinity Hall [Cambridge] 23 August 1763
My ever dear Friend,—I received your very affecting letter, and sympathize with you from the bottom of my soul. I sincerely pity the unhappy disposition of your mind, and would give the world to relieve you. But, my dear Boswell, if you pay any regard to your own character, if you have any affection for me, I beg you may endeavour to act a part more becoming yourself. Remember your resolutions before we parted, allow reason to reassume her dominion, think of Johnson, and be again a man.

Recollect what answer you sent me a few days before you left England, when I wrote to you in rather an unmanly style. You told me I was under the influence of the demon melancholy, and that study and reflection would infallibly cure me. I took your advice and am well. Allow me in my turn to prescribe the same regimen to you (which I have a better right to do, having experienced its effects), and I make no doubt of receiving in a very short time a letter very different from your last.

You may take my word for it that your sole disease is idleness, and that when you have once got into any settled way you will find yourself as well as ever. You say dissipation has unfitted you for study. Read six hours a day but for one week, and on the contrary, you will tell me that study has made a perfect pedant of you and spoilt you entirely for jollity and riotous mirth. Here comes in again my old doctrine of habit to convince you that you may still be whatever you please. To talk of relinquishing all hopes of attaining a consistent character and acquiring a name is unmanly and dishonourable. . . .

But why do I talk to you in this manner? You blame your weakness as much as I can do, and are solicitous to conquer it. Only continue to be so, my dear friend, and all will be well.

I am not at all surprised at your quick removes from one place to another. It is the natural consequence of the present state of your mind. However, I would not be long thus, but would certainly return to Utrecht against winter, were it only to oblige my father. Though his notions with regard to some things are not perhaps altogether right, yet he is a sensible, good man, and has nothing more at heart than your welfare. You should gratify him therefore a little, even though it might somewhat punish yourself. You know our situation here is such that we cannot always do what we would. There are many relations and dependencies to which a proper regard must be paid. A father is a character to which much is due. If it be possible, then, endeavour to please him and make him happy. I am sure he would not desire you to stay longer than one winter at Utrecht. . . .

I am here without a soul in college but my brother and one of the dullest doctors in the University. Nicholls left us last week.

I have had the honour to drink tea twice with Mr. Gray;[4] once at Nicholls's rooms and once at his own. I have also since paid him a morning visit, and have met him two or three times at the coffeehouse. He is very civil, and my idea of his greatness is not at all diminished by knowing him. He is the best bred man and the most agreeable companion in the world. I long to know him more.

It gave me much pleasure to find Mr. Johnson accompanied you to Harwich. Pray let me know what passed. . . .

I hope Mr. Dempster will meet you at Brussels. If Count Byron be there, you will mention me to him. Probably he is at Vienna.

Pray let me hear from you very soon, and believe me, my dear Boswell, your truly affectionate friend,

WILLIAM JOHNSON TEMPLE.

[Boswell to Temple]

Rotterdam, 2 September 1763

MY DEAR TEMPLE,—I cannot express the happiness which your letter gave me. I had been so bad as to consider myself good for nothing and utterly contemptible. I have found now the reverse.

[4] Thomas Gray the poet, author of the famous *Elegy*. He lived in Pembroke College, Cambridge.

I wish I could support myself by its recollection in my hours of gloom.

As I imagined Dempster would not come to Brussels without first writing to me, I delayed going thither and took a jaunt through Holland, and returned to Utrecht, where I received a letter from Dempster·telling me that he had left Paris immediately on receiving my melancholy letter and had made a journey of sixty-two leagues in thirty hours to Brussels, where he was extremely disappointed not to find me, but could not wait till I should come. Was not this a high instance of generosity? I assure you, it flattered me much; and I was much vexed to think that he had taken so much trouble without seeing me. However, to find his regard so strong has done me much good. He has since written me a long letter, in which he has given me his advice to stay some time at Utrecht and then go to a French academy. But, like a too lenient father-confessor, he bids me follow my inclinations and allows me to return to my chambers in the Inner Temple, as nobody could blame me for living where I can have *mens sana in corpore sano.* This doctrine I could with satisfaction imbibe and put in practice, were I to yield to my weakness.

But your letter, my friend, rouses my spirit. You tell me that "my sole disease is idleness"; that you was bad; that you applied to study regularly, and are well. I am convinced that you are in the right. But you must make some allowance for a gloomy cast of mind which I unfortunately have.

I like your mentioning six hours a day. To mark out an exact scheme is taking. I am determined to do what you propose. But I waver about the place of my residence. At Leyden I shall be within three hours of The Hague. I shall have the youngest Prince of Strelitz, and Mr. Gordon, Lord Aberdeen's brother, for my companions.[5] At Utrecht I hear of no agreeable companion. Count

[5] The Prince of Strelitz was a brother of the Queen of England. Both he and Gordon were young, he only fifteen and Gordon eighteen. Gordon later became an officer in the Army.

Nassau is a man in years, though very polite. Utrecht has assemblies. But I am told they are most exceedingly dull. Add to this the shocking disgust which I have taken to Utrecht. I would therefore incline for Leyden. But, then, I came over with an intention to stay at Utrecht; and Sir David Dalrymple would not be pleased if I should forsake his favourite place.

What I am now resolved to do is this. I shall go up to Utrecht and stay a week, and force myself to study six hours a day during that time. After that, if I find that I still give a strong preference to Leyden, I will go thither, and I make no doubt but what my father and Sir David will pardon my altering their plan a little. My grandfather and father both studied at Leyden. I have a kind of innate prejudice in its favour. But, my dear Temple! I am very weak and fickle, and am of different minds in the same day. I will endeavour to summon up resolution, and yet will make myself a man.

I am very happy to hear that you have at last got acquainted with Mr. Gray. I hope you will cultivate his friendship and that when I return to dear England you will present me to him.—Mr. Johnson is ever in my thoughts when I can think with any manliness. I keep an exact journal which I shall send to you when I can find proper opportunities. . . . Make my kind compliments to Bob. I rejoice to hear such accounts of him. I ever remain yours,

JAMES BOSWELL.

I am not yet quite myself again. You may observe that I write heavily. I sometimes regret that I left England. Would it not have been better for me to have stayed in the Temple in winter and in Cambridge in summer? I might have formed better into a manly character with you and Nicholls and Claxton.[6] GOD bless you all. I am a benevolent being. I rejoice at the felicity of others, even when distressed myself. Since I am come abroad, I will make the best of it. I will resolve to do well. Encourage me from time to time.

[6] Like Nicholls, an intimate Cambridge friend of Temple; a lawyer and an antiquary. Temple named his third son John James after Claxton and Boswell.

I am sorry to make you pay postage for so poor a letter.[7] I hope to give you better by and by. Continue to write to Mr. Stewart's care.

[Events following 30 August, Boswell to Johnston, continued]

Utrecht, 23 September 1763

... I met with several papers in *The Rambler* describing the wretchedness of a mind unemployed, a peevish and gloomy fancy indulged. I began to think that I had no title to shelter myself from blame under the excuse of madness which was perhaps but a suggestion of idle imagination. I read another of his papers, where he talks of patience as the noble duty of a man and of a Christian; and he pushes fortitude of mind so far as to doubt if "a mind well principled will not be separated before it is subdued."[8] I was roused with so noble an idea of human nature. I met with another paper on the power that a man has over his ideas, and how he may harden himself against being unhinged by little evils; with another where he shows how much happiness is gained by cherishing good humour, and with another where he shows that mental employment and bodily exercise are absolutely necessary to keep our frame easy and well. Thus prepared I resolutely determined to return to Utrecht, to fix myself down to a regular plan, and to persist with firmness and spirit, and combat the foul fiend. I have done so; and thanks to Mr. Johnson, whose precepts (with the favour of GOD, to whom I earnestly prayed to assist me) I am quite well. . . .[9]

[7] At this time, and for long after, postage was paid not by the sender but by the recipient. The rate for a "single" letter (one sheet) from the United Provinces was 10d.; for a "double" letter, 1s. 8d., for a "treble" letter, 2s. 6d. This was a single letter.

[8] No. 32, "The Art of Bearing Calamities": "I think there is some reason for questioning whether the body and mind are not so proportioned that the one can bear all that can be inflicted on the other; whether virtue cannot stand its ground as long as life; and whether a soul well principled will not be separated sooner than subdued."

[9] Boswell lost track of his construction.

[Dempster to Boswell][1]

Dundee, 29 October 1763

DEAR BOSWELL,—I thank GOD for your recovery. I am a complete physician for the spleen, and on the strength and faith of my skill, I foretell you will not only soon be well but you never will have more trouble from that cause. Spleen is like a bullying boy at school: insupportable till he is once heartily thrashed, and for ever after your humble servant. It is but six years since I drubbed the dog to his contentment, and he has never disturbed me since.

Make no apologies for bringing me to Brussels. I seldom give myself much trouble about any one for whom I would not go much farther when much more inconvenient, to assist or relieve. Let it be the basis of a solid and durable friendship, which will produce much good and a great deal of pleasure and fun. And on this last I set a high value.

Pray indulge your sceptical turn. You are already convinced of the insignificancy and uncertainty of things. By scepticism you will soon discover that some things are less insignificant and uncertain than others. Believe me, dear Boswell, Revelation is nonsense. GOD never manifested himself but by his works. Disbelieve whatever the clergy have invented to enfeeble and debase mankind and to aggrandize themselves. My study is to be perfectly moral while I live and indifferent when I die. You can't conceive what magnanimity the very pursuit of these objects inspires. Enthusiasm is madness, superstition folly, and faith a farce.

I only write this to congratulate with you on your recovery, and to assure you of my secrecy. Your letters are smoke long ago,

---

[1] Because of Dempster's departure for London and Scotland, Boswell did not write to him for almost two months, and Dempster's reply, though written promptly, was delayed by various accidents and did not reach Boswell until 26 November. In this case it seems better to depart from the usual arrangement of this volume (which is to print letters to Boswell under the dates on which he received them), and to insert Dempster's next letter at this point.

and what they contained as the shadow that leaves no impression. When I come to London, I'll write you at more length; nay, perhaps indulge you with a dish of politics. Till then, believe me to be, with most sincere affection, your

DEMPSTER.

MONDAY 5 SEPTEMBER [Rotterdam] Set out immediately with little trunk for wagon to Ter-Gouw,[2] and then take *schuit* to Utrecht with *Rambler* to read. Be resolute to try one week six hours' reading, two walking, &c. Mem. Father's " 'od help me,"[3] and try to compose ideas. Act with fortitude.... Be glad you've taken no rash steps. Repress fastidiousness and encourage good humour.

THURSDAY 8 SEPTEMBER [Utrecht][4] Breakfast after having read Ovid and Tacitus, and wait for the tailor and get first a Leyden suit of green and silver. See François and send him to take the house and have it furnished; he will find you all sorts of things.[5] You may have green coverings on your tables and two large candles. Go there this evening. Read much and write journal and persist in your good plan.

[Received *c.* 8 September, Archibald Stewart to Boswell]

Rotterdam, 7 September [1763]
DEAR BOSWELL,—Though you promised to write me so soon as you got to Utrecht, I can easily pardon the neglect, imputing it to

[2] He left his large trunk at Rotterdam "till further orders."

[3] In two other memoranda Boswell counsels himself to remember this remark of Lord Auchinleck's, but gives no further details. ("Mem." in these notes stands either for "remember" or "memorandum.")

[4] Boswell wrote this memorandum in French except for the last two words.

[5] "François" is Boswell's servant, just engaged. His last name was Mazerac. The "house" (Boswell is using the word in the Scots sense of a flat or set of rooms) was in an inn called the Cour de l'Empereur (Keiserhof). A register of transfers and mortgages of the city of Utrecht describes this under date of 28 November 1792 as "a large mansion ... standing on the Cathedral Square opposite the Cathedral tower, having its egress by a certain alley giving on the Fishmarket."

the Dom,[6] bell, psalm-tune, &c., &c. However, I hope you have ere now made yourself master of the town and silenced the *dreadful bell*.[7] Gordon came to me the same day you left this[8] and told me he hoped you would "resolve to *pess* the winter at Leyden. I should," said he, "*mennege* him finely by making him read a little, walk, ride, and talk a little." The more I am in company with Gordon the less proper I think him for comforting you. Last night Gordon, Hay,[9] and I supped together at Mrs. Gennet's, where the two former were once or twice at daggers' drawing. If I had not season-ably interposed and made up matters, I should certainly have seen our friend Hay put his right foot before his left with that grace peculiar to himself.[1]—More of this at meeting.

As you have often told me that in the most trifling incidents of life you are unwilling to determine without advice, I think it my duty as your sincere friend to lay the following plan before you for your way of living at Utrecht.—Supposing you were to follow Dempster's advice to make no more sallies into the streets, you ought to rise generally about eight o'clock or a little before it. So soon as you have huddled on your clothes, open your chamber window and throw your head out, keeping your mouth wide open in order to feast upon the fresh air. In this posture remain for near the space of a quarter of an hour. Then proceed to bodily exercise by dancing and capering about your room for near twenty-five minutes. After spending forty minutes in this manner, devour about a Scotch pint[2] of porridge and milk (if to be got) for break-fast; after which turn up Erskine[3] and study him with attention, considering that every sentence of his you make yourself master of will add at least a year to your father's life and may come to

---

[6] Cathedral.   [7] *Othello,* II. iii. 175.   [8] "This place": a Scotticism.

[9] Not certainly identified. An Alexander Hay of Edinburgh was enrolled in the University of Leyden in 1765, but as Hay is not again mentioned in the letters or memoranda it is perhaps more probable that he was some Scot merely passing through Rotterdam.

[1] That is, draw his sword and put himself in the attitude of defence.

[2] Three pints British, 3.6 pints U.S.

[3] A manual of Scots law. See p. 32 *n.* 5.

immortalize your own. For recreation read a chapter now and then of the *Great Man* or honest Spec.[4] Your tongue and p——k are the only two members I have not instructed you how to exercise. The former of these you must satisfy by half an hour's vociferation at your servant, forenoon and afternoon. As to the latter, I believe he requires very little exercise, as he seldom or ever of late has been seen to move at all. . . . Excuse this damned nonsense, and believe me sincerely—

I was just going to finish when your letter was presented me by the trusty Mollison.[5] I am very glad to find that you have raised your good friend Reason to the dignity of Governor of Utrecht and Commander-in-Chief of all your other passions. He is a worthy fellow and deserves this preferment. Your trunk shall be sent as you direct, as shall your letters. Burn this and you'll oblige, yours affectionately,

ARCH^D. STEWART.

FRIDAY 16 SEPTEMBER. . . . Latin till breakfast, something till eleven, then dress and at twelve French, then walk and dine. Afternoon, journal, &c. But next week you go to lectures, which will employ two hours and one in writing notes, about which you need not be exact. Mem. worthy father. Guard against liking billiards. They are blackguard, and you'll have high character with Count Nassau, &c., if you don't play. Be easy and natural, though a little proud. Write out full mem. that this is your winter to get rid of spleen and become a man.

[*c*. 16 SEPTEMBER. FRENCH THEME][6] In acquiring any language, it helps to write a great deal, because by doing so one learns spelling, without which the knowledge of a language is very imperfect. But, besides, when one writes, one must understand the grammar perfectly or make many absurd mistakes which, although they may pass unnoticed in the rapid flow of conversation, will certainly be discovered at once by the reader. For this reason I have resolved to write a little every day; and although in the begin-

---

[4] Dr. Johnson's essays or *The Spectator*.   [5] Stewart's clerk.
[6] Translated; see pp. x, xv, xvii.

ning I shall make sad work of it, I hope by practice to make myself
a good French scholar. This first time I have written without looking up the words in the dictionary because I began too late; but
after today I shall apply myself as assiduously to the attainment of
elegance in this renowned language as if I expected a prize of a
hundred thousand pounds sterling from the Academy of Sciences
at Paris.

SUNDAY 18 SEPTEMBER. Be shaved and dressed at half-past
eight, and then breakfast and go to the French church, and after
that walk and come home and write journal, and at two o'clock go
to the English church and be modest but not affected, and then
drink tea with Mr. Brown,[7] and in the evening, coffee and journal.[8]
Keep up to plan. Hear Rücker, &c. on Tuesday. Guard at first with
students. Be resolute and hear soon from Temple, and write him
about Miss S. But be not foolishly engaged in sombre hours. Be a
man always.[9]

You find now that you have been able (with GOD's favour) to
make yourself happy even in the most trying circumstances. Let

[7] The Reverend Robert Brown (1728–1777), British agent in Utrecht and
minister of the English (Presbyterian) church there. He was a Scot who had
spent some time at Geneva, and while there had entered sufficiently into
Genevan polemics to get mentioned sharply by Voltaire in a footnote to his
poem *La Guerre Civile de Genève*. He had recently married a Swiss girl, the
daughter of an expatriate Scots baronet, Sir James Kinloch. Belle de Zuylen,
who will figure prominently in this volume, was fond of Brown and of his
wife and sister-in-law, whom she described in 1765 as the only women in all
Utrecht she went to see. Boswell made arrangements to dine regularly at
Brown's to improve his French conversation, and carried his French exercises
there to read aloud. Brown was, throughout Boswell's residence in Utrecht, a
useful and reasonably sympathetic friend. Though Boswell found him anti-
pathetic, he had to admit that he was "a generous and clever little man"
(below, 7 April 1764).—French Protestant services are still held, as they
were in Boswell's day, in St. Peter's church, a few hundred yards to the east
of the Cathedral. The English services were held a few hundred yards to the
west of the Cathedral in St. Mary's, the most important Romanesque church
of Utrecht. It was demolished about 1840.

[8] The original of this memorandum is in French up to this point.

[9] The four following paragraphs are undated in the manuscript, and the
order in which they were written is uncertain.

this be always a sure and steady proof to you. This is a chimera. Your happiness is not produced by dissipation and gaiety, and so may vanish suddenly. It is wrought out by philosophy and pious resolutions of doing your duty as a man, with fortitude. Never forget this strong period of your life.

Write to Temple full account of your mental cure. Tell him that you allowed your mind to be disturbed by frivolous objects, yielded to slight gloom, not thinking of dignity and moral duty. But that you exerted spirit and found the noble bliss of acting with propriety, which even in your dark hours gave satisfaction; and it will increase the longer you act so, as it will give a longer retrospect. Bid him keep this to be a constant check on you.

Consider, pray, the morality of the Gospel; and if you find illicit concubinage forbidden, abstain from it and keep yourself strong for marriage. You can smile and say, "I was once an infidel. I acted accordingly. I am now a Christian gentleman. You can't blame me: I'm young and strong." Mind not trifling jokes on virtue.

Write to Temple and to Johnston on Friday, and advise about Miss S. Say as you are to be a good old Scotch gentleman, if you should neglect the opportunity of a woman sensible, amiable, well bred, who has lived in London. Who can read and talk. Who would entertain your friends, and whose harpsichord would charm your soul. If your friends think your scheme good, you can talk to Stewart and proceed finely and gently. If it does not succeed, 'tis another adventure.

MONDAY 19 SEPTEMBER. Write your mems always in English. You can write French in versions. Resolve never to remit plan a moment of being a philosopher and having a mind well principled. Your plan does in all weathers and all circumstances. You *must* do well and be a good, worthy, respected man. You are now forming into proper character. Learn not to talk of yourself. To be moderately reserved and never extravagantly merry. You will get a right set for life. . . . Tomorrow, hear all lectures, &c. Write for trunk tonight. Write to Johnston tomorrow.

TUESDAY 20 SEPTEMBER. This is the day on which you are
to take trial of professors. Try and be shaved and dressed by nine;
then hear Rücker, and at ten breakfast, and at eleven hear Trotz,
and at twelve hear Wesseling.[10] You need hear only law lectures,
and rather have fencing master. Two days a week you may want[1]
dinner, which will be for health and pay fencing. Attend either
Rücker or Trotz and no more. But read much privately and continue firm to plan. . . . Resolve now no more billiards. Be not hasty
to take music master, and consult Count Nassau about concert. Be
frugal, calm, and happy, and get wine soon.

[Received *c.* 20 September, Lord Auchinleck to Boswell]

[Auchinleck, *c.* 3 September 1763][2]
DEAR SON,—I have received yours of the 12th ult., and bless
GOD for the accounts you send me of your safe arrival in Holland
and of your progress towards Utrecht, where I suppose you are now
happily and comfortably fixed.

It was with great pleasure I read your account of my very dear
friend Mr. Gronovius[3] and the kind reception he gave you. It shows
me I was not mistaken in contracting friendship with him, for that
is the proper mark of a friend—to be constant and steady and to
show friendship to the connections of their friend. I cannot say that
any with whom I entered into friendship ever deceived me. Our

10 Rücker, Trotz, and Wesseling all gave lectures on law. After the Continental custòm, Boswell plans to hear the opening lecture by each and then select
the course he wishes to attend. He finally settled on Trotz.
1 "Go without."
2 Undated by Lord Auchinleck; endorsed "9 September 1763" by Herries,
Cochrane and Co., bankers, in London, through whom it was forwarded. See
below p. 26 *n.* 6.
3 Abraham Gronovius (1695–1775), distinguished classical scholar and Librarian of the University of Leyden. Boswell had called on him on the 12th of
August to present a letter from his father, who had contracted a friendship
with Gronovius during his student days at Leyden. Lord Auchinleck had kept
up his interest in Greek and Latin and had unusual competence in both.

friendships were contracted upon a mutual esteem and confidence and after being well apprised of one another's characters.[4]

I hope as you are now gone to another country—I had almost said another world, for Holland is altogether different from any other part of the globe that I know—that you will endeavour to follow out the good resolutions you set out with, apply hard, and make yourself a man of learning. At first after so much dissipation it will be irksome, but every day it will become more easy, and very soon will be more entertaining than any scene you have yet gone through. Pray, be on your guard as to your company, and don't take up with odd people or with vicious people. Count Nassau will be of great use to you, and the professors will be good company. I beg it of you to be cautious against contracting intimacies with people you know nothing about. This is a foible you should from experience arm against. I know that you were taken in at London by that weakness and cheated of your money.[5] In every country there are rogues who keep a sharp lookout upon every young fellow that makes his appearance, and, if they can, will take advantage of him. . . .

. . . There is in this country the appearance of a plentiful crop, and we have now very fine weather for harvest, which is begun. The country is in great beauty. I am busy dressing the ground about the House, and have made a good progress.

I set out for Inveraray upon Monday. Lord Prestongrange is my colleague and takes Stirling by himself, and I take the other two by myself. . . .[6] Your mother is in her ordinary state of health and remembers you with affection. I forgot to mention that your credit on Holland is for £30 every six weeks. That is the sum you draw for,

[4] An implied criticism of Boswell's friends Johnston, Erskine, and Temple, of all of whom Lord Auchinleck entertained a low opinion.

[5] The *London Journal* records no instance of Boswell's having been cheated of his money through contracting an intimacy with some one he knew nothing about. But there is that mysterious Army officer whom he told Belle de Zuylen he relieved and sent home to his friends. See p. 309.

[6] This reference makes it possible to give the letter an approximate date. The Court sat at Inveraray on Thursday 8 September.

and the exchange will be <deduct>ed by the banker. It was Sir
David Dalrymple's way. Farewell, <my dear so>n, and may GOD
bless and preserve you. I am your affectionate father,

ALEXR. BOSWEL.[7]

[Received *c.* 20 September, Temple to Boswell]

Trinity Hall [Cambridge] 13 September 1763

MY DEAR BOSWELL,—Your last letter gave me as much pleasure
as your first did concern. It is as I thought; your bad spirits pro-
ceeded entirely from your unsettled situation and the loss of
England. The first inconvenience is already removed, the latter is
your own choice, and for your benefit. It affords me inexpressible
satisfaction to find you determined to return to Utrecht. I know
there is nothing too difficult for you, and I make no doubt of your
remaining there without any restraint to yourself, after having
spent a little time in the manner you propose. . . .

Indeed you are a benevolent being. I know you are and I love
you for it. I know you can rejoice at the happiness of your friends,
however miserable you may be yourself. But how can you imagine
those friends can be happy, when they know you are not so? For
the sake of all those then that love you, let me beg of you, my dear
Boswell, to sum up all your resolution, and no longer to act a part
that is unworthy of you. You know I must always love and esteem
you, but unless you break in pieces the fetters of dissipation and
sloth, how can I ever entertain a high idea of your character? I long
to see your journal. I consider it as the history of your mind as well
as travels, and shall be as much entertained with its ebbs and flows,
its elasticity and lassitude, as with the variety of characters, of
places and of objects which you will describe.—Bob continues to
do well. He desires to be remembered to you affectionately. I had
more to say but my paper admonishes me to conclude. I am, my
dear Boswell, your sincere friend,

W. J. TEMPLE.

[7] Lord Auchinleck had dropped one *l* from the family name. One of Boswell's
first gestures of independence was to restore it.

It is unkind in you to apologize for your letters. If you were capable of writing a dull one, you know it could not be unacceptable to me. To hear that you are well is worth the postage of fifty letters. Let us write freely what we think, and never dress up our letters as if they were going to the press. . . .

[Boswell to Temple]

Utrecht, 23 September 1763

MY DEAR TEMPLE,—If my last letter gave you pleasure, this must give you much more, as I can now inform you that I have put my good resolutions in practice. Your letter first gave my mind a proper direction. Mr. Johnson confirmed and carried me on. I have received the most valuable instruction from his *Rambler*. Several papers seem to have been just written for me. I shall make out a *cento* (if I may use the expression) of philosophy for the happy conduct of life from his works. He is the ablest mental physician that I have ever applied to. He insists much on preserving a manly fortitude of mind, and maintains that every distress may be supported. But I shall not now begin to my *cento*.

When I was once roused to exert my spirit, I went up to Utrecht. I fixed myself down to a regular plan and in a day or two grew almost well. I am now settled in the best manner. I have got a neat house of my own and an excellent servant. I get up every morning at seven. I read Ovid till nine, then I breakfast. From ten to eleven I read Tacitus. From eleven to twelve I am shaved and dressed every day. From twelve to one I hear a lecture upon Civil Law. From one to three I walk and dine. From three to four my French master is with me. The rest of the day is spent in reading different books and in writing. This day I began to set about recovering my Greek. I have taken Cebes's *Table* and shall next read Xenophon, and so advance to greater difficulties.[8]

[8] Boswell began studying Latin while a small boy, and maintained a very good command of it all his life. He began the study of Greek at the University of Edinburgh when he was fifteen, but perhaps then went through no more than the elementary course. One gets the impression that in spite of this re-

My dear friend! how noble is this! Good GOD, what a change! Luckily I did not write to my father during my miserable state of mind. Honest man, he is pleased to think of my being on a prudent plan, and knows nothing of what has happened. And now that it is over, there is really no harm done. To be sure, I endured a most dreadful shock. . . .

I have for some time past been in a sad course of dissipation. I hope to get rid of that and to form habits of study and manly conduct which will make me happy all my life. Instead of thinking myself in a dreary solitude, I am in a foreign university-town, acquiring knowledge, learning French, living among foreigners. There is not another English student here. Count Nassau is very polite, and tells me that by and by we shall have fine parties. My dear friend, how strange is this affair! I look back on my late situation as on a horrid dream. I can scarce believe it. Should I be cast down with the recollection of it? or should I not exult at having obtained a complete victory, and never dread a return? I must however remark that I have a little natural disposition to be melancholy. But I will bear it like a man; and it never lasts long. How near was I doing some dreadful extravagant thing! But I thank GOD I have escaped. I have been much obliged upon this occasion to Stewart.

And now, my friend, you must not smile when I tell you what I am at present amusing my fancy with. Stewart's sister is sensible, amiable, has been several winters in London, is perfectly accomplished. She is not handsome, but is extremely agreeable and what you would call a woman of fashion. She and I were always good friends; and when I was in Scotland, she was the only woman I could think of for a wife. Stewart and I have been talking much of her, and I have heard more and more of her good qualities. I begin to think that I should not let such a prize pass without knowing if I might have her. I could write postscripts in her brother's

view in 1763–1764 he retained in after life only about enough of the language to identify a Greek passage with the aid of a translation. Cebes's *Table,* a dialogue on education formerly held to be the work of a disciple of Socrates, was much used in the eighteenth century as an elementary text.

letters, and take many ways to find out how she would like the scheme. Pray excuse this. I can conceal nothing from you; nor will I ever take a step of any consequence (except an intrigue or a quarrel) without your advice. Tell me if it would be agreeable to have such a scheme in view after my travels, and if I would not make the tour of Europe with high satisfaction while I considered that I should have the honour to take the most accomplished woman in Scotland by the hand upon my return. You know I have always wished to marry an English woman. But should I neglect to obtain a lady who would be an honour to my family, entertain my friends, and be a constant companion to myself? My dear friend! From this indistinct story you may guess my present sentiments. In the stillness of Utrecht, this scheme appears very fine. Tell me truly, is it just a whim? Would it embarrass me for some years yet to think of marrying? Should I set myself at ease and let some worthy man have her? Shall I have as good some time hence? Or will it fix me to a rational plan, and shall I begin to beat about the bush? Pray write me fully about it. For you shall determine me.[9] My kind wishes to Bob. I ever am, my dearest Temple, yours most affectionately,

JAMES BOSWELL.

Write soon.

[Boswell to Johnston, concluded]

Utrecht, 23 September 1763

... Consider, my friend, what a noble discovery I have made, that melancholy can be got the better of. I don't say entirely. But

[9] This sort of thing was an old story to Temple, to whom Boswell had been turning for years for serious advice concerning matrimonial schemes. The first letter of Boswell to Temple now known to exist, a letter written when Boswell was some months short of eighteen, confides his passion for a Miss Martha White, an heiress of £30,000, who later married the Earl of Elgin. Between this date and 1769, when he finally married, Boswell wrote at great length to Temple about at least four other young ladies whom he had more or less serious thoughts of making Mrs. Boswell. The woman he *did* marry was not of the number.

by vigorously opposing it, I have a conscious satisfaction even in
my dark hours; and when I have the "sunshine of the soul,"[1] then
I am doubly blest. My dear Johnston! this is a strange letter. I had
not room to be full enough. But from what I have said you may by
the assistance of your fancy have matter of thought for some time.
Pray let my victory have a proper effect upon you. I shall think this
late shock a fortunate affair if it help us both to a method of preserving constant satisfaction of soul. I shall write more to you on
the subject. I continue my journal, and much entertainment will
it afford. I shall transmit it to Temple; and when I return, we shall
read it together. O my dear Johnston! felicitate your poor friend
restored to comfort! This last affair appears now almost incredible.
Luckily I did not write all the time to my father. I hope now to be
in no danger.

Pray take care of Charles.[2] Temple will send you a bill for
some money soon. Write immediately, before you leave Grange
for old Edina. . . .[3] I ever am, my dear Johnston, affectionately
yours,

JAMES BOSWELL.

Address A Monsieur, Monsieur Boswell à la Cour de l'Empereur à Utrecht. Write fully your thoughts about my scheme of
Miss S——.[4]

Take care and open this letter nicely, or you'll tear the writing;
especially the two little seals on the sides.

P.S. Write freely on S. scheme. It is the only Scots one I can

[1] Pope's *Essay on Man,* IV. 168.

[2] Boswell's natural son, at this time about ten months old. He had been born
shortly after Boswell left Edinburgh in November, 1762, his mother (Peggy
Doig) being apparently a servant. Before his departure, Boswell had arranged with a Dr. Cairnie of Edinburgh to put the child in the care of a
foster-mother, and had provided funds for his maintenance. Johnston visited
him regularly and sent Boswell reports. See *Boswell's London Journal, 1762–
1763,* 1950, p. 324 *n.* 6.

[3] The omitted passage refers to Miss Stewart in much the terms of the preceding letter to Temple.

[4] What follows was written on the outside, after the letter was folded and
sealed.

think of. For I have always thought of some fine English one. Should I banish this whim and have a run of several more years?

SATURDAY 24 SEPTEMBER. This day regular plan. Ovid till breakfast, Tacitus till eleven, dress till twelve, then either Trotz or visits; dine Plaats Royaal. ... Three to four, French; four to five, Greek; then coffee; then notes of law, and history, and journal, and Erskine's *Institutes*. ... Get Corpus Juris.[5] Billiards is the only *mala fama* here. Make resolve against it. Write Stewart at night. Miss S. is again evaporated. You see how vain a fancy. You must not marry for some years, unless Temple bids. Write him on Tuesday, long composed letter, sensible and on a subject of learning mostly. Persist firm and noble.

[Boswell to Temple]

Utrecht, 25 September 1763

MY DEAR TEMPLE,—Although I wrote you a very long letter last post, yet I must now again have the happiness of talking to my friend. My last was written somewhat in a hurry, as I had put it off till the post-night, which is very short here, as the bag is shut at eight. I was so full of my own affairs that I could talk of nothing else; and even of them I wrote but an undistinct account. I think our correspondence should be perfectly the result of inclination. Let us write whenever we feel a desire to do so; and then our letters will be truly valuable to each other, when they flow from the heart and are not laboured. At the same time, if a particular subject starts up, we may take some pains to pursue it, and so may now and then contribute to the mutual improving of our understandings, as well as to the gratification of our affections.[6]

[5] The great collection of Roman law which he was studying with Professor Trotz. John Erskine's *Principles of the Law of Scotland,* which Boswell and his father call "Erskine's *Institutes,*" was a manual of Scots law, now obsolete. The much more important work by Erskine now known as "Erskine's *Institutes*" was not published till 1773.

[6] The three paragraphs following are in reply to the middle section of Tem-

It gives me very great pleasure to think that you are upon so good a footing with Mr. Gray, and that you find him as high a character as you formerly conceived him to be. The contemplation of such a man must rouse every noble principle. For he was not born so. By study and by reflection he has attained that dignity of mind and elegance of sentiment. I leave his poetry out of the question. A genius like his can seldom arise to show humanity how high it may be. But there are few men who by proper cultivation may not become very noble beings.

My dear Temple! may not even I make myself a respectable character? I am particularly happy to find that you have talked freely to Mr. Gray of your situation, and that he has given you his advice as a friend. This is a matter of great consequence. Pray let me know particularly how you consulted him, and what he said. You observe with great justice that speculation is not enough, and that a man ought to engage in some scheme of active life that may render him useful to society and happy in himself. You must be sensible that the mind of most men will grow uneasy without some actual plan. Such is the constitution of the world that if we speculate too much about it we shall see all human pursuits in insipid or ridiculous views. But let us once heartily engage in some course of action and all these imaginations vanish. We are filled with desires, with hopes, and with fears that excite our powers and render us vigorous by their exertion. We ought to consider that God has placed us here as in a state of probation, where we have got abilities, which if we exercise properly, we may have immediate happiness, and may raise our minds more and more towards that state of perfection which all noble souls have ever had ideas of. Another great incitement to a life of action is the exercise that it affords to the social virtues. He who lives in a studious retirement is almost necessarily somewhat selfish, for solitude gives him a habit of attending only to his own good; whereas by taking a part

---

ple's letter of 13 September (above, p. 27), omitted in this edition. Since Boswell repeats so much, not merely of Temple's ideas but of his language, one of the two disquisitions seems sufficient.

in life, we have constant opportunities of doing service in some way or other to our fellow-creatures. And I must add that the studious and retired hours of an active man are by far the most agreeable. The great point is to have a proper mixture of action and speculation, and this I should imagine every man in tolerable circumstances may continue to enjoy.

Now, my friend, these are very good general reasonings. But how are they to be applied? I am anxious to hear of your determining upon some plan of real life. I am sure it will do you infinite service to be fixed. I like to hear of the mitre dancing before your eyes. Will you then determine to be a clergyman? Shall I really see Dr. Temple's handsome equipage at Auchinleck? Or is the bar unwilling to quit hopes of having your presence? Indeed, I am seriously of opinion that it would be too dry and laborious a business for you. There is no doing things by halves as a lawyer in England. However, I shall be happy to have your particular ideas. I am grown quite keen that we should both take our posts in the warfare of life. I persuade myself we have spirit enough to make good soldiers. Let us never yield a moment to mental cowardice; if we do, we shall think meanly of ourselves. Let us persist with an unremitting fortitude.

I will lay my present schemes clearly before you, and so you can consider them properly. After some time passed in idleness, dissipation, and fickleness, I have now resolved to pursue a rational plan of life. I am born to an estate of a thousand a year in Scotland, which has been transmitted through several generations of worthy men who held a good rank in the country. I think myself under a natural tie to keep up this family upon the old estate; to improve and beautify it, and to live well with all my neighbours by being upon an agreeable hospitable footing with them. This may be sufficient employment for some months in the year. But I must have more occupation. I am therefore acquiring knowledge of the Civil Law and of the law of Scotland, that I may be one of the Faculty of Advocates, a very respectable society. That I may have it in my power to do service as a man of business and may be in the road to preferment as a judge, which is no chimerical project. By this means I have a conscious satisfaction that I am acting a proper part. I have respect; I have an addition to my fortune. I have time enough to cultivate the elegant studies, which I am determined never to neglect. I can pass some months in London every year, and so be quite a man of the world, by being at the Metropolis often enough to keep up acquaintance with all my English friends, who would value me more as a man of some consequence than as a mere agreeable companion, and would perhaps take jaunts to see me at Auchinleck. For I must mix some of my gay schemes with all this propriety and rational consideration. I would have interest, and so be able to serve my friends in many ways. Perhaps I may be fortunate enough to obtain a seat in Parliament. That would put me upon a very fine footing; and perhaps I might get a good place in London, and so pass my winter in London and summer at Auchinleck. But these last schemes I cannot promise so much upon, nor would I fix my imagination too strongly upon them. The others are very attainable. By this means I shall give satisfaction and comfort to my worthy father, who has suffered much uneasiness from my former levity and inconsistency,[7] which to a man of his prudence and uniform conduct appeared much worse than to other people.

I am now at a foreign university, or rather in a foreign city where I have an opportunity of acquiring knowledge. I am at a distance from all my dissipated companions. I may attain habits of thought, study, and propriety of conduct. I am next to travel through Europe. I shall always be upon my guard to persist in the proper course, and hope to return to England so confirmed in it that I shall be able to proceed through life with unaffected rectitude.

I wrote to you in my last that I had taken it into my head to think of Miss Stewart for my wife. You know my precipitant impetuosity when I am pleased with a new fancy. Perhaps you have

[7] The manuscript reads *inconstency*. Boswell may have meant *inconstancy*, but the spelling would be most unusual for him.

smiled sufficiently at this. But you must write to me gravely about it. For it has really got a pretty firm hold of me. By talking with her brother I have been reminded of her many perfections. She is of a good family, and has £5000 for her fortune, and I am sure would be agreeable to my father. I never was in love with her; that is to say, I never felt any of that inflamed fancy for her which is intoxicating while it lasts but never can remain long. I always considered her as a sensible, affable, well bred woman that I chose to be with as a companion, though at times I could discern a kind of tender affection glancing through my mind. Pray give me your advice fully. Is this scheme merely the suggestion of a rich imagination in solitude, which ought to be laughed at and dismissed? Or is it an excellent plan which ought not to be relinquished?

As I must at any rate pass some months at Auchinleck, do you think that an English woman would like that (Miss Floyer for instance),[8] or should I not try to secure a lady who would support a character of dignity? I could easily see by writing postscripts to her and talking to Stewart if she liked me. My pride will scarcely allow me to doubt it. At any rate, 'tis an adventure. If it be a foolish scheme, check it freely. I shall do you the same kind office in the like situation.

I continue quite well. O Johnson! how much do I owe to thee! I now see that I can conquer my spleen by preserving just ideas of the dignity of human nature and never allowing sloth and idleness to get the better of me. I have cured it when it was at its worst. Pray remember this, and never allow me again to plead a real distemper.—If you think my general plan of life good, approve it and keep me firm to it, and let us remember that at any rate we shall be a third of the year together and with higher satisfaction if we are doing well.

[8] Frances Floyer, daughter of a Governor of Madras and cousin of Norton Nicholls, "whom" (says Boswell in a later journal) "I had seen in London in the year 1763, when my friend Temple admired her much." Miss Floyer, it turned out, had no objection to Scotland, for she married Captain John Erskine, heir of the attainted earldom of Mar, and went to live at Alloa.

And now for honest Robert. Remember me most affectionately to the dog. Tell him how great a man I am with my house and my servant; and tell him that I have got two suits: of sea-green with silver lace, and scarlet with gold.

Pray let me know how much a letter from this costs you. We must not write too often. Here again I am talking absurdly. Pray leave a bit of paper clean for your seal, as I always tear some of the writing. I ever remain yours most affectionately,

JAMES BOSWELL.

P.S. Pray forward the letter that was left for me at my chambers in the Temple.

[*c.* 25 SEPTEMBER. FRENCH THEME] At present I rise every day early, a practice which contributes much to the preservation of health, for it knits up the nerves and gives hardiness and vigour to the entire constitution. There are many people who have made themselves weak and sickly simply by sleeping too much, or rather by a vile habit of wasting the precious morning hours in lazy slumber. But as for me, I have given orders to my servant to wake me every day at half-past six o'clock, and my orders are always obeyed with marvellous exactitude. It is not usual to find a watch that runs so true as François, and I am quite ready to lay a bet on him against all the clocks in the country. As soon as I am awake, I remember my duty, and like a brisk mariner I give the lash to indolence and bounce up with as much vivacity as if a pretty girl, amorous and willing, were waiting for me.

SUNDAY 25 SEPTEMBER

> Ten lines a day I task myself to write,
> Be fancy clouded or be fancy bright,
> Sure, no Egyptian task; for unconfin'd
> Let Genius range the forest of the mind,
> And, as Apollo grants him vigour, grub
> The tow'ring cedar or the lowly shrub.
> I seek not sallies elegant and terse,

But to acquire the power of making verse;
And sure by practice I may freely hope
To turn a line like Dryden or like Pope.

MONDAY 26 SEPTEMBER. Let your first care each morning be to look at your mems. Then to your plan for the day. But frequently review week's mems each Saturday, as you often forget useful hints. Pray mark in journal, "Governor Reason and the banditti."[9] Pray keep to plan and have mind well principled.[1] Tell [François] not to shave against grain for fear of scurvy. Bring up journal hard today. Write Johnston on Tuesday, if post comes not, and Dempster next week. Write but seldom, and read much.

TUESDAY 27 SEPTEMBER. Yesterday was rather irregular. 'Tis true you read Latin, Greek, French, and did a little at Erskine. But you have much journal to bring up. Write as few letters as possible. Hear first from Dempster and keep yourself quiet, retired, and studious. Persist vigorous in plan; never remit. Make it out full for pocket-book. Write French before ten each morning, and lay out hours exactly. Spend not so much time in sauntering. Be firm to be always employed, and be not just immediately entertained; but have constant eye to future life and being Laird of Auchinleck and Baron. Never want dinner. You will hurt your health. You can if you please have it sent to you. Mark Tacitus always. Never indulge fits and starts. Have no flute master to interrupt.

SATURDAY 1 OCTOBER. Get commonplace-book, like Gray. You was irregular yesterday by supping out to have Professor Cas-

9 Probably related to the following passage in one of the French themes: "Mr. Sheridan, teacher of oratory, comparing the human mind to the political constitution of Great Britain, found many similarities between them. Reason, said he, is the king; Imagination and its train of Fancies represent the nobility; and the Passions represent the people." See also the final paragraph of Archibald Stewart's letter, p. 22. Boswell has perhaps thought of an extension of the figure in which *some* of the passions have set themselves in lawless opposition to the state?

1 An echo of Johnson's "soul well principled": see above, p. 18 *n.* 8.

tillon's company,[2] which was not amiss. But you gained little by
it. You was pretty much upon your guard. But you rather indulged
high spirits too much and spoke too much. Besides, you spoke too
much of yourself and too laughably of Dominus Trotz. Guard
against approaches to familiarity with Brown or Rose,[3] and try to
fix dining with Brown, so as to be in the way of a family always.
This day, just set it apart to bring up journal, and then you'll be
clear; and after this all will go regularly on. Never remit plan.
Apply much to Voltaire. Think to hear Trotz on feudal system.

TUESDAY 4 OCTOBER

Sure I resolv'd three days ago and more
By noon to have my rhyming business o'er,
But the resolves of mortal man are vain,
For now I must begin at night again.
A night like this so early in the year
To my five senses never did appear:
My soles resemble much—or let me die—
Two smoothing-irons which have long lain by,
And, I protest, my fingers with the cold
Are so benumb'd I scarce my pen can hold.

WEDNESDAY 5 OCTOBER. You laboured hard yesterday at
journal, and you have brought it up well. You have only Sir

[2] J. F. Salvemini de Castillon (or Castiglione), Professor of Mathematics at
Utrecht, became next year professor at Berlin. He had made translations
from Pope and Locke and had edited the minor works of Newton. Belle de
Zuylen said he was the only man she enjoyed discussing metaphysics with.

[3] Our knowledge of Rose, who was, all things considered, the most intimate
of Boswell's male associates in Utrecht, remains disappointingly vague. He
was of a junior branch of the distinguished Scottish house of Rose of Kilravock, according to Boswell, a first cousin of the reigning laird; and was later,
at least, in holy orders, but whether in the Church of Scotland or the Church
of England is uncertain. What he was doing in Utrecht is equally obscure.
He seems to have felt himself in some sort an exile, and was glad to accept
payment for tutoring. Boswell went to him for lessons in Greek, and he gave
Professor Trotz instruction in English. He rented a room in Brown's house.

William Forbes and the adventure with the Dutch students to mark.[4] The rest will be merely your studies of Greek, &c. *From this time* let plan proceed: seven to eight, Ovid; eight to nine, French version; ten to eleven, Tacitus; three to four, French; four to five, Greek; six to seven, Civil Law; seven to eight, Scots; eight to ten, Voltaire. Then journal, letters, and other books. Learn by all means *retenue*[5] and being easy without talking of yourself, and guard against ridicule; so don't encourage viewing objects in ridiculous lights. Write Father soon. Dine Brown Sunday and be moderately grave. Keep fixed general plan still in view. Sir David, Johnston, Arthur Seat.[6]

[Received 5 October, Sir David Dalrymple to Boswell]

Knaresborough, Yorkshire, 26 September 1763

MY DEAR SIR:—I have been so great a wanderer of late that you need not be surprised at my not having wrote to you. I was at Inverness upon the Circuit when I heard that my youngest sister, who was here for the recovery of her health, was dangerously ill. I lost no time, but came here. I found her rather better, but still in a dubious way.

This evening I got your letter of the 8th September, which both surprised and afflicted me. I am glad however to find that the foul fiend (as you call it) has left you. Your friend has very justly told you the name of this spectre; it was Idleness. Sometimes

[4] "Yesterday you was necessarily and properly taken up with Sir William Forbes, a Scotch knight, and who has care of your brother" (Memorandum, 22 September 1763). Boswell's fifteen-year-old brother David had recently been apprenticed to the banking-house of which Forbes was a partner. Forbes later became one of Boswell's most trusted friends and was executor of his estate. The "adventure with the Dutch students" is unexplained.
[5] "Reserve."
[6] "I next stood in the court before the Palace [of Holyroodhouse, Edinburgh], and bowed thrice to Arthur Seat, that lofty romantic mountain on which I have so often strayed in my days of youth, indulged meditation and felt the raptures of a soul filled with ideas of the magnificence of GOD and his creation" (*Boswell's London Journal, 1762–1763*, 1950, pp. 41–42).

she appears like an *improba Siren*,⁷ amusing to destroy; at other times she arms herself with whips and stings and torments her votaries. If you continue to fill up your time with study and exercise, she will have no opportunity of assailing you with success. Your application to GOD was a right and a wise method of relieving you from your distress, but you must not suppose that GOD will operate upon your mind without your using the proper means for your own relief.

The means you are using are excellent. To tell you the truth, I am not much surprised that at your first arrival in a strange place your mind was uneasy. That however is but a momentary sensation of uneasiness, and you will get over it presently if you follow that excellent regimen which you prescribe to yourself. Pray make yourself master of French as soon as you can, without neglecting exercise. When the weather is bad, get into a wagon or chaise of some kind, and jolt off your listlessness. As soon as the weather sets in for frost, learn to skate. You will find a master for that exercise where you are. Skate in company and you will run no danger of drowning, nor much of ducking.

There was a shoemaker, an eminent professor in skating, at Utrecht when I was there; his name Lebonk. Let me recommend him to your acquaintance. He is an accomplished personage, speaks both French and English, and has as high ideas of his own significancy in his way as Mr. Pitt or any statesman of them all can have. Let him tell you the story of his having skated before the King of France. But perhaps I am speaking of one who is no more. I hope you will have no occasion of consulting Dr. Tissot.⁸ He speaks the languages, and is no mean original in his way.

It will amuse you to take a college on the *Notitia rerum publicarum*.⁹ I just suggest such things as I think may entertain you till you come to have facility in understanding and speaking French.

⁷ "Immodest siren" (Horace, *Satires*, II. iii. 14).

⁸ A doctor of medicine. Boswell did consult him on 25 May 1764.

⁹ "The idea (or conception) of state property," for example, highways, rivers, and harbours. In Scotland the word "college" (Latin *collegium*) retained until the nineteenth century the continental meaning, "course of lectures."

I think some time hence you should give your good father a general idea of the situation of your mind on your first arrival at Utrecht; however, of this you yourself must judge. You should not forget your good friend the Christian philosopher, Mr. Johnson. He has studied the human mind so much and so well that your case will not seem extraordinary to him. Will you allow me to joke with you so far as to remind you of Dr. Swift's chapter on the diseases of the Yahoos?[1] There is also a consultation of Martinus Scriblerus in a case something resembling yours.[2] You will find from those passages that your Cambridge friend has truly pronounced your late disease to have been Idleness. Adieu, dear Sir. Believe me most sincerely yours,

Dav. Dalrymple.

THURSDAY 6 OCTOBER. This letter to Mr. Johnson is a terrible affair. Don't take any more time to it. But either send him a short substantial one or copy out the large one; 'tis natural, though rude. He will like it, and you can correct your copy and make it very pretty, for there are fine, strong, lively passages in it. Copy

[1] The seventh chapter of "A Voyage to the Houyhnhnms" concludes: "My master likewise mentioned another quality which his servants had discovered in several Yahoos, and to him was wholly unaccountable. He said, a fancy would sometimes take a Yahoo to retire into a corner, to lie down, and howl and groan, and spurn away all that came near him, although he were young and fat, wanted neither food nor water; nor did the servants imagine what could possibly ail him. And the only remedy they found was, to set him to hard work, after which he would infallibly come to himself. To this I was silent, out of partiality to my own kind; yet here I could plainly discover the true seeds of spleen, which only seizeth on the lazy, the luxurious, and the rich; who, if they were forced to undergo the same regimen, I would undertake for the cure" (*Gulliver's Travels,* Part IV).

[2] Scriblerus diagnoses "the case of a young nobleman at Court, who was observed to grow extremely affected in his speech, and whimsical in all his behaviour" as an occurrence of the very common disease self-love, and prescribes, among several remedies, that "it would not be amiss if he travelled over England in a stage-coach, and made the tour of Holland in a trackscoute" (*Memoirs of Martinus Scriblerus,* Chapter 11, by Dr. John Arbuthnot and others, in the *Works* of Alexander Pope).

out today the first business you do. Then lay the copy by, not to
be looked at for a long time, and seal the letter comfortable, and
send it off.³ You'll never have such a task again.

FRIDAY 7 OCTOBER. You go on charmingly. Be steady and
firm. You have told Brown your story, and he will assist you. Begin
on Sunday to dine with him. If you please, and the day is good,
put on scarlet and gold, and please humour with cockade. Send
today for book of maps and read Xenophon with more pleasure.
Make commonplace-book of a quire, but don't bind it. Do like Castillon; mark where different subjects are to be found. Extract from
Tacitus, Ovid, Xenophon, Voltaire, and so pick up treasure as you
go on. Push scheme of Society.⁴ You must allow three hours every
evening for amusement. Six hours are enough a day for labour.

[*c.* 7–9 OCTOBER. FRENCH THEMES] Last evening I was honoured with the company of the celebrated Professor Trotz. Although the weather was horrible, he was so good as to venture out
and come to see me, which puffed up by a great deal more the vanity which I naturally possess in a supreme degree. I offered him a
glass of wine, but he told me he was suffering from a bad cold and
had a pain in his chest and that wine would not be good for it. I was
very sorry to hear that he was ill and that we could not have the
pleasure of drinking a glass together, which would have made us
lively and inspired us with cordiality. Then I proposed tea, and he
told me that it would be very agreeable to him. I was surprised to
see that he took sugar like an Englishman, because I had heard so
many jokes about the narrowness of the Dutch in that article.

Professor Trotz is a very learned man. He gives excellent lectures on the Civil Law, which he explains, not drily like a pedant,
but like a philosopher. He now and again intersperses ingenious

³ His Register of Letters shows that he did send the letter off next day. But
neither the original nor the copy has been recovered, and he printed no part
of it in *The Life of Johnson.*
⁴ A literary society of students which met on Wednesday evenings and spoke
only French. From this memorandum it appears that Boswell was the
founder, or one of the founders.

moral observations and amusing historical anecdotes, and his college is truly a school of liberal knowledge. He was formerly professor in Friesland, and when he was invited to Utrecht the Frisians begged him to stay; offered him *carte blanche* and the dignity of a Senator. But Mr. Trotz thanked them very much and preferred Utrecht because his wife's family were there and because it was a very elegant city; and as life is short, he wanted to pass it pleasantly. I laugh heartily to myself to see so striking an instance of the fact that all our pleasures are relative. That same Utrecht which appeared so gloomy to a man from London was considered a seat of felicity by a man from Franeker.

Looking out of my window this morning I saw a very odd figure. It was a big Dutchman, very fat and very clumsy. He had on a blue garment, thick and long, a wig of amazing size, and a terrifying sword at right angles to his body. He was holding a book with both hands, raised almost to his eyes, like a Scots precentor. He held himself perpendicular, and he walked with measured steps, pursuing his studies. I was greatly diverted and wished much that Hogarth, the famous painter of comic scenes, could have seen him. He would no doubt have given us a fine burlesque picture. Or if Butler, the author of *Hudibras*, had seen him, he would have given us most excellent comic rhymes on a subject so full of ridicule.

SUNDAY 9 OCTOBER. If the day is good, put on your scarlet clothes and behave with decency before fair lady[5] at French church. Home till half an hour after twelve at journal, and then go to Brown and dine and be cheerful and happy. After church, journal all evening, to bring it up once clear. Then you'll be quite regular. Never desist an hour from plan. Be always like Lord Kames, doing something, and never divert people here like Carnegie.[6] Write out Plan. Bring up Van Eck and go on with Erskine. Indulge not whims but form into a man.

[5] Unidentified.
[6] Lord Kames, like Boswell's father a judge in both the supreme courts of Scotland, was a voluminous author on a variety of subjects. "Carnegie" is not identified.

TUESDAY 11 OCTOBER. From this day follow Mr. Locke's prescription of going to stool every day regularly after breakfast.[7] It will do your health good, and it is highly necessary to take care of your health. This morning read from breakfast till college, Van Eck, so as to bring him up. It is reading Latin, and will serve for a day instead of Tacitus. Take notes when you can on Pandects, and get a *Corpus Juris;* perhaps Brown can let you have one. Buy Trotz *De memoria;*[8] get an Erskine for him. Be temperate and rise at seven each morning. Take some negus at night to prevent damps. It is necessary. Take constant exercise.

[*c.* 12–14 OCTOBER. FRENCH THEMES] I like exceedingly to wash my feet in warm water. It gives me a kind of tranquillity. I am not joking; I speak from experience. I have often done it merely for pleasure. But if I receive so much delight from washing my feet, how great must have been the luxury of the Romans, who solaced thus their entire bodies. The warm baths which they had everywhere contributed greatly to felicity. . . . Truly, without exaggeration, one cannot imagine anything more consoling than after a day of annoyance and fatigue to undress and stretch one's self out at full length in fluid warmth, to have one's nerves gently relaxed, to enjoy indolent ease and forget all one's cares. I experienced a little of that enjoyment when I was at Moffat in Scotland for the mineral waters. But my pleasure was very crude because I was taking the baths for my health, and there were no conveniences for bathing for pleasure.[9] I was put into a horrible tub, a scanty covering

[7] " . . . if a man, after his first eating in the morning, would presently solicit nature, and try whether he could strain himself so as to obtain a stool, he might in time, by a constant application, bring it to be habitual" (John Locke, *Some Thoughts Concerning Education*, Section 24).

[8] "Van Eck" was a Latin comment on the Roman Civil Law, "arranged in the order of the Pandects," that is, of the digest of excerpts from the writings of the Roman jurists prepared at the order of the Emperor Justinian. Trotz's work appears to have been a method for memorizing the Roman law.

[9] This happened in his twelfth year. In the sketch of his life which he afterwards wrote for Rousseau, he says that he had a bad cold which left him with nervous indigestion and scorbutic complaints.

was thrown over me, and in that state I was obliged to remain for half an hour. I had as my supervisor a barbarian of a Presbyterian preacher, who called out from time to time in a harsh voice, "Take care, you rogue! If we see the least disobedience to our orders, we shall proceed to instant punishment." And that was why I kept quiet, though I was extremely bored.

A warm bath is, I confess, a most agreeable kind of luxury, but luxury is very dangerous. . . . Above all things a young man should guard against effeminacy. I would advise him to avoid warm baths and accustom himself rather to the cold bath, which will give him vigour and liveliness. When I was at Edinburgh, I used to take a cold bath every morning, even in the severest winter. I met there the most shameless flatterer I ever saw. He was the bath-keeper. He said to me, "Mr. Boswell, if you should choose to join the Army, there is no doubt that you would be accepted for any rank lower than that of General." He always flattered me without limit. He had a prodigious stock of gross compliments. But, indeed, though I always laughed at his amazing effrontery, I liked to hear him run on. The most obvious flattery has in it something agreeable.

FRIDAY 14 OCTOBER. This is the great day of Count Nassau's dinner. Dress in scarlet and gold, fine swiss, white silk stockings, handsome pumps, and have silver-and-silk sword-knot, Barcelona handkerchief, and elegant toothpick-case which you had in a present from a lady. Be quite the man of fashion and keep up your dignity. Don't think it idle time, for while abroad being in good company is your great scheme and is really improving. Only take care and never be merely idle, but employ some hours a day in study. Bring up journal clear, and after this clear it every three days.

FRIDAY 14 OCTOBER

> Let other bards compose majestic songs:
> My humble subject is a pair of tongs;
> Not those slight things which ladies use at tea,
> But what you may by ev'ry chimney see.

Boswell's Inviolable Plan, drawn up at Utrecht, 16 October 1763.

My surly tutor[1] in my wayward youth
Made me submit to punishments uncouth.
And, as a dreadful penance for neglect,[2]
Oft made me take the tongs about my neck.
But I to wear the tongs was always vain,
And thought them grander than a mayor's chain.

SATURDAY 15 OCTOBER. This day resolve to bring up journal, so push it on smartly but prettily and fully, and be sure to give Count Nassau's dinner as a specimen, &c. You was rather too high last night. Always try to attain tranquillity. Every time that you gain an advantage over bad affections, you'll be stronger. Write out Plan fully today for certain, and write obligation to Father with answers to all objections, and make him keep you to it. Take French version every day to Brown. Have Carron Monday, Wednesday, Friday. Learn *retenue*. Pray do. Don't forget in Plan: when once you're fairly at business, you'll go on.

SUNDAY 16 OCTOBER. You did a great deal yesterday. You made out your Plan,[3] and you brought up near a whole week of journal. This day bring up the rest, and then you'll always after this be clear and easy. 'Tis true you sat up a little late, but that must now and then happen in important cases. Read your Plan every morning regularly at breakfast, and when you travel, carry it in trunk. Get commonplace-book. Be one week without talking of self or repeating. The more and oftener restraints, the better. Be steady.

[1] Lord Auchinleck provided for his children a series of domestic tutors or coaches—all young men preparing themselves for the ministry of the Church of Scotland—who lived in the family and drilled the boys in their lessons. "Surly tutor" sounds like the second of these, the Reverend Joseph Fergusson, who came when Boswell was twelve.

[2] "Neglect," "respect," &c., regularly dropped the final *t* in Scots pronunciation of the eighteenth century.

[3] This portentous document, headed "Inviolable Plan, to be read over frequently," has been preserved, and is in some respects the theme song of this volume, but Boswell has anticipated so much of it in his memoranda that it seems best to print it in an appendix. See the facsimile opposite, and p. 387.

SUNDAY 16 OCTOBER

> For three full weeks, I can with pleasure say,
> I have not fail'd to write my lines-a-day;
> And what is more, though careless oft and rude,
> Johnson himself would call them very good.
> At diff'rent seasons diff'rent poets sing:
> Great Milton's fancy brighten'd in the spring;
> And Shakespeare's noblest pow'r in winter came,
> For then the playhouse brought him gold and fame.
> Sure, I am blest with a melodious mind,
> Who ev'ry day poetic ardour find.

[*c.* 17–18 OCTOBER. FRENCH THEMES] "Holland certainly has a very harsh climate, dangerous to strangers who have been brought up in a temperate region. There are horrible fogs and excessive cold, but especially a continuous dampness, except in the summer months." Thus a discontented man might describe the United Provinces, and, I confess, with considerable justice. But when one has actually made the experiment of living there, one finds that there is no great difference between Holland and other countries; that is to say, if a stranger lives well, eats well, drinks well, and dresses well—and also takes a good deal of exercise, which in Holland is absolutely necessary to give a brisk circulation to the blood and consequently an agreeable liveliness to the mind. If one lives after that fashion and has a suitable occupation, one can be very well satisfied. I speak positively, for I speak from experience.

Nevertheless, I dare not be so bold as to deny that in Holland it begins to get cold early in the year. I have had experience of that too. If I should deny it, my hands and feet would cry out against their master and give him the lie. The fact is that I had made a resolution not to have a fire in my rooms before the month of November, and for several evenings I have studied three or four hours on end shivering like an Italian greyhound, and sometimes I have sat up to one o'clock in the morning enduring the most disagreeable sensations. But finally I had the honour of dining with the Count of Nassau, the Grand Bailiff of Utrecht, where I found a good fire so comfortable that I began that same evening to indulge myself with the like satisfaction; and tell me if I have not done well!

TUESDAY 18 OCTOBER. You was a little irregular yesterday, but it was but for one day to see the Utrecht concert. You don't like it, and you're not to go any more. . . .

WEDNESDAY 19 OCTOBER. After this let your mems give first a little sketch of the former day. Mark what was right and what wrong, and then give directions for the following day. Yesterday you was not up till nine, and so was a little hurried. You did not give strict enough attention to Civil Law, which is very necessary as an elegant study to be kept in mind. You talked too *drôle* at Brown's, and your version is too much a piece of diversion to the company.[4] You talked too much in vivacious style to Rose, and a little too much to Guiffardière.[5] You sat up too late. Today return to the charge. Ever remember your sad shock, and you'll never fall into cold, insipid indolence. Ever remember duty. Read version comic today after dinner, and to Carron, but after this to Brown alone before dinner. Take care; *retenue*.

[*c.* 20 OCTOBER. FRENCH THEME] A nightcap is a most excellent invention, for nothing is more wholesome than to have the

[4] He had made a collection of unfamiliar French words for several days, and then had written a nonsense story to get them all in.

[5] "The subject of my next discourse is Monsieur Guiffardière, a truly curious and wonderful subject. This young man is a native of Hainault. He has never been in England, and yet he can not only read but speak the English language perfectly well. He has been a great deal in the company of English people, but I have seen several foreigners who have spent a long time in England and yet could not speak so well as Monsieur Guiffardière does. He has a great deal of vivacity, and I am told that in his youth he was an amorous and gallant man who always loved the society of ladies, and perhaps was sometimes a worshipper in the temple of Venus. But now he has become a reverend priest [i.e., a Protestant clergyman]" (French Theme, *c.* 28 September 1763). Guiffardière later became French reader to Queen Charlotte and instructor in history to the royal princesses: he appears in Fanny Burney's *Diary* as "Mr. Turbulent." His levity always shocked Boswell, a situation which he was aware of and deliberately exploited.

head well covered from the dampness of the night air, especially
when the pores are open and the whole body relaxed by sleep. It is
highly necessary in order to preserve the teeth, and the teeth are
highly necessary to man. Without those useful members he cannot
speak gracefully; for he whistles like an old woman of eighty. And
besides (a thing even more to be deplored) he cannot eat meat.
Monsieur Castillon, although a very learned man, is a sad example
of this. His teeth are so bad that for several years he has eaten
nothing but hash. Unknown to him are the robust joys of greedily
devouring a great piece of beef or mutton. Poor man! he is going
to Berlin. I hope with all my heart that that jesting rogue the
Marquis d'Argens[6] never sees him eat, for fear that he will turn
him to ridicule.

SATURDAY 22 OCTOBER. You did very well yesterday, only
you transgressed a little in talking of yourself. Let your memorandum always give a just review of the past day, and that will assist
you to regulate the future. . . . Think no more at present of marriage; rather take a little freedom like the patriarchs. But at present
study is enough. This day is market-day. Walk, finish first book of
Xenophon. Read much of Clarke, and be ready to write to Temple
clearly in favour of Revelation.[7] Bring up journal.

SUNDAY 23 OCTOBER

Th' approach of Sunday still I can't but dread,
For still old Edinburgh[8] comes into my head,

[6] The Marquis d'Argens, French miscellaneous writer and friend of Voltaire,
had become chamberlain to Frederick the Great and Director of Fine Arts in
Frederick's Academy at Berlin.
[7] On 24 May 1763 (*Boswell's London Journal, 1762–1763,* 1950) Johnson
had recommended to Boswell the reading of Dr. Samuel Clarke's *Discourse
Concerning the Being and Attributes of God,* a famous work in defence of
"the Truth and Certainty of the Christian Revelation." Boswell in Holland
put into practice a great deal more of Johnson's program for him than has
hitherto been realized.
[8] Read as two syllables. "A robust Caledonian was telling in the Scots pronunciation that he was born in *Embro.* 'Indeed!' said an English physician:

Where on that day a dreary gloom appears,
And the kirk-bells ring doleful in your ears.
Enthusiasts sad, how can you thus employ
What your Redeemer made a day of joy?
With thankful hearts to your Creator pray,
From labour rest, be cheerful and be gay.
Let us not keep the Sabbath of the Jews;
Let generous Christians Christian freedom use.

SUNDAY 23 OCTOBER. Yesterday you was still too jocular and talked of yourself, particularly of your whoring, which was shameful; however, you continue your plan of study, and you make no great deviations. Lesser things must come by degrees. Try firmly this week never once to speak of yourself. It will be great. Go to French church. Then home and read Xenophon and bring up journal clear today. You have a good deal to insert. If you can once be silent and have habits of study and manly thought and conduct, you will do well and may marry a woman of the best family in England. Bravo! But be prudent.

[*c.* 24 OCTOBER. FRENCH THEME] ... But in England there are the oratorios of Handel, which are truly most sublime.[9] My friend Mr. Sheridan,[10] who is always charmed by the music of these oratorios, used to regret that Handel was a foreigner and did not perfectly understand the English language, because as a result of his ignorance the music is sometimes not well fitted to the words. In *The Messiah* they are always singing, "Who *is* the King of Glory?"

'upon my word, the prettiest abortion I ever saw' " (*Boswelliana*, ed. Dr. Charles Rogers, p. 213, where Boswell records that he had the story from Patrick Craufurd of Rotterdam).

[9] The three themes preceding this have all been on the subject of music.

[10] Actor, theatre-manager, and (by preference) teacher of elocution; father of the more famous Richard Brinsley Sheridan, who was at this time a boy of twelve. Boswell had adopted Thomas Sheridan as his mentor in Edinburgh in 1761, where Sheridan had come to give a series of lectures, and had been much in Sheridan's house during the period covered by the *London Journal*, *1762–1763*.

and "I *am* the King of Glory," and so lose the noble sense of the words entirely by putting on *"is"* and *"am"* the accent which ought to be on *"Who"* and *"I"*: *"Who* is the King of Glory?" *"I* am the King of Glory." We also have plenty of very good church music, and for English songs Mr. Arne is certainly excellent. Indeed, his opera *Artaxerxes* has abundance of merit. We have besides a number of other musicians of whom I will speak in my next theme.[1]

[Received 24 October, Lord Auchinleck to Boswell]

Auchinleck, 8 October 1763

MY DEAR SON,—Since you went to Holland, I have had the pleasure to receive two of your letters: the first from Leyden, to which I wrote an answer addressed, as you desired, Au Neuf Château d'Anvers; the other, which is dated from Utrecht the 8th of September, is now before me. I am glad you are settled to your mind, though I suspect that upon trial you will find inconvenience in having a house by yourself. Lodgings in a discreet family are comfortable, give less to do in the affair of housewifery, and give more opportunity for converse without ceremony; and the only way of acquiring a foreign language is to speak it *hardiment,* as the French say. And the French people have no disposition to laugh at a blunder in a stranger when attempting to speak their language, an absurdity that is remarkable in the English; nay, they are so shy to let a stranger know he has blundered that in place of a formal correction, they will repeat your question, putting it in good French that you may thereby learn how to express the thing on another occasion. This I have often remarked; and therefore it is absolutely necessary for you to attend not only to the subject, but to every word that is spoke.

I think you did well to take a little tour before the colleges sat

[1] He mentions Karl Friedrich Abel and Felice di Giardini. "Mr. Abel," he says, "is a German, and he does not take it in good part when people say he composes Italian music. He said to me, 'Sir, that is not Italian music or German music: it is music that comes down from heaven.' "

down. Amsterdam is a fine city. The Stadthouse, which is a noble edifice, was all built with stones furnished by your great-grandfather, the Earl of Kincardine. I have the contract between him and the burgomasters in relation to it.[2] There was a namesake of ours, James Boswell, a turner, an old acquaintance of mine who was fixed there; and one of the ministers of the English church there, Mr. Longueville, was born in Dickstoun, the next house to Tenshillingside, a very worthy man who is by marriages in opulent circumstances and would have shown you great civility had you called on him and let him know who you were.

You desire to know my landlord's name at Leyden. It was Ramach; he lived *op de hoek van de Vliet* in the street called the Rapenburg. My landlady, with whom I stayed before she married him, was called the Widow Boene. He was a tailor to his trade.

Your plan of passing time for your improvement is proper. When you read and take notes regularly, you'll find great profit, for the taking of notes ascertains your attention and at the same time rivets the thing in your memory. I would recommend to you as the best preservative against melancholy and vice never to be idle but still to be employed in something; this is the only specific against these maladies. And for that reason you should endeavour to acquire a taste for as many things as you think you may in after life command as is possible. Reading is the great point indeed. But as you are now in a country where gardening is in perfection, you should be at pains to learn it, and by that means when you come home can execute many pretty things. You'll likewise see the method the Dutch manage their cattle, and take notes of it. I would wish to be informed of the method by which they keep their cows so clean, for my remembrance of it is dark. They had a contrivance

[2] Alexander Bruce (d. 1680), second Earl of Kincardine, was an eminent royalist who followed Charles II into exile. In 1659, at The Hague, he married a Dutch heiress, Veronica van Sommelsdyck; their daughter, Lady Elizabeth Bruce, married James Boswell of Auchinleck. Lord Auchinleck got from Lord Kincardine his Christian name of Alexander. Lord Kincardine owned quarries of stone and of marble at Culross in Fifeshire.

for making their dung no way offensive to them, and a way of
watering them in a trough, as I think. Write me as to this and
mention the measures, that so one might execute it here.[3] You'll
be frequently, I hope, with Count Nassau, who is, I hear, a fine
gentleman.

Sir David Dalrymple is either married or just on the point
of being to Miss Brown, Lord Coalston's daughter. We are all here
in our ordinary, and all join in compliments to you. Harvest is
mostly over; it has been good and plentiful. May GOD bless and
preserve you. I am your affectionate father,

ALEXR. BOSWEL.

WEDNESDAY 26 OCTOBER. Yesterday was an excellent day.
Remember it with satisfaction. You did all your business well and
with spirit. You talked freely to Brown and bid him be a monitor to
warn you of deviations, and he agreed to do so and gave you high
applause for your conduct. Pray persevere. Consider that this happiness is wrought out by study, by rational conduct, and by piety.
It is the natural effect of these causes; and you may ever be so. Be
fixed in your general Plan, and never admit fancies to lead you
from it. Send today at ten for your discourse for the Society,[4] and
prepare little repast and pipes. Never forget your Plan a moment.
Always be improving.

[*c.* 26 OCTOBER. FRENCH THEME] There is a musical society
in London called the Catch Club ... There are many members,
among them many people of quality and fashion and also some of
the best singers in England. They give every year a prize of ten
guineas to the person who submits the best song, both as regards
words and music. They have a truly excellent collection. The
subjects are gay: they celebrate the pleasures of wine and of love.
The words are for the most part spirited and the accompanying
tunes match them in liveliness. These songs are composed in three

---

[3] "So that one might build the same things here."
[4] See above, p. 43 *n.* 4. He had perhaps left it with Brown or Carron to be
corrected?

parts, and when properly executed have really a very agreeable
harmony. Lord Eglinton[5] is one of the most famous members of
this society. He sings in charming taste. He had the goodness to
teach me some songs. When I return to England, I hope to learn
more. My Lord did me the honour to say that there were not three
better ears in the whole society than mine. How many happy evenings have I passed at his house, singing! But he is not merely a
singer. He is truly a man of distinguished mind. I could celebrate
his perfections here, but we must always keep to our subject, and
mine at present is music. There is a very pretty kind of music in
Scotland: it is sweet, melancholy, and natural. They say that David
Rizzio, the musician of the Scottish queen, the fair Mary, is its
author. Perhaps that ingenious Italian did mingle the airs of his
country with those of Scotland. I mean, that he gave the airs of
Scotland a little of the tenderness of Italy. In the mountains of
Scotland they have music that is undoubtedly original. Their slow
airs are very pathetic and their quick ones (*reels*) have an astonishing vivacity. They are the best dance-tunes in the world.

    FRIDAY 28 OCTOBER. You did charmingly yesterday. You
attended well to everything. . . .

    SUNDAY 30 OCTOBER

> The farther up the hill of life we rise,
> The less we feel the passion of surprise.
> Our wonder deaden'd by successive change,
> We come at last to reckon nothing strange.
> Had any cunning man foretold as how
> I should become enamour'd of a *vrouw:*
> That my keen eyes with warmest love should rove
> O'er features parch'd by fumigating stove,
> Even at the age when I was flogg'd at school,
> I should have thought him a consummate fool.

[5] A rakish but able Scots nobleman who had been very kind to Boswell
during both of his visits to London and had "introduced him into the circles
of the great, the gay, and the ingenious." See above, p. 1.

MONDAY 31 OCTOBER

> And yet just now a Utrecht lady's charms
> Make my gay bosom beat with love's alarms.
> Who could have thought to see young Cupid fly
> Through Belgia's thick and suffocating sky?
> But she from whom my heart has caught the flame
> Has nothing Dutch about her but the name.
> Let not an ear too delicate recoil
> And start fastidious when I say "De Zoile";
> So mere a trifle I can change with ease:
> Your tender niceness will "Zelida" please?[6]

MONDAY 31 OCTOBER. Yesterday you did not at all keep to rules as you ought to do. You had sat late up and rose irregular. You went to Guiffardière at eleven and talked too foolishly and too freely. At night you was absurdly bashful before Miss de Zuylen. You went up to Rose's room to read Greek; you laughed too much. You are sure you was not behaving properly when Rose talked of you by the name of Boswell before your face.[7] You put on foolish airs of a passion for Miss de Zuylen.... Be always candid to censure in your mems, and you'll amend.

[6] This is Boswell's first reference to Isabella Agneta Elisabeth van Tuyll van Serooskerken, concerning whom his heart was to be in a state of alternating attraction and repulsion for the next four and a half years. For a full note on the relationship, see p. 293. She seems generally to have preferred to be known by the familiar name Belle de Zuylen, the name Zélide, by which Boswell always addressed her after they really became intimate, being a self-conscious literary style which she adopted in writing her "portrait" of herself (see p. 184) but appears not to have used elsewhere. "Tuyll" is the family name, "Zuylen" (modern Dutch Zuilen) the name of the village near Utrecht from which her father took his principal title of nobility. Boswell very seldom uses the family name, his ordinary designation being "de Zuyl." In this instance he wrote "de Zoile," and that spelling has been allowed to stand because it looks like a better rhyme for "recoil." The correspondence of sound was in fact fairly close.

[7] That is, when he allowed Rose to refer to him as "Boswell" rather than as "Mr. Boswell."

[31 OCTOBER. FRENCH THEME] It is certain that I have the greatest desire to learn French, but I fear that I am not learning it quickly. Perhaps my keen desire makes me think myself worse in acquiring the language than I am. I certainly take a great deal of pains to improve. I write two pages of a theme every morning.[8] I read for two hours in the works of Voltaire every evening. When I do not understand words perfectly, I look them up in the dictionary, and I write them down with their meanings. Every Wednesday I have the pleasure of passing the evening in a literary society where it is not permitted to speak a word of anything but French; and I dine at Mr. Brown's, where there are two ladies who do not speak English, and where for that reason it is always necessary to speak French. Yet I cannot observe that I am making rapid progress. In writing, I am slow and clumsy, and in speaking I have great difficulty in expressing myself and often make terrible blunders. Instead of saying, "Would you like to play at shuttlecock?" (*volant*), I said, "Would you like to play at robber?" (*voleur*); and instead of, "Mademoiselle, I am entirely at your service" (*tout ce qu'il vous plaira*), I said, "Mademoiselle, I am something (*quelque chose*) that will please you."[9] Such blunders make a man very ridiculous. But I must not be downhearted. Very soon I hope to acquire propriety of language. I confess that we do not speak French at Mr. Brown's as assiduously as we ought. Laziness disposes us to speak English and sometimes barbarous Latin.

[8] He had started with one, and even at this period sometimes managed only one; on other occasions he probably wrote several to make up. But his *plan* was to write exactly two pages each day, Sundays included.

[9] About this time he drew up in French a list of the "howlers (*bévues*) made by Monsieur Boswell in learning to speak French," but neglected to continue it. Besides the two *bévues* mentioned above, he records the following: *Je suis trop recherché* for *Je cherche trop mes mots; Je suis bien chaud* for *J'ai bien chaud; Les magistrats d'Utrecht ont besoin de faire allumer la ville* for *illuminer*, &c.; *En Suisse les fourneaux sont bien peignés* for *peints*. His *Je suis tout ce qu'il vous plaira* is hardly more idiomatic than his admitted *bévue*. He could have said *Mademoiselle, tout ce qu'il vous plaira* or *Je ferai tout ce qu'il vous plaira*.

But after today (Monday 31 October) I am determined never to speak except in French. Let us see if I have any resolution.

[Received 31 October, John Boswell, M.D., to Boswell][1]

Edinburgh, Monday 17 October 1763

MY DEAREST SIR AND KIND NEPHEW,—However long I may have been in writing you, yet can assure my good friend he has never been out of my heart as well as memory since I left him at the entry to St. Paul's.[2] One accidental meeting there, and one parting bottle at the tavern there, I can never forget; and indeed, the whole of one unexpected (to me lucky) meeting at London will ever be remembered by me as one of the most agreeable incidents of my life, as it was then I had confirmed to me the former opinions I had conceived very early of you. I hope however the friendship that is begun will increase; and although never could Mason say more heartily than you and I, "Happy to meet, happy to part," yet above all, happy on the thought to meet again. . . .[3]

I delivered your letter and paid the money mentioned to your friend Mr. Johnston, and find him a man according to our own hearts after the flesh, and hope to have him for an agreeable friend so long as I shall stay here. He is now at Annandale. I bid him send his letters either to me (for you) or to direct them for you as I've done this.

I have scarce ever been settled since I came home, and my

[1] Boswell's uncle, Lord Auchinleck's only surviving brother, a physician of Edinburgh. He and Boswell resembled each other in temperament much more than either resembled Lord Auchinleck. Dr. Boswell had been in London during part of Boswell's recent stay there.

[2] 24 July 1763: see *Boswell's London Journal, 1762–1763*, 1950, p. 323.

[3] Boswell had been admitted a Mason in Canongate Kilwinning Lodge, No. 2, Edinburgh, as early as his nineteenth year (Dr. Boswell at the time being Depute Master), and had already served as Junior Warden of his lodge. He later became R. W. Master of Canongate Kilwinning and finally Depute Grand Master for Scotland. One of the marks of the congeniality of temperament existing between Boswell and his uncle was that they were both ardent Masons. Lord Auchinleck held the Craft in contempt.

brother and I have scarce ever exchanged a word on any subject. Only in general I have, I hope, given both he and lady satisfaction concerning a son of theirs now at Utrecht. I beg you'll make my compliments to him and tell him I hope he'll not allow me to be classed amongst the bad judges and prophets.

I long to hear you are pleased with Holland, and Utrecht in particular, and that you are satisfied now I was not imposing upon you when I commended it as a polite, literatury[4] place. There is one Boswell there, a bookseller, whom you'll certainly find out and inquire his origin. Hopes you'll write me a full account of all the celebrated professors now there, and also who are the first toasts. Did you see Gaubius. . . ?[5] How did you like Leyden? Do you begin to roke[6] a pipe, Mynheer?

We are now here very quiet, but on Friday first there is to be a grand procession of all the Freemasons from the Parliament House to the North Loch in order to lay the foundation stone of the new bridge.[7] We have had very inconstant weather, only these two or three days bypast better than any we had in July or August. I beg you'll write very particularly and give me all your arguments for a certain friend of yours[8] settling at London, &c. All your friends at Affleck[9] were well last week. . . . I'll endeavour to write you a better letter next time. May God eternally bless you, &c.

B.

[*c.* 2–3 NOVEMBER. FRENCH THEMES] . . . But after all these profound reasonings on breeches,[1] I should like to know what is the best material to make them of. I am now wearing a kind of black

---

[4] An adjective from "literature"; a useful invention of Dr. Boswell's.

[5] Jerome David Gaubius was a physician of some distinction at Leyden. Dr. Boswell knew him well and had probably been his pupil.

[6] Smoke (Dutch, *roken*).

[7] The North Bridge, the first effective outlet from the City across the North Loch and first step in the formation of the New Town.

[8] Dr. Boswell himself.

[9] Dr. Boswell's spelling is here preserved as indicating how the name Auchinleck was universally pronounced in the eighteenth century.

[1] A page and a half on breeches precedes this extract.

stuff made, I think, at Utrecht. It is composed of linen and silk, but it is extremely thin and does not wear well. I have worn breeches made of this stuff only three or four weeks, and they are already miserably torn. I am much ashamed of them. When I play at shuttlecock with our young lady,[2] I sweat for fear she will discover so excellent a subject for teasing me. It surprises me, indeed, that she has not discovered it before now, because they are torn between the legs, rather before than behind, and when I play warmly, I straddle like a very Colossus. But she is a modest girl and does not wish to see such shameful things, and if by chance she had seen them, she would pretend the contrary. I commend her much for not looking at my torn breeches, but I should commend her more if she would have the goodness to mend them.[3] She can do it without risk when I have taken them off. Breeches are improper only when they are on my backside. In themselves they are no more than simple and innocent objects. If Mademoiselle would do me the favour I ask, no one could find anything to blame her for, except perhaps a superstitious prude whom nobody should pay any attention to. I myself have known an old maid who was so very scrupulous that she would not for anything in the world pronounce the word "breeches" in English, which was her native tongue. She would not pollute her lips by saying "a pair of breeches," but would only pronounce the first letter. She always said, "A pair of b——s."

I undertake to be Mademoiselle's knight-errant if she will kindly mend my breeches with her own fair hand. I have the honour to say that it is not the first time I have asked and obtained such a favour. My breeches have been mended by ladies before now. They have been mended by the most famous beauty in the north of Scotland, and even when I had them on.[4] I must admit, however, that it was only in one of the knees.

SUNDAY 6 NOVEMBER. Let your Inviolable Plan be read only

---

[2] Mrs. Brown's younger sister, Marguerite Kinloch, about twenty-one years old.
[3] Boswell wrote all this planning to read it at Brown's in Mademoiselle Kinloch's presence.
[4] Boswell gives no further clues as to this lady's identity.

every Saturday morning, and judge by it impartially how you have passed the week. Resist not every good impression. This night you wrote this when just returned from Mr. Brown's at twelve at night. You felt high satisfaction at looking back on two months spent in study and in propriety. You found real satisfaction in religion and piety. You determined never to relax in your warfare; and always to have a consistent conduct, and by rehearsing to prepare for real life.

This night, when you are in your best moments, sound in understanding and contented and happy, you are sensible that you deal too hardly with yourself at times. Remember this. If you are mindful of your duty to God, repent of your offences, endeavour to raise your mind by piety, by thinking on the certainty of death and on the dignity of human nature, and if you do your duty as a student and be guilty of no folly, you are very well. You are subject to gloom, as the prettiest men have been. You are not then to judge of yourself. You are to be patient.

[*c.* 8 NOVEMBER. FRENCH THEME] I have certainly caught a cold. I feel its dreadful effects. My nose is stuffed, I breathe with great difficulty. I have a sad headache, and I have severe chills all over my body. A "cold" is really a fever. It is often the beginning of the most dangerous illnesses. I must take care of myself now: I should not like to die in this country of fogs. Simonides says that it is all one where one dies, because there is "everywhere a passage to the other world." But although I have great respect for that excellent philosopher, I cannot be of his opinion on this subject. For my part, I hope to die at Auchinleck, in London, or in Edinburgh, and in my last moments to have an Anglican clergyman to read me the divine service and aid me in lifting my soul to God and in meditating on the felicity of glorified spirits. . . .

[Boswell to Temple]

Utrecht, 9 November 1763

MY DEAR TEMPLE,—That Mr. Gray advises you to go into the Church, I am much rejoiced to hear. I know that his opinion will have the weight with you which the opinion of a man of distinguished good sense, learning, and worth ought to have. Besides, there is a secret satisfaction, a gratification of vanity not unworthy of the best, in having so great a bard for a counsellor, which may also incline you to pursue the path which he points out.

Indeed, my friend, you are born to be a clergyman. Your amiable dispositions and mildness of manners are excellently fitted for that character. You are devoted to study, to virtue, and to friendship.

You tell me that you have a material objection. You are very doubtful with regard to Revelation. That is indeed material. There are, to be sure, many infidels in orders, who, considering religion merely as a political institution, accept of a benefice as of any civil employment, and contribute their endeavours to keep up the useful delusion. But, my dear Temple, you have too much delicacy of sentiment to entertain such an idea of duplicity, and too much honour to think of propagating fraud, though dignified with the name of pious. . . .[5]

And now at last I have time to talk of myself. I am much indebted to you for your concern in my welfare. (Upon second thoughts, the expression "indebted" ought not to be used between real friends. Let me not get into the polite expressions of the Continent, where friendship is little known.) I am convinced that I ought to have hopes of enlarging my plan, and of being in Parliament. I am convinced too that my rising in the world must depend in some measure on my marriage. Your mentioning an alliance with an English family of rank and fortune gave a spring to my ambition. Let me not despair of making such an alliance.

My late scheme of matrimony I am sensible was a bad one. I must not think of that important step for some years, especially as I have yet to travel and to settle my conduct in life. I had inflamed my imagination by thinking on the amiable Miss Stewart, and did not see the whimsical appearance which a courtship in postscripts must have made. I have a strange turn towards marriage. I have

[5] An extended and earnest defence of the Christian revelation follows.

distressed you with consultations upon that head from the beginning of our friendship. While I have such a friend to whom I can lay open even my weakest fancies, I shall be happy. My flourish about intrigues and duels was an intemperate sally of high spirits. . . . I ever remain your most affectionate friend,

JAMES BOSWELL.

[*c.* 9–10 NOVEMBER. FRENCH THEMES] . . . In speaking of [a cold], the French have only one word to express the fact that they have come down with one. But the English have two: "I have catched cold" and "I have got cold." In my youth I lived for a time in the house of the Earl of Eglinton in London, where I had the honour to be known to H.R.H. the Duke of York.[6] One day I was arguing with him about these expressions concerning a cold, and I maintained that we should say "catch cold" for the present or imperfect, but to indicate some time past we should say, "I have got cold." The Duke laughed, and was quite willing to confess himself beaten.

In my last theme[7] I exposed my ignorance of the French language. I said that they had only one word to express having a cold. But Mr. Brown, my instructor in French, has told me that there are several phrases equally proper in such circumstances. I had a strong desire to introduce my conversation with the Duke of York, and I admit that I dragged it in by the hair. It rarely happens that a young man who has no relations at Court has the honour to be known to a prince. My vanity was much flattered by that honour.

[6] Younger brother of George III, a year and a half older than Boswell, and heir presumptive to the throne when Boswell met him in 1760. He was a violinist of some distinction, a rake, and what the eighteenth century called a "rattle." Horace Walpole, writing in 1751, described him as "a very plain boy, with strange loose eyes." Boswell had offended him by dedicating to him in 1762 a doggerel poem, *The Cub at Newmarket,* without asking his permission.
[7] The preceding paragraph. It must be remembered that by "theme" Boswell means his daily exercise of one or two pages, not all the pages dealing with a single topic.

It was a great matter of pride for a Scot when he returned to his
own country to speak of the conversations which he had had with
his Royal Highness. And indeed the thing was well known in Scotland; and as all rumours, whether good or ill, but especially ill, are
greatly exaggerated, this one was too. The solicitors[8] of Edinburgh,
as they drank their punch, said that I was quite the companion of
the Duke of York, that we ran together through the streets of
London at all hours of the night, and that we made no ceremony
with each other: it was just "James" and "Ned." At the age of nineteen when I was raw and a dreamer, it was certainly not wrong of
me to be puffed up with pride because I was known to a prince. But
now, when I have some experience and begin to be a real philosopher, how foolish it seems to me to pique myself on a thing so
trifling! The Duke of York was not a man of dignity nor of extraordinary genius. He was sunk in debauchery and sometimes made
himself the companion of the vilest of the human species. I knew
him only very little and he never did me the least service. . . .

SATURDAY 12 NOVEMBER. Yesterday was an irregular day.
You passed three hours at Brown's with Miss de Zuylen. You was
too much off guard, and gave way too much to instantaneous fancy,
and was too keen about the Highlanders. You was a little light-
headed; however, you must not be too severe. For if you never
mimic, never censure, never talk of yourself, and have piety ever
in mind, you cannot go wrong. So learn to sit in company and have
command. Trifle away no time. Be busy this day to atone. At Greek
hour never speak till 'tis over. Be hard to that. Speak French with
Rose to learn as soon as possible. Mark German baron learning
d'être vif.[9] Keep firm to study and propriety.

[8] *Procureurs.* Boswell's actual English word would have been "writers,"
the Scots term for lawyers who are not admitted to plead at the bar.

[9] A story told him by Belle de Zuylen, recorded in his *Boswelliana* as follows (p. 220): "A dull German baron had got amongst the English at
Geneva, and being highly pleased with their spirit, wanted to imitate them.
One day an Englishman came into the Baron's room and found him jumping
with all his might upon the chairs and down again, so that he was all in a
sweat. 'Mon Dieu! Monsieur le baron,' dit-il, 'que faites-vous?' ('Good God!
Baron,' said he, 'what are you about?') 'Monsieur,' replied the Baron, wiping

[Received 12 November, Lord Auchinleck to Boswell]

[Auchinleck, ? October 1763]

My dear Son,—Your letter of the 7th of October, which came
in due course, gave me uncommon satisfaction, for as I know your
veracity and can confide in the accounts you give of yourself, I
now bless God that I have the prospect of having comfort in you
and support from you; and that you will tread in the steps of the
former Jameses, who in this family have been remarkably useful.

I quite approve of your plan of study. You may, by the assistance of Professor Trotz, come to be thoroughly master of the Pandects, which is the most rational system of law extant, and the
reasonings in it the most acute and accurate; and Mr. Erskine's
Institutes of the Scots law are well composed. It will be an entertainment to compare the two laws of Scotland and of Rome, and
you'll see that we have in most things followed that great and wise
people.

Your returning to the study of the Latin and Greek authors
secures to you a mine of unexhaustible knowledge and entertainment. There is a peculiar strength of thought and of expression in
the ancients, a *je ne sais quoi* which strikes those who understand
them with reverence. By falling into this way you will find constant entertainment, and that is the only thing can dispel gloom
and low spirits. When I have nothing to do, which happens when
I am from home visiting, time passes heavily; but when I am occupied, I repine that it is so short. You'll too in Holland probably
acquire a taste for gardening and send me home some instruction
about it. In my last I put a query about a Dutch cow-house or byre
which I suppose you'll solve me in.

You inquire, and properly inquire, about our Dutch relations,
that you may be in condition to talk with them when you meet
them. I shall tell you what I know, and I know a good deal. The
first of the family of Sommelsdyck who made a conspicuous figure
was Francis. I shall say nothing as to him, but remit you to a noted

down his temples with a handkerchief, 'j'apprends d'être vif' ('I am learning
to be lively')."

book entitled *Mémoires pour servir à l'histoire de Hollande*, par. Monsieur de l'Aubery du Maurier, who does not speak well of that gentleman because you'll see he outwitted the author's father. The next person was Cornelius, of whom Monsieur de l'Aubery gives a great character, and indeed he was a great good man. He was my great-grandfather and among the richest men in Holland. He had one son, who was murdered in a mutiny at Surinam, of which he was at the time Governor; for you must know the family has the property of a third part of that valuable island, and power to put in the Governor *per vices,*[10] or every third vice along with the States of Holland. And, besides that son, Cornelius had seven daughters who got great fortunes; four of them were married: one to the Earl of Kincardine, my grandfather; her name was Veronica van Aerssen van Sommelsdyck. I have their contract of marriage in my possession, signed by the Earl and her and by her father, Cornelius. . . .

The late Admiral Sommelsdyck, to whose civilities I was much obliged when in Holland in the years 1727 and 1728, was son to him who was murdered in Surinam. He left one son, Francis, who is the present Heer van Sommelsdyck, and three daughters, one of whom is dead, unmarried; the other two are married to nobles; but Monsieur Chais, to whom I shall get you a new letter,[1] will inform you more particularly, as he was and is a great intimate in the family. . . .

I have only to add that I approve of your dining with Mr. Brown; he has a good character. Your mother remembers you with affection, as does Johnny. I must cut short for making my letter close.[2] Farewell, my dear son, be steadfast in the good way. I am your affectionate father,

ALEXR. BOSWEL.

I have no room to mention books to be bought.

[10] "In turn."

[1] The Reverend Charles Pierre Chais, Swiss Protestant clergyman and author, was pastor of the French church at The Hague. Apparently Boswell's letter of introduction to Monsieur Chais had miscarried or been mislaid.

[2] That is, "must stop writing so as to leave enough blank paper to cover my letter when it is folded."

SUNDAY 13 NOVEMBER. Yesterday you did extremely well. You received a letter from your worthy father which warmed your heart and gave you new vigour to pursue a proper course. . . .

[c. 14 NOVEMBER. FRENCH THEME] There is a dreadful uproar in Great Britain because the Tories are in favour at Court. "Tory" was a jeering word used to express an Irish savage, and the republican faction gave that appellation to the loyalists[3] in England. Mr. Johnson in his *Dictionary* defines a Tory thus: "A man who adheres to the ancient constitution of the State, and the apostolical hierarchy of the Church of England," and certainly that is a good definition. The Court undoubtedly does well to show favour to so respectable a party, who are in truth the firmest friends of the Constitution. . . . They have been discontented for several reigns, because they hoped to restore the House of Stuart. At the present time they are convinced that such a revolution would not be for their country's happiness. They see that the succession is well established in the House of George, and they have become its friends, and, thank GOD, by that change we may hope for a well regulated government. When I speak of the reigning house, I always say "the House of George." It is perhaps a prejudice, but although the family of Brunswick or Hanover is a distinguished family, I do not like to recall that the king of our glorious nation is merely a prince of Germany, with one of those barbarous names—Guelf,[4] I believe. But George the Third is born a Briton, and he has the heart of a Briton. He is a perfectly amiable man; perhaps his virtues are more amiable than great. There has as yet been no occasion to determine his character.

SATURDAY 19 NOVEMBER . . . . You have struggled, you have conquered. . . .

WEDNESDAY 23 NOVEMBER. Yesterday you did upon the whole very well. Your version, your Dutch, and your Greek went

---

[3] That is, to those loyal to the House of Stuart; to the Jacobites.

[4] Boswell originally spelled it "Wolfe"; "Guelf," though possibly in his own hand, was I think a correction by Carron or Brown. "Guelf," as a m :ter of fact, is an Italian spelling of the German name Welf.

well. You plagued Mademoiselle a little and made the ignorant
being think you impertinent. Guard against seeming so. At night
you had truly an adventure. You saw an entertainment of Dutch
students; a concert; all keen on meat and drink; then marching like
schoolboys with *Kapitein* and frightening the street. Then home;
then saw the masks, and one like woman; then house again con-
ditionless drank roaring—songs. King George.[5] Compliments paid
you, &c. Mark all in journal. Be *retenu* but amusing at Brown's.

THURSDAY 24 NOVEMBER. Yesterday you recovered very well
after your riot with the Dutch students. But remember how near
you was to getting drunk and exposing yourself, for if you had
gone on a little longer, you could not have stopped. You have important secrets to keep. Though you are sorry for the crimes,[6] yet
preserve a warm affection and gratitude to the persons and show it
when you meet, disinterestedly; and in the mean time always shun
drinking, and guard lips. . . .

[*c.* 24–26 NOVEMBER. FRENCH THEMES][7] . . . Soon my Lord
Bute was made Groom of the Stole, as they say in England, a very
honourable office. He is master of the King's wardrobe. In these
themes I can never resist anything laughable that presents itself,
whether there is occasion for it or not. In this I follow the example
of Rabelais, Tristram Shandy, and all those people of unbridled
imagination who write their books as I write my themes—at random, without trying to have any order or method; and for that

[5] The writing is crowded and the transcription not altogether certain. I
interpret the passage to mean that he joined a group of students who were
drinking and singing noisily; that every person present had unconditionally
to drink all the toasts and propose one himself; that Boswell's toast was
King George.

[6] A reference to his intrigues in Scotland with women of fashion and reputation. Before he met Samuel Johnson he would not have used the word
"crime" to describe these amours.

[7] The themes from which this extract has been taken form a digression in
a long series detailing the current political situation in England. Lord Bute,
George III's unpopular favourite and prime minister, had resigned office
in the previous April.

reason they have acquired great reputation among people of un-regulated vivacity who do not wish to give themselves the trouble of thinking even in their amusements. . . . I recall that when I was very young in Scotland I believed that the office of Groom of the Stole was Groom of the Stool: that is, I thought the office of master of the wardrobe (*garderobe*) was gentleman of the close-stool (*selle*), because the English words for those very different things are almost the same; and I supposed that every time his Majesty honoured the temple of Cloacina with his presence, he made use of a piece of fine cambric, or rather that it was assigned to him for such an occasion and that the gentleman of the wardrobe furnished a sufficient quantity of soft paper and took the fine cloth as a per-quisite for himself, or rather for his wife; and that it is not impos-sible that many ladies of quality in England have worn that cloth when their husbands were in the honourable office of gentleman of the wardrobe—that is to say, according to the conjecture I made in my youth. Made, do I say? No, I did not make it; I got it from chambermaids, and they perhaps got it from their mothers, and so on, *ad infinitum*. It would be a task worthy the most famous anti-quary to discover the origin of that conjecture: that is to say, to find the person who first made it.[8]

SATURDAY 26 NOVEMBER. Yesterday you did very well. You did your morning business. You dined with the Countess of Nassau, and she showed you much respect. The young Count d'Ouwerkerke is lively, good-humoured, and quite a little man of the world. The governor is a sensible, pretty man. All was elegant and fine.[9] You

[8] The laughable etymology which Boswell rejects is in fact the correct one, "stole" in the title "Groom of the Stole" being the mediaeval form of "stool" and having nothing to do with garments. The Groom of the Stole had as his original function the oversight of the chamber containing the king's close-stool. The more refined etymology preferred by Boswell and others may have been encouraged by the fact that in mediaeval English *garderobe* meant both "wardrobe" and "privy."

[9] The Countess of Nassau here mentioned was not the wife but the sister-in-law of the Grand Bailiff of Utrecht, and was sometimes called Beverweerd or Nassau Beverweerd to indicate as much. Since it does not appear that

observed her Ladyship's inquisitive temper. But you had *retenue.*
You said nothing of Madam Brown but *"fort aimable"* and of Mr.
Brown but "an excellent *homme,"* and you was discreet in talking
of Miss de Zuylen. You took much, was quite as you could wish.
The Countess takes you under her protection; all will go well. . . .

SUNDAY 27 NOVEMBER. Yesterday was a charming day. You
waited on Countess Beverweerd in the morning, quite sweet and
pretty, as in London. You received your list of ladies.[1] You then
read three pages of Greek; then dined decently, although a little
flighty, but you restrained your elation. Brown and Rose foretold
that the ladies and gaiety would make you negligent. But you replied with Spanish pride that you had seen too much of these
things. You then made your tour, quite the man of fashion; was received at two places a little awkward, but made your way, happy to

she had any living children at this time, "the young Count d'Ouwerkerke"
was probably a nephew of her husband and also of the Grand Bailiff, her
husband's brother. "The governor" was no doubt the young Count's tutor.
The Count of Nassau Beverweerd (whom Boswell seems not to have met
until 4 December) was approaching seventy. The Countess, at this time
about thirty, is the subject of a characteristically brilliant and caustic pen-
portrait by Belle de Zuylen, written about a year later than this: "The
Countess of Nassau has been brought to bed; people laugh and talk. As for
me, I see nothing certain in the matter except the pleasure which having a
child will bring to a woman who otherwise has nothing but an old fool of a
husband; and without spoiling by vague conjectures the sentiment which
makes me share her joy, I shall go and congratulate her sincerely. I am
rather fond of that woman, and I do not know why: her lectures bore me, her
curiosities are a burden, I am assured that she is not at all my friend although
she puts on a show of being so—and in spite of all that she interests me. The
singular thing about her, if she really is *galante,* is that she has none of the
defects and none of the charms which ordinarily accompany *galanterie.*
No jealousy, no bickerings, nothing of the nonchalant self-forgetfulness so
dangerous but so attractive: her mind is inflexible, she descants, she sub-
divides, she talks politics in a tone which seems to testify that she does not
know how to speak of love." By 1766 the Countess's indiscretions had become
so notorious that Belle was avoiding her company.
[1] A list of ladies of rank and fashion to whom he might pay his respects,
and so get invited to the assemblies, which were about to begin.

hear such a fine character of Sir David; ambitious to imitate it. You then had eight pages of version corrected, which was well written, and behaved easily. Then you waited on *la Comtesse* and went to *les Comtesses* d'Aumale. Struck at first entry, &c. Behaved well. Home with *la Comtesse* and supped charming, and received instructions, &c., &c. . . .

[List of Ladies Given Boswell by the Countess of Nassau]

> Madame de Tuyll   1[2]
> Les demoiselles d'Averhoult   3
> Madame d'Amerongen   2
> Madame Maleprade   1
> Les Comtesses d'Aumale   2
> Madame Wachtèndorp   1
> Mademoiselle Assenburgh   1
> Les demoiselles de Bottestein   2
> Madame van den Heuvel (dans le Trans)[3]
> La Comtesse d'Efferen   1
> Madame Roosmalen   2
> La Comtesse de Boetzelaer   1
> Madame Sichterman   1
> Mademoiselle de Tuyll   1
> Madame de Zuylen   2
> Madame de Guy   1
> Madame de Lockhorst   2

[Received 26 November, Dempster to Boswell]

Manchester Buildings [London] 19 November 1763

DEAR BOSWELL,—The enclosed letter[4] you will perceive by the date was intended for you long ago. I wrote it in Scotland, trans-

[2] The numbers after the names presumably indicate the number of cards to be left.

[3] A street in Utrecht, still extant, south of the Cathedral Square, in the immediate neighbourhood of the University.   [4] Printed above, p. 19.

mitted it to Fordyce at London, who was by that time on his way to Edinburgh. There I received it from him again, brought it up with myself, and in the hurry of Parliamentary affairs, have carried it a week in my pocket. All this to prove you may be long of hearing from Dempster without being forgotten or neglected by him.

I just came to town time enough to witness the prosecution against Wilkes.[5] The King insisted on his ministers bringing him to punishment, which I am informed they were in some doubts about the possibility of. However his Majesty has found the House of Commons more zealous and unanimous than any of his ministers expected.

The whole House condemned *The North Briton*, No. 45, and three hundred of the members voted it all the hard names which Lord North, Norborne Berkeley, Chace Price, or Bamber Gascoyne could bestow upon it. In the course of the debate, Martin of the Treasury said the author of that paper in which his character was traduced and in which he had received a stab in the dark was a coward and a scoundrel. Next morning Wilkes sent him that *North Briton* with his name at bottom. Martin then challenged Wilkes. They met in Hyde Park, both parties behaved gallantly, and at the

[5] John Wilkes, the famous demagogue, a Member of Parliament, had conducted a scurrilous anti-ministerial periodical called *The North Briton*, in the 45th number of which he had called the recent speech from the throne (19 April 1763) "the most abandoned instance of ministerial effrontery ever attempted to be imposed on mankind," and had insinuated that the King had deliberately countenanced a lie in reading it. The Government had ordered Wilkes to be prosecuted, and had actually committed him to the Tower of London, but because of the bungling methods used by the secretaries of state in arresting him and Wilkes's privilege as a Member of Parliament, the Lord Chief Justice of the Common Pleas had ordered him to be discharged. It was therefore necessary for the Government, if it wished to continue its prosecution, to transfer its activities to Parliament; and this it did on the very first day of the next session (15 November 1763). Dempster's letter carries on from this point. He knew that Boswell would be interested in the news, for Boswell had struck up a personal acquaintance with Wilkes in London the previous spring.

second shot Wilkes received a wound in his lower belly, of which, though not in danger, he is at present very ill. Proceedings have been stopped against Wilkes till his recovery.

You must know that Wilkes was just about publishing twelve or thirteen copies (printing, indeed, more properly) of a most extraordinary work entitled *An Essay on Woman,* a parody on *The Essay on Man,* to which he had likewise added, to complete the burlesque, Warburton's notes. The work was inscribed to Fanny Murray, and consisted chiefly of a parallel between that courtesan and the Blessed Virgin, much in favour of the former. Instead of *The Universal Prayer* was subjoined a parody of *Veni Creator.* In point of obscenity and blasphemy, nothing can surpass this work. The Bishop of Gloucester (Warburton) complained of a violation of his character and of a breach of privilege. The House of Lords have addressed his Majesty to have the author prosecuted according to law. Poor devil, how thick misfortunes fall upon him! How lucky your *jeu d'esprit* and Erskine's never was published.[6] It is, you find, a serious affair to laugh at a bishop; and so it should, else their white wigs, lawn-sleeves, sycophantish dispositions, and hypocritical lives would render them eternal subjects of ridicule and contempt.

Adieu, you immense rascal. May you and all your posterity be damned; may the United Provinces be again reclaimed by the Zuider Zee; and if by chance you should escape the deluge, may you be doomed to study law in the next town in the world that resembles Utrecht. Yours very affectionately.[7]

MONDAY 28 NOVEMBER. Yesterday you did very well. You walked an hour. You was prudent at Mr. Brown's, and talked genteelly of your assemblies; after dinner you joked him too broadly on Calvinism. Let him alone. He is a very good man in his way. Behave politely to him, and you will reap advantage. Remember, you entrusted him with your story. Make him warn you. But be

[6] No copy of this *jeu d'esprit* has as yet been found. See p. 13 *n.* 1.
[7] No signature.

retenu. . . . You went at six to the Grand Bailiff's. . . . You played a party[8] with a prince and Miss de Zuylen. You was shocked, or rather offended, with her unlimited vivacity. You was on your guard; at supper you was *retenu*. After it you spoke a little too much. But you was decent, and better than you imagine. You talked like Johnson against *Comtesse*. How different from two years ago! . . .

[Received 28 November, the Reverend Charles de Guiffardière to Boswell. Original in French]

Tilburg, 26 November 1763

SIR:—It is with real pleasure that I remember having promised to let you hear from me from a country where all the inhabitants, to my way of thinking, are aborigines—so difficult is it for a foreigner to like it. This is, however, the place of my exile, a place which is certainly worthy of the Getae and Massagetae of poor Ovid.[9] It would need only a poet to sing of it to make it as frightful as the coasts of the Black Sea. Judge from all this, lucky man! you who live in indolence and pleasure; who every day see Mademoiselle de Zuylen, who play shuttlecock with *la belle sœur*[1] an hour every day; you who read Xenophon with the virtuous and chaste La Roche,[2] judge, I say, if deprived as I am of all this, I am not to be pitied? In vain I call up my virtue and bravely face all the rigours of my fate; my weaknesses and passions speak louder still, and there is not a street-porter in Utrecht whose life I do not envy.

[8] That is, a *partie*, a game of cards.
[9] The poet Ovid was exiled to Pontus for having written inflammatory verses (his *Ars Amatoria*) and for being privy to some Court intrigue the details of which remain unknown; he wrote his *Tristia* there in an effort to secure his pardon.
[1] Mademoiselle Kinloch, Brown's sister-in-law.
[2] La Roche, "the Rock," is a nickname for Rose, who was of the family of Rose of Kilravock (pronounced Kilróck). But unless the whole passage is ironical, I do not know why the pleasure of his company should be grouped with that of meeting Mademoiselles de Zuylen and Kinloch.

What enchantment, what delicious intoxication, to be every day with her whom one loves! to speak to her of love! to listen to an adorable mouth uttering with infinite grace the ravishing words, "I love you"; to read in her eyes your sentence, your happiness, her desires, her uneasiness, and your victory! Ah, Sir, if I am not very much mistaken, you are going shortly to triumph over the charms of the fascinating De Zuylen and find yourself often in a situation to prove the sweet transports that a fond heart feels at the feet of the adorable object of its wishes.

However, when you are sure of your conquest, do not fight with useless scruples, thinking that your mistress's honour consists in her chastity! Above all, no timidity. And if she ever takes it into her head to faint during a tête-à-tête, do not call for help. She would not be at all grateful to you for such officiousness. Do not be afraid of becoming fickle: a gallant man may be so in love. This passion has no other bounds than those set by a vivid imagination; and the ability to succeed with many women, excuses, believe me, a fault which they even find charming.

This is, my dear Sir, a French lecture which perhaps will not be agreeable to an Englishman's taste: I am far from supposing that you need any lessons in love, you who are a hero in gallantry, but one loves to talk about what one has frequently felt with such delight. Ask La Roche if he does not agree with me. Only heaven forbid that he should put in practice the impure morality that he so ably addresses to women!

I beg you to warn Brown of what is going on; I fear greatly for the innocence of La Roche and our *belle sœur*. It would be frightful if poor Brown had to maintain them.

Adieu, my dear Sir; always preserve some <regard> for a man who congratulates himself on having known you, and who will always esteem you and asks for your friendship. I have the honour to be, Sir, your most humble, most obedient servant,

De Guiffardière.

My address is, In care of M. le Comte de Hogendorp de Hofwegen, à Tilburg.

TUESDAY 29 NOVEMBER. Yesterday you did moderately. You disputed the misery of life boldly and well against Brown. You found him out to be a cunning, hard little man. You must not let him attempt to take too much liberty with you. Neither must you be disgusted at him, but remember your character will depend much on what he says. Fight out the winter here, and learn as much as you can. Pray, pray be *retenu*. O man, thou hast a sad inclination to talk; now is thy time to cure it! . . .

[Received 30 November, Temple to Boswell]

Inner Temple [London] 23 November 1763

MY DEAR BOSWELL,—Your letter was sent to me from Cambridge. You see I am once more returned to my old habitation. I have been here about a month. Though I should prefer London to all places in the world if I had a handsome independent fortune, yet in my present circumstances it is far from being agreeable to me. I do not enjoy life here. My acquaintance, though sensible, are very few in number; it is not convenient for me to purchase the books I want; nor can I indulge so often with an opera or a play as I could wish. In short, when I have read till I desire some relaxation, I can find none, and often feel myself very miserable. Indeed, I am now convinced that there can be no happiness without business, without something that may enhance and give a sort of zest to the pleasures of study, which makes me more solicitous to get into orders, or some way of life or other, as soon as possible. . . .

I am much obliged to you for your last letter. I shall consider the subject of it with attention, and hope soon to send you an answer that will please you. As Lord Hertford is now at Paris as our ambassador, and as Mr. Hume is with him,[3] do not you think it would be more for your advantage to spend part of the winter there than in the dull uniformity of Utrecht? You will see the

---

[3] David Hume, at the height of his fame as an historian, had accompanied the Ambassador as unofficial secretary. (He later secured the official appointment, and for a time in 1765 was *chargé d'affaires*.) The French had received him with unparalleled enthusiasm.

best company, you will hear the French tongue spoken in its greatest purity, and obtain the acquaintance, perhaps friendship and familiarity, of the Buffons and D'Alemberts of France. Indeed, I think it the luckiest incident in the world for you; and you certainly would be much to blame to slight it. However, I would not have you by any means leave Utrecht without your father's consent and approbation. If he should be against this step at present you can take it in the summer months.

I am very glad to hear you speak so candidly of your matrimonial scheme, and hope yet to pass some months with you at your venerable mansion house in Yorkshire,[4] as well as at Auchinleck. . . .

A sensible history of the reigns of James I and Charles I came out the other day, written by a lady: Mrs. Macaulay, Dr. Macaulay's wife.[5] The style is not good, but she defends the cause of Liberty better than any of our historians. This is the character Mr. Gray gave me of it today, for I have not seen it myself. It will appear odd enough if the most constitutional history of England should be written by a woman. She intends carrying it down lower. By the by, I have finished Rapin and the *Anabasis*.

I make no doubt of your mixing the polite French authors with your severer studies. Mr. Gray thinks very highly of them. In France, he says, a genius is no rare thing; in England we can scarcely produce one in a century. I expect you will be my preceptor in French literature.

[4] See pp. 30, 36.
[5] Mrs. Catharine Macaulay, daughter of a wealthy country gentleman of anti-aristocratic principles, had been privately educated on the Roman historians, and wrote "Whig" history in opposition to Hume's "Tory" volumes. She was the object of a good deal of ridicule, not all unjustified. Johnson had talked to Boswell of her shortly before Boswell's departure for Utrecht: "Sir, there is one Mrs. Macaulay in this town, a great republican. I came to her one day and said I was quite a convert to her republican system, and thought mankind all upon a footing; and I begged that her footman might be allowed to dine with us. She has never liked me since. Sir, your levellers count down only the length of themselves" (*Boswell's London Journal, 1762–1763,* 1950, p. 320).

We are all in a combustion here. Mr. Wilkes has been wounded
in a duel by Mr. Martin of the Treasury. It was occasioned by
some reflections in *The North Briton* and some words that passed
in the House of Commons. Mr. Wilkes is better. No. 45 is voted
a false, scandalous, and seditious libel, and is to be burnt by the
hands of the hangman. It is expected Mr. Wilkes will be expelled
the House tomorrow. The House of Lords are then to send him to
Newgate for a profane pamphlet <which>, however, he never
published; but they say printing in the eye <of the law> is
publishing, and it seems the Ministry have discovered by low
<bribery that> he had printed thirteen copies for his own use. It is
imagined he will leave England and disappoint their revenge.[6]
The pamphlet was written by the late Mr. Potter, and is entitled
An Essay on Woman. The notes are Mr. Wilkes's, but he supposes
them the Bishop of Gloucester's. The frontispiece is a Priapus with
this inscription: Σωτὴρ Κόσμου.[7] The Lords proceed against him
for a breach of privilege in using the name of one of their house.
But perhaps this is no news to you. . . .

Do not draw a bill upon me for the guineas, but tell me to
whom I must pay it, and I shall do so as soon as ever I can. This
is not grammar, but it does not signify. I shall return to Cambridge
about the end of next month. Pray write to me soon, and believe
me, my dear Boswell, your most affectionate friend,

                          WILLIAM JOHNSON TEMPLE.

Does Mr. Johnson write to you? Churchill is to be examined
today by the House of Lords about Wilkes's pamphlet. He ran
off the other day with a beautiful young lady of fifteen, but is

[6] This proved to be correct. Wilkes, as soon as he was able to travel, eluded
those set by the Government to watch his movements, and went to Paris to
visit his daughter, who was in a school there. He intended to return to plead
his case in the House of Commons on 19 January 1764, but a relapse prevented
it. The Government refused to accept the evidence of his illness, and caused
him to be expelled from the House. Being convinced that he was sure to be
convicted in the prosecutions for libel, he resolved not to return. He was consequently outlawed, and remained in exile for four years.

[7] "Saviour of the World."

already returned. When the afflicted father asked him when he would send back his daughter, he answered perhaps he would *have done with her* in about ten days. Such a monster![8]

Nicholls has changed his plan and is to take orders. . . .

WEDNESDAY 30 NOVEMBER

> Men must not still in politics give law;
> No, Kate Macaulay too her pen must draw,
> That odious *thing*, a monarch, to revile,
> And drawl of freedom till ev'n Johnson smile.
> Like a Dutch *vrouw* all shapeless, pale, and fat,
> That hugs and slabbers her ungainly brat,
> Our Cath'rine sits sublime o'er steaming tea
> And takes her dear Republic on her knee;
> Sings it all songs that ever yet were sung,
> And licks it fondly with her length of tongue.

[*c.* 1 DECEMBER. FRENCH THEME] I have just been speaking of our House of Commons like a regular scold. I have just been making the most outrageous invectives against its members. I use the expression "I have just been making" (*je viens de faire*) because so far as space is concerned these invectives are very close to what I am now writing. They occur in the last page before this. But at the same time it must be added that they are not so close in point of time. I wrote them yesterday morning. I am devoted to order and ceremony. I have established a decree as irrevocable as the laws of the Medes and the Persians to write two pages in French every morning, and not to write more. That is why I often break off my subject when I am perhaps in the middle of a sentence. I have an excellent

---

[8] The behaviour of Wilkes's partner in *The North Briton*, Charles Churchill, the reigning poet of the day, was especially scandalous because he was in holy orders and had not resigned his charge until the previous January. It may be recorded to his credit that he did not desert the "beautiful young lady" (a Miss Carr) but continued to protect her, and when he died, about a year after the date of this letter, tried in his will to provide an annuity for her as well as for his wife.

memory, and I always remember the next day what I would have said if my paper had been long enough. In saying this, I have no intention of making you believe that I think by rule, that my sentences are so exact that they resemble a circle, which you have no difficulty in completing if you have made a segment of it. No, on the contrary, my sentences have no regular shape. My arguments, if you will, are sometimes circular, but my sentences are very much out of the ordinary. They are like curious porcelain, which the lady of the house has extreme difficulty in matching, so as to keep her set complete, when by ill luck a cup is broken. The same difficulty in finding a match is observable among excellent things; and, truly, I have reason at least to doubt whether my sentences are not very fine rather than very odd. Oddity itself is sometimes a kind of excellence. But at present I wish to argue for true genius. Here are pretty trifles! However, I come back to the cause which makes me remember so exactly the subject on which I had been writing twenty-four hours previously, and that is simply a good memory.

THURSDAY 1 DECEMBER. . . . This day at eleven call on *la Comtesse* and return thanks for her great politeness, and tell story, and take advice about society; but be prudent. *Think* in time; remember Johnson. Pleasure ruins the mind. All will be gone if you grow loose. Be quite constant as an admirer, and pray learn to conceal your feelings. Keep to Plan and you'll be happy; how great if you stand!

FRIDAY 2 DECEMBER. Yesterday you did very well. You was agreeably surprised to hear that *la Comtesse* was not a woman of gallantry, and yet you was sorry somehow that your virtue was not to be put to the trial. . . .

SATURDAY 3 DECEMBER. Yesterday you did very well, and you conducted yourself charmingly at the Assembly. Only you was a little absent at whist. *Hoc age:*[9] let that be your motto. Be like the Duke of Sully, always active. You are now happily free

[9] "Do the thing at hand."

from sickly ideas of vice. Pursue piety and goodness. In a political light, you must preserve your vigour to have fine, lively, healthy sons. *La Comtesse* is charming, delicate, and sentimental. Adore her with easy affability, yet with polite distance, and acquire real habits of composure. This day bring up journal much. . . .

[Boswell to Temple]

Utrecht, 6 December 1763

MY DEAR FRIEND,—By the date of this letter you would imagine that it was written upon the sixth of this month, but in reality I now sit down at one o'clock in the morning of Sunday the fourth by a comfortable German stove to talk to you a little before I go to sleep.[1] I am in charming spirits. Friends like you and I should participate everything. I have shared my grief with you. Let me share my joy also.

How like you this kind of style? It is gay, to be sure. But is it not flashy? Should a man indulge himself in it? Would it not spoil his taste? People may talk of David Hume as they please. I maintain his style is far from being good. He fritters it away like a French *marquis*. Read the work of Mr. Johnson. There indeed is style; there indeed is the full dignity of an English period.

"What is the matter with him now?" you will probably have said. O Temple, I wish this letter may come to you at a pleasant moment. If you receive it at the dreary hour when you have just stepped out of Clifton's with the cold depression which hangs upon us for an hour after dinner, woe be to it. But if Mrs. Legg or Edwards's lad,[2] or peradventure the barber should bring it in at the

[1] Tuesday the 6th was probably the next post day. He planned to write in instalments and finish his letter Monday night or Tuesday morning. But if the entry in the Register of Letters is correct, he did not actually get the letter off until Friday the 9th.

[2] Clifton's Chop-house, Butcher Row, Strand, was the favourite London din-

cheerful hour of noon, when you have just closed your Tully, and, filled with noblest sentiment, sit musing in your easy chair, happy will be its fate. It will be read with sweet attention and relished with lively joy.

My dear friend! After two months of a life almost solitary, you need not wonder that the smiles of the ladies' faces and the beautiful figures on their chimney pieces should have very great effect upon me. I now find Utrecht to be what Sir David found it. Our *noblesse* are come to town and all is alive. We have card-assemblies twice a week, which, I do assure you, are very brilliant, and private parties almost every evening. Madame la Comtesse de Nassau Beverweerd has taken me under her protection. She is a lady that, with all your serenity, would make you fall upon your knees and utter love speeches in the style of Lord Shaftesbury's *Rhapsody*,[3] and that would please her exceedingly, for she delights in Shaftesbury's benevolent system. I really trembled at the transition which I made last week. But I stood firm, and recollected so as to hold the reins in my hand.

I have changed my plan a little. I allow three hours every evening for amusement. I am come abroad to see foreign manners as well as to study. While I am in the company of foreigners of fashion, I am always receiving some improvement, at least in language. Madame de Nassau has shown me more civility than can well be imagined. I am getting more acquaintances daily. When once you are well in the gay world here you may be very happy. So it appears to me at present. I hope it will continue to

---

ing-place of Boswell and Temple; Mrs. Legg, Temple's laundress in the Inner Temple. Boswell described her in the London Journal of 1762–1763 as "an old woman who has breakfast set every morning, washes our linen, cleans the chambers, wipes our shoes, and, in short, does everything in the world that we can require of an old woman." Edwards was a stationer at Temple Gate in whose care Boswell sent his letters to Temple.

[3] *The Moralists, a Philosophical Rhapsody,* 1709, later included (as Treatise V) in *Characteristics of Men, Manners, Opinions, Times.* It is a dialogue between a sceptic and an "enthusiast."

appear so. However, I am taking care to be independent of it, for my great support is study.

Your proposal for me to go to Paris this winter would be thought terrible by my father. Indeed, without a mine of money an Englishman can do nothing at Paris. I have no intention to pass much time there at all. I shall see everything that is to be seen; but for living there long, I have not enough. Besides, I want to take a winter's course of Civil Law, and to acquire habits of application to render me fit for being useful in life. Think you that I would learn prudence for my conduct in this world at Paris, or would D'Alembert and the other infidel Academicians help me on in my journey to happiness in the next?

I revere Mr. Gray. But I will not subscribe to all his tenets. I believe there are more good authors in France than in England. But I believe we have some authors that would weigh against half a dozen of their best. And does the pensive Bard really commend Catharine Macaulay's *History of England?* Will you allow me a play of words? Two blacks won't make a white. Neither will two Grays. Low enough but true. Believe me, Temple, that an English republican is either a weak or a wicked politician. I thank GOD we have got a monarchy, limited as much as a true patriot or true lover of order could wish. I rejoice to find that the King begins to show real firmness. I hope he will make it be remembered that *The Crown* is the head of our Constitution.

Poor Wilkes! Sad dog as he is, who will not be sorry for him! I long to hear his history. . . .

I am glad that Nicholls goes into the Church. It will be another inducement to you, and I hope will be an agreeable situation for him. I expect to be supported by you two in your mitres like King Richard in the play. Keep up your spirits, my dear Temple. Be ever busy. Strengthen your mind by study and by thought, and pray try to stir up some desire in your breast for worldly advantages. That would give you a greater degree of agitation, which is always pleasant. I am vexed that my paper is so

small. Tell me your opinion of my alteration in living. I am timorous. I have no friend here to open my mind to with that unlimited
frankness which you have heard. Adieu. I ever am yours most
sincerely,

SUNDAY 4 DECEMBER   JAMES BOSWELL.

> O had I here a maid, upon whose lap
> I might recline my head and take a nap,
> The gentle heavings of her lovely breast
> Might soothe my senses to oblivious rest.
> In the dead hours I journalized last night,
> My eyes all fretted with the candle's light.
> How can a man write either verse or prose,
> Whose drowsy eyelids every minute close?
> Without the least delay to bed I'll creep,
> And warm and quiet take a pull of sleep.

MONDAY 5 DECEMBER. Yesterday you did surprisingly well
after your severe late-sitting. But be firm to go to bed always at
twelve, or before it, and never to eat suppers.[4] You drank tea with
honest Carron. Then you went to *la Comtesse's*. You was a little
awkward, but you cleared up at cards. You was presented to Count[5]
at supper; you was hurt by Albinus, a coarse Dutch wit. You did
not like to speak. However, you was a little in the *tumbling* humour, and affected to be too much the great man. Never allow one
minute's affectation. The Comtesse showed a lowness, a Dordt mer-
cantility[6] in suspecting that you understood Hollands, and repeated. Have a care; never say a word of it. You was disgusted, but
see how things turn out. Be independent.

[4] In England (and also presumably in Holland) in the eighteenth century
people ate breakfast at ten in the morning, dinner at three or four, and drank
tea at six. Supper, if served at all, came late in the evening.
[5] Presumably Hendrik Carel, Count of Nassau, Heer van Beverweerd, the
Countess's husband. As indicated above, he was twice her age.
[6] The Countess had been born in Dordt, or Dordrecht, a wealthy trading city
of the Netherlands.

TUESDAY 6 DECEMBER. . . . Your Sunday evening continued to disgust you. You was uneasy and you could not but show it, though moderately. You talked to Brown of the rudeness of Albinus. He agreed, but you heard hints of his intrigue. Good heaven! What is the world! You was shocked; you hated her. And yet it is not true. What a weak mind have you! Fie! Yield not thus. Command your passions and be ever in good humour. You went to bed very soon. You was not well. You made good resolutions to sleep off chagrin, and obstinately learn a proper *retenue* and conduct.

WEDNESDAY 7 DECEMBER. Yesterday you did very well. You was really *retenu,* and at Assembly was agreeably surprised to find Albinus complaisant, speak much, and tell you, "It's not every Englishman who is well received,"[7] and ask you to dine with him. His card first surprised you. You have here another instance: never take disgusts at first. Visit him tomorrow. You was quite mistaken in being discontent on Sunday; all was well. Return to the charge. At ten, send to Comtesse if she chooses to walk, and go to her at eleven. . . .

THURSDAY 8 DECEMBER. Yesterday you walked round Utrecht with *la Comtesse.* How delicious! You spoke charming French. Had no servant. She gave the characters of Monsieur d'Amelisweerd, a rough squire, but jealous of his lady, a charming little woman. You joked her at his not dreading the English as gallants. Talked of jealousy. She said she was happy at your being recommended to Count Nassau. She could take you everywhere. All this looked like address. Also, she gave hints of Madame Amelisweerd. Told she was married at seventeen, when one does not know the consequences; said marriage was unequal. Said going to The Hague, Paris, London was *un peu trop fort.* Was not this confidence in you? You was very prudent. At night Brown told you how she had found you out about disgust at Albinus. She is

---

[7] This sentence is in French in the original. It may be assumed without further notice in all the memoranda that follow that both sides of direct conversations with Hollanders were recorded by Boswell in French, and appear in this edition in translation.

very penetrating. But you have her for all that. Be very *retenu*. She gave you no cautions to try you. Have a care. Don't alter.

FRIDAY 9 DECEMBER. Yesterday you visited Albinus. The day was passed so-so. It was indeed devoted to the Society, as it was your night. You made a very good discourse; copy it fair and send it to Father. Have a care. You are not quite right at present. Your health is not perfect. That disorder of the stomach distresses you. Be more regular to go to bed. Eat a lighter dinner; drink less wine and a good deal of water to give a clear digestion, and never miss the Mall once a day.[8] Lay your hand on your heart. Pause. Withstand pleasure or you will be dissolved. Attend to Trotz. Resolve it, to fill your mind. See how you can acquire that habit. Pay *la Comtesse*.[9] Never give up general Plan. Be *retenu*.

FRIDAY 9 DECEMBER

> Yet Holland gave—ay, there's the cruel sting—
> Gave to Great Britain, gave, ye gods! a king.
> Ah, name him not; no more our shame disclose,
> Nor on our coins point out his monstrous nose.
> O let the mem'ry of the villain rot;
> Be on his reign an everlasting blot.
> True, in his youth the phlegmatic *Mynheer*
> Display'd the brutal courage of a bear;
> 'Tis true he made the mighty fam'd reply,
> "Rather than yield, in the last ditch I'll die."

[*c.* 9–10 DECEMBER. FRENCH THEMES] I have not written any themes for three or four days. Have I then been negligent?

---

[8] "The Mall is esteemed the principal ornament of Utrecht, and is perhaps the only avenue of the sort in Europe still fit to be used for the game which gives its name to them all. The several rows of noble trees include at the side both roads and walks, but the centre is laid out for the game of [*pall-*] *mall*, and though not often used, is in perfect preservation. It is divided so as to admit two parties of players at once, and the side boards sufficiently restrain spectators" (Charles Campbell, *The Traveller's Complete Guide through Belgium, Holland, and Germany*, 1815, p. 97). The game was played with a wooden ball and mallets, like croquet.

[9] What he had lost to her at cards.

No, not at all. But I have been busy writing a discourse according to the directions of the literary society of which I am a member. This discourse is in French. Tell me, then, if I have wasted my time. Tell me if a man would not profit as much by writing a French dissertation as by writing a French theme. Perhaps there are subtle differences between them; for my part, I do not understand them. I am content to make my judgments on obvious appearances. I do not seek to refine. Lord Kames, a man of great knowledge and true genius, was nevertheless a little too refined. When he published his *Elements of Criticism,* in which he exhibited much thought and even original taste but too much subtlety, Mr. Love the actor said, "My Lord Kames is not content if you show him a fine room, perfectly elegant; he wants always to scratch behind the panelling and analyze the plaster of the walls." He might have added, "And perhaps taste it," for Lord Kames is a deep chemist and has conducted some very curious experiments in that science. He wished to apply his science of chemistry to agriculture. Some malicious rogues would persuade us that he has tasted all sorts of dung with a truly philosophic palate, in order to acquire a perfect knowledge of the most effective ways of fertilizing the soil. He entertained for some time a pretty fancy that one could make an extract of the essence of dung and so save the expense of carts, which now cost us so much to carry our dung to the fields. Major Dalrymple, brother of my Lord Drummore, says that, following the same principles, one could have the essence of wheat, so that a man could carry his harvest home in his snuff-box.

We have completely lost sight of the Earl of Bute, concerning whom I began to write with so much formality in these themes. Never has one seen more irregular compositions than the present. If after two thousand years they are found by some antiquary, he will not gain much. I defy him to understand them. They are really in cipher, partly because of the badness of the writing, partly because of the astonishing variety of matter, so that one page has very little connection with another. They are as well hidden as an essay of high treason would be in Turkey or a dissertation containing matter against the Catholic Church in Spain. However, I do not doubt that they will be highly esteemed by antiquaries. The manuscripts which have been found amongst the ruins of Herculaneum, concerning which these gentlemen have made so much ado, have almost the same obscurity.

SUNDAY 11 DECEMBER. Yesterday you did very well. You read an immensity of Greek. You was *retenu* yet cheerful at table. It was a dismal day and you eat too much wild duck, so was a little gloomy. However, you said not a word of it, nor have you said a word of it near these three months.... Take long walk today to brace you, and do so every day. Eat less....

MONDAY 12 DECEMBER. Yesterday you did delightfully. You did not commit one fault in any respect the whole day.... You was *retenu* at dinner. You admired *la Comtesse* in church, but not imprudently. You supped happy and cheerful. In short, for all yesterday you enjoyed *tranquillitatem animi*. There is a fine tale to tell. Persist. Relax not propriety, yet torment not yourself with trifles to be an old woman ... Go to bed exact at twelve. Pick teeth with wood; make toothpicks. At six Madame Maleprade. Be easy and gay. Approach not love....

TUESDAY 13 DECEMBER.... Consider what a different man you are now from what you have been for some years. Instead of idle dissipation, you read Greek, French, law; and instead of drollery, you have sensible conversation. You also mix gay amusement with study.... Wait on Grand Bailiff to let him know that you are to leave the town for some time.[1] Write to Guiffardière short—only two pages and a quarter and no nonsense, only a gay recital of assemblies. This day continue; don't always be mending yourself in trifles like a boy his shuttlecock: he spoils it. Be fine at Assembly. No love; you are to marry. But *la Comtesse*, charming and friendly. You are forming charmingly; you are no buffoon, you only want calmness.

WEDNESDAY 14 DECEMBER. Yesterday you did just as well as you could wish. Upon my word, you are a fine fellow.... Bravo! Go on....

[1] He is planning to spend his Christmas holidays at The Hague.

[Received 14 December, Samuel Johnson to Boswell][2]

London, 8 December 1763

. DEAR SIR:—You are not to think yourself forgotten or criminally neglected that you have had yet no letter from me. I love to see my friends, to hear from them, to talk to them, and to talk of them; but it is not without a considerable effort of resolution that I prevail upon myself to write. . . . Whether I shall easily arrive at an exact punctuality of correspondence, I cannot tell. I shall at present expect that you will receive this in return for two[3] which I have had from you. The first, indeed, gave me an account so hopeless of the state of your mind that it hardly admitted or deserved an answer; by the second I was much better pleased. . . .

You know a gentleman, who, when first he set his foot in the gay world, as he prepared himself to whirl in the vortex of pleasure, imagined a total indifference and universal negligence to be the most agreeable concomitants of youth and the strongest indication of an airy temper and a quick apprehension. Vacant to every object and sensible of every impulse, he thought that all appearance of diligence would deduct something from the reputation of genius; and hoped that he should appear to attain, amidst all the ease of carelessness and all the tumult of diversion, that knowledge and those accomplishments which mortals of the common fabric obtain only by mute abstraction and solitary drudgery. He tried this scheme of life a while, was made weary of it by his sense and his virtue; he then wished to return to his studies; and finding long habits of idleness and pleasure harder to be cured than he expected, still willing to retain his claim to some extraordinary prerogatives, resolved the common consequences of irregularity into an unalterable decree of destiny, and concluded that Nature had originally formed him incapable of rational employment.

[2] From *The Life of Johnson*, where Boswell published the letter in full. The original manuscript has not been recovered.   [3] Not recovered.

Let all such fancies, illusive and destructive, be banished henceforward from your thoughts for ever. Resolve, and keep your resolution; choose, and pursue your choice. . . . This, my dear Boswell, is advice which perhaps has been often given you, and given you without effect. But this advice, if you will not take from others. you must take from your own reflections . . .

Let me have a long letter from you as soon as you can. I hope you continue your journal . . . I am, dear Sir, your most affectionate servant,

Sam. Johnson.

[Received 14 December, Dalrymple to Boswell. Original in French]

Edinburgh, 2 December 1763

My very dear Friend,—The progress which you have made in the French language shows me what can be done by a man of brains as soon as he settles down. I assume that your mind is quiet at the moment because I see that you are busy with your studies. Believe me, I have known people who chattered in French without stopping to draw breath, though their knowledge of it was not equal to yours. You have committed yourself to the road and must now hurry straight on, without being stopped by the obstructions that may present themselves. Though I myself am but a barbarian, I make bold to praise you for acquiring what I understand with difficulty and seldom speak.

I find you infatuated with Fatality. Since neither Clarke nor Johnson has been able to dissipate these clouds which overshadow your mind, how could *I* persuade you that you are a rational being? Tell me, however: when you do good, do you not believe yourself free? And is it not merely when you wander astray in the paths of Folly or when you reflect on your follies—is it not then that you believe yourself led by the hand of an invisible fatality?

Don't you remember what was said by Prior, a man of the world who could think like a philosopher too:

> That when weak women went astray,
> Their stars were more in fault than they?[4]

Milton gives these metaphysical problems to his devils to debate: they amuse themselves by reasoning on "fixed Fate, free Will, Foreknowledge absolute."[5] It is the devil's business to occupy one's self with thoughts that have no outcome. Make up your mind that God is just and that the soul is immortal, that virtue is lovely and vice harmful to society. All the other truths will follow from principles so certain and agreeable to well disposed hearts as these. For my own part, I find in myself such repugnance to the dogma of Fatality that I assure you *non persuadebis etiamsi persuaseris*[6] that I am not free.

You are reading the *Universal History* of Voltaire. Keep a sharp look-out: he is the most intrepid retailer of fables to appear in Europe since the century of Varillas, Leti, and Raguenet. Some time I shall amuse myself by writing the life of Cromwell, drawn from French authors, without including in it the slightest morsel of truth. The truth can sometimes be found in Monsieur de Voltaire, but it is found either rouged or daubed or in ridiculous disguise. It would be impossible to praise too much his facility and his delightful turns of phrase, but for the rest I ought to hold my tongue, as the old song says, for I have never seen it.

It may well be that you have found Dutch civility a little dry, but remember what I have often told you, that you must accustom yourself to the usages established in the countries where you may find yourself. The Dutch do not give dinners, they do not put themselves at the trouble of paying visits. Try to meet the Count de Nassau on the Promenade or in public places, and you will find him a friend without disguise or artifice. May I venture to say that he is in some sense the Governor of the City, and that one may excuse him from making visits of ceremony.

[4] The quoted lines are in English. Prior wrote "That *if*," etc. (*Hans Carvel*).

[5] Milton, *Paradise Lost*, II. 560.

[6] A Latin version of Aristophanes's *Plutus*, 600: οὐ γὰρ πείσεις, οὐδ' ἢν πείσῃς,"You shall not convince even if you should convince me."

Here I am married, as your father has told you. I am happy; I go my way in peace; I apply myself to the duties of society, and in filling the empty places of my brain with useful studies, I close it to metaphysical chimeras. Do thou likewise, my dear friend, and be happy; as happy as your very humble and most affectionate

DAV: DALRYMPLE.

Please have the goodness to make my most sincere compliments to Monsieur le Comte de Nassau.

THURSDAY 15 DECEMBER.... You was indeed a great man yesterday. You received letters from Lord Auchinleck,[7] Mr. Samuel Johnson, Sir David Dalrymple. Mr. Johnson's correspondence is the greatest honour you could ever imagine you could attain to. Look back only three years when you was first in London with Derrick.[8] Consider. He is the first author in England. Let his counsel give you new vigour. Return still to the charge....

FRIDAY 16 DECEMBER. Yesterday was a lukewarm sort of a day.... You forgot temperance, which you seldom forget. You eat too much beef and drank too much wine.... This day write law and version, and at eleven Rose, and give a good brush at Greek. At one, walk; after dinner, more Greek. At night, Assembly. Then journal. Saturday set apart to clear all up. Let journal be completed, short. Write to Johnson easy. Prepare all for Hague. Persist.

[Boswell to De Guiffardière][9]

Utrecht, 16 December 1763

MONSIEUR:—By the address of this letter you will see that I intended to write in French. By the address I mean the exordium,

---

[7] Not recovered.

[8] A rather disreputable Irishman, later "King" of Bath, who had been Boswell's first instructor in the ways of the town, or, to use his own words, had shown him London "in all its variety of departments, both literary and sportive."

[9] Reprinted from *The Letters of James Boswell*, 2 vols., 1924, with the kind permission of the editor, Professor C. B. Tinker, and of the Oxford University Press. The original was in the Adam Collection and is now in the collection of Mr. and Mrs. Donald F. Hyde.

Monsieur. I did indeed fully intend to have written to you in that language, of which you know so much and I so little. But I recollected that my French letters are as yet but mere themes, and that I should not be doing you a great kindness to give you the trouble to correct them.

Although I cannot correct the language of your letter, yet I think I may take upon me to correct the sentiment of it. Your French morality, Guiffardière, is "lighter than vanity." A generous Briton gives it to the wind with a smile of disdain. To be serious, your amorous sentences are vivacious. But are they proper from a son of the Church? Indeed, Doctor, I am afraid not. Believe me, Sir, such sallies are dangerous. They glance upon the mind and dazzle the eye of discernment. Morality is permanent, although our sight be wavering; happy are they who can keep it constantly in view. I have experienced a good deal of variety, and I am firmly convinced that the true happiness of a MAN is propriety of conduct and the hope of divine favour. Excuse me, Guiffardière. I am domineering over you, I allow. But don't you deserve it? When you left this, was you not resolved to acquire "intellectual dignity"? I desire that you may remember your resolution. You have now a fair opportunity to become a real philosopher. If you improve your solitude as you ought to do, the rest of your life may be passed in cheerful tranquillity. Take this as it is meant, and you will thank me.

I now find Utrecht to be the same agreeable place which my friend Dalrymple found it fifteen years ago. We have brilliant assemblies twice a week and private parties almost every evening. La Comtesse de Nassau Beverweerd has taken me under her protection. She is the finest woman upon earth. She has shown me the greatest civility, and has introduced me <upon> the very best footing <into the> gay world of this city. I <begin to> make acquaintance with the people of fashion, and hope to be agreeable to them. There are so many beautiful and amiable ladies in our circle that a quire of paper could not contain their praises, though written by a man of a much cooler fancy and a much smaller handwriting than myself.

I have stood upon my guard and have repelled dissipation. I

am firm to my Plan, and I divide my time between study and amusement. "Happy man!" you will say. Our vacation begins this day. I shall go to The Hague next week, and expect to pass there some weeks of felicity. Do not allow yourself to weary in your present retreat. Acquire fortitude and all will at least be supportable in this changeful world. I am, Sir, your sincere well-wisher and humble servant,

JAMES BOSWELL.

Last post I had a long letter from MR. JOHNSON.

SATURDAY 17 DECEMBER.... You are coming quite into the style here. Only you was a little too *young* with Madame de Nassau in giving a kind of jump when you heard she was to be at your two next parties. You cultivated acquaintance with Madame[1] de Zuylen. Never be in the least foolish. Harden....

SUNDAY 18 DECEMBER. Yesterday you did perfectly well. You read much Greek and finished *The Anabasis,* and you had twelve pages of version examined, which was excellent. You was quite genteel and gay at Assembly, and had much conversation with Madame de Nassau and Madame Amelisweerd. *La Comtesse* told you of intrigues at The Hague. She said your calling her *Protectrice* would look strange. She said, by the by, that *Terie* said you was *extrêmement gouté.*[2] You saw how things were. You are a happy dog.... But you talked rather too much. Have a care of being *étourdi.*[3] This day at eleven call on Grand Bailiff. Then have fire in stove and great table in next room. Send to Brown you can't dine, and bring up journal....

MONDAY 19 DECEMBER. Yesterday you did charmingly. You brought all up clear; only you left your letter to Johnson and your journal to furnish you occupation on jaunt and prevent you from

[1] The manuscript has "Mad.", which in these memoranda may mean either "Madame" or "Mademoiselle." "Mad. de Zuylen" is in almost all cases Belle de Zuylen, but here I think her mother was meant.
[2] "Very much liked." "Terie" (which might also be read "Jerie") was probably the nickname of Madame d'Amelisweerd or one of the other ladies.
[3] "Giddy."

the fretful gloom of idleness. You may write, or at least sketch, in *schuit.* . . . This morning get all ready. Forget nothing. Take papers and Butler[4] or *Gil Blas* to read in *schuit.* Be firm. . . . From first to last be temperate. See how well you can go on. Be quite *retenu,*, pious, and careful. Amen.

FOR HAGUE JAUNT. Your going to The Hague is of more consequence than you imagine. You are to wait on Mynheer de Sommelsdyck, of whom you have heard so much from your infancy, and who may be of infinite use to you. Your father considers this as a matter of great moment. So do your best. You have now a rational system. Formerly you made your general plan yield to the present moment. Now you make the present moment yield to the general plan, as it soon passes. Think before you enter The Hague. Learn the usage of life. Be prudent and *retenu.* Never aim at being too brilliant. Be rather an amiable, pretty man. Have no affectation. Cure vanity. Be quite temperate and have self-command amid all the pleasures. Would Epictetus or Johnson be overturned by human beings, gay, thoughtless, corrupted? No; they would make the best of them and be superior. Have real principles. You have acquired a noble character at Utrecht. Maintain it. . . .

TUESDAY 20 DECEMBER [Leyden] Yesterday you did charmingly. You supported the tedious nine hours in the *schuit,* and though you grew cold and gloomy, you stood firm. You talked Dutch with the jolly dog and his two daughters. You arrived at Leyden, dreary a little. But you drank coffee, read the English news, wrote good verses and a noble letter to Mr. Johnson.[5] Thus it is that you are happy. You are formed for regular decent life. You have deviated into the road [of] vice and have been miserable. Take care now you are a Christian. *Think.* Be firm. Admire still *la Comtesse.* But not vicious, for though 'twould inflame your fancy, 'twould fever your heart and ruin your *Plan.* See Abraham

[4] Bishop Joseph Butler's famous *Analogy of Religion, Natural and Revealed, to the Constitution and Course of Nature,* 1736.

[5] The original has not been recovered. A rather uninteresting fragment of it was printed in *The Life of Johnson.*

Gronovius today. Take pen and ink in *schuit* and copy letter. Be at *Comédie* by six. Be *retenu* with Gordon. Try it now. Remember your Templar oath.[6] It is at such a time as this that gloom appears. Then resist it. Go to Maréchal Turenne not to be with Gordon, who is pert.[7] Allow no sad idea to seize you. Take exercise. Be independent.

WEDNESDAY 21 DECEMBER. [The Hague] Yesterday you waited on honest Abraham Gronovius and passed an hour with him, quite Dutch, commentaric, and comfortable, and promised to come and dine with him on a Saturday and copy the notes on the *Graecae Lyrici*.[8] You hired the roof[9] and wrote your letter cleverly

[6] Probably an oath which Boswell took just before leaving the Temple in London to go to Holland.

[7] The Maréchal Turenne was an inn or hotel at The Hague. Gordon had probably invited Boswell to share lodgings with him.

[8] "I wish you would inquire for me whether there is in the library of the University at Leyden any manuscript notes or corrections relating to the fragments of the Greek lyrics. Your father told me several years ago that he had a remembrance of some such things, but he could not give me any particulars. I think he also mentioned a manuscript of Anacreon. I want to know its age and the first line of each poem in it. The librarian, if he is not a notorious blockhead, will be able to inform you of all those particulars. It has been long my intention to procure an edition of the fragments of those lyrics, not of every single word or of imperfect sentences, but an edition containing such pieces as may convey an idea of the style and manner of each author and of the measure in which he wrote. This, though a simple plan, has never yet been executed" (Sir David Dalrymple to Boswell, 28 July 1763). Boswell's *Graecae Lyrici* is a slip for *Graeci Lyrici* or *Graeciae Lyrici*.

[9] That is, *roef*, the deck-house of the barge. "In [the *roef*] there are four oblique windows, which move up and down, and a table in the middle with a long drawer, filled with pipes. There is also a spitting-box and a little iron pot containing burning turf, for accommodating the smokers with a light. The seats are covered with handsome cushions. The *roef* is generally occupied by the genteeler passengers, though the price is but about threepence an hour. So steady is the motion of the vessel that a person may read, write, or even draw in it. . . . A person may hire the whole of the *roef* to himself by giving proper notice" (Charles Campbell, *The Traveller's Complete Guide through Belgium, Holland, and Germany*, 1815, p. 17).

to Mr. Johnson.[1] You was a little unhinged by the novelty of The
Hague. However, you did all right: waited first on the Ambassador,[2] then went to Comedy, where you was pleased. Came home,
read Tacitus and wrote journal. You felt gloom, but you bore it,
and are ever resolved to bear it. You was peevish a little to poor
François. Poor honest, quiet creature, be good to him. Don't consider him as a servant here, but as a careful body to look after your
things. Never once use him sullenly. Give general order: never in.
. . . Starve and keep off spleen.

WEDNESDAY 21 DECEMBER

DIALOGUES AT THE HAGUE[3]

Scene, the street

BOSWELL. Le Jeune.

VALET.[4] Sir? What is your pleasure?

BOSWELL. Show me where Colonel Spaen[5] lives.

VALET. This way. He lives in the Prinsesse-Gracht.

BOSWELL. Have you served in the Army?

[1] He had already written it (see the previous memorandum), but he now
copied it carefully, no doubt making some improvements as he copied.

[2] Sir Joseph Yorke. Boswell was presented on 26 December.

[3] These dialogues are recorded entirely in French.

[4] A *valet de louage* or local servant whom Boswell has hired for the period
of his stay in The Hague.

[5] Alexander Sweder, Baron von Spaen, of a noble German family, was a
favourite of Frederick the Great in his youth, and had been involved with two
other young officers, Lieutenants Katte and Keith, in Frederick's plot to
escape from his father's control by fleeing from Germany in 1730. The plot
being discovered, Keith saved himself by flight, but Katte was arrested and,
by express command of Frederick's father, was beheaded. Spaen, who is said to
have swallowed the one incriminating paper in his possession, got off with a
brief imprisonment and exile. Entering the service of the States-General, he
rose to the rank of major-general. His wife was a niece of the Count of Nassau.
Boswell had a letter of introduction to her from the Countess of Nassau
Beverweerd.

VALET. Not in the last war, Sir.

BOSWELL. You have certainly been in the Army, because you march in line so well. Please to walk either in front of me or behind me.

VALET. Sir, I beg your pardon. But I will tell you the reason. It is a custom of us servants *de louage* to walk in that position, because foreign gentlemen have many questions to ask and do not wish to put themselves to the trouble of shouting to us. I hope that I did not offend you.

BOSWELL. O no. Follow the custom. I merely noticed that you had been a soldier.

Scene, the Maréchal Turenne

FRANÇOIS. Sir, here is a card from Colonel Spaen, who has been here. He has invited you to dine at his house. He will wait for you till three o'clock.

BOSWELL. Ah! give me my scarlet suit and go directly for the hairdresser. Wait a moment. What time is it?

FRANCOIS. It is a good quarter after two. Sir, you can go as you are. It is not a grand dinner.

BOSWELL. Then I will. Listen: if any one inquires here for me, always say that I am not at home, except when I give you orders to the contrary.

Scene, Monsieur Spaen's house

MME SPAEN. Mr. Boswell. I am delighted to see you here.

BOSWELL. Madame, I received Monsieur Spaen's card very late. I did not have time to dress. I took the liberty to profit by your civility, as you see. I hope you will excuse me.

MME SPAEN. Sir, you look very well. I expected you today or tomorrow. Have you seen this town? Is it not very pleasant?

BOSWELL. It is very pretty indeed. But I have not yet seen much of it. I have been here only since five o'clock yesterday evening.

MME SPAEN. Have you been at the playhouse?

BOSWELL. Yes, Madame.

MME SPAEN. Were you well amused?

BOSWELL. Very well. But as I am not used to hearing French

spoken rapidly, I missed a good deal. It appears to me that you have excellent actors here.

COLONEL SPAEN. Sir, I am glad to find you here. I have been at the Maréchal.

BOSWELL. Sir, I had the honour of receiving your card.

COLONEL SPAEN. But, Sir, I have been there just now, to bring you in my carriage.

BOSWELL. Sir, I am deeply grateful.

COLONEL SPAEN. Well, Sir, will you sit beside my wife?

BOSWELL. If I may venture to *part*[6] the ladies.

MME SPAEN. I am afraid, Sir, that my hoop is in your way.

BOSWELL. Not at all, Madame, but I fear that I am in the way of your hoop.

MME SPAEN. And how do you find Utrecht?

BOSWELL. Very pleasant, Madame. Our assemblies began three weeks ago.

COUNTESS DE NASSAU OUWERKERKE. I believe the first assembly was at my aunt's house.

BOSWELL. Yes, Mademoiselle. Your brother was my good friend. He taught me all the etiquette. He is always gay. He speaks French well. He speaks very fast.

COUNTESS DE NASSAU OUWERKERKE. Sir, he speaks altogether too fast.

BOSWELL. Oh, it is a sign that you understand a language well when you speak fast. I should be very happy if some one should say to me, "You speak French too fast."

MME SPAEN. Have you been in an argument yet?[7]

[COUNTESS DE NASSAU OUWERKERKE.][8] He has argued against Madame de Nassau Beverweerd that there is more evil in the world than good.

BOSWELL. Yes, I argued for Evil while drinking good Burgundy;

[6] "Partager." The company is sitting down to table, Boswell between Madame Spaen and the Countess of Nassau Ouwerkerke. Their skirts are so wide that he has to (or pretends that he has to) push his way to the table.
[7] A dig at the fondness of the Countess of Nassau Beverweerd for arguing and lectures. See p. 69 *n.* 9.   [8] This speech is not assigned in the manuscript.

and I remember that she said to me, "Sir, if you go on like that, I think you will become a partisan of Good."

CAPTAIN REYNST.[9] Really, women are very deceitful. A girl adapts herself to all the humours and all the caprices of her lover, but when he is her husband, all at once she snaps him up: "You're mine!" There, Madame!

MME SPAEN. As for me, I live in great tranquillity. I try to do the honours of the house for Monsieur Spaen, when he is good enough to bring in good company. I never play. I never sup abroad. Yet I am very fond of having supper at home, and people have the goodness to come. That is very flattering. Self-love enters into everything. Rousseau is right.

BOSWELL. Has my carriage come?

SERVANT. Not yet, Sir.

CAPTAIN REYNST. Have you ordered a carriage, Sir?

BOSWELL. Sir, may I have the honour of giving you a lift?

CAPTAIN REYNST. If you will be so good as to take me.

COLONEL SPAEN. Mr. Boswell, we have a Society here, a morning club made up of people of the highest fashion where one chats or plays or makes the acquaintance of everybody. Sir, I will introduce you there as a foreign member. Sir, I leave you master of the house.

BOSWELL. It is necessary, Sir, always to have a carriage?

CAPTAIN REYNST. Excepting in very good weather. But really you must count on a carriage most of the time.

BOSWELL. How much do they ask here per day for a carriage? A ducat?

CAPTAIN REYNST. I believe it is about a ducat. But Monsieur Molin, your host, will give you complete information about all those things. He is a worthy man. Have you seen Sir Joseph Yorke?

BOSWELL. Not yet. I left a card and a letter for him from one of his friends in London. Must I go to his house a second time without waiting for him to call on me? I have heard Sir Joseph's character, that he is—

[9] A naval captain, later a lieutenant-admiral. He knew Belle de Zuylen well.

CAPTAIN REYNST. He is a little stiff. But go a second time. Do not be lacking in your attentions. If he is not at home, ask for his secretary and tell him you are English, that you wish to see the world, that you have friends here who are ready to introduce you everywhere, but that you wish to be presented by the Ambassador if it is convenient for him.

BOSWELL. That will show the Ambassador what footing I am on.

CAPTAIN REYNST. Yes, Sir. Ambassadors will show you a great deal of civility when you don't need it.

WEDNESDAY 21 DECEMBER

> Fashion, of all that mortals ever wear,
> Takes most delight in sporting with the hair.
> Just now the town admires a bushy top,
> And for a head the pattern is a mop.
> Pass and begone! the whimsy strikes the Court,
> Hair to look well can never be too short.
> Like powder'd negroes grown a little pale
> Fine fellows seem, though never yet in jail.[1]
> In its full shape the bullet pate appears,
> And, bless us! what a quantity of ears!

THURSDAY 22 DECEMBER

DIALOGUES AT THE HAGUE

Scene, the ordinary at the Maréchal Turenne

BOSWELL. This a very pretty town.

1 CAPTAIN. You have not been here long?

BOSWELL. Only one day.

1 CAPTAIN. You have acquaintances here?

BOSWELL. Yes, Sir. I have the honour to be known to the Baron de Spaen. I dined at his house yesterday.

1 CAPTAIN. O Sir, you were balloted on at our Society today, and you were admitted. So you may go there whenever you please.

[1] Because the heads of convicts were cropped?

BOSWELL. It is my misfortune to speak only a very little **French**, but I have been only three months at Utrecht—that is, at a place where I have had the opportunity to learn it.

2 CAPTAIN. Sir, you speak very well. You are quite intelligible.

BOSWELL. That is something.

1 CAPTAIN. You know Madame de Nassau Beverweerd at Utrecht?

BOSWELL. Yes. I have the honour to be well received in that family. She is most engaging.

1 CAPTAIN. She is very good looking.

BOSWELL. Yes. I am learning French in the company of two ladies from Switzerland, the wife of our English minister and her sister. I dine at their house. I hear a great deal about Switzerland. They are extremely fond of their country and their countrymen.

2 CAPTAIN. That gentleman there is from Switzerland; he is an officer in the Swiss Guards.

BOSWELL. Sir, you are Swiss?

3 CAPTAIN. Yes, Sir, from the Pays de Vaud,[2] from Lausanne.

2 CAPTAIN. I should be extremely fond of your country of Switzerland. You are very high up, you don't run much risk among your mountains; I mean, you can of course fall from your cliffs and break your neck, but that is something you can avoid. But here we are always in danger from the sea, and we cannot have certain protection.

BOSWELL. Yes, perhaps one day you will have to swim.

2 CAPTAIN. Yes, we shall have a Deluge. I shall be like Deucalion. I shall throw stones to renew our nation.[3]

BOSWELL. But, unfortunately, Sir, you have no stones in this

[2] Boswell, who had a good ear but did not yet know much about Swiss geography, got this down as "païs de veaux de Lusanne": "the calf-country of Lausanne."

[3] In the Greek version of the Deluge, only Deucalion and his wife Pyrrha survived. They created a new race by casting stones behind them. Those thrown by Deucalion produced males, those thrown by Pyrrha, females.

country. Nature has undoubtedly passed a fixed decree that Holland shall be completely lost, for it has not given you the means of renewing yourselves.

Scene, the house of the Countess of Degenfeld[4]

BOSWELL. I am unlucky in not being able to speak. I know very little French.

COUNTESS DEGENFELD. You know enough, I should say, to get by with.

BOSWELL. Not bad for three months.

REYNST. You have a very good accent.

COUNTESS DEGENFELD. It is not the time now to see The Hague at its best. For that one must be here in the summer. But you see the people of fashion now.

BOSWELL. Yes, Madame.

FRIDAY 23 DECEMBER. . . . Good dinner at ordinary. Countess Degenfeld, sweet, handsome, amiable. Comedy, well entertained. Good dance. Home. Sat up too late. You stood it, but it hurts stomach. Do it seldom; rather do less an hour than ruin constitution. [Go to bed] exact at twelve. This day at eleven, Club; dine here and let chance next declare. Be pious, prudent, *retenu,* firm. "Separated sooner than subdued."[5]

FRIDAY 23 DECEMBER

> Sure, by all rules of reasoning, tonight
> I must with more than usual fancy write;
> For I sit down to write in spirits gay;
> To my charm'd ears how sweetly sounds "La Haye"!
> On the firm base of rational content—

[4] Another Countess of Nassau, niece of the Grand Bailiff of Utrecht; she later accompanied her husband to Vienna, where he was sent as Ambassador, and died there. In 1763 she was between thirty-five and forty. A very grand lady. Her character is freely discussed by Constant d'Hermenches and Belle de Zuylen: D'Hermenches thought her empty and affected, Belle saw better qualities in her.   [5] See p. 18.

For three good months in useful study spent,
For having acted on Religion's plan,
And done the serious duties as a man—
Is my fair castle built of solid joy,
Which vice and pleasure dare not to destroy.

SATURDAY 24 DECEMBER. Yesterday was a great day....
Reynst ... carried you to Parade, where you saw the Dutch
Guards, and was animated a little with old ideas. But considered
how superior you was now with civil views than when a dependant
for a commission. You felt yourself above Prince and all, and
wondered how you had been so foolish. Write this to Father. You
was then presented to Monsieur Sommelsdyck: amiable, soft,
genteel....

DIALOGUES AT THE HAGUE

Scene, the Parade

REYNST. It's a fine regiment, isn't it?

BOSWELL. It truly is. Well, after all, it must be confessed that
there is something in a corps of gallant soldiers that strikes us like
nothing else. I have the soul of a soldier, but—your Highness, I
am charmed to have the honour.

PRINCE OF HESSE. Where are you lodged?

BOSWELL. At the Maréchal Turenne. And where are your Highness's quarters?

PRINCE. Oh, I am on duty here,[6] but I shall have the honour to
pay you a visit.

BOSWELL. Sir, the gentlemen in the Service like to change.[7]

REYNST. Well! Monsieur de Sommelsdyck, Mr. Boswell, a Scotsman, a relation of yours.

SOMMELSDYCK. Sir, I am charmed.

[6] "O, je suis de la parade."

[7] "Changer." I suppose it means either, "like to get away from their military
quarters," or, "like to have a change of duty."

BOSWELL. Sir, I should have had the honour to pay you my respects before this. But I was waiting to be presented by Monsieur Chais, who was good enough to promise to perform that courtesy for me.

SOMMELSDYCK. Your father is living and in good health?

BOSWELL. Yes, Sir. He has the greatest respect for your family. He received many civilities from the Admiral, your father, thirty years ago when he—my father, that is—was studying at Leyden.

SOMMELSDYCK. You are at Leyden?

BOSWELL. No, Sir. I am at Utrecht. I really had the keenest desire to have come first to The Hague to pay my respects to my relations, but the fact is that we English are very negligent; and to tell you the truth, I could not speak French and I did not wish to present myself as a dumb cousin.[8] But after having been three months at Utrecht and worked hard, I have got enough to get by with after a fashion.

SOMMELSDYCK. Sir, I shall have the honour to present you to my wife. Will you dine with us today?

BOSWELL. Sir, I am engaged.

SOMMELSDYCK. Tomorrow, if you please?

BOSWELL. I shall have the honour.

Scene, Mr. Maclaine's[9] house

MACLAINE. Gentlemen, you will have but a poor dinner.

BOSWELL. What should one reply to that?

CHAIS. "It can't be helped," I suppose.

BOSWELL. Well, it is beginning well, all the same. This soup is excellent.

[8] "Cousin Muet." Perhaps an allusion to a play currently being performed at The Hague. A young man who is presented by some girl as a "dumb cousin" but who is actually her lover was a stock figure in French comedy.

[9] Archibald Maclaine, north-Irishman, co-pastor of the (Presbyterian) English church at The Hague. He was very learned and for a time served as preceptor to the Prince of Orange. James Maclaine, the famous "gentleman highwayman" hanged at Tyburn in 1750, was his brother.

MACLAINE. Mr. Boswell, there is *vin rouge,* Rhenish, and Burgundy: ask for which you prefer.

BOSWELL. Do you know that Mademoiselle de Zuylen is in town? She is our *bel esprit* at Utrecht.

MACLAINE. I have met her only once. I'm afraid a young lady like that is not a natural character.

REEDE.[1] Oh, your fear is most unjust.

MACLAINE. What's that you say, Baron?

REEDE. I was saying that Mademoiselle de Zuylen is very likable. She writes verses, but she is not ill natured. She jests . . .[2]

SUNDAY 25 DECEMBER. This is Christmas day. Be in due frame. Only hear prayers at Chapel, but don't take sacrament except you can see Chaplain before.[3] Yesterday . . . you . . . went a moment to Society, then to Monsieur Sommelsdyck's, where you dined and passed all the afternoon and evening, quite *en famille,* no brilliancy but all friendship. The *family tree.* Write for him name and titles and small tree of your family. . . .

MONDAY 26 DECEMBER. Yesterday you waited on Mr. Richardson, Chaplain to Sir Joseph Yorke; found him affable and decent. Took you up to his room, told you, "Our Church leaves it to every man." Presented to Ambassador. . . . Took with him. Then Chapel. "Grace and truth":[4] fine sermon. Then received the

[1] A brother of Frederick Christian Reinhart van Reede, fifth Earl of Athlone, a Hollander bearing an Irish peerage title conferred on his ancestor by William III. "Young Reede," as Boswell afterwards calls him, was a close friend of Belle de Zuylen.

[2] The dialogues break off here at the bottom of a full page, with a catchword for a succeeding page. But it is not at all certain that anything is lost. See p. 79.

[3] Boswell, who had never previously made his communion in the Church of England, presumably wished to know whether he was expected to make confession and abjuration of heresy as he had done when received into the Roman Catholic communion. See p. 1.

[4] The concluding words of the gospel for Christmas: "And the Word was made flesh, and dwelt among us, and we beheld his glory, the glory as of the only begotten of the Father, full of grace and truth" (John 1. 14).

blessed sacrament solemnly professing myself a Christian; was in devout, heavenly frame, quite happy. The first time that I received the communion in the Church of England. . . . This day, in all forenoon and bring up journal and letter to Father . . . Be firm and consider you're quite independent of Father, &c.

TUESDAY 27 DECEMBER. . . . You dined splendid at Wilhem's. That is all. You was quite easy. You went home and wrote two hours. You returned and supped. She[5] talked of Madame de Beverweerd: the length of her neck and the inequality of her eyes, her *fausses couches*[6] and her thinking herself handsome. But you was prudent. When you return to Utrecht, be just as you was with her, only more guarded, since you have taken the sacrament. . . .

WEDNESDAY 28 DECEMBER. . . . Went to Maclaine's and talked with him on religion and morals, particularly women. He maintained you must sacrifice something for virtue. He answered all quibbles. In France and Italy, 'tis encouraging vice, contributing your quota; for every single individual will make the same excuse. You cannot make a woman an equivalent for loss of character, as you must consider the world's opinion. If she agree, it is taking £500 from a child. . . .

[Received 28 December, Stewart to Boswell][7]

Rotterdam, 27 December 1763

MY DEAR SIR:—I am this moment favoured with yours of the 26th current, in consequence of which I send you here annexed a pair of my finest laced ruffles. They are by no means Brussels, yet they are so far from being plain that I protest they cost me fifteen ducats. I recently got rid of four pair of my handsomest ruffles, otherwise I would have sent you genuine *point d'Alençon.* I am

[5] Madame de Wilhem. She was first cousin to Belle de Zuylen.
[6] Miscarriages.
[7] The original starts in English, drops into French, and then reverts to English.

delighted to see that you are having the reception that your merits deserve. I am really happy to see that you *are so*,[8] and shall be very glad to see you here, being, in haste, yours affectionately,

A. STEWART.

If the parcel should not have come to hand, please to cause inquiry be made at the market-boat.

[Received 28 December, Lord Auchinleck to Boswell]

[Auchinleck, December 1763]

MY DEAR SON,—I wrote to you last week a letter in your own form and answering to Juvenal's description: *plena iam margine et nondum finita.*[9] When one begins to write to a friend, they think they have little or nothing to say. But as they write, they warm, and fresh matter presents itself. At present I write this only to let you know what I suppose would occur to yourself: that it is quite necessary when you go to The Hague that you wait of[1] Sir Joseph Yorke, the British Ambassador there. When I had occasion to be with my Lord Privy Seal (Stuart Mackenzie, Esq.) the time of my being at the last Glasgow Circuit, he said that many of our countrymen neglected to get recommendations to the King's Minister at the places where they went; which, he said (and no man has travelled more nor knows the world better), was a great loss to them, for that a man who was not known to the Ambassador was looked upon as being a low man in his own country. In order therefore to your being introduced to Sir Joseph, I have got application to be made by means of my Lord President[2] to Mr. Yorke, late Attorney General, for a letter to introduce you to his brother Sir Joseph, and I expect it will be sent you under cover to Utrecht. In

---

[8] That is, are happy.

[9] "Full even to the margins and even then not finished" (*Satires*, i. 5–6). This letter, which Boswell received on 14 December, has not been recovered.

[1] A Scotticism.

[2] Robert Dundas, the presiding judge of the Court of Session, of which Lord Auchinleck was a member.

case you be left that place before it comes, you'll leave orders for any letters that come to you to be sent after you. If again by any accident you should be disappointed of that letter, you'll get somebody of respect in The Hague to introduce you. . . .

Be sure to make my best compliments to Mynheer van Sommelsdyck. I remember him very well, but he won't remember me, for it is thirty-four years since I saw him, when I went to take leave of his worthy father and mother, and he was then but about five years of age. I doubt if his sisters will remember anything of me, though I remember them well. Make also my compliments to them. . . .

In my last I said in general that we are pretty well supplied with the classics, and now they are put up in the library room, they make a good show. However, if you fall upon any of the very old editions before the 1500,[3] and get them cheap, it is worth while to take them; for as they were printed directly from the manuscripts, frequently discoveries may be made from them. There is one book in your own way that I think you should buy and read over with care. It is entitled *Causes célèbres et intéressantes*, in twenty-six or twenty-seven octavo volumes. It contains the proceedings of the Parliament of Paris in a number of curious cases which came before it; vastly instructive as well as entertaining, fit for every gentleman who aims at making a figure in public life; and as that is your aim, it is proper you direct your studies to things that conduct to it.

As for abstruse points in law, philosophy, or divinity, it is in vain for a man to break his brains upon them. The point is to be in condition to do our duty and to do it with diligence. We cannot know everything, so let us attach ourselves to the most useful things.

I applaud you for not condemning the Dutch language; our countrymen commonly do. One good reason for it is that they don't understand it. It is not a polite language, 'tis true, except in the mouth of a handsome woman. I must make this exception, for I

[3] A Scotticism.

remember well when I have heard a pretty lady saying "O hemel!"[4] I thought it musical. But one thing we must own, that the English is a good deal borrowed from it—or, which is the same, from its mother, the High Dutch. If you want to know a little of it speedily so as to divert yourself with Jacob Cats when you come home, you had best take a master to teach you the reading of it.[5] I did this for a month with success.

My compliments to Mr. Brown, of whom I hear a mighty good character. His wife's father is my Lady Coalston's brother; but, poor man, he was unhappy, having a wife in this country still alive, to whom he was married before he married Mrs. Brown's mother. I mention this to you in confidence; don't speak of it. Mrs. Brown may be a good woman notwithstanding this *macula natalium*,[6] so it should not be published. All here remember you with affection. Sir David Dalrymple and his lady are to dine here next week.[7]

THURSDAY 29 DECEMBER. Yesterday you sat in all day writing.... You was dull, but you did not yield. You grew better at Sporck's.[8] Madame Maasdam[9] told you how *la Comtesse* was taken to Utrecht, as there were strange suspicions. "She is a little *galante*, but do not whisper it." I said, "She is my mistress—in French." ... Pray be *retenu* and stand out. This day at ten, Maclaine, House in Wood.[1] ... Be cheerful but on guard. Let exercise drive off spleen; call up every principle.... Write lines soon. Have a care or you'll alter. Have a care.

[4] "O heavens!"

[5] One of the proud possessions of the Auchinleck library was a large Dutch folio book of emblems by Jacob Cats (1577–1660) which had belonged to Veronica van Sommelsdyck, Lady Kincardine.   [6] Stain on her birth.

[7] There is no signature, but nothing has been lost.

[8] Rudolph Ulrich, Baron Sporck or von Sporken, envoy extraordinary to The Hague from Hanover.

[9] Monsieur de Sommelsdyck's sister. Her husband was a general of cavalry.

[1] The Huis ten Bosch, a royal villa erected in 1647 for the widow of Prince Frederick Henry of Orange, grandfather of William III; one of the showplaces of The Hague.

FRIDAY 30 DECEMBER. Yesterday at ten, you went with Maclaine and saw House in the Wood: fine paintings. Senses not deceive, but reason wrong on their reports.[2] . . . Then dine Spaen; by
Madame Degenfeld; grow fine; say you'll break appointment.
Then all afternoon. Spaen favourite of Prince; privy to English
jaunt; taken up, bread and water. Katte beheaded. Comes to Holland, gets troop, as they would serve King's friend; returns, asks
rank would have had if not served King. Offered majority, not see
for thirty years till last year at Cleves; all *retenue* for some time.
King sorry, squeezes hand: "Any commands at Berlin?" "Nothing,
only that I've the same heart now as thirty years ago."[3] Then
Yorke's . . . Not dance, wrong. Gordon picks at your coat; don't
answer him. "You're the strangest boy I ever saw." 'Twas little to
be thus moved. . . .

FRIDAY 30 DECEMBER

> Last night at eight o'clock to Yorke's I went,
> And seven long hours in dissipation spent,

[2] "The dining-room is embellished with grisailles by De Wit (1749) of
Meleager, Atalanta, Venus, Adonis, and Genii, painted in imitation of bas-
reliefs and producing an almost perfect illusion" (Baedeker).

[3] This section of the memoranda, though not the easiest of reading, is presented to show the way in which Boswell has begun to convert his memoranda into rough notes for his journal. See pp. 49, 50. The latter part presumably means, "He came to Holland and was offered the command of a troop
of cavalry (a captaincy), the Dutch saying that they wished to serve a man
who was the friend of a king. He thought it over, went back and asked them to
give him the rank he would have had if he had *not* served the King of Prussia.
He was then offered a majority, accepted it, and did not see Frederick for
thirty years. Frederick visited Spaen last year at Cleves, where Spaen's estate
is: the King was for some time reserved, but finally showed that he was
sorry for his coldness to so close a friend of his youth," etc. According to
Dr. Eduard Vehse (*Illustrierte Geschichte des preussischen Hofes ... bis
zum Tode Kaiser Wilhelms I*), Frederick was very gracious and familiar,
reminded Spaen of many episodes of their youth, but never mentioned their
conspiracy. Spaen afterwards used to remark, "The King has a splendid
memory down to the year 1730."

Where all was valued merely by the eye,
And glitt'ring blockheads made a sage stand by.
As I have been but little time abed,
Weak are my limbs and dizzy is my head;
My jaded muse, all drowsy and all faint,
Like Dr. Young's must utter her *Complaint;*
And must the bane of manly virtue call
What foolish mortals idly name a ball.

1764

SUNDAY 1 JANUARY. Yesterday you was very splenetic. ...
Dined ordinary. Then idle. Billiards by self. Then home, coffee,
&c., and grew well. Madame de Wilhem's, easy and happy. Came
home well. ... You have stood this. Be firm.

[Received *c.* 1 January, Stewart to Boswell]⁴

Rotterdam, 30 December 1763

MY DEAR FRIEND,—I am truly delighted to see by your esteemed letter that you have at last taken notice of what every one
who has the honour to know you saw from the beginning: namely,
that you are full of wit and good humour, besides being remarkably handsome.

I think I hear the fine ladies of The Hague saying to one another as they see you pass, "There's a proper young man, one can
see that straight away from his face; he is very good-looking, eh!
don't you think so, my dear?" "Yes, most assuredly, and he is certainly English, for he is too well set-up for a Dutchman." "Oh! it is
evidently that young English lord recently come from Utrecht who
Mademoiselle Boetzelaer told us was full of wit, very gay and
extremely likable: he has also a great deal of fine manners without
the least affectation. His name is Bossel or Bosvel; they say he is
very rich—"

I can assure you that your French is very good. It is true that
there are some small mistakes here and there, and without putting
yourself to much trouble you will find many more in the letter

⁴ The first three paragraphs of the original are written in French.

113

before you, for I have really forgotten my French, it has been so long since—[5]

As it is possible I may be obliged to go in a day or two to Amsterdam, I beg you will send me my sword, if you can spare it, and you'll oblige yours affectionately,

A. STEWART.

Though I am very scarce of paper, I must see to make you laugh. I happened to be reading one of your letters to Sally, and when I came to that passage wherein you say "that candour and openness which constitutes my character," Sally says, "Faith, I think he only wants a razor now." "Why that?" replied I. "Because," returned she, "he has already soaped his own beard."[6]

MONDAY 2 JANUARY. Yesterday you heard Maclaine preach on being strangers on earth. You was very gloomy. Then you went to Society; played at billiards with Prince of Strelitz. Then at loo with him. Gordon still snappish. Said to him, "What's the matter with you?" It had effect. Dined Maasdam, still gloomy; tea Houston's, quite Scotch. Was galled, but said not a word.[7] . . . You are now a little jaded with all this idle, unnatural, sickly dissipation. Be firm on guard these three days, so as to depart sound. Never be moved with trifles. Be manly and silent.

[5] Stewart forgot on turning the leaf to finish his sentence.

[6] After his return from London in 1760, Boswell had founded at Edinburgh a jovial society known as the Soaping Club. In the jargon of this society "to soap a person's beard" meant to puff his vanity by flattery; to "shave" him or "to apply the razor," to deflate him with cutting wit. "Sally" is the wife of Stewart's clerk Mollison; she had formerly been the maid and perhaps more. In his memorandum for 12 January 1764 Boswell, then at Rotterdam and in a bad temper, refers to "the clerk and his wife, erst maid and w——re."

[7] One illustration out of many that could be chosen from these memoranda of the invariable effect of Scots familiarity and sarcasm on Boswell. Colonel John Houston was an officer in the "Scots Dutch," that is, in the brigade of Scots nationals in the Dutch service. "Gordon" is the Honourable Charles Gordon (see p. 16), who, like Boswell, had come to The Hague for the vacation. Boswell had previously called him "pert," and "snappish and envious," and had drawn from him the remark, "You're the strangest boy I ever saw" (above, p. 111).

[Boswell to Stewart][8]

S'Haag's, 2 January 1764

MYN HEER EN VRIND,—Ik heb niet mar en cleyn Beytie Hollans, en Ik heb niet een Dictionarie myn te helpen; mar Ik heb een groot lust in dat taal te schryven, en Ik sal het probeeren. Mynheer can lauchen, als hy beleeft: Waarom niet? Ik lauch ook. Te lauchen is heel goed voor de Gezontheid. Ik ben seer verplight te mynheer voor zyn degen; en als it niet necessaar is tway degenen te hebben Ik zend it met groot plaisir. Sarah heel vroolic is te zegen dat ik moet een scheirmess hebben, om dat ik heb myn baard gezeepen. Mar mynheer it is wonderlyk dat Sarah noch niet van ue huys vertrecken is; heb mynheer niet een andere vryster engageerd, Sall mynheer van Lainshaw een Jong kneght van Schotland niet gezenden? En zoo Mynheer naar Amsterdam te gaan is. Maar hy moet secker bin gow rug te komen, voor it sall speyt me seer, him niet te vinden in fyve daagen t'Rotterdam. Mynheer moet myn een brief schryven, maar in Hollans niet. Ik bin, Mynheer &c.,

JACOBUS VAN AUCHINLECK.

[8] This "Dutch" letter, which Boswell dashed off at top speed, is printed in the text exactly as he wrote it, for his writing in Dutch is the whole point of the jest. Readers who know a little German will be able to decipher most of it without a dictionary. For those who dislike puzzles, a literal version follows: "My [dear] Sir and friend:—I have but a small bit of Dutch, and I have not a dictionary to help me; but I have a great desire to write in that tongue, and I shall try it. Mynheer can laugh if he pleases. Why not? I laugh too. To laugh is very good for the health. I am very much obliged to Mynheer for his sword; and as it is not necessary to have two swords, I send it with great pleasure. Sarah is very merry to say that I must have a razor, because I have soaped my beard. But, Mynheer, it is strange that Sarah has not yet left your house. If Mynheer has not engaged another girl, shall the Laird of Lainshaw not send a young lad from Scotland? And so Mynheer has gone to Amsterdam. But he must be sure to come back quickly, for it will grieve me sore not to find him in five days at Rotterdam. Mynheer must write me a letter, but not in Dutch. I am, Sir, &c., JACOBUS VAN AUCHINLECK." The "Laird of Lainshaw" (in Ayrshire) was Boswell's first cousin, brother of his future wife.

[Received 5 January, Stewart to Boswell]

[Rotterdam, *c.* 4 January 1764]

YOUR LAST LETTER, my dear Boswell, cost me more than all the other letters you ever wrote me, as I was obliged to employ a *Tovenaar* or *Sorcier,* what the Scotch commonly call second-sighted people, to explain it to me, and he assured me it took him all his skill to decipher it. I need not tell you how extravagant these sort of people are when they know you can't do without them, which was really the present case. I shall be glad to see you five days hence, I mean from the date of your last *Mystery.* Yours, &c.,

A. STEWART.

FRIDAY 6 JANUARY. Yesterday you went with Yorke and was presented to Prince of Orange.[9] You was melancholy to a degree. You heard Gordon talk all his system of folly on Plan, &c., and you told him he was ill-tempered. You dined Sommelsdyck's and was happy enough to be very cordial, and parted from him in great friendship, happy to have *fait connaissance,* &c. You said not a word of your gloom, and stood firm. This day dress immediately in brown. Pay visits to Spaen, Maasdam, De Wilhem, Yorke. Give orders if Gordon sends to say not at home. . . . Pay bills calmly and leave Hague with full satisfaction, having acquitted yourself as a man.

SATURDAY 7 JANUARY. . . . Came drowsy in *schuit* to Leyden; eat light supper, was well and easy. Keep so. This day Abraham Gronovius; copy notes for Sir David; dine and be temperate and cheerful. You must take care of your stomach; eat always some toast and drink a little negus at night, so as not to clog stomach at one meal. Tonight or tomorrow, Stewart, fine and happy, but *retenu.*

[9] Holland was at this time headed by a "Stadtholder," the office being hereditary in the House of Orange. But William V, the Prince of Orange to whom Boswell was introduced, was still a boy of fifteen. He had first been under the regency of his mother, the Princess Royal of England, daughter of George II, and now had for tutor the Marshal Duke of Brunswick-Wolfenbüttel.

SUNDAY 8 JANUARY. Yesterday you passed the morning with Mynheer Gronovius first, then Prince Strelitz. Could not dine, but saw him quite young student. Then walked with Abrahamus. Then dinner, daughter and *juffrouw*.[1] Quite full remembrance of Father. Then looked at his rooms with pleasing concern. Then Gordon, walk with him. Then evening at Prince's. . . . Loo; gained; was happy and temperate; and home in good spirits, and reflected with joy on four months well spent. . . .

MONDAY 9 JANUARY. Yesterday you breakfasted Gordon, quite fine, with ideas of Duke of Gordon, Lord Aberdeen, &c. Saw his books; read *Spleen* and Dodsley's *Collection,* and recalled fresh and warm ideas of London poetry.[2] Gordon was vastly pliant and fond of you. . . . Walked, then took leave by a short shake of the hand of Abraham Gronovius; then surveyed Leyden as Father's old town. You have really an affection for Holland. Played at night and lost, just expense on travels. You see world. . . .

TUESDAY 10 JANUARY. Yesterday you left Leyden early in the morning, dark and solemn, and kept up spirits well in *schuit,* though rainy. Arrived at Rotterdam at half after one; hearty reception by Stewart. Glad to see the house again where you endured so much. . . . Don't go out, but sit in all evening at brag. 'Twas wrong. This day breakfast, then dress, then journal, then walk, then dine, then journal and bring up. You have great materials. If you don't hear from Brown today, set out tomorrow. . . .

[Received 10 January, the Reverend Robert Brown to Boswell]

Utrecht, 8 January 1764

DEAR SIR:—By the inclosed, which I thought I could not do better than send you both for information and amusement, you

[1] Probably not Madame Gronovius, who, being a professor's wife, would have been designated by the more polite *Mevrouw,* but some young woman attendant on the daughter.

[2] *The Spleen* was a popular eighteenth-century poem by Matthew Green. Dodsley's *Collection,* perhaps the most famous of English anthologies, was first published in 1748. See *Boswell's London Journal, 1762–1763,* 1950, 105.

will see that I have executed your commission, and that you have all the time you desire. Whatever day you come, I beg you'll do us the pleasure of eating a bit of supper at our house, to make up for the bad (or rather no) dinner you shall have had upon the road.— All here desire their best compliments to you, and offer you many sincere New-Year wishes. As you do, so shall I refer all news till meeting; and so, having had a very hard day's work of it, consisting of two sermons and the administration of the sacrament in English and Latin, I shall take my leave, with assuring you that nobody can be with more esteem and real regard your friend and servant than

ROBERT BROWN.

P.S. The *dies Martis* is Tuesday sennight. I beg my compliments to Mr. Stewart.

[Received 10 January, Professor Christian Heinrich Trotz to Brown][3]

[Utrecht, *c.* 7 January 1764]

VIRO PLURIMUM REVERENDO BROUWNIO, PASTORI MERITISSIMO, S. PL. D.   C. H. TROTZ.

Terminus collegiorum est dies Martis post septimanam sequentem. Habebit itaque amicus noster satis adhuc spatii, quo res suas disponere valeat. Reliqua inter dulcia colloquia, cum redierit amicus noster communis, tractemus. Ceterum felix sit iter, felix etiam anni exordium, felicior progressus, et sequentium felicissimus exitus. Vale faveque tuo.

[3] The original of this letter is printed in the text, in order to remind the reader that in the eighteenth century professors in Continental universities still lectured in Latin and even used Latin naturally for epistolary correspondence. The letter may be translated, "C. H. Trotz sends his compliments [S.P.D. = *salutem plurimam dicit*] to the Reverend Mr. Brown. The term begins a week from next Tuesday. Consequently our friend will have plenty of time yet to put his affairs in order. The other points you raise we will discuss in friendly conversation when our common friend has returned. I add the wish that his journey may be happy, the New Year also happy, happier its progress, and most happy the issue of the years to come. Adieu; think kindly of your [humble servant.]"

THURSDAY 12 JANUARY. Yesterday you deviated sadly. You passed the forenoon with Stewart writing a little and talking without force or spirit. You did well at dinner in speaking Dutch. In the evening you resolved to bring up journal; and instead of that you sat seven hours at cards with the clerk and his wife, erst maid and w—re.[4] For shame, this was very bad.... You have not been on guard here as at Hague.... Make a firm resolution, a *promise,* never to play but when necessary, as 'tis low and unworthy....

MONDAY 16 JANUARY. Yesterday you recovered. You went to Church of England in the morning. Then you wrote, then walked. You was gloomy. But you kept your post and did not own it even to Stewart, who knew it all so well formerly. So you see that silence is your great refuge. You dined too hearty. Restrain stomach, and by custom you'll have easy temperance.... This morning, up at six. Pay washing. Letters. George, Betty, Sally.[5] Barber.... Set out at eight, full of spirits as after trial ...

TUESDAY 17 JANUARY. Yesterday you took leave of Stewart and had good drive to Ter-Gouw; there, was a little peevish, but checked it. Then *schuit* to Bodegraven.... Arrived happy and comfortable; felt affection for Dame,[6] &c.; supped Brown, all happy. Gaiety universal; heard that you was well amongst the people here; heart better than head; quite happy. This day resume with courage; dress immediately and pay visits. First, to *la Comtesse.* Then Trotz;[7] then visits; then dine; then walk; then Greek. Begin first day so as show true great man, and go to Assembly in satisfaction and composure. Be extremely *retenu.*

WEDNESDAY 18 JANUARY. Yesterday Mademoiselle de Zuylen. Yesterday you paid visits and read some Voltaire in forenoon. You received long letter from your worthy friend Johnston. Get large sheet of good paper and answer it immediately. Mem. Arthur Seat, Thom's, Macbeth, all your old ideas. Now being firm and

---

[4] Mr. Mollison and Sally.   [5] "Give tips to the servants."
[6] Probably his landlady.
[7] Shortly after writing this memorandum, he received another Latin note from Trotz saying that the "college" was deferred to the nineteenth.

retenu, try to help Johnston and give him abstract of history since coming abroad. . . .

THURSDAY 19 JANUARY. . . . Then Monsieur Trotz, and shake hands with *condiscipuli,*[8] and return quite in train. This day shake off sloth and resume studies. . . .

FRIDAY 20 JANUARY. Yesterday you began Trotz. After dinner Brown and you, &c., went and heard Hahn on nitre.[9] You said fatalists should be hanged and sceptics whipped. Greek went on. In the morning you visited Brouwer[1] and saw Icelandic. You talked on scheme of Scots dictionary.[2] Pursue it while here. Brown will assist you. It is not trifling. 'Twill be an excellent work. But be prudent with it. This day conclude letter to Johnston. Write Dutch song. Cheer up; take exercise and resume firmness; you must combat nervousness.

[Boswell to Johnston]

Utrecht, 20 January 1764

MY DEAR SIR,— . . . The whole of your letter shows me the continuance of that warm friendship which I hope shall never cease to fill the hearts of us both. Your complying with my request in writing from Grange pleases me much. Such little agreeable circumstances are not to be neglected. We should think no innocent gratification, however small, beneath our enjoying. Let us lighten our moments in this state of existence every lawful way we can.

You have given me the advice which I expected from you with

[8] Fellow pupils.
[9] Johannes David Hahn, M.D., was Professor of Philosophy and Natural Sciences at the University of Utrecht. He practised medicine, and was Belle de Zuylen's physician. Boswell later consulted him about his own health.
[1] So far unidentified. Boswell spells the name Brower.
[2] An ambitious scheme of compiling a dictionary of words peculiar to Scots English which will occupy a great deal of his thought in the weeks following. He describes the project at length, below, p. 162.

regard to my matrimonial scheme. Often and often have I consulted you upon such projects; and I really believe that had it not
been for your prudent counsel, I should have been a husband two
winters ago, and by that means should have ere this time been a
very unhappy man. This last scheme was founded on the same
principles with my former ones; and now I am equally glad at my
not having attempted to realize it. . . .

If I remember right, I gave you in my last a very full recital
of the severe fit of melancholy which I was seized with upon my
first coming to Utrecht, as also of my having taken a manly resolution to conquer it, and of my having succeeded. . . . I told you
that my honoured friend Mr. Samuel Johnson had supplied me
with the weapons of philosophy. It was in *The Rambler* that I
found the causes of my woe described and cures pointed out. I beg
you may get that book. It costs twelve shillings. But it is worth
much more. Study it, and endeavour to preserve the noble sentiments which it inspires. It is the best book that England has produced for such people as you and me. It proceeds upon the supposition that we are here in a state where there is much gloom, and
fortifies the mind to enable it to support the evils which attack it.

I have got so much to say to you that I should not dwell too long
on any one topic; and yet again, I find I have much to say on every
topic. I must do my best, and give you as much as I can, till my
paper be filled. . . .

I have found Utrecht to be a most excellent place. I have here
excellent opportunity to study, and at the same time to see foreign
company. There are a number of noble families who reside here in
the winter. I have been received into their assemblies, where I pass
two or three evenings a week improving in French and in politeness. At Christmas we had a month of vacation. I then went to The
Hague, where I passed three weeks in the most brilliant gaiety. The
style of living there is much in the manner of Paris. I found my relations there to be people of the first rank, and was treated by them
with the utmost civility. I had recommendations to a variety of

people. I was presented to the Prince of Orange and the other princes there, to all the foreign ambassadors—in short, to everybody.
I passed a couple of days at Leyden, where I supped twice with the
young Prince of Strelitz, our Queen's brother, once at his own
house, once at the house of Mr. Gordon, Lord Aberdeen's brother;
and now I am returned to this seat of the Dutch muses and have
resumed my studious regularity with much satisfaction.

Formerly such a change of life used to unhinge me quite. Now
I am firm and keep my post. I shall ever reverence Utrecht, for it
was there that I first began to act upon steady and manly principles. I am already not a little altered. But altered for the better.
However, I must guard against extremes. No longer ago than last
winter I was the ardent votary of pleasure, a gay sceptic who never
looked beyond the present hour, a hero and philosopher in dissipation and vice. Now I am all devoted to prudence and to morality. I
am full of the dignity of human nature; and so far am I from indulging myself in mimicry and ludicrous jocularity that I must
always have some grave or some useful subject. Perhaps I am too
much an enthusiast in rectitude. But candour makes me own that
rectitude has to me all the charms of novelty. You see then in what
situation your friend now is. Are you not happy to be informed
of it?

On Christmas day I was at The Hague and received the blessed
sacrament at the Ambassador's chapel. His chaplain is just that
genteel, amiable, Church-of-England clergyman whom I have
heard you say that you would like to have in your house, were you
a man of great fortune.

I have no room to write you remarks on this country. I must
refer them till meeting, when you will be entertained with my
foreign journal, which contains already 310 pages. In the mean
time, I would have you read Sir William Temple's *Observations on
the Netherlands.* They are short and entertaining, and will give
you some idea of the country where your friend is. Into whatever
nation I shall go, I must have you to read an account of it. Sir William Temple in his *Observations* says something particularly ap-

plicable to you and me. You cannot miss it; so your mentioning it to me will show me that you have read the book.[3]

I think it is a pity to take off the embargo on my papers. However, I indulge you with liberty to read my letters: but let the journal be reserved till I am sitting at your fireside.[4] I hope my papers are safely preserved. Lest they should grow damp, I would wish to have them taken out of the box sometimes and exposed to the air in a room where there is a good fire. By the by, my father's opening my four bundles dwelt so in my mind that I took the liberty to mention it to him in my last letter. I have not as yet had his answer. My intention was that he should ask pardon as a friend, which I hope he will do.[5]

[3] "Strangers among [the Dutch] are apt to complain of the spleen, but those of the country seldom or never; which I take to proceed from their being ever busy, or easily satisfied. For this seems to be the disease of people that are idle, or think themselves but ill entertained, and attribute every fit of dull humour, or imagination, to a formal disease which they have found this name for; whereas such fits are incident to all men at one time or another, from the fumes of indigestion ... or from some changes or approaches of change in winds and weather.... Yet this effect is not so strong but that business or intention of thought commonly either resists or diverts it; and those who understand the motions of it let it pass, and return to themselves" (Chapter 4).

[4] During Boswell's stay in London, 1762–1763, he had sent Johnston weekly instalments of his journal, each accompanied by a letter. He had stipulated that after Johnston had read journal and letters once, he was to put them away in a box, not to be looked at again until Boswell returned to read them with him.

[5] After Boswell had gone to London in November, 1762, he sent back to Edinburgh directions that certain sealed bundles of his private papers, then lying in his father's house, should be delivered to Johnston. On Johnston's reporting that some one had opened the bundles, Boswell wrote an angry letter to his father, whereupon Lord Auchinleck broke off correspondence and talked of selling the estate. See *Boswell's London Journal, 1762–1763*, 1950, p. 274 *n.* 8. Not a single letter from Boswell to his father has as yet been recovered. It is not known whether Lord Auchinleck did "ask pardon as a friend." We can give him the benefit of the doubt, for a letter from him received by Boswell on 1 February is missing.

I have not passed so *sound* a winter these six years. Yet I am not quite content; for I do not enjoy enough. I am afraid to resign myself to pleasing sensations lest I should be too susceptible of uneasy ones. I am really of too anxious a temper, for I dare say you will think I have no reason to fear my having too hardened a soul.

My dear Johnston, never allow yourself to doubt of my friendship for you. Go to Arthur Seat, where we have often walked and where I hope we shall walk yet oftener. Recall every agreeable hour, and be assured that as long as that old mountain stands, so long shall my friendship last.

You give me great comfort by your accounts of Charles. I trust him entirely to you. I left £20 in the hands of Herries and Cochrane. I shall write to them soon, so as that they may answer your draught for £10. I shall write in a week or two, so that you may have the money before you go to Annandale.

I am happy to find that you are so well with the worthy Doctor.[6] ... He writes me much good of you. Davy gives me uncommon satisfaction. He will be a man. Tell him I shall write to him soon. Let me hear from you often, and send your letters to your friend in London.[7] I ever remain, my dear Sir, your most affectionate friend,

JAMES BOSWELL.

Dic[8] mihi ubi habitas hoc anno. An floret theatrum Edinburgense? An Dominus Digges adhuc in scenam prodit? Amicos nostros communes meo nomine saluta. Solus sum Anglus in hac

---

[6] Dr. Boswell.   [7] This friend remains unidentified.

[8] This postscript was written on the only portion of the sheet still remaining blank except the rectangle that Boswell had reserved for the address. When the sheet was folded and sealed, the postscript was exposed on the outside. Hence the mild disguise of a learned tongue. It may be translated as follows: "Tell me where you are living this year. Does the Edinburgh theatre flourish? Does Mr. Digges still hold forth on the stage? Greet our common friends in my name. I am the only Englishman in this university, and consequently I am every day in the company of foreigners. I hope to pass jovial nights with you at Thom's, that excellent host." "Thom" was a vintner in Edinburgh; the Soaping Club met in his house.

Academia et igitur cum exteris consortium diurnum habeo. Spero noctes hilares tecum tenere apud Thomam hospitem illum excellentem.

FRIDAY 20 JANUARY

> Not the consummate laziness of swine
> Is greater than this laziness of mine.
> Were you to lay me in a dirty stye,
> My limbs I'd stretch and say, "Do let me lie!"
> By my warm furnace I lethargic sit,
> And ease much rather choose than lively wit.
> Luxurious living any man will spoil
> And make him puny and averse to toil.
> Now drowsy Morpheus deadens all my powers;
> For once I'll sleep me full eleven hours.

SATURDAY 21 JANUARY. Inviolable Plan today. Yesterday you was at Assembly *chez* Mademoiselles Bottestein. You was surprisingly uneasy with awkwardness; you must force off this. You played good party, that's all. At night you was quite lazy, and you indulged it to complete week after vacation; and now begin firmness; swear it. Lethargic gloom is now attempting you. But by exercise till you sweat, drive him off. Eat less and drink more. This day, journal till one. Then Brown, and much version. Then home, journal till eight. Then Trotz, fine. You're engaged next assembly with Mademoiselle de Zuylen; cheer up.

SATURDAY 21 JANUARY

> With the same ease that blackguards feed on tripe
> Have I, James Boswell, learnt to smoke a pipe:
> For I am now a very Dutchman grown,
> As all at Utrecht cannot fail to own.
> My father smoked full thirty years ago,
> And I most wisely in his footsteps go.
> While in my grate the wood is blazing seen,

> Upon a table I my elbow lean,
> And with a visage most composed and bluff,[9]
> Steams of tobacco solemnly I puff.

[*c.* 22 JANUARY. FRENCH THEME] Laziness is my true enemy,
and indeed is the enemy of all the virtues that can ennoble a man.
One may as well cease to be as to be lazy. I will go further. It is
.better not to be than to be lazy, because if a man does not exist
and consequently has no good, he has also no evil. But laziness is
worse than a privation of existence, for it is impossible to be lazy
without being depraved. Man was created to be busy, and all his
faculties, of soul as well as of body, become useless and spoil in
idleness. Well! Why do I make these reflections just now? The
reason is a curious one: because just now I am lazy myself. I
have a natural disposition to that vice. I am fat, and I have a
temperament so constituted that although I have plenty of fire
I have also a good deal of sluggishness. It is a rather extraordinary
constitution. An officer in the English military service[1] gave a
very ingenious illustration of it. He said that I was like a great
stone couched on the slope of a mountain, and while I stayed there,
I was lumpish and heavy; but when I was once set in motion, I
went with amazing velocity, so that it was impossible to stop me
until, the projectile force being exhausted, I came again to rest.
Indeed, it is a very apt illustration, for when I am in company, it
is equal odds that you will see me taciturn and sombre, and on the
other hand, if I begin to speak, you will hear a brilliant vivacity,
a rapidity of thoughts; if I may use that expression, a fire of
language of which you have not often heard the like. It is the same
in my actions. For example, when I have been some days without
studying, I have a shocking disposition to indolence. I am wretched
when I am idle, but I have not enough force of mind to return

---

[9] "Bluff" in the eighteenth century meant rather "surly, blustering, domineering" than "roughly but good-naturedly frank." Mr. Ernest Weekley has
conjectured with much plausibility that the general shift in meaning was
effected by Sir Walter Scott, who always gave the word its "modern" sense.
[1] Unidentified.

promptly to work, and it is only through the pangs of *ennui* that I am obliged to take a road which I am sure leads me to happiness.

TUESDAY 24 JANUARY.... Yesterday you began to recover. You got up in good time, brisk, and shook off sloth. This is really part of the disease of your bad constitution, and you must use the constant regimen of early rising and exercise to strengthen your weak nerves and make your sluggish blood circulate. It will grow easy and pleasant, and you'll harden more and more. You was gloomy during the day, and owned to Rose amid his gloom that the climate oppressed you.... This day push on. Recover more and more. Read law in morning. Learn to rise at six and labour truly. Beware slovenly study.... Assembly, fine, and play with *Veuve*,[2] &c....

[*c*. 26 JANUARY. FRENCH THEME] To be learned is undoubtedly very pleasant. We all have natural curiosity, and the satisfaction of that curiosity is very agreeable; it is also flattering, because when we make comparisons between ourselves and others who are ignorant of what we know, there results a gratification of our pride, a gratification by no means contemptible. On the contrary, it is perhaps one of the greatest gratifications that human nature is capable of. I confess for my own part that I have a great deal of pride, too much, in fact, not to feel pain from it sometimes, for my pride, like the vanity of Mademoiselle de Zuylen, is *boundless*,[3] and consequently is often shocked. It is not enough merely to be proud or vain; it is necessary at the same time that other people should think we have a right to be so....

SATURDAY 28 JANUARY.... At Assembly you was easy with *la Comtesse*, but saw her piqued. You must make up this by

[2] The very rich and lovely young widow, Madame Geelvinck, who will figure prominently in the memoranda from this point on. She was born in 1738, her maiden name Catherina Elisabeth Hasselaer; married Lieve Geelvinck in 1756, and became a widow the next year. She was a close friend of Belle de Zuylen.

[3] "*Sans bornes*," underlined in the original. Boswell is quoting from Belle's character-sketch of herself called "The Portrait of Zélide": "Naturellement vaine, sa vanité est sans bornes." See p. 185.

easy complaisance, as she can do you more service than Zélide, whom, however, you must be a good friend to. You played at cards with Madame Geelvinck—charming indeed. You said to Zélide, "I love Sue, &c.[4] But the contrary is true with you and me." "No," said she, "I was prepossessed in your favour." "But I was not in yours." Too severe, &c. . . .[5]

SATURDAY 28 JANUARY

> Since the strange ev'ning that I first began
> To write ten lines a day on stated plan,
> Ne'er have I been in such a woeful plight
> As that in which I find myself tonight.
> Of learned Trotzius I have been the guest,
> And with his heavy supper am oppressed.
> Lazy and hot, most sensibly I feel
> That I have eat roast rabbits and roast veal;
> And though impatience goads my fretful brain,
> Not one idea can I thence obtain.

[29–30 JANUARY. FRENCH THEMES] . . . To confess the truth, I was badly brought up. I was taught the ancient languages, but I was not taught things. I had naturally an excellent memory, and that memory became still better through cultivation. But, alas! what was it that I remembered? It was a mass of phrases, of rules of grammar, and perhaps a few little stories. But I was not trained to think about what I was reading; on the contrary, I acquired a habit of skimming through a book without extracting any ideas from it. I remember perfectly how my mother promised to make me a present of a Confession of Faith of the Church of Scotland, provided that I read it from beginning to end. A Confession of Faith

---

[4] *I love Sue* was a song currently popular. I know it only by title. The words probably say that the lover had loved Sue before he had ever met her.

[5] "Too severe," since the words are recorded in French, may be Belle's rejoinder.

was at any rate a book. I had a great desire to form a library, and I used every legitimate means to fill my shelves. I therefore read as quickly as I could that collection of absurd unintelligibility, but my mind did not receive the least impression from it. Election and Reprobation and Irresistible Grace were to me as unknown as the systems of the votaries of Vishnu, Ishvara, and Brahma in the East Indies.[6] All the same, I read the book and my mother was satisfied. But there is no doubt that if we are not taught to give our attention to what we hear and what we read, we acquire bad habits and lose the power of acquiring knowledge from books. Another very bad usage in Scotland is to take children to church before they can understand what the minister says. This creates a habit quite contrary to Nature, namely, a habit of listening to a man speak for half an hour at a time without attending to a word he says.

Today is the 30th of January, a day which the Church of England has set apart for a day of fasting; and if Britons will only think seriously on the melancholy occasion of this fast, they ought to think that it merits observation in Great Britain for ever. It was on this day in the year 1649 that impious rebels put King Charles I to death; and to increase their horrible crime, they committed it under pretext of law and liberty. Thus all the principles of religion and government were violated by the murder of our amiable and pious Sovereign, who with much justice has acquired the title of martyr. We admit that he had faults, or rather made mistakes. But when we regard them as the causes for which those scoundrels led him to the scaffold, they appear to us like slight stains on an exalted reputation. I do not wish now to dispute with the Whigs, that is, with those who love republican principles so much that they forget the true British Constitution and have small respect for the King, who nevertheless is, as we say, at the head of our Constitution. I address myself solely to those who have been called

---

[6] Ishvara, "(the) Lord," is a familiar title of the god Siva. Boswell's actual spellings are *Vistnou* and *Eswara*.

Tories: that is, to those who maintain true loyalty. I use these
ludicrous terms because the fact is that they have been in use so
long that they give us instantly the ideas of these different parties
and give it even with a particular force which explanation does
not give. . . . We have been accustomed to hear these words from
our earliest youth in a particular sense. Consequently they make
a more lively impression on us than a long argument.

I ask you, my friends, if so shocking an event ought not to be
called to mind every year by the people of England. The Whigs
are in agreement with us on the point, but they wish the day to be
observed for a very different reason than that of the Royalists.
When the present Earl of Dundonald was a member of Parliament, he went into a church in London on the 30th of January,
although he was a violent Whig. Sir Watkin Williams Wynn, one
of the Tory leaders, came in. "Ah!" said he, "Cochrane! Is it you I
see? What! Do you wish to celebrate this day?" "Yes, Sir," replied
he. "I think that this day ought to be celebrated in England from
century to century, to remind our king that he has a joint in his
neck." . . .[7]

[7] This Earl of Dundonald, a blustering old Army officer, was Boswell's great-
uncle; he succeeded to the peerage unexpectedly at the age of nearly seventy
when a young cousin was killed at the siege of Louisburg. His retort (allowing for the fact that we cannot know its exact form in English) will be recognized as identical with that which Lord Auchinleck is said on the authority
of Sir Walter Scott to have made to Dr. Johnson when Johnson asked him
what good Cromwell had ever done to his country: "Good, Doctor! he gart
kings ken that they had a lith in their neck." I have in at least two places pronounced this report of Scott's (which was first written down in 1829) to be
apocryphal. Since it now appears on unimpeachable evidence that the remark figured in a family anecdote long before Scott's time, we must conclude
that Scott may have been in receipt of a true tradition after all. Scott's manuscript, a letter to John Wilson Croker now in the Yale University Library,
clearly reads, "God, Doctor!" and so the retort was printed by Croker. I do
not hesitate, however, to adopt the brilliant emendation proposed to me by
Dr. Marshall Waingrow, "Good" for "God." Scott's letters, particularly those
written towards the end of his life, show many inadvertent omissions of words
and letters.

[Received 30 January, John Mollison to Boswell]

Rotterdam, 26 January 1764

Sir:—By order of Mr. Stewart, I have sent you herewith the cake he promised you; he˙wishes you may eat with as much pleasure as he sends it. He also begs you will return the small trunk, as he will have use for it soon.—Sally begs to be kindly remembered to you. On the morning you left this, she gave you change for a ducat, but you omitted to give her the ducat. No doubt you will recollect this circumstance, which she only puts you in mind of that it may not be forgot.—I salute you kindly, and am, Sir, your most obedient humble servant,

John Mollison.

TUESDAY 31 JANUARY. Yesterday you did not strictly keep the Fast, as not being in Britain. You may be a Tory and have most warm loyalty for King George. But beware Jacobitism. Beware lest you slide to it imperceptibly. After dinner you disputed fairly with Brown on religion and found him a cold, low body. He was vulgar and rude. You laughed and said you'd never again dispute with him. . . . This day, law and journal. Write short to Stewart[8] and to Mollison. Tomorrow begins spring and rising early. . . .

WEDNESDAY 1 FEBRUARY. . . . At Assembly you appeared in sea-green and silver and was really brilliant—much taken notice of and like an ambassador. You begin to be much at your ease and to take a true foreign polish. Madame Geelvinck was charming. You told her you expected to see her character by

---

[8] At the end of February Stewart left for England on business, and did not return to Holland until after Boswell's departure. Boswell wrote to his father, Sir Michael, giving him a good report of Archibald's behaviour, and received a grateful acknowledgment from Archibald himself, but the two appear not to have met again for many years. In 1770 Stewart purchased an estate in Tobago. Boswell, who saw him in London in 1772, says that he had acquired a fortune (part of it by gambling), but that he was badly deformed with rheumatism. He was killed at Tobago in 1779 while defending h⸱s plantation against the crew of an American privateer.

Zélide.⁹ She said, "It is not interesting." You said, "Oh, do not say that to me!" She said, "You, who are so sincere!" She saw what you meant. You played whist well. After it, you felt, for the first time in Holland, delicious love. O *la belle Veuve!* She talked low to you

⁹ A written character, a character-sketch, in French. There is what I take to be a copy of it in Boswell's hand among the Boswell Papers. From it we learn that Madame Geelvinck had a slight cast in one or both of her eyes, which were pretty, brown, and gentle; that her complexion was brilliant, her teeth handsome, and the lower part of her face pretty, but that her general expression was more fetching than any of her features taken separately.—"You have intelligence and discernment; you grasp immediately what is said to you, and you draw the right conclusion provided that no prejudice gets in the way. You do not believe that you know everything, and you like to learn. Your conversation is lively and easy, never affected, never too positive, subject to no prevailing taste which causes too frequent a return to the same subjects. You speak with an agreeable negligence and informality; you listen with flattering and intelligent attention. Your *badinages* have an amusing vivacity; but, as nothing is perfect, they sometimes lack delicacy and taste. How fortunate are those whom you love! Your way of letting them know it is so natural, your caresses have an indescribable something so sincere and naïve that they cannot but be infinitely sensible of it....—You show less good opinion of yourself than you do a wish to make yourself approved by others: less of pride than of vanity. That vanity, which is still very childish, unrefined, and spontaneous, causes a too great attachment to trifles: to physical beauty, to fashions and dress, and a too visible attention to everything concerning yourself. Others would concern themselves about you more readily if you thought a little less about yourself: if you forgot yourself, at least occasionally. You are very easy to please, but you never think of inspiring love, your coquetry is all in your manners, never in your intention. You have no more of it than you allow to be seen.... You adopt a little too readily and without enough examination the ideas of others, whether as concerns your conduct or your opinions.... But ... a character of this sort ... has ... advantages: ... it is the cause of your complaisance, ... it contributes more than anything else towards making you loved. Men love nothing so much as that which flatters them; and you cannot flatter them more sensibly than by imitating them; nothing ... will give you greater assurance of their esteem, their friendship." It is very important to remember that *la Veuve* was only twenty-five years old.

and close, perhaps to feel breath.[1] All the *Heeren* looked blue. You took her hand to the coach, and your frame thrilled. . . .

[1 FEBRUARY. DUTCH THEME][2] Since I plan to learn the Dutch language; that is, since I wish to learn at least a little, so that I can converse with the natives of this country, I have resolved to write a little in that language every day. Because today is the first of February, I am beginning with the greater pleasure, for it is the beginning of a month and also the beginning of spring.

These pages which I shall write will have a great deal of imagination, but I fear that they will have no coherency. The Reverend Mr. Brown plans to correct them, and I hope he will not be ill-natured. Indeed, I must confess that my subjects are very defective, as well in matter as in style. But that is only the beginning, for with practice I shall write like a very Dutchman. . . .

THURSDAY 2 FEBRUARY. Yesterday you got up at seven, but uneasy by having lain with clothes on. You wrote law, but you did not attend enough to Trotz. . . . Yesterday you spoke too much of *Veuve* and sat up late against rules. Beware. This day, labour. Swear *retenue* and manners, and seek not ease by talking; it gives it not. Try silence one week. Think no more of *Veuve;* 'tis sickening to noble mind.

[*c.* 2 FEBRUARY. DUTCH THEME] The city of Utrecht is a fairly large one. It is not very wide, but it is long. It is encircled by ramparts, and I believe it was fortified under the Spanish rule. It is a very good place to study in; there are various excellent *hoogleer-meesteren* there. I am well aware that for the most part they are called "professors." But that is to borrow a French word, and I shall never do that. The Dutch have no more need of French words than of French money; of that I am sure. We shall not borrow from the Monsieurs. The Dutch language is an old, strong, rich language; and since I boast that I have Dutch blood in my veins, I say that a Hollander should scorn the language of a Frenchman when-

---

[1] "To see if your breath was sweet." *Feel* meaning *smell* was once common in English.   [2] See pp. x, xv, xvii.

ever it is compared with his own. It has annoyed me to hear so much French mixed with the Dutch. It is a scandalous business that free peoples should in that fashion decline every day from the sober strength of their respectable ancestors.

[*c.* 2 FEBRUARY. FRENCH THEME] When I came home yesterday evening, I scolded my servant, not at all harshly but with proper restraint. I said, "François, really you don't know how to pack coats; just see how this one is wrinkled. You must fold the collar over and not this part, because although it gets a little crumpled at the neck, when one puts it on, the shoulders stretch it out and the wrinkles don't show; but it takes a long time for this part to come smooth. What do you call this part?" "Sir, it is the *pans* (skirts) of a coat. But I assure you that I packed them well on your trip. The coat was longer than the trunk, though not much, and I did fold it over a little at the collar. So I am sure that the skirts could not have been rumpled in the trunk. I must have folded it badly in the drawer here after you came back from The Hague." After a harangue like that I had nothing to say. I undressed in great tranquillity and set myself to read Monsieur Voltaire....

I take credit to myself for having been so reasonable with my servant in a situation where passionate people like yourself would have beaten him.[3] You say to me, "Why not strike a servant sometimes, when one feels like it? It is an amusement of a sort, it relieves one's spleen to punish the cause of it. The desire to avenge ourselves on those who have offended us is universal; and Nature herself shows us that it is right. You observe that a child, when he falls on a stone that hurts him, is angry and kicks it or beats it with a stick, and it is only afterwards that he is appeased." Sir, I must reply to your lesson in philosophy, but do not expect a word-for-word reply. Be content, Sir, if I refute you in the large. I assure you that I should not find any amusement in beating a poor man who dares not make any resistance. It is in my opinion a shameful act of cowardice to behave like that.... Nature, I admit, does inspire

[3] Many of the French themes are impassioned arguments with an imaginary interlocutor. See pp. 48, 79.

us with sentiments of vengeance, but the same Nature inspires us also with sentiments of forgiveness towards those who have offended us. On the one sentiment is founded the other, and judge for yourself which one of these two sentiments is the more amiable. That same child whose example you are so much inclined to follow, when he begins to reflect a little, is filled with remorse for having caused pain to another—"even to that poor stone," as he says, with a simplicity that is also very natural. I have myself seen a child, who, after having beaten his nurse for some offence which had greatly irritated him, poured out floods of tears when she moaned. . . .

FRIDAY 3 FEBRUARY. . . . At Society, Des Essar[4] gave queries as to beasts, which were not answered. But the Society disputed the *optimus mundus*.[5] Brown pushed the place of such a being in the scale as man. It was said there was no necessity for a scale: we might have been all angels. "Come," said I, "we would not take up more room as happy beings than as unhappy." "But," said Brown, "the space must be filled up." "No, let it be a vacuum, a lumber-place, and, if you please, cram your *malum*[6] into it and so have the rest clear." You called Pope a blockhead, &c.; 'twas heedless. . . . This day resolve firm to be man. Be on guard for French and no ridicule. Make your best of your worst winter. . . .

[4] For an account of Des Essar, see p. 203. The Society was now meeting on Thursday evenings.

[5] Whether this is the best of all possible worlds; the argument of Pope's *Essay on Man*:

> Of systems possible, if 'tis confessed
> That Wisdom Infinite must form the best,
> Where all must full or not coherent be,
> And all that rises, rise in due degree;
> Then, in the scale of reas'ning life, 'tis plain
> There must be somewhere such a rank as Man;
> And all the question, wrangle e'er so long,
> Is only this, if God has plac'd him wrong?
>
> I. 43–50

[6] Evil.

SATURDAY 4 FEBRUARY.... At Assembly ... you spoke long time to *belle Veuve*. She stood up and she whispered and she corrected your French delightfully. She said she'd give you Zélide in her own writing.[7] You told her 'twas strange—'twas the very thing you wished. She said, "I am glad that we meet." You said you was physiognomist. She said, "I reveal little, but I am very sincere." You are much in love. She perhaps wishes to marry rationally. But have a care. Mention never a word of her. Seem at ease, till perhaps in long time you mention it to her. . . .

[*c.* 4 FEBRUARY. DUTCH THEME] "Dag, Mynheer!" ("Good day, Sir!") That is a proper Dutch salutation; and if you wander through the streets of Utrecht, you will hear it a dozen times between morning and evening. The Hollanders also say, "Dienaar, Heer!" ("Your servant, Sir!"), but with such quick enunciation that a foreigner will think that it is "Ja, Mynheer" ("Yes, Sir"). When I first came to Holland, I thought it was that, and I always said, "Yes, Sir." ... It is amazing that so many Englishmen have studied in Holland without having learned any of the language. It is said that the Dutch language is a language for horses. Monsieur Castillon said so, after having lived in Utrecht for several years. He was on the Amsterdam *schuit* when he made that comparison, and if there had not been a man there who knew him, I believe that a stout Dutchman would have thrown him into the canal.

SATURDAY 4 FEBRUARY

> The cloudy vapours from my brain to drive
> And make me feel that I'm again alive
> (For sleep has ever been compar'd to death,
> And nothing parts them but a little breath),
> Around my room I vigorously strut
> And then a score of sprightly capers cut;
> Next on my flute most pleasantly I play,
> And as I feel myself grow light and gay,
> I make the house with charming music ring,
> And only wish that you were there to sing.

[7] "Would lend you 'The Portrait of Zélide' in Belle de Zuylen's own hand."

SUNDAY 5 FEBRUARY.... You advance well in dictionary. At dinner you was really on guard and *retenu,* and spoke French. * * * [8] Stay, stay. Between one and two *la Veuve* was at Madame Amerongen's door. You approached her timidly. She was quite a goddess. She said, "Do you wish to go in?" You went with her and was presented to Monsieur and Madame Amerongen and to Monsieur de Natewisch.[9] The sister was cold and backward, and seemed to dread strangers and designing foreigners on the *Prize.* You was composed and polite, though timid. *La Veuve* looked all elegance and sweetness. You sat half an hour; you was charmed; you concealed even this. Bravo! You do right never to speak of a thing till long after; and if you speak only French, you'll learn *retenue,* for you don't blab in French. . . .

MONDAY 6 FEBRUARY.... This day, public academical oration, then Greek, then walk; then dine and for one week eat moderate, more than usual, and few fruit; and pray be *retenu* to avoid Scotch sarcastic jocularity. Never be so rude as to try it. At four Mademoiselle de Zuylen. Be modest and on guard; *now* on trial. Study harder. Have prudent plan.

TUESDAY 7 FEBRUARY. Yesterday you heard Hennert's *oratio.*[1] He was lively and eloquent, and you really saw something like an university: the professors all in gowns, the crowd of students, and the noble music.[2] At dinner you was *retenu,* only looked so that Mademoiselle[3] said [you had an] ironical air. Beware of this. You drank tea at Monsieur de Zuylen's. He took you cordially by the hand. All was *en famille* and fine. Mademoiselle de Zuylen

[8] The asterisks appear in the manuscript. I do not know what they mean.

[9] Madame Amerongen was Madame Geelvinck's sister; Monsieur de Natewisch, Monsieur Amerongen's brother.

[1] On the departure of Castillon for Berlin (see p. 39 *n.* 2), Johan Frederik Hennert had been called to Utrecht as Professor of Philosophy, Mathematics, and Astronomy. This was his inaugural address, *De Ingenio Mathematici.*

[2] "Utrecht has a university, but with as little appearance of such an institution as that of Leyden. The students have no academical dress; and their halls, which are used only for lectures and exercises, are formed in the cloisters of the ancient cathedral" (Charles Campbell, *The Traveller's Complete Guide through Belgium, Holland, and Germany,* 1815, p. 95).   [3] Kinloch.

was more agreeable than ever, for she was moderate and tempered and in plain, comfortable style. You talked of your dictionary. He said one Pell published a collection of Dutch and English, but he should like to see the Scotch. She roasted you about it as being trifling. But you told her all was to be liked that was useful—even turfs.[4] She put the dictionary under that. You said the words were your children, and you'd protect your family. You was fine but rather too gay. Bonnet came in; you spoke Dutch, and he politely offered book. . . .

[EVENTS OF 7 FEBRUARY. DUTCH THEME] Last Monday I drank tea at Heer van Zuylen's. He was very polite; indeed, he received me even in the style of a friend. His daughter was highly amusing; yet she told me later that she was not in good humour. It is certainly amazing how a young lady can pretend so well; but then it is commonly said that women are extremely shrewd and can make men believe whatever they choose. Also the two[5] sons of the gentleman were there: one of them a naval lieutenant in the service of Holland (although he has been for three years on an English man-of-war), the other a young fellow who has not yet chosen his vocation. It was very pleasant to see the way in which the father and the sons conducted themselves towards one another. I did not see there either testy imperiousness or timid subjection, but the genteel ease which ought always to be found in a family. Heer van Zuylen is one of the most ancient noblemen in the Seven Provinces, and he is very wealthy too, for he married an Amsterdam lady, a merchant's daughter, with a great deal of money.

After we had been sitting some time, Mynheer Bonnet, the Professor of Theology, came in. I was very much surprised to find him a lively and cheerful man. I tried to speak a little Dutch, and thus we became excellent company. Heer van Zuylen mentioned my Scottish dictionary, and the Professor said that he had

[4] Probably with a gesture towards the container of peats for the stove or fireplace. *Turf* means peat in both Dutch and English.

[5] There were actually three, but the eldest, Willem (aged twenty-one), was not at this time in Utrecht. Of the two that Boswell met, Diederik, the sailor, was twenty and Vincent, seventeen.

a dictionary in which the connection between the Low Dutch, the Old Saxon, the Icelandic, and the Latin languages is exhibited. The author's name is Lambert ten Kate, and the book is in two volumes.[6] I expressed a wish to see this book, and the Professor with great politeness said, "Sir, I shall send it to you tomorrow." I thought I could not do less than pay the Professor a visit. So I went there, and found him at home, and was very well received. We spoke both Latin and Dutch, and we agreed to meet sometimes.

At six in the afternoon I sent my servant to the Honourable Professor, and he brought me the dictionary, which is indeed a treasure. It is written in Dutch, and I do not yet know Dutch well enough to understand it entirely. But the Reverend Mr. Brown, agent for H.M. the King of Great Britain and pastor of the Scottish church at Utrecht, was at my house and looked at it. After reading in it for half an hour, he threw up his hands and exclaimed with great admiration, "Well, Sirs! I have never seen a book that pleased me more. Here we have four languages; and here we also have many good dissertations upon language in general. The author shows how all languages have come from one original, and it must be granted that he supports his opinions with many strong proofs."

Mr. Brown intends to translate the book, but he has so much else to do at present that he does not have enough spare time. Nevertheless, he will in the mean time translate into French a few bits of it which he will read before our Thursday Philosophical Society. It will be a very good subject for discussion by the learned members. It will introduce us to many curious considerations. We shall quote various maxims from ancient history, and we shall make many observations concerning the formation of languages. We shall try to show how mankind has been changed by a small difference in pronunciation. I do not expect that we shall all be in accord, for the proverb says, there will be as many opinions as there are men.[7] And besides we are of different nationalities: French, English, and German.

[6] It had been published in 1723, one of the most penetrating works in Germanic philology to appear before Jacob Grimm.

[7] "Quot homines, tot sententiae" (Terence, *Phormio,* 454).

WEDNESDAY 8 FEBRUARY.... Yesterday you sent note to Madame Geelvinck, quite young man of fashion, easy and lively like Digges.... At Assembly you was quite at ease. You begin really to have the foreign usage. You said to Zélide, "Come, I will make a pact of frankness with you for the whole winter, and you with me." You talked freely to her of prudence. But you talked too much. They all stared. Be on guard. This day, go on: journal, but not too full. Mem. religion.

[*c*. 8 FEBRUARY. FRENCH THEME] Again I must complain of Indolence: she is a tyrant who oppresses me, who confines me in bed as criminals are confined in their cells. In vain I try to rise. I am weighed down with the heaviest of fetters. I have freedom of motion only to stretch my legs and fold my arms; my very eyes appear to be held shut with fine chains. What witchcraft! How can that she-demon exert such influence over a man, especially a man who boasts of having an extraordinary portion of celestial fire? O earthly body, it is you who cause me thus to be brought into bondage. Troublesome burden, it is to you that I owe almost all my ills. My immortal soul is so bound to you that it suffers all your pains, that it can barely resist your desires; or, to express myself more precisely, your appetites. That great philosopher, that noble Christian the Apostle Paul, complains of you with the enthusiasm of a lofty soul which finds itself shut in a gloomy prison. "Wretched man that I am, who shall deliver me from this body of sin and death?" Illustrious saint! You suffered much in the war of the spirit, but you attained to unending felicity and glory. Yes, it is true that in heaven we shall always be happy. GOD in his goodness has told us so, and we must believe it. No doubt we are unable to form an idea of that felicity. Eye hath not seen, nor ear heard, neither have entered into the heart of man, the things which GOD hath prepared for them that love him, those who by patient perseverance in their Christian course seek glory, honour, and immortality. These are animating words. Do not speak to me of the gloom of our religion. This life, I confess, is gloomy; and if it were not for the hope of another, we should be in most deplorable

case. But then we are assured that we are but strangers here, that
we are only in a state of probation, and if we show ourselves
good soldiers of Jesus Christ, if we do our best to elevate our souls,
after death we shall be received into the company of the angels and
of GOD himself.

THURSDAY 9 FEBRUARY (A triple memorandum).[8] Yesterday you did not attend enough to Trotz. Amend this. At dinner
you was on guard. It was fine, cheerful day. At four young
De Zuylen came for you, and you went quite easy; was well with
Mademoiselle, Bernard, and Rose, but was really hurt with her
imprudent rattling and constant grin. You was angry for having
thought of putting any confidence in her, for she blabbed, "It is
your continual study to check your imagination." She is really
foolish and *raised*. Be her friend, but trust her not. You had first
been at *la Comtesse's*, who was snappish but polite enough; only
pretended to understand your French worse than she did—vile
spite, low cunning. At concert you was charmed with bassoon.
You was timid, but at last went to Madame Geelvinck. She said,
"Our faces are not unfamiliar to each other." A little after, you
said, "Nor our sentiments." Love was introduced, how I know
not; perhaps on such occasions the little god jumps in between
the parties. She said, "I believe there is more evil than good in the
world, and consequently more evil in love." You said, "There
is only jealousy; that is horrible."[9]

MME GEELVINCK. Yes, I am as jealous as a fury.

BOSWELL. But when others are jealous, have you charity enough
to do nothing to increase it?

MME GEELVINCK. Sir, if one found fault because I stood before
the window, &c.[1]

---

[8] That is, one filling three pages instead of the usual one.

[9] This dialogue, like most of those in the memoranda, does not give the names
of the speakers and sometimes does not separate one speech clearly from
another.

[1] "That would depend on the kind of behaviour on my part that made one

BOSWELL. Then if both parties follow that rule of action, jealousy has no influence, and love can be preserved always.

MME GEELVINCK. But after love comes *ennui*.

BOSWELL. Madame, I am too frank not to confess that I fear that too, yet I hope it is possible to guard against the evils of love.

MME GEELVINCK. I believe that one can truly love only once.

BOSWELL. Are you sure of that, Madame? I am not.

MME GEELVINCK. But you have been in love?

BOSWELL. I thought it was true love, but the lady was fickle. I am much indebted to you for having introduced me to true love.[2]

MME GEELVINCK. Are you sincere?

BOSWELL. Yes, I assure you that I am. Are you sincere too? Come, will you make a pact of sincerity between us?

MME GEELVINCK. Yes.

BOSWELL. You see I speak without fear.

MME GEELVINCK. You are wrong if you are afraid of me.

BOSWELL. Well! I can speak to you quite openly?

MME GEELVINCK. Just as you speak when by yourself.

BOSWELL. Permit me merely to say, "I admire you," from time to time.—What must one do when one is in love?

MME GEELVINCK. I don't know.

BOSWELL. You are in a peculiar situation: beautiful, pleasant, and, what is generally more important, rich. Can you tell if people really love you?

MME GEELVINCK. It is difficult.—You must not repeat this conversation.

BOSWELL. Madame, I am discreet. I would that my heart were plucked out for you to see.

MME GEELVINCK. Are you good-natured?

BOSWELL. On my honour. I am a very honest man with a very generous heart. But I am a little capricious, though I shall cure that. It was only a year ago that I was the slave of imagination and

---

jealous. If a man found fault with me for doing something quite harmless, such as showing myself at the window, I would not change my behaviour to please him."   [2] "Pour m'avoir fait entré."

talked like Mademoiselle de Zuylen. But I am making great advances in prudence.

MME GEELVINCK. Have you good principles?

BOSWELL. Yes. When I say, "That is a duty," then I do it. Mademoiselle de Zuylen says that I am never bored, but I do get bored, though I never show it.

MME GEELVINCK. Have you any faults?

BOSWELL. Yes, I sometimes suffer from very bad humour, but it doesn't last long.—But, Madame, is this not much to my honour? Ought I not to be proud that you show so much kindness for me? But how can you have so much confidence in a stranger whom you have seen only very little? Truly, that flatters me.

MME GEELVINCK. My sister says she would like to know you better.

BOSWELL. I shall do myself the honour to call on her.

MME GEELVINCK. And Madame d'Amerongen, sister to Monsieur Mossel,[3] wishes to make your acquaintance. When she gives a supper, you shall be invited.

BOSWELL. Every one here is looking at me with envy.

MME GEELVINCK. We must speak no more at present. Talk a little to Madame d'Amerongen.

After this you stood with imperial dignity while the grinning Dutch were all blue around you; then went to English Society and was moderate. This day swear *retenue* except to Madame, and keep strictly to it, and tell her so. . . .

THURSDAY 9 FEBRUARY

Last night again I sat me up till three,
Which all the world may by my visage see;
In my dull head my fretted eyes are sunk,
And gaunt I look like a Cistercian monk;
My nerves unstrung and spirits quite depress'd,
Cold gloomy vapours rob me of my rest.

[3] Not Madame Geelvinck's sister; another Madame d'Amerongen.

If for amusement I would read, I tire
And catch myself a-dozing o'er the fire.
Yet sure as cock at dawn of morning crows,
My ev'ning verses I must still compose.

FRIDAY 10 FEBRUARY. Yesterday you did very well. On
Wednesday you sat up very late, being all agitated with love and
fiery imagination. You sprung out of bed, and upon your bare
knees swore not to speak of yourself, except to Madame Geelvinck,
for eight days. You forgot this once or twice yesterday. However,
you'll keep to it more and more. You was hurt by want of rest. Your
nerves were unhinged and spirits very low. But you kept it to self.
Be more grave, and you'll support it with manly dignity. You must
not tire at Brown's. All the world would seem insipid to each other
after dining a number of months together. But you're at Utrecht
to improve. So keep on. Sometimes you may fast or go to Plaats
for a week. . . . At night be soft, polite, and guarded, and be gentle
with *Veuve*. Swear not to mention it. Be slow, and see if it lasts.

[10 FEBRUARY. FRENCH THEME] . . . I have been out this
morning, and I am going to tell you why. I went to see the Hereditary Prince of Brunswick pass with the Princess Royal of England,
his wife.[4] Yesterday evening I saw them pass, too, but it was so late
that I could not see their Highnesses, although there were torches
enough. It is very seldom that one sees a parade at Utrecht; for that
reason a great crowd had assembled at St. Catherine's Gate to see
their Highnesses disembark and enter their carriages.[5] A great

[4] "Hereditary Prince" (translating German *Erbprinz*) means "heir to the
reigning prince," who in this case was the Duke of Brunswick-Wolfenbüttel.
Karl Wilhelm Ferdinand succeeded his father as Duke in 1780. In 1792, because of his reputation for liberality and benevolence, he was offered the
supreme command of the French Revolutionary Army, but refused, and instead commanded the opposed Prussian forces. He was mortally wounded at
Auerstedt, 1806; his son and successor, Friedrich Wilhelm, was killed at
Quatre Bras. Karl Wilhelm's Princess was Augusta, eldest sister of George
III; they had been married in London on 16 January.
[5] They had come by water.

many people, including even people of high fashion, had been waiting several hours. Most of them were on foot, but some who had better sense and more money had carriages, in which they had sat quietly protected from the cold. They had good footwarmers and perhaps something to eat, with a bottle of good wine. So they nourished their bodies and chatted very happily. But we had a clash between some of our people of distinction. The Grand Bailiff had ordered the *dienders* (that is, the police of the city) to place themselves on the bank of the canal to open a way for their Highnesses and prevent the crowd from pressing upon them. The officer in command of the troops came with a detachment of carabineers and ordered these silly *dienders* driven away. The Grand Bailiff was violently enraged at this, and hurled insults at the officer. The soldier, however, was a man of resolution; and placing his hand on his sword, said, "Sir, I do not wish to hear any more of your outrageous remarks." The Count of Nassau, who showed himself no better than a puppet, then quieted down, but insisted that the commanding officer of the garrison should arrest the officer who had driven away his worshipful *dienders*. The commanding officer would not engage in the business, and the Grand Bailiff threatened to write to The Hague.

Since I wrote the last page, I have seen one of the nobles of Utrecht, who has told me that the commanding officer of the garrison has followed the orders of the Grand Bailiff, and has actually arrested the offending officer. . . .

SATURDAY 11 FEBRUARY. Yesterday you saw Prince and Princess pass. You was still cold and bad, really distemper of body. You told Brown you never would say where you dined, that he might not know when you fasted. Let this be observed. A message to dine with Monsieur d'Amerongen set you a-going. You dressed neat. At dinner you was gloomy, but kept your post and grew very cheerful, though still on guard, and spoke French and Dutch, and was temperate. You are growing firm. Amerongen, worthy man, said, "I invite you to our dinner, as you see,[6] to show that we shall

---

[6] "Comme vous le voyez."

be happy to see you from time to time." He repeated this as you went away. 'Twill be an excellent house. Cultivate there. You went at five and read Greek—O noble! But you once or twice brought in self. Assembly *chez* Mademoiselle de Zuylen. You are growing quite easy; only err in wanting to speak[7] to lady of house at first. Madame Amelisweerd said, "You are very romantic and are in love with Madame Geelvinck." You said, "I was romantic, and everybody is in love with her." Then you told *la Veuve* what she said, and said, "To relieve me now—will you come back?"[8] "Yes, for at least two months. We must not talk," &c. This was really hints. See what she really is. Take care. . . .

SUNDAY 12 FEBRUARY. Yesterday you did very well. You had dreamt of *la Veuve*. You brought up a good deal of journal. After dinner you talked on Baxter's scheme of invisible spirits, and maintained that it was not an improbable theory.[9] You was *retenu* and much on guard. You said you had been in company every night this week. Brown said, "You do very well." Indeed, 'tis true, for 'tis part of your plan in coming abroad. At Mademoiselle de Reede's you was gay, yet had dignity. *La Comtesse* talked of white suit and why you had got it. You said, "It would puzzle all the academies of Europe to give a reason why I had that suit made." This was like Slavonic to her. After cards she said, "You talked two hours with *la Veuve*, and then she did not talk with any one yesterday evening. If you can secure a prize like that in Holland, you can go home (*thuis*) satisfied." "Yes, Madame, that would certainly be worth a concert."[1] "Yes, that would be a concert for the whole of life." "In unison, in harmony, I hope." There you triumphed. . . .

MONDAY 13 FEBRUARY. Yesterday you waited on Grand Bailiff after prayers and talked long with him and well. After this, be more neat in journal, nor mark little usual accidents. You had

[7] That is, in failing to speak.   [8] She was planning to go to The Hague.
[9] Andrew Baxter, a Scotch philosopher who died in 1750, had argued that dreams are caused by the action of spiritual beings.
[1] Probably with reference to the saying of Henri IV that Paris was worth a mass. The long dialogue of 8 February had taken place at a concert: see p. 141.

Madame Brown, &c., to pass the evening and sup. The young *Comte*[2] was with you some time and jumped and sung and played tricks and whist; all went well. The supper was elegant. You were all gay and in good humour. You sung and played on flute. Yet did you retain your decent firmness and hope of pleasing God. Nor was you buffoon. All was well. After they went, you *thought:* "What! am I yielding thus? Can my firmness not stand against love? Is not this a delirium? If Madame Geelvinck was to delay answer for two months, would I die with impatience? Yet, would I engage for life?" Fie, fie! Till you are serene, you cannot think of it as a man. Tell her, "You said to me that you would tell me my faults. That is to treat me as a friend. Do you wish me to write to my father?" Be gentle and once sure of her. Today fast. Journal; *partie;* study.

TUESDAY 14 FEBRUARY. Yesterday you got up in good time, and was fresh and healthy. You did not attend enough to Trotz. Go exact at the hour after this, and force attention. You fasted and stayed at home from one to five. You read Voltaire. You wrote journal. You had prayers. You renewed resolutions of virtue and piety. At the *partie* you was too merry in saying that Madame Roosmalen would *vous batter*. It seemed strange.[3] They are stupid, low, censorious. Be not free with them. Take up, keep your own counsel, and show that you're quite independent. You supped elegant at Mademoiselle de Zuylen's with the General,[4] &c. She said, "You write everything down." Have a care. Never speak on that subject. Madame was there. O how charming! You and she exchanged looks and that was all. This day study firm nor lose balance. *Retenue* at dinner; at Assembly, on great guard. If *She* is there, ask her if you behaved right yesterday. Ask religion. Then

[2] The son of the Grand Bailiff?

[3] Because he should have said *vous battre* ("beat you"). *Batter* would probably have been heard by accurate speakers of French as *bâter*, and *bâter l'âne* ("saddle the ass") carried an indecent meaning.

[4] Belle's uncle, Hendrik Willem Jacob van Tuyll, Lieutenant-General of Cavalry.

her life, in confidence. Take care; restrain. Be busy and see. Let not
Satan tempt you as Cupid. . . .

TUESDAY 14 FEBRUARY

> I thought my time of trial had been o'er,
> And am'rous torments hop'd to feel no more;
> Yet most severely my mistake I find,
> For fiercest love is raging in my mind,
> And like the good Sir Roger I appear
> A charming widow's gallant cavalier.[5]
> And dost thou think, O Cupid, to enslave
> By thy bewitching wiles a soul so brave?
> As Epictetus firm, I will disdain
> To own thy sharpest darts can give me pain.

WEDNESDAY 15 FEBRUARY. Receive the pleasure of recollection that you did remarkably well yesterday. You walked in cloisters before nine, and renewed good resolutions after sweet meditation and solemn thought. You attended well at Trotz's. You was
retenu at dinner. All was well. At Assembly you kept close on
guard, though the mean beings began to joke rudely about *la
Veuve.* You was quite reserved. But is it not strange that she was not
there? You was a little sombre on that account. Tomorrow call on
her *après dîner.* She's perhaps trying your patience. If you don't
see her ere Hague, you'll have time to cool. 'Twill be noble not to
mention it to mortal but herself. Study harder, three days certain.
. . . Write to Temple of *Veuve.* Separate fiery passion. Tip her valet.
If you persist in this *retenue,* you'll be quite man of fashion. 'Tis
easy, too.

[*c.* 15 FEBRUARY. DUTCH THEME] It has been thirty years
since my father studied at Leyden. He studied Dutch with great
diligence and in a short time had mastered it so well that he was

---

[5] Sir Roger de Coverley, in the *Spectator* papers of Addison and Steele, kept
"himself a bachelor, by reason he was crossed in love by a perverse beautiful
widow of the next county to him."

able to make himself understood. He took lodgings in a Dutch home. His landlady was a widow, and had a sister who lived with her. The widow was courted by a tailor, but the sister was no friend of the lover, which the widow took greatly amiss. One morning at four o'clock she waked my father in a state of great excitement. "O Sir," said she, "Sister's dead." "What did you say, Ma'am?" answered he. "Is she dead?" "Yes, indeed, Sir," said the landlady. "She kept a bottle of brandy in her room every night, and I fear that she drank too much." My father got up in alarm and went downstairs and found Sister dead for certain; but he had suspicions that the widow had helped her out of the world when she married the tailor immediately afterwards.

[Received 15 February, Temple to Boswell]

Trinity Hall [Cambridge] 7 February 1764[6]
MY DEAR BOSWELL,— ... Have you wept over Germanicus yet, or attended at the conference of the philosopher and his pupil? Does not the character of Helvidius Priscus rouse your emulation and kindle in your young breast the flame of glory? No man but a fool or a knave ever read Tacitus without improving both his head and heart. His reflections are universally allowed to be as deep, and founded as much in a knowledge of human nature, as those of the greatest politicians. His love of liberty and virtue is enthusiastic, he everywhere censures the bad with boldness and indignation, and praises the good with rapture. He paints with the imagination of a Raphael, and his style is the abrupt sublime. When shall a Tacitus arise amongst us to write a history of a House of Stuart, to damn a race of tyrants to eternal infamy?

[6] Misdated by Temple 7 January. But the postmark is 9 February, and Boswell's reply (below, p. 193) shows that he had received no other letter from Temple between 6 December 1763 and 23 March 1764. This letter is included to illustrate one of the more puzzling aspects of the extremely close friendship between Boswell and Temple: the diametrical and passionate opposition of their political views.

O Sidney![7] thou friend to mankind, thou foe to oppression, thou scourge of tyrants and guardian of liberty, citizen, philosopher, hero, what can atone for thy sufferings, what expiate thy blood? The souls of departed patriots still call aloud for justice on thy inhuman murderers. And they shall be revenged; some future historian shall record your virtues and their crimes.

Your notions of government surprise me. They are slavish and unworthy of an Englishman. All power is derived originally from the people, and kings are but the servants of the public. They are chosen to govern nations, not for their own private good, but for the general good of the governed. If they do their duty, if they show themselves the first in virtue and ability as well as in station, they will be revered while living and lamented when dead; their fame will live for ever in the minds of a grateful people. But if otherwise, if they crush the subject race whom kings are born to save, they shall be abhorred and punished by their much injured masters; they shall live in dishonour and die in infamy; their names shall be blotted out of the annals of their country.

The English government is not a monarchy; it is a mixed republic where the supreme power is equally divided amongst the three estates. The executive power of the laws is in the King, the power of making laws in the people or their representatives, the Lords and Commons. (For I reckon the King's assent as nothing, since no king of England, not even the worst of them, ever dared to put his negative upon a bill passed by both Houses of Parliament.) I am as zealous for prerogative as you, but a king of England has no prerogative but to do good by supplying the deficiencies of the laws, the most honourable and glorious of all prerogatives, which whenever he shall be found again to abuse, I trust there will not be wanting other Hampdens and other Sidneys to pull the tyrant down and trample him [in] the dust.

You seem to laugh at a woman attempting to write a history of

---

[7] Algernon Sidney, English republican leader, executed in 1683 for favouring the succession of the Duke of Monmouth. It is thought that he may have helped William Penn in devising his Pennsylvanian Constitution.

England; and indeed it appears absurd enough, for one would be led to expect from such an historian a panegyric on royalty and the effeminate pleasures of a court, rather than a hatred of tyrants and a just encomium on virtue, frugality, and public spirit. I have read Mrs. Macaulay and have been most agreeably disappointed, for I find her the very reverse of what I expected. She begins at the accession of the Stuart line, and is to conclude with the election of the House of Hanover. You say Locke has made you a Christian; read his immortal treatise on Government and be no longer a slave.

Mr. Mason[8] has been here some time; he went to London last week. He has published a new edition of his poems, and has left out *Isis* and the ode on the Duke of Newcastle's installation. The volume is dedicated to Lord Holdernesse in a sonnet prefixed. The frontispiece is rather vain; it explains in too full a manner what he entitles himself (A.M.) and makes him indeed master of all the arts. I spent several evenings with him and Mr. Gray at a coffee-house here. He has a dull, heavy look, and a particular cast with his eyes, but is very entertaining in company, altogether free from affectation, and more affable than Mr. Gray. I did not know he had so good preferment in the Church; he has near six hundred a year.

I long much to hear from you. Pray write to me soon and very particularly. Utrecht must be a dreary place at present. It rains here almost without intermission. Have you been chaste since you left us, or do Dutch women feel it all o'er as ours do, and is human nature in that respect everywhere the same?[9] Strange questions these, Boswell, but not unnatural ones. Believe me ever, my dear friend, yours with the sincerest affection,

W. J. TEMPLE.

THURSDAY 16 FEBRUARY.... Temple's letter gave you spirits. This day, Civil Law, &c., in good order; two other volumes of Voltaire. *Retenue* more and more. You are now fine. At five, *la*

[8] William Mason, poet, friend of Gray. Boswell greatly admired his verse plays *Elfrida* and *Caractacus,* written in imitation of classical models.
[9] I suppose, "are Dutch women as frail as English?" the implication being that Boswell's only hope of chastity was not to have opportunity.

Veuve; if not in, tea Rose. You are beginning to calm a little. Take care. If you're easy, you'll do more with her, and let it be an elegant penchant, and perhaps, &c. . . .

[*c.* 16 FEBRUARY. DUTCH THEME] (I shall for once try to write a half-leaf just as I speak. I shall use no dictionaries, but shall introduce only words that come into my head. I must also admit French words, because I hear them so much every day in all companies.) I have been very unfortunate in the article of stockings, for they are flimsy and do not last long. I have found many holes in them, sometimes when it was less than five minutes to twelve o'clock, when I should have been starting for Mynheer Trotz's college on Roman Law. François, my servant, can darn the holes very capably, and that is convenient. My shoes are excellent. I have bought no shoes since I have been in Holland. I brought six pairs of shoes from London, most of them Scotch shoes.

FRIDAY 17 FEBRUARY. Yesterday you did very well; you was truly on guard and had command of yourself. What is strange, you already are calm with respect to *la Veuve.* You see what a little absence does. You said that from the Spartan Republic we may see as from an experiment what men may be brought to; and though we have not need for such excess of hardy virtues, we may mix them with our elegant politeness. . . . Fast today, or be only *maigre*[1] by having two rolls at breakfast. Give poor woman double hire.[2] Send to Rose: no Greek till tomorrow. Bring up journal, obstinate three hours. At Assembly play part like Digges. Be collected. Ask [*la Veuve* about her] religion, ask confidence, ask advice, ask line from Hague. Swear silence, yet court *la Comtesse* with address. Mem. constant piety, nor yield to any tyrant passion.

FRIDAY 17 FEBRUARY

> The great Apostles bid us often fast;
> And think you, Christians, that its use is past?
> Think you no more your bodies to subdue
> And your resolves of virtue to renew?

[1] That is, eat no meat.   [2] His cleaning woman?

Think you that riot and incessant mirth
Can fail to chain you grov'ling to the earth?
For me, whose gen'rous and aspiring mind
Is now to solemn piety resign'd,
I shall keep Friday as a holiday,[3]
And as the Church directs me, fast and pray.

SATURDAY 18 FEBRUARY. Yesterday you did very well. You brought up much journal. You fasted; you read prayers; you was in sweet, gentle, calm humour. At Assembly you was immoderately awkward. Your fine suit embarrassed you. Some of the ladies joked you on your sword knot and such trifles, just like Edinburgh lasses. They are mean. But you kept ground, being quite *retenu*. You durst not go to Madame Geelvinck for a long time. Your heart was torn with love. You played party very absent, and she showed with her eyes that you had touched her; yet there's no being sure. You asked when she went and returned, confusedly. She said, "I am sorry. I am not strict." . . . You yielded too much to your passion, for consider: you, who have been so often in these love scrapes, have not so much to plead. At any rate, for marriage love must be gentle and calm and constant, and not fiery and melancholy. So, at any rate, you will do well to bring it to a philosophical temperature; and then you are indeed fine fellow, and can take your measures lastingly, and keep Hollanders much at distance. But, oh, affect not passion and oddity! But confound them by ease and cheerfulness. This day a true adventure: call on Grand Bailiff and tell him you'd be glad to see the dance; if not in, write neat.[4] Go tell her you are devoted to her, she alone knows it; hope she'll be generous, and see the event. Ask if any hope and say you can't promise yourself; say it boldly and firm; and ask write from Hague. . . .

[3] The manuscript has the alternative, "I shall at seasons set apart a day," probably to avoid the impropriety of calling a fast a holiday, that term in ecclesiastical usage being reserved for feasts.

[4] From the next entry it appears that this was a party for children. Boswell knew that Madame Geelvinck would accompany her son there; he wanted another chance to talk to her without interruption.

SUNDAY 19 FEBRUARY. Yesterday you called on Grand Bailiff. Not in; very well. You read Greek and then walked in Mall. But you had not *retenue* enough. You talked of love, and how a philosopher ought to subdue it. This showed Rose that you was at least a little struck. You was too much opened by the fine weather. You must keep under arms in the fairest summer days. You walked with young Geelvinck.[5] You said, "He is a spark from the sun in heaven." ... At four, Bailiff's in fine humour; heart rejoiced to see all the young folks; was quite at ease yet not too forward. Had long and important conversation with Madame Geelvinck:

BOSWELL. At what age, &c., did you first truly fall in love?

MME GEELVINCK. Really![6] That is certainly being frank.

BOSWELL. Oh, how happy I am! And since you became a widow, have you been in love?

MME GEELVINCK. No. Really![6]

BOSWELL. But, Madame, I am very much in love. I adore you. Will you make a distinction between Madame Geelvinck and my friend, and give me your advice?

MME GEELVINCK. Yes. But I am truly sorry. I advise you to cure your passion.

BOSWELL. But, Madame, how?

MME GEELVINCK. You have been in love before?

BOSWELL. Yes, I have been in love before, but those passions had no foundation. I always had the help of reason to cure them. But I believe I have never really been in love before now.

MME GEELVINCK. Oh, fancy that!

BOSWELL. But, Madame, is it impossible for you to fall in love?

MME GEELVINCK. I shall never do so.

BOSWELL. There is more good than bad in love.

MME GEELVINCK. I am happy as things stand. I am free. I can go from one city to another. One ought not to give up a certainty.

BOSWELL. But, Madame, have you no thought of a pleasure you have not yet tasted? Only think how you could begin a new life.

---

[5] Madame Geelvinck's son, six or seven years old.   [6] "Non?"

MME GEELVINCK. Really, I am sorry that you are like this; it will make you unhappy. I will be your friend.

BOSWELL. Will you be my friend always, for the whole of your life?

MME GEELVINCK. Yes.

BOSWELL. But did you not know that I was in love with you?

MME GEELVINCK. No, really. I thought it was with Mademoiselle de Zuylen; and I said nothing about it.[7]

BOSWELL. Oh, my dear Madame, what heavenly pleasure I have at this moment in looking at you. I am speaking as you told me to— as though I were alone. I can trust in you; you will not expose me?

MME GEELVINCK. No, I assure you on my conscience.

BOSWELL. You believe that I am in love? I swear it to you by all the hope I have of happiness in this existence or the other. You believe that I am sincere?

MME GEELVINCK. If you are not, you are horrible.

BOSWELL. You believe me, then?

MME GEELVINCK. Yes, I believe you when you say it.

BOSWELL. But I ought not to despair. One must have a little indulgence. Oh, if you please, say only that perhaps——

MME GEELVINCK. That would be to behave like a coquette.

BOSWELL. But say that perhaps——, something like that.— But what do you think on the subject of religion?

MME GEELVINCK. Have you not the same religion in Scotland as we?

BOSWELL. Yes, but I have found women here who thought themselves wiser than other people, women who did not believe it.

MME GEELVINCK. At any rate, those who have the hope of another world lose nothing. Those who do not believe it must be in a bad way.

BOSWELL. But do you believe that GOD has given a revelation of his will?

MME GEELVINCK. Yes.

---

[7] Reading as *dit* ("Je l'a dit point de tout") a word that has been written over and could be almost anything after the first two letters.

BOSWELL. Oh, I am glad of it. Yes, Madame, you have [in the Christian faith] a system conformable to the perfections of GOD, confirmed by proofs which are sufficient to comfort us.

MME GEELVINCK. Yes, and there are mysteries; but although I do not understand mathematical problems, am I to deny the truth of mathematics?

BOSWELL. Madame, can you believe that only six months ago I was completely heedless, and gave great concern to the most excellent of fathers? I changed completely. Have I not made progress?

MME GEELVINCK [changing the subject]. I would sacrifice myself for my son.

BOSWELL. That is a delicate sentiment. I could not love you so much as I do if I did not love your child.

MME GEELVINCK. If I should marry again, my husband could not love my son like his own, and perhaps I should not love my other children so much.

BOSWELL. But if you should find a man of whom you can be certain that he loves you sincerely, and that through duty and affection he would do everything for your son—is it not possible to find such a man?

MME GEELVINCK. It is possible.

BOSWELL. Think, Madame, you will lose half your life. You will leave the world without having tasted of love.—Will you have the generosity to write me only one or two lines from The Hague? That will convince me that you are sincerely my friend.

MME GEELVINCK. Yes, provided that you do not answer.

BOSWELL. You are afraid that I would say something so tender as to touch your pity. But I have permission to write if I am reasonable?

MME GEELVINCK. Yes.

BOSWELL. Tell me, everybody is looking at me with envy: is it right to be vain?

MME GEELVINCK. Um.

BOSWELL. Do you know my address?

MME GEELVINCK. Yes, *chez* Bart.[8]

[8] The proprietor of the hotel (the Keiserhof) where Boswell had his rooms.

BOSWELL. I am happy now, but when I am alone, I shall think of a thousand things I ought to have said. How happy I am to have had an opportunity to confess all this to you. It is, I suppose, necessary for it to remain unknown?

MME GEELVINCK. Yes, do not tell it to any one.

BOSWELL. It gives me some relief to have confessed it instead of letting it lie in gloomy silence. What must I say to people who ask me questions?

MME GEELVINCK. Oh, you have wit enough to parry such questions.

BOSWELL. But after you have come back from The Hague, if I cannot forget my passion, what will you do? But I must not ask. Say only, "We shall see." Are you fickle?

MME GEELVINCK. No, I do not have that kind of disposition.

BOSWELL. As for me, I am very fickle, so much so that I am never sure of myself; and I assure you, if you were in love with me, I should advise you not to be.

MME GEELVINCK. That is most extraordinary.

BOSWELL. It is a pity you are so rich, although I am very fond of money.

MME GEELVINCK. Shame!

BOSWELL. But listen. I am not greedy, yet, after religion, my chief aim is to uphold a respectable and ancient family of which I am the representative, and so—

MME GEELVINCK. I leave my heart with you.

This was truly an adventure, and you did an immense deal. She is delicious but impregnable. You said, "My ambition is roused to win a heart that has never been possessed." MME GEELVINCK. "For shame! That is like a coquette." BOSWELL. "No. Coquettes have not suffered the pangs themselves." . . . This day resume. Be more on guard and try to recover easy cheerfulness, nor lose time by any black passion. Stand firm.

MONDAY 20 FEBRUARY. Yesterday you was sick and gloomy, as it was the day after you declared your passion and the day before Madame goes. Yet you was quite guarded, nor could any mortal discover it. Rose told you of Williamson a Liverpool merchant's being crossed in love, and he said that melancholy people affixed some particular idea, as love, &c., merely to distemper. That is too true. . . . You supped at Brown's very splendid, and you sustained character. Yet you have not had so severe a conflict at Utrecht. This day, get up, go to Porte and see her pass, as that is a Spanish piece of gallantry; but conceal yourself, or you're ridiculous. Then think: this is spleen—expel it. You're miserable with it. 'Tis not, then, generous, and it may grow frivolous. Recover clear, firm tone, nor allow fretful passions to have habit. You are fortunate your mistress is your friend and confidant, and you can from time to time talk to her. But she'd tire of a whiner. Come, be manly; resolve, and be worthy of her, and see if you could be a sensible husband. Expel sloth. Speak no more of her. . . .

TUESDAY 21 FEBRUARY. Yesterday after a sad night of sickness from stomach disordered, you sprung up before seven, and taking dram, went out to St. Catherine Porte, where you made interest with honest German carabineer and got into his box and saw Madame pass. She looked angelic, and that glimpse was ravishing. You then treated sentinel with Geneva.[9] You stood on ramparts and saw her disappear. You was quite torn with love. Then you entered to fencing. You was very bad all day. Yet you was silent. At Madame Nassau's you was cheerful, yet on guard, but affected a little gloom. Mem., ill-humour is a crime; combat. Mademoiselle[1] said you had much *bonheur,* and thought you content. Keep that character. Love has now fairly left you, and behold in how dreary a state you was in. At night you was listless and distressed and obliged to go drawling to bed. This day study hard; get firm tone; go on. Mademoiselle will be your friend.

[*c.* 20 FEBRUARY. DUTCH THEME] I go every morning to a fencing-master. He is ninety-four years old. His father taught William III, Prince of Orange, to fence. He was an Italian. His name was   and the name of his son is   .[2] He crossed with

[9] Gin.   [1] Belle de Zuylen.
[2] Blanks in the manuscript. Boswell later gives the name of his master as Cirx

Prince William into England and Ireland, and so did his son. Consequently this man cannot be less than ninety years old (the son, I mean, my master), and he has assured me that he is ninety-four. He was at the famous battle of the Boyne. He was also in Scotland, and has travelled in France, Spain, and Italy. It is indeed amazing to see the old carle.[3] He is as healthy and spry as a man of thirty, and he can fence with all the agility in the world. I can assure you that his hand is stronger than mine. We tried it, and he won.

[*c.* 20 FEBRUARY. FRENCH THEME] I like much to lie with my head very high. I think it is healthy to do so. At home I always have a couple of pillows, and if I am in a strange house, the first thing I ask is whether I can have a couple of pillows. I ask it without the least ceremony, whether of gentlemen or of ladies. When I was at Laird Heron's in Galloway, I said to the lady of the house, "I beg you, Madam, let me have your best bedroom and a couple of pillows." She could not grant me my first request, but she saw to the second. Likewise, when I was at the Earl of Galloway's, my Lord Garlies[4] was so polite as to show me to my bedroom and say, "Mr. Boswell, you will have the goodness to mention it if there is anything you lack." I walked very softly over and looked at the bed. "My Lord," said I, "there is nothing lacking but a couple of pillows, and I hope I shall have enough interest to procure them." Sometimes I have forgotten to ask for my pillows, or have asked for them when it was too late; when the housekeeper had gone to bed and had her keys in her pocket carefully placed under her head. In

---

or Cirkz, which certainly does not look Italian. But the name of the son may have been Hollandized, and Boswell may have heard it wrong. Dr. Breuning tells me that in 1740 the Town Council of Utrecht gave permission to one Frans Dirxen (i.e., Dirk's son), drum-major of the regiment then occupying the garrison, to give lessons in fencing. One suspects that this was Boswell's master.

[3] *Carle* ("fellow") in the original. Boswell kept the Scots spelling, though he no doubt meant the Dutch cognate form *kerel*.

[4] Boswell visited both Patrick Heron at Kirroughtrie and the Earl of Galloway at Galloway House during the autumn of 1762. Lord Garlies was Lord Galloway's eldest son.

such a case I have been extremely embarrassed. I have been at my wits' end. However, I have always found some expedient. I have sometimes put my clothes and sometimes a cushion in place of the pillows. I would rather use a stone than sleep without having my head well raised. It is said that to hold the head high is a sign of pride; and perhaps you will accuse me of hauteur even when I sleep. . . .

WEDNESDAY 22 FEBRUARY. Yesterday you was lethargic and still hippish[5] and gaunt, but you stood ground and played whist not amiss at Madame Lockhorst's.[6] That's all for journal. You are really not well at present. Some course must be taken, or you must wait with patience. You are weak, relaxed, insipid, and gloomy. These trials you laid account[7] to meet with. You stand them and are silent. That is truly noble, and will yield you solid pride yet. So have patience as not to be uneasy to others. This day fencing, or stay in. Write for Society. You've had too many metaphysical subjects. Complain not of evils which you can help. Poverty a great [evil]; used as a phrase: "*Poor* devil."[8] Force activity and drive off this gloom. Sit not scorched o'er the fire. Be silent, and see some time hence how your heart is.

[23 February, opening paragraphs of Boswell's French discourse, given before the Literary Society at Utrecht]

Since I have had the honour to be a member of this learned Society, we have concerned ourselves mainly with lofty speculations of metaphysics or subtle refinements of morality. We have heard certain of our members present specimens of rich imagination and penetrating judgment. I say "imagination," because in subjects so elevated that we hardly have faculties for comprehending them (or at least where we find very few propositions substantiated by

---

[5] Depressed. The word is formed from *hyp(ochondria)*.
[6] Belle de Zuylen's aunt and godmother.   [7] "You expected"; a Scotticism.
[8] This and the preceding two sentences are notes for his address, a portion of which is printed after this entry.

"data," as they say)—in such subjects, we owe a great deal to the liveliness of our minds, which aid us by making handsome fictions where realities desert us. Forgive me, gentlemen, if I appear to treat our important speculations too airily. Far from holding them in scorn, I respect them after my fashion, superstitiously, with a devotion like that which is born of ignorance. I never find myself prouder of my existence than when I walk with my head swathed in the solemn cloud of abstraction. This evening, however, I wish to cheer us up a little by proposing a subject into which there will enter nothing but common sense and observation.

We complain a great deal of the evils of life, but we ought to consider how many of these ills can be prevented by human attention and care. Poverty is perhaps the evil that we fear the most. This has even passed into a proverb. When we wish to speak of a man in a pitiful plight, we use the expression, *"Poor* man." But doubtless it is through some fault in political science that poverty exists in society. Let us trace briefly how it comes about. . . .

THURSDAY 23 FEBRUARY. Yesterday you did very well. You was still gloomy and indisposed in health. But you was resolute and went on. You was, however, a little lax with Rose in joking in a sort of desultory, imperfect way, and too feeble with Brown in being uneasy for fear your discourse should not be liked, and pleased when he liked it. Mean is he who thus depends on others. Reverence GOD, and have a standard in your own mind. At night you had Rose and Hungarians.[9] They talked fine Latin. It was wild and romantic with old Scythians, and your spirits brightened, yet temperate. Every Saturday they're to be with you. . . .

FRIDAY 24 FEBRUARY. Yesterday you was still gloomy and unhealthy. But you stood firm: was *retenu.* Polished your discourse,

[9] "The number of students, one year with another, is seven or eight hundred in each of the universities of Leyden and Utrecht. . . . They all live in private lodgings, except thirty or forty Poles and Hungarians, who have a college in each of the universities, where they are maintained at the public expense, which are the only endowed foundations here" (*Description of Holland,* 1743, p. 337).

read it well, and did your duty fully at Society. What more would you have? You *must* suffer. Cursory chat of Des Essar on *la Veuve* —her fifty admirers, her husband having not behaved well to her —seized your attention. However, you are really prudent. After Society you cured dire gloom merely by dancing. You see how corporeal.... No fast, as twice last week....

[*c.* 24 FEBRUARY. FRENCH THEME][1] ... When I enter an assembly, I appear to be a young man of family on my travels, elegantly dressed in scarlet and gold. I am seen to chat pleasantly with the ladies of wit and beauty; I am seen to play a game of cards and to be as fashionable and as frivolous as the rest. No doubt, therefore, it would seem safe in talking to me to make fun of the author of a dictionary as being a heavy man; it might even be supposed that in talking thus one would be paying a compliment to a man of vivacity, and that he would be charmed to hear the most piquant witticisms directed against a man so different from himself. It might seem that in abusing the blockhead one would be praising the man of genius. But how taken in they are when they learn that the blockhead and the man of genius are one and the same! How surprised they are when they learn that I am writing a dictionary myself!

... It is a Scots dictionary. You must know, gentlemen, that Great Britain was peopled by the Gauls, the same people who came from Scythia and occupied a part of France, and then passed into Ireland and Britain.... Some centuries later, the barbarians of Scandinavia, especially the Saxons, invaded Great Britain, and having been victorious, the true ancient Britons were driven from the most fertile parts of the country and established themselves in the country of Wales, the neighbouring country of Cornwall, and the islands and mountains of the West and North of Scotland. The

[1] The placing of this long but important section of the French themes at this point is somewhat arbitrary, for though the series (some thirty pages in all) devoted to dictionaries, and especially to Boswell's proposed Scots dictionary, must have been begun about this time, it obviously was not all written at a sitting.

Saxons, the Danes, and the Normans spread over the rest of the kingdom. Thus the inhabitants of England and of the Lowlands of Scotland were all the same.

Consequently the language was the same in South as in North Britain. But as it was made up of a variety of dialects, of which the Saxon was the chief, there were bound to be some differences: some words were kept in one district which were not kept in another. According to the proportion of Danes, of Saxons, or of Normans, a proportion of their dialects was bound to be preserved. Which of these peoples was most numerous in the migrations into Scotland, I cannot determine; but doubtless there was a difference of number. In this way can be traced the origin of some of the differences between the tongues of the two districts of Great Britain. Add thereto the imperceptible corruptions which were introduced by time, and we shall see another very fertile source of variation. Both divisions of the people had their peculiar corruptions, and thus drew away little by little from each other. The ancient Britons spoke Old Celtic. But the different divisions of even that people have acquired a diversity of dialects. The Welsh and the Scots Highlanders often differ in their manner of speaking. It is true that it is principally in pronunciation, but by degrees that makes a great difference. A century after such changes, when the words in question are not only pronounced but spelled differently, it is difficult to see that they are actually the same. The majority of people never see it. It is known only to those who apply themselves to the study of antiquities and of orthography, or rather of etymology.

It is thus that has arisen the greatest difference between English and Scots. Half the words are changed only a little, but the result of that is that a Scot is often not understood in England. I do not know the reason for it, but it is a matter of observation that although an Englishman often does not understand a Scot, it is rare that a Scot has trouble in understanding what an Englishman says: and certainly *Sawney* has an advantage in that. It is ridiculous to give as the reason for it that a Scot is quicker than an Englishman and consequently cleverer in understanding everything. It is

equally ridiculous to say that English is so musical that it charms
the ears and lures men to understand it, while Scots shocks and disgusts by its harshness. I agree that English is much more agreeable
than Scots, but I do not find that an acceptable solution for what
we are trying to expound. The true reason for it is that books and
public discourse in Scotland are in the English tongue.

I do not know what influence Celtic could have had on these
composite languages of Great Britain. That would depend on the
communication between the ancient and the new Britons. It is also
a question whether Celtic has mixed more with the English language or the Scottish. I am inclined to think that one would find
more of it in Scots. There was more communication between the
inhabitants of the Lowlands and the Highlands in Scotland than
there was between the English and the Welsh. . . .

There are several English dictionaries, especially the excellent
work of Mr. Johnson; and doubtless to have such a work is a thing
of great importance, for English in time will become the universal
language of our isle. We have not a single Scots dictionary. Really,
that is amazing. I believe there is not another language in Europe
(or dialect, to use that terminology—they are all dialects) of which
there is not some sort of lexicon. Allan Ramsay, a Scottish poet who
has written some very pretty things in his mother-tongue, has
given us a little glossary in which he has explained some words,
but very few of them. Nor has he made the least attempt to give
etymologies. There was an excellent reason for it: he could not. He
had been bred a wig-maker, and for some years followed his trade
in Edinburgh. His genius soon showed itself in little verses and
rude ballads. Afterwards he read translations of the ancient poets
and began to cultivate his mind, and finally he became a poet of
real merit in several kinds of composition. He did not know any
foreign language, and so was incapable of making a dictionary of
his own.

We have several Scots authors, properly so called: that is, authors who have written in the Scots language. We have the histories
of Knox and Calderwood; the lives of the authors and warriors of

Scotland by Abercrombie; and several treatises in law, in antiquities, and in religion. But our most esteemed works are those of our poets, among whom must be mentioned King James V, Bellenden, Ramsay the Elder and Ramsay Junior, besides several others who have written detached pieces. In the works of these poets may be found the finest strokes of genius of every sort.[2]

People in England do not know how much wit there is in Scottish authors. It must be confessed that these authors make only a very small number. All the same, it is well worth while to preserve them. The Scottish language is being lost every day, and in a short time will become quite unintelligible. Some words perhaps will be retained in our statutes and in our popular songs. To me, who have the true patriotic soul of an old Scotsman, that would seem a pity. It is for that reason that I have undertaken to make a dictionary of our tongue, through which one will always have the means of learning it like any other dead language. I confess that I look forward some centuries from now and see with romantic pleasure the Scots of that day applying themselves to the study of their ancient tongue as to Greek or Latin, and considering themselves much indebted to the work of Old Boswell, who has made it possible for them to taste the excellent works of their brave, happy, and venerable ancestors. . . .

Here is the plan which I propose to follow in compiling this work. I shall not put into it a single word which is recognized as English; and to determine that, I shall not count as English any

---

[2] Boswell's knowledge of Scots literature apparently did not extend back of the end of the sixteenth century, and consequently he misses the authors who would now be considered the most important: Barbour, King James I, Henryson, Dunbar, and Sir David Lindsay. John Bellenden (known in the main for prose translations from the Latin) seems an odd representative of the glories of Scottish verse. Allan Ramsay's son, also Allan Ramsay, was a distinguished portrait painter and wrote a good deal of occasional verse, but little of it was ever published, and none of the pieces that survive is of high quality. Even for the authors he names, it is probable that Boswell is affecting more knowledge than he really had, and that he knew little more of Scots verse than its popular songs.

word which has not been ratified by the authority of Mr. Johnson. To qualify myself to trace the etymologies, I am applying myself to the European languages, and I hope to acquire a sufficient knowledge of them. But I shall not stop there. I shall not trust to my own labours alone. I shall establish a literary correspondence with scholars in different countries. I shall send them from time to time lists of words, and they will send them back to me with conjectures on their origins. Besides that, I have another idea which is perhaps a bit fantastic, but which nevertheless may be practical. I am thinking of publishing in a Scottish newspaper similar lists of words, begging all those who can give derivations to send them to my publisher. In that way I should have countless conjectures, from which I could choose those which appeared to me the most ingenious and plausible. Those who granted me the favour would have to send their conjectures anonymously; in that way I should be at full liberty to choose without partiality; and I hope that no one would be offended if his derivations were not accepted. In taking this precaution, I should be following in some sort the famous printer Henry Stephanus, who posted in public places the proofs of his New Testament, sheet by sheet, and offered a reward of two pennies for each error that should be discovered. By that means he gave us an edition so correct that it contains only one misprint, and that in the introduction. I myself do not intend to offer prizes, for it is not a question of mechanical perfection concerning which the vulgar can judge. But by doing as I have just described, I can have the general assistance of my learned countrymen.

I shall make a careful collection of dictionaries in all languages. I shall consult them all, and I shall enter in my dictionary all the words which have any resemblance to the Scots words: that is, which not only resemble them but have the same meaning or practically the same, either literally or figuratively. In this way we shall get a general view of the connection between languages so far as Scots provides a basis of comparison. I shall not debate the origin of language. . . .

As for the languages of the present day, there are doubtless some which have not the least connection with the others. The Hungarian language is entirely different from the other European tongues. It has almost no borrowed words. I have had an opportunity to hear it spoken by Hungarians themselves, some of whom come to study at Utrecht. They pride themselves greatly on their language, and maintain that it has no connection even with Slavonic. The Chinese language is entirely unique. In a word, there is without doubt a diversity of tongues in the world, a diversity that cannot be denied, though no reason can be given for it. . . .

To return to my dictionary. . . . As Mr. Johnson has already given us full definitions of the English words, I should give only the bare English word for a Scots one, and should send my readers to Mr. Johnson's *Dictionary* to get the definitions. Consequently my task will not be nearly so great as if I had followed Mr. Johnson's method. Excuse me, I am in error. I should not have more work, for I could copy his definitions exactly; but the work of printing will not be so great, for my dictionary will be a third the size of his.[3] There are however several Scots words for which there are no English equivalents. There are words to express usages and customs peculiar to our country; and also original words, to express the complete sense of which the English have no terms. And there is my plan for a Scots dictionary. Courage!

The Scots dictionary of which I have been speaking at such length ought certainly to be an excellent work. Well and good. But when shall we have it? As to that, gentlemen, I cannot give you any reply that will be very illuminating. For the fact is that I do not know myself how much time I shall take to compile it. I have many other things to do which are more important to me and which I am resolved not to neglect. My dictionary will be merely the task of my leisure hours. Since I wish very much to do a thorough piece of work, I shall not hurry. I shall go quietly on, with all the help I can get, and I hope that in time you will see it done very satisfac-

[3] Boswell appears to have lost the thread of his argument, and to have written this sentence as though the preceding had said that if he included definitions, his labour would be greater than Johnson's.

torily. My indolence shudders when the idea of so laborious a work presents itself, but consoles itself when it considers that the labour will be shared, and that it will be necessary to do only small bits of it at a time. In this way horror is dissipated, my mind is calmed, and I am at peace. Without having peace of mind one cannot accomplish much. It is true that the poet says *Facit indignatio versus.*[4] But I doubt that *indignatio* will help us in a long work.

I have spoken so much of my dictionary that you must surely be bored with it. I am dreadfully bored with it myself. Let us drop the subject. . . .[5]

FRIDAY 24 FEBRUARY

> If you do love me, my enchanting fair,
> Pray let me have a tender Scottish air.
> Sing of some faithful swain or warrior bold
> Whose names were famous in the days of old.
> Sing me such music, which when Rizzio play'd,
> The beauteous Mary's sorrows were allay'd.
> Ah, let your voice be moderate and slow
> When you express the solemn notes of woe,
> Nor rudely spoil by an affected trill
> The sweet and simple *Lass of Patie's mill.*[6]

SATURDAY 25 FEBRUARY. Yesterday you did very well. You was sensible, prudent, *retenu.* You stood gloom; recollected how many, many years you have been attacked by it, and in what a variety of ways, and resolved in silent pride to maintain your dignity, conscious that the Quakers' Meeting, Donaldson the painter, and all other objects just remain the same. (These are mentioned

---

[4] "Indignation gives birth to verses" (Juvenal, *Satires,* i. 79).
[5] Boswell continued to refer to this great project for many years, and in 1769 showed Johnson a specimen of it, but he never brought it to completion. The manuscript (which probably was not very extensive) was sold for sixteen shillings in the sale of the library of his son James in 1825, and has not been reported since.   [6] An old Scots air, the lyric by Allan Ramsay.

because they please by an association.)[7] At Assembly you was fine
with Mademoiselle de Zuylen. She was amiable. She said you
might see her at home at least once a week. You said pride after a
certain pitch became affable; and that emulation was necessary,
for as you went up hill, you saw those before you. She said *la Veuve*
had no passion, and often ill humour. This girl trusts you; like her.
You heard that assemblies will end in March. Bravo! You'll study.
. . . Shun marriage. Today, honey for cold.

SUNDAY 26 FEBRUARY. Yesterday you did very well, although distressed with severe cold. In the morning you had fervent
devotion, saying, "O great and beneficent Being, let me not have a
slavish dread of thee, but an exalted respect; and at last I will be
happy." You was a little too merry after dinner, and in a bizarre
way. Shun always this. At Madame Lockhorst's you made Madame
de Nassau talk. She said you'd be *arrêté*.[8] You said, " 'Twould be
hard in this world, where there are so many fine women, if a man
cannot adore and escape too." The little Amerongen said, "He is in
love with my aunt."[9] This day be on guard; go on. You must hold
at duty of both churches, or perhaps indulge one Sunday. At any
rate, sup not at Brown's. Check these regular whims. . . .

MONDAY 27 FEBRUARY. Yesterday you stayed in all forenoon, thus showing that you act not from whim but reason. You
brought up much journal. You had dreadful cold. Rose said wars

---

[7] "I can find benefit from religious assemblies of various denominations of
Christians; least indeed from those of Presbyterians. But my mind is disposed
to quiet, mild communication with heaven in a Quaker meeting, as it is
stirred and elevated in a church where there is solemn external worship"
(Boswell's Journal, 12 September 1777). The Quakers' Meeting was probably
pleasantly associated with his mother, "a lady of distinguished piety," who
seems to have taken him there as a child. In his journal for 16 December 1775
he refers to a memorable scene in the year 1759 at Prestonfield, the pleasant
country house of his elderly friend, Sir Alexander Dick, at which Donaldson
the painter had been present.

[8] "Arrested" (in his mental and moral development if he married Madame
Geelvinck).

[9] Joost, Baron Taets van Amerongen, Madame Geelvinck's nephew, was at
this time not more than three years old.

were going out, from their mildness nowadays. ... You went timeously[1] to bed. This day, hard study; attend Trotz. Mem. Father, more and more manly behaviour. ... Home at five and have much journal. ...

TUESDAY 28 FEBRUARY. Yesterday you began your new course of *retenue* to accustom yourself to constant useful conversation, with mild and grave dignity, and only to relax at times to merriment. This character it is not difficult to form. Only lay restraint for a little at first. You see it is not observed when you do it. ... This day *rouse*. Cold is better; indulge it no more, lest you hurt nerves and fall into old-womanish complaining. Fix hours better and labour harder. Make the most of Brown: Dutch and geography. But above all, *think*, and get manly ideas. You will be pretty gentleman. Write Madame Geelvinck. If you are always employed, you can never fall back to idle vanity as with Eglinton.

[*c.* 28 FEBRUARY. DUTCH THEME] This is the worst winter that has been seen in Holland for many years. We have had scarcely any frost, which is surely the best winter weather in this land. Whenever it freezes hard, so that the canals are covered with good ice, the Dutchmen are happy; then everybody goes out to skate. But this winter we have had nothing at all but rain and wind and thick fogs; weather indeed so unhealthy that a foreigner cannot stand it.[2] I myself have had a bad cold for ten days. I had a severe headache, but I am so regular that I have not been absent a day from my college. Mynheer Trotz also had a cold, yet he gave his lectures, and I thought that it would be highly scandalous if the student should indulge himself more than the professor, who is much older. ...

Mynheer Trotz is certainly a most unusual man. He is a Prussian. But he has been many years in the Seven Provinces, first at Franeker in Friesland, then at Utrecht, having been professor of law in both places. He is an excellent jurist, having a profound knowledge of Roman and Dutch law, and having also much knowl-

[1] Betimes, early. A Scotticism.
[2] This explains why Boswell has made no mention of skating.

edge of history and philosophy. He is very lively and mingles many entertaining stories with his lessons. He has a great desire to learn English. He began it some years ago, but he neglected it. However, he has begun it again. Mr. Rose is his teacher, and goes to him twice a week, and really it is amazing to see with what attention and spirit the old professor can read.

WEDNESDAY 29 FEBRUARY. Yesterday you dozed in bed till near ten, having been disturbed with dismal dreams by reason of your severe cold. You was indolent and could do nothing with spirit. Yet you stood calm and firm, and was master of yourself. You dined with Monsieur de Zuylen. The invitation gave a turn to your spirits. You was grave yet agreeable, and had address. You dined too full and was clogged. This is a sure effect of a known cause; so determine obstinate temperance so as never to take more than you can. . .

WEDNESDAY 29 FEBRUARY. This day, for the first time since 25 September 1763, I wrote no lines, having kept my bed with a cold.

THURSDAY 1 MARCH. Yesterday you lay abed all day at ease to cure cold; read three hours Voltaire, and was tranquil. *Raro fiat.*[3]

[Received *c.* 1 March, Trotz to Boswell][4]

MY HONOURED FRIEND:—I am very sick of the kold and my Doctor have counselleth to keep for my[5] these day en morning, because my health; but there is no great danger. Nevertheless i must pardon me for this time, we shall bi diligent into the following week. I wish jou heartily a good dinner, being your most faithfull Friend,

C. H. TROTZ.

My Compliment to Maester Brouwn en us Friend my Teacher. Condonabis, Amice, balbutienti; at juvat tentasse et sufficit ridendi

[3] "Let it happen seldom."
[4] Except for some slight additions to the punctuation, this letter is printed just as the learned professor wrote it.   [5] "To restrain myself," "to stay in."

materiam vobis praebeam. Valete. Venam mihi secuerunt, hinc calamum vix dirigere valeo.[6]

FRIDAY 2 MARCH. Yesterday you got up better. You was however still distressed, and at Brown's was weakish and joked on *l'amour*. You forget that at those weak seasons, care is to be taken to preserve chain of uniformity. At Society you had excellent dispute on natural and moral causes to make national character. This day, French and Dutch versions; home at five, and journal all night. No more indulgence—vapours. Forget not that in all religions and systems, firmness of man is noble.

SATURDAY 3 MARCH. Yesterday you lay too long. This cold is made an excuse for laziness. You finished Campbell and had clear proof for Christian miracles.[7] At dinner you was very well and read Dutch and Greek well. But talked too long with Rose, and was too indolent. Mem., *now* is the time to acquire habits for all your life; you're always ready to plead some indisposition. But even then be firm. . . .

SUNDAY 4 MARCH. Yesterday your cold was bad, and you was miserably gloomy. You walked with Rose in the sun, who said an infidel must be uneasy, for he is always asking questions on religion. After dinner you said 'twas hard that in this world of woe your greatest quantum of happiness had been enjoyed in vice. This was very rash. Brown said, "What! have you been happier in vice than in virtue? BOSWELL. "Yes." BROWN. "Come, you've got the cold; your humours are thick; you're wearying." He said it without impertinence. At night you had Hungarian, learned Tokay (mark it), and grew well.[8] Your dreams last night were sad. . . .

[6] "Friend, you will pardon one who lisps; but there is pleasure in having tried, and it will suffice if I furnish you matter for laughter. Farewell. They have blooded me, so that I am scarcely able to guide a pen."
[7] George Campbell, D.D., Principal of Marischal College, Aberdeen, had published *A Dissertation on Miracles* in 1762.
[8] "I pretend to a little judgment in this wine; because during a winter that I lived at Utrecht, I was a member of a club of Hungarians, one of whom had a vineyard in Tokay, and used to entertain us with it very liberally." (A

[Received *c.* 4 March, Trotz to Boswell][9]

Sunday 4 Marsch 1764

Much Esteemed Friend Maester Boswell:—I am very glad to receive of your hand one agreable letter, full of civilitie and affection. But, do you believe, my dear Friend, that any body of mine scholars have the same meinds, for the study as Mr. Boswell? No, no, there is a certain sort of lazi fellows, called on the Dutsh-men: Luy-Zakken[1] or belli homines,[2] which run rather into the Coffeehouses or publick meeting hauses to hear news and read the Gazes. Truly, they buried themselves in much fruitless conversation. But let us leave that odious People. Concerning my Health i was let blood yesterday, and since i find myself much better, i thank God. Therefore i shall morrow morning, or monday mine lectures begin again. My Doctor a wise and experient Man, Maester Woerdman, have it permit: for jou knowst well, wath the Lawyer say in t. 26 D. de oper. libert. Medicus imperat.[3] Now my Friend, you are to much obliging towards my: for you force me to be uncivil and troublesome to you. Surely you kindlet and encouraget me, like a Socrates at the virtue, to the frequent exercise of the English tongue, whom i esteem and love. In earnst, i schould desire, if you would do me the favour, to explain me de faults, they i have made, whyle i self several have found, it might be to my advantage. Fare well, till i have the honnour to see you again I am with respect Your ever obliged and faithfull Friend,

C. H. Trotz.

---

deleted passage in Boswell's autograph manuscript of *An Account of Corsica.* He later gives the name of this Hungarian as Jánosi.)

[9] Printed without any editorial interference except for the addition of one or two marks of punctuation.

[1] Literally, "lazy sacks."

[2] "Polite men," "men of the world." It is not impossible that Trotz intended a pun with English "belly."

[3] "Title 26 of the Digest, concerning the power of a physician to command his freemen to stop practising medicine." The allusion seems very far-fetched.

4. *March* 1764

My Compliments to all our Friends Mr. Brouwn and my Instructor Mr. N. N.[4]

MONDAY 5 MARCH. Yesterday you was gloomy but better.
Rose drank coffee with you, and you related to him your having
shaved.[5] This was wrong. Never repeat past follies but to very intimate friends. You talked of Smith's Sympathy,[6] and said that when
passion rose high, you had a faculty in your own mind called
Reason; you appeal to that. You find he disapproves; you dare not
act. This is all within yourself. If you act, he condemns you. There
is no occasion for a far-fetched appeal to others, which at best is but
vague; and if others are bad, must be bad. Envy cannot be accounted for on Smith's principles. Think on this. At night you grew
easy and renewed resolves of patience and firmness. This day . . .
finish Johnson's letter.

TUESDAY 6 MARCH. Yesterday you got up vigorous and well,
your cold gone and health and joy bounding through your frame.
Mem. schellings to the fencing master. . . . You was cheerful at
dinner. After it you reproved Brown for indecent talking. . . . You
walked long with Rose, and talked on the unalterable obligations of
virtue, and pushed them well; next on the Christian morals, and on
the precepts being temporary, otherwise hard to be understood. . . .
On the whole, it was an idle day. This day . . . improve in memory.
You resume foreign *beau monde*. Be prudent; mem. Father. . . .

WEDNESDAY 7 MARCH. Yesterday you did very well. You
thought that Smith's system was running mankind, melting them,
into one mass in the crucible of Sympathy. Whereas they are separate beings, and 'tis their duty as rational beings to approach near
to each other. You are to give an analysis of Smith's book. 'Twill be
fine. Write out sketch of *Female Scribbler:* old, surly squire; weak,
ignorant mother; light, trifling lover whom she does not care for;

[4] "Mr. Nomen Nescio" ("Mr. I-don't-know-his-name"), i.e., Mr. Rose. It is
rather odd that Trotz had not learned his instructor's name.   [5] See p. 114.
[6] Boswell is reading *The Theory of Moral Sentiments* (1759) by Adam Smith,
better known later as the author of *The Wealth of Nations*. Smith had been
his teacher in Glasgow, 1759–1760.

foolish maid; heavy, covetous bookseller; generous, sensible lover,
&c.[7] You went at three and heard Professor Trotz. You was well and
firm and reserved at Assembly. Pray speak not of self. Be good to
Rose while here. Write short and genteel to Sommelsdyck, Madame
Spaen.[8]

THURSDAY 8 MARCH. Yesterday you did very well. Having
finished Xenophon, you began Plutarch. You drank tea with
Madame Brown, with Madame Sichterman, whom you found
agreeable, and was pleased to see the lady to whom Sir David has
poured forth his plaints. You mentioned him. But she waived the
nice subject. At eight you was at Zélide's concert, fine, really
charmed and soothed; she, sweet and mild. You're to go every
Wednesday. This day at ... four, Zélide; ask if you may show
Portrait to Rose;[9] if so, make him copy it. Journal by degrees. ...
No neutral time. I beseech you, gain calm behaviour like Temple,
nor be uneasy at its not appearing.

[Received 8 March, Andrew Erskine to Boswell]

Edinburgh, 16 February 1764

MY DEAR BOSWELL,—Have you forgot me, or have I forgot you?
The latter I can assure you is not the case; I'm afraid the former is.
You took so ill my not writing to you before you left London that
when you went abroad you did not so much as tell me where you
was going. Till I met your friend Johnston about a month ago in
this place, I was ignorant whether France or Japan, Italy or Peru
contained the body of James Boswell, Esq. How could you use so
barbarously a man whose only crime was being in low spirits? My
spirits, I thank heaven, are now recovered, and I never was so
happy in my life.

I will give you a short but substantial account of my life and

---

[7] Apparently a play or *conte*, based to some extent on the character of Belle
de Zuylen. If ever written, it has not yet been recovered.
[8] He is planning in about a month to revisit The Hague, and wishes to prepare
the way for his arrival.   [9] Her character-sketch of herself: see p. 184.

adventures since I left you. I came to Edinburgh, where I was in the deepest low spirits. I went to the Highlands, where I grew better. I went to Kellie, where I relapsed.[1] I went again to the Highlands, where I improved. I returned to Edinburgh, where I am at present, perfectly delighted. I bathe every morning, and every morning your friend Mr. Rankeillor wishes you saw me go in, I perform the operation so wonderfully well. His language is quite soaring when he talks of my plunging.[2]

Talking of language, I must here make my apology for writing to you in one which by this time you can't possibly understand. I had some thoughts of going down to Leith and trying to prevail upon a Dutch skipper to translate my English into his own beautiful lingo, but as I'm just going to begin studying French, that shall be my language for the future. I suppose by this time you can talk Dutch to a Frenchman and French to a Dutchman, in the same manner as when you was in London you spoke Scotch to Englishmen and English to Scotchmen.

I come now to the most material part of my history, at least to you. You may remember two or three years ago I told you of a little plot I had contrived for a farce. I wrote it (the farce, I mean) when I was in the Highlands the beginning of this winter. Soon after I came to town, I enclosed it in a letter to Digges. He was extremely pleased with it. I dined with him and Mrs. Bellamy soon after.[3] I found them, I think, the most agreeable couple I almost ever saw. . . . The farce was first played on Monday the sixth of February to a very full house; it was received with more applause than I expected. . . . The run . . . was stopped by Digges's being obliged to

[1] "The Highlands" means the residence of his brother-in-law the Laird of Macfarlane on Loch Long; Kellie, the mansion house of his brother, the Earl of Kellie, in Fife.

[2] An ominous sentence. In 1793 Erskine, in a fit of depression, filled his pockets with stones and drowned himself in the sea.

[3] The famous (or notorious) actress George Anne Bellamy. She and Digges were living together. She was the illegitimate daughter of Lord Tyrawley, he (by legitimate descent) the grandson of Lord Delawarr.

go to London to see his brother, who is just dying. Donaldson was my publisher; it sells well. . . .

Pray tell me your plan. What say you to a visit from me at Utrecht this summer? Direct to me at Macfarlane's house in the Canongate. Lady Betty and Lady Anne remember you.[4] I dined with Johnston lately very agreeably. I have got much acquainted this winter and I cut up well.[5] Tell me all about yourself, your spirits, your designs, &c. Farewell. Yours very affectionately,

ANDW. ERSKINE.

FRIDAY 9 MARCH. Yesterday you rose well; after breakfast you received a letter from Johnston with accounts of the death of the poor little child.[6] Alas, what is the world? You was distressed and sunk. Rose sympathized. You hesitated if to mourn. Rose said 'twas only external ceremony, and none but yourself knew. You was low at dinner; Brown saw it. After dinner you talked of it to him. He was sensible and hardy. You drank tea with Zélide. Madame well.[7] She sweet, mild, agreeable. . . . At night you sat late. You was strange. Do so no more. You had letter from Erskine. How much altered are you! Answer him grave, yet cheerful. . . . This night Mademoiselle de Zuylen; bid her be calm, to show you if she could be your companion in grief, but only say dead *parent*. . . .[8]

THURSDAY 8 MARCH

Man is, indeed, O Job, to trouble born;
Oft must his bosom with distress be torn.

[4] His sisters: Lady Betty was married to Macfarlane.
[5] In the United States the usual figurative meaning of *I cut up* would be "I am boisterously mischievous"; in England, "I leave a (large) fortune." Neither meaning seems to fit here. Perhaps merely, "I serve as a satisfactory object for severe criticism"? Erskine was notoriously shy and awkward in company.
[6] His son Charles. See pp. 31 and 124; also *Boswell's London Journal, 1762–1763,* 1950. p. 324 *n.* 6.   [7] Madame de Zuylen, Belle's mother.
[8] "Relative." Boswell actually wrote *parents*.

Affliction strange, but, ah, how very keen!
I weep for him whom I have never seen.
For in my heart the warm affection dwelt,
For I a father's tender fondness felt.
All the firm precepts that the Stoics taught
Cannot dispel my dreariness of thought.
Now in the time of serious solemn grief,
I from religion only find relief.

FRIDAY 9 MARCH

Perplexed reas'nings may the best deceive,
But what we see, we surely may believe.
Let not wild fancy sceptically range
And doubt of facts because she finds them strange.
At the twelfth hour on Wednesday, dreary night!
Shone at my window a strong glow of light;
It vanish'd twice, as it had twice been seen,
And left me musing what this light could mean.
I can protest that I was broad awake,
And that my joints with terror did not quake.[9]

SATURDAY 10 MARCH. Yesterday you got up more composed,
but sickish from late sitting up; never do so again. At dinner you
was grave yet easy. You was of *partie* with Zélide at Assembly. You
told her you was distressed for the death of a friend, and begged to
see if she could be company to the distressed. She said yes, but she
soon showed her eternal laughing. You talked to her plainly that
she did not use her *raison:* that she would tell the minister, "I don't
love my children," to shock the poor man.... You told her she
never had a better friend. She said, "I believe it." This day *retenue;*
be firm and only silent. What a world is this! ....

SUNDAY 11 MARCH. Yesterday you was melted with tender

[9] Boswell (who was superstitious and showed a lifelong interest in the second-
sight) appears to have believed that this was a portent of his child's death—or
rather, of his receipt of the news.

distress. You walked musing in the Mall. You would fain have persuaded yourself that it was not true, that Charles was still alive. At dinner you was faint and gloomy, and you read Greek feebly. At night you had Hungarians. You made the divine talk over the Calvinistical doctrines, and he displayed unintelligible perplexity. Did you not determine to keep mind fixed to real objects, and to expel *speculations,* which you *know* to be uncertain? This day at ten, Jesuits' church. . . . Sup not tonight. Have unaffected serious sorrow. Let your religion be just and manly.

MONDAY 12 MARCH. Yesterday you got up very dull. However, you dressed and went to the Jesuits' church, where the solemn worship put venerable ideas in your mind, not without many strange recollections of past life and philosophical ideas at present.[1] You stayed at home and dined not. You was easy at church.[2] After it, Rose and you walked. You owned that you was very uneasy. He said, "We must lay our accounts with such things." He advised you against dining at ordinaries; said it would be talked of and would do you little good. You talked on *Liberty* and on GOD's omniscience, and he owned he could not answer but fled to ignorance. You had *partie* at Madame Pester's with Zélide, fine and mild. She said she was *friande.*[3] Then all mild with grief. You supped Brown's. Rose and he disputed *vacuum* and *plenum,*[4] one not understanding other. Just enough to show absurd metaphysics. This day just begin anew firm, real study. You have kept your honour. Be silent, nor joke. Don't go *partie;* Madame Amelisweerd deserves a little neglect.

TUESDAY 13 MARCH. Yesterday you saw the horse-market, one of the greatest in the world. The day was sweet and mild, and

---

[1] The only reference to attendance at Roman Catholic worship during Boswell's residence in Holland. He clearly wished to attend mass and pray for the repose of his child's soul. There was no Anglican congregation in Utrecht.
[2] Brown's church.   [3] "An epicure."
[4] The problem of whether or not all space is filled with matter. Johnson had discussed it on 22 July 1763, no doubt because Boswell had then brought it up. See *Boswell's London Journal, 1762–1763,* 1950, p. 318.

you walked charming. At dinner you was on guard, and after it you read Dutch, and Hall and Sterne's letters.[5] You read Hume till you was sick. At Madame Amelisweerd's you was pretty well. You found yourself at eleven so sleepy, your attention so gone, your nerves so unstrung, that you yielded to indulgence of luscious sleep. But as fine weather now comes, be firm and fill up each day. Tonight, cheerful silence. Zélide.

WEDNESDAY 14 MARCH. Yesterday you lay abed at ease. You was still dreary and was glad as a relief to make Bourier[6] chat. You was thus amused insensibly. At dinner Brown's Scots indelicacy hurt you. Rose and you talked of it as very disagreeable. At Assembly *chez* Madame de Zuylen you was *tranquil*. Vassell said, "My sister knows very well that you are sorry that she is ill." *La Comtesse* was truly chagrined. But you knocked a pair of ducats out of her pocket at cards. This turned up her Dutch nose.[7] At night you was pretty well. After dinner you said imprudently you had so bad a view of life that you could almost do anything. . . .

[5] In manuscript. Brown had told him on 26 January that he was acquainted with Laurence Sterne's friend, John Hall-Stevenson, "whom he used to sit up with till three at Geneva," and that he had a letter from Sterne. Boswell had met Sterne in London in the spring of 1760.

[6] This name does not occur elsewhere in the memoranda. Because of the ambiguities of Boswell's script, it could equally well be transcribed Bounier or Bourien.

[7] "Vassell" is apparently a nickname for Belle de Zuylen's youngest brother Vincent. (Diederik was called "Ditie.") Belle was certainly ill at this time (see p. 183), but may for all that have been present at this assembly. Boswell's "Livre de Jeu à Utrecht" under date of 13 March 1764 records 10 guilders 6 stivers (approximately 18s. 10d., $4.60) won from "Mademoiselle de Zuylen" but nothing won from the Countess of Nassau Beverweerd. The amount, however, is about two ducats. It is easy enough to suppose that Boswell posted the account from memory, but a little hard, after his ungallant glee at turning up the Countess's Dutch nose, to suppose that he had forgotten whom he had won it from. (For converting Dutch money into English in these notes, I have made use of a table in Thomas Nugent, *The Grand Tour*, 3d ed., 1778, i. 51. For the further conversion into American currency, I have arbitrarily set the pound sterling at $4.87.)

WEDNESDAY 14 MARCH

> O Temple, say what method shall I find
> Still to preserve my dignity of mind?
> How shall I gain that firm internal force
> Which makes a man move steady in his course;
> By good not soften'd, nor subdu'd by ill,
> Pursue his journey up high Virtue's hill?
> Oft I the warmest resolutions make
> That the great road I never will forsake,
> But oft I find that I have gone astray,
> Nor can I tell how I have lost my way.

THURSDAY 15 MARCH. Yesterday you was still uneasy. A letter from your worthy father full of strong sense, of spirit, and of affection, animated you to new endeavours;[8] yet was you feeble. At dinner it was dull; but as you observed to Rose, few would have supported it so well. You talked over gaming—bad from its consequences. You kept Brown to French. He began course of geography. You stayed tea with Rose, and talked of madness and spleen and lying abed; you yielded too much to indolence. Resolve no more English speaking. Sustain character of country gentleman. Keep mind to self. In a month you go to Hague, and after that you need not dine. Be good-humoured. Despair not, nor be proud of chagrin . . .

THURSDAY 15 MARCH

> To you, my friend,[9] I fear not to disclose
> My real sorrows or my fancied woes;
> For you can all my dreary stories hear,
> Nor make me fretful by a galling sneer.
> To you, whom from my earliest youth I've known,
> Not ev'n my faults am I asham'd to own.
> Doom'd to a life of sadness from my birth,
> I live a weary stranger on the earth;

---

[8] Not recovered.   [9] Still addressing Temple.

In vain I struggle to escape my doom;
In vain I struggle to be free from gloom.

FRIDAY 16 MARCH. Yesterday you was better. Brown disputed against Hume's happiness of little miss and orator being equal.[1] BROWN. "They are both equally content. But surely it is possible to make beings more happy than merely content. We can compare feelings and pronounce some more noble and happy than others. It is by comparing absent ideas with present that we judge of size and many other things. The miss and the philosopher have their desires equally satisfied. This bottle and that glass are equally full. But the bottle holds more." Des Essar gave thoughts on translation—very good. This day rise brisk. Write Temple; tell him all circumstances. Ask if 'tis weakness; ask his advice. Push always some subject, nor suffer spleen a moment, nor be cast down at woe which you only knew of. . . . Never dispute on religion with Brown; you'll leave him soon.

SATURDAY 17 MARCH. Yesterday you got up at seven. You wrote a long splenetic letter to Temple. You tore it; you did well. Write him a neat manly one, and talk of your gloom as past.[2] You was honoured with a letter from Monsieur van Sommelsdyck. You was quite the man of distinction. You attended to Trotz *de Probationibus*.[3] At dinner you was bad, but stood it. . . . After it you complained to Rose of the insipidity. He said you could do no better, and you owned you did not expect *agréments*[4] at Utrecht. Rose said he was very unhappy, and that he had never had such uneasy feelings before he came to Utrecht. . . . At four, Zélide.

SUNDAY 18 MARCH. Yesterday you did pretty well. You wrote

[1] "I mentioned Hume's notion that all who are happy are equally happy; a little miss with a new gown at a dancing-school ball, a general at the head of a victorious army, and an orator after having made an eloquent speech in a great assembly. . . . I remember this very question very happily illustrated in opposition to Hume by the Reverend Mr. Robert Brown at Utrecht. 'A small drinking-glass' . . . " (*Life of Johnson*, 12 February 1766).
[2] An indication of the fact that in the memoranda we have a truer picture of the actual state of Boswell's spirits than in his journal or letters.
[3] On Proof.   [4] "Comforts," "amenities."

genteel letter to Monsieur van Sommelsdyck. After dinner you
disputed with Brown on Omnipotence and Evil. He said he was
settled, and that you must travail in birth with such notions for
some years. "Stuff!" Rose sneered, and said, "If I read Bayle, I
would be as wise as when I began."[5] You walked with Rose, but
could make little of him. You was so bad as really to think of despairing. You drank tea with Zélide; father and mother very good to
you. She bad, but quite friendly and charming. You chatted easy;
saw her in good humour. She said she could have a husband that
she would not tire of if he had something to do. Hungarian talked
physic,[6] and bid me let blood to render *agilis*. You grew quite easy.
This day . . . copy Portraits and send to Zélide.

MONDAY 19 MARCH. Yesterday you awaked as dismal as
mortal could be. You grew better. . . . You walked with Vincent,[7]
who amused you with stories of the family *s'ennuiant*. Rose walked
with you and agreed that Dr. Clarke had made the proofs for the
Being, &c., strong, but advised a course of Natural Philosophy. You
said that contingencies are supposed in the Scriptures, and so things
are accounted for consistently. You receive a revelation from a
Being whom you have the strongest proofs that he is,[8] and he
promises to make the good happy. Just keep to this. Be quiet and
never own waverings, for then you're moulded by every hand. Let
principles be in your own mind. Pursue Plan. . . . No *partie* tonight, but letters and Zélide. Say not another word to Rose on
speculation. He goes soon. Be genteel, nor own uneasiness.

[5] Pierre Bayle (1647–1706), a Frenchman, was brought up a Protestant, became a Roman Catholic, and then returned to Protestantism of a decidedly
rationalistic cast. He had been professor at Rotterdam, but had been removed
from his chair there because of his sceptical tendencies. His *Dictionnaire
historique et critique* (1697) analyzed and criticized in a rationalistic
fashion all these doctrines which Boswell and Brown were debating. If Brown
recommended Bayle, he could hardly have been a strict Calvinist. Boswell
hated the doctrine of predestination and wished with all the power of his
being either to forget or to disprove it, but whenever he was seriously depressed, he found it at once fascinating and irrefutable.   [6] Medicine.
[7] Belle de Zuylen's brother.   [8] Boswell lost track of his sentence.

[Received 19 March, Madame Geelvinck to Boswell.
Original in French]

The Hague, 17 [March 1764]
EXCUSE MY SILENCE, DEAR SIR. The reasons which have compelled me to put off writing are too long and too boring to write
down. The Hague is not a place for correspondence, as you know. It
has been impossible for me to copy the Portrait, but I hope to atone
for my idleness by sending it to you in the hand of the author.[9] I
have seen your friend Gordon and judge differently of him than
Mademoiselle de Zuylen does. You will soon see me again at
Utrecht, where I hope to repeat face to face how much I am your
servant and sincere friend,

H.[1] VEUVE GEELVINCK.

My pen and ink are both excessively bad, and my scribbling is
worse.

PORTRAIT OF ZÉLIDE

Compassionate by temperament, liberal and generous by inclination, Zélide is complaisant only on principle. When she is
mild and affable, be grateful to her; she is making an effort. When
she remains for any length of time civil and polite to those whom
she does not care for, redouble your esteem: she is a martyr.

[9] There are among the Boswell Papers two "portraits": the first the well-
known "Portrait of Zélide" by Belle de Zuylen herself, the other (I think)
of Madame Geelvinck, also by Belle de Zuylen. (See p. 131.) A translation of
the "Portrait of Zélide" is printed after this letter. I have followed Boswell's
text rather than Godet's (*Madame de Charrière et ses amis*, i. 59–61) except
for one or two places where Boswell clearly made an error of transcription.
Professor F. W. Hilles has helped me generously in the phrasing of the
translation, and I have borrowed half a dozen words or so from Geoffrey
Scott's brilliant version of part of the portrait in *The Portrait of Zélide*,
Constable (Scribner), 1925.
[1] The H here seems odd. Madame Geelvinck's Christian names were Catherina Elisabeth and her family name was Hasselaer.

Her vanity is boundless and boundless by gift of Nature, but if it had not been, her experience of mankind and her resulting scorn would soon have made it so. She has already come to see that fame is nothing if purchased at the expense of happiness, but she would still submit to much for the sake of fame. When will the light of the intellect direct the inclinations of the heart? When it does, Zélide will cease to be a coquette.

Unhappy contradiction! Zélide, who would not needlessly strike a dog or crush the vilest insect, would perhaps in certain moods enjoy making a man unhappy, and unhappy for her own amusement; merely for a kind of prestige which does not deceive her intellect in the least and tickles her vanity only for an instant. But her feeling of superiority is short-lived: the first glimpse of triumph brings her to herself. She no sooner recognizes the scheme in her heart than she despises it, loathes it, and wishes to renounce it for ever.

You will ask me perhaps if Zélide is beautiful, or pretty, or merely passable. I do not know. It all depends on your loving her or her wishing to make herself beloved. She has a beautiful neck; she knows it, and displays a little more of it than modesty allows. Her hands are not white. She knows that, too; she jokes about it, but she would be happy not to have this cause for joking.

Affectionate in the extreme and even more fastidious, she cannot be happy either with love or without it. But where did Friendship ever find a temple more hallowed, more worthy of his presence, than Zélide's heart?

Realizing that she is too sensitive to be happy, she has almost ceased to hope for happiness. She flees from remorse and pursues diversion. Her pleasures are rare, but they are lively. She snatches them, she relishes them eagerly. Aware of the futility of planning and the uncertainty of the future, she seeks above all to make the passing moment happy. Can you not guess her secret? Zélide is something of a sensualist.

Too lively and too powerful feelings; too much inner activity with no satisfactory outlet: there is the source of all her misfortunes. If her organism had been less sensitive, Zélide would have had the character of a great man; if she had been less intelligent and rational, she would have been only a weak woman.

Addition to the Portrait of Zélide

You insist: the portrait of Zélide must be reconsidered. If it were only a question of making another, the thing would be easy. Zélide's friends say that it would be possible to make twenty, all like the original, all differing from one another. But the task is more difficult than that. The author of the portrait must erase certain lines from an old sketch, dashed off carelessly to fill the vacancy of an evening in autumn—a sketch that was intended only for the eyes of a single woman friend and that ought never to have been given to the world. She would have retouched it if she had intended it to be circulated, but almost before she had read it over, it escaped from her hands. Many people assure her that she was unfair to Zélide in saying that she is good-humoured only on principle. She herself now enters an appeal against a judgment of which she once approved.

If to be kind is to weep over the unfortunate, to place beyond price the happiness of every sensitive being, to be willing to sacrifice one's self to others but never to sacrifice others to one's self, Zélide is kind by nature and always was so. But if it is not enough to observe scrupulous fairness with a heart that is compassionate and sensitive; if to be kind one must also dissimulate one's dislikes and disgusts, must not speak out when one is right, must respect the weaknesses of others; must make those who have tortured us by their wrong-headedness forget the points in which they were wrong—then Zélide has always hoped to be kind, and is becoming so. Her heart is capable of great sacrifices; she accustoms her temper to small ones. She tries to make every moment of those who approach her happy, for she would like to make their lives happy, and moments make life. Though she is too sensitive to be happy herself, those who associate with her profit by her un-

happiness. Her existence ought not to be useless; and the less it
appears a good to her, the more she wishes to make it a good for
them. When she feels like crying, she tries to make others laugh;
she forgets her own afflictions in order to soften those of others.
She wishes to be happy in the happiness of others when she cannot
be happy in her own. For the rest, to do her duty is the first of con-
solations, as it is the sweetest of pleasures; and Zélide believes that
the happiness of those to whom Providence has joined her destiny
is a charge which has been entrusted to her.

Second Addition

If enough justice has not been done her on the score of kindness,
perhaps on the score of friendship she has been too generously
handled. There is no friend more active than she, but must one
have a strong liking for a person in order to be zealous in his service? There is no confidant more discreet than she, but would Zélide
betray an enemy either? Gay and bantering, she is reproached
for mocking at every one. She sees without prejudice what is ridiculous, and she laughs at it without scruple. Love himself could not
bind her eyes. But Zélide does not stop loving those who move her
to laughter; she never expected to find human beings without
weaknesses. A man who is ridiculous amuses her but cannot make
her angry. She is very far from preferring vice to absurdity. To
views unfortunately narrow, one small blemish ruins the most
beautiful picture; to eyes that are truly kind, ridicule does not in
the least efface the splendour of merit. Even vices do no harm to
virtues: one should see mankind trait for trait. Her confidence, it
is said, is not flattering; it is too general, and perhaps if it were be-
trayed, Zélide would not be much surprised. I have read that men
cannot hide their own secrets nor women the secrets of others, but
in this Zélide is not a woman. Another's secret is for her a sacred
charge; her own is in her power. She disposes of it according to her
fancy; or rather, Zélide has no secrets. What would she not reveal
to amuse herself and shock others? She is forced by a memory from

which nothing is effaced, by a heart which never forgives itself anything, to respect everything that concerns others. To risk other people's goods would be unjust; unceasing regret would be her punishment. But she makes sport of what concerns herself alone. She always sacrifices the future to the present, and as soon as the present has become past, it too [is sacrificed].[2] She rarely thinks she has paid too much for a gratification. But if a brief amusement cost her long vexation, her repentance would be merely that of a bad economist who had made a poor bargain. What a difference between him and the wretch who has robbed the public or ruined his wards! It is her lack of concern for the future that has caused Zélide to commit a thousand imprudences. If she had reflected an instant, her portrait would not now be running about the world. She would have realized that almost half of mankind is malicious, and that that half speaks for the other, which cannot read. Fortunately the blame of a thousand fools and of a hundred thousand prudes is not worth a moment of regret. Every day Zélide grows more insensitive to the judgment of the blind multitude. She would despair if those who know her well quitted her without regret, or met her again without pleasure, or spoke of her without esteem. Would it show self-love if she questioned whether that would ever happen? She is not always greatly loved, but people always choose to be with her rather than away from her. This is precious to her: it ought to be. It assures her that she deserves esteem, and she is very glad to deserve it. But how does it concern her happiness if people should admire or blame her at a distance on hearsay, on vague reports, on remarks half understood? Can she think either more or less highly of herself because of such things?

Blest Sensibility! Zélide will never disown thee, thou sole offset for the misfortune of nice discernment and exacting taste. Thou who causest her to cherish the sweets of Nature, thou who dost bind her to the Arts much more than capricious Vanity! Thou art highly dangerous, perhaps, but thou art always a positive good.

[2] Boswell left a blank, probably because he could not read the word in Belle's hand. Godet does not print the passage.

Bad luck to them who know no innocent delights of sense! It is not for them (as the author of *Émile* says), no, it is not for them that I write.

TUESDAY 20 MARCH. Yesterday you lay abed purely to have a little present ease. You called on Brown; told him you was not well. Said he, "You are melancholy." You asked if he would not take amiss your dining elsewhere some days. He said, "By no means," with true frankness, and bid you amuse yourself. At ten you had letter from *la Veuve*, sweet and elegant. Yet, alas! it did not elevate your gloomy soul. However, be proud of it. She's the finest prize in the Provinces, and you'll be well with her. You dined at Koster's[3]—blackguards. You was direfully melancholy and had the last and most dreadful thoughts. You came home and prayed. You read Greek, and Voltaire on the English. This day, spring up. Resolve this. You can't be worse, and it may harden. You have not owned too much. Return to Brown's; resume and improve; don't joke.

[*c.* 20 MARCH. FRENCH THEME] . . . I am in doubt whát is the best breakfast. Some people take soup, others take meat. But the most general mode in Europe is to take tea or coffee. But still there are difficulties. What is best to eat with tea and coffee? In Switzerland you have hot cakes well covered with butter. In London you have muffins, which are much the same thing, or sometimes butter-toast, that is, bread and butter toasted together. Sometimes you are given bread, either toasted or not, and left to put the butter on it yourself; and in some slightly more luxurious families, you are also served honey and preserves. After all, in breakfasting each must follow his own taste. There is no truer proverb than that which says that one man's meat is another man's poison.

The opinions of mankind are fairly well agreed in the matter of dinner. Every one at mid-day wishes to eat something substantial and hot. There is, however, a great difference as to the number

---

[3] A hotel in the Oudkerkhof, not far from the Cathedral Square. The point is merely that it was a new eating-place for Boswell, and that he did not like it.

of dishes and the manner of dressing them. I myself do not like a
mixture of meats. I like a good soup, a slice of beef or mutton, and
a little green stuff or pastry; and there is my dinner.

There is a diversity of opinion as to supper. In France and in
several other countries they have a heavy meal at night. In England people eat almost nothing. I think it is much more healthful
not to eat supper, or to take only something very light. However,
I admit that that depends principally on habit, for there are people
who eat supper, even a hearty supper, yet who are perfectly well.
Again, each man to his own taste. . . .

WEDNESDAY 21 MARCH. Yesterday you told Mr. Brown that
you would not desert him; that one in gloom thinks to be relieved
by changes, but that they are vain. He said you would do well after
Mr. Rose goes to change about. You said you could not be so well.
At dinner he amused you with Sir W. Aston and his family. Facts
are most entertaining. Sir W. asked in the Presbyterian church,
"Pray, what is it? Is it a worship?" . . . He said a melancholy man
should marry a woman who is not so. You attended well to geography and to Greek but joined with Rose against Utrecht; 'tis infectious. At Assembly *chez Comtesse* you behaved well, though
with brutes. . . . Be pious like Pitfour. . . .⁴ All will come well.
Journal at night.

[21 MARCH. FRENCH THEME]⁵ I will try to relate in passable
French Mr. Brown's conversation at dinner yesterday. "We once
had at Utrecht," said he, "the most uncouth English family that
one can conceive. Sir Willoughby Aston⁶ had an estate of £5000
a year in the west of England. He spent a great deal of money to
win an election, which he lost after all; and he lived on too splendid
a footing. He found his affairs somewhat embarrassed, and resolved to pass some years in foreign countries in order to save. He

---

⁴ James Fergusson of Pitfour, a prominent member of the Scots bar, an
Episcopalian and reputed Jacobite. Boswell often sets his learning and piety
up for imitation.

⁵ The French original of this theme is printed below, p. 391.

⁶ Sir Willoughby was the nephew of Dr. Johnson's favourite, Molly Aston.

was a great hog, an enormous lout. He squinted horribly, but he was not without a kind of rude common sense; and as he had been justice of the peace for several years, he knew all about *the poor's rates*. His wife was the most ridiculous and disgusting of beings. She was nearly fifty and dressed like a girl of sixteen. She was affected and vain and insipid and capricious. Her brother, Mr. Pye, a merchant of Amsterdam, detested her. He had engaged to come and dine with her and to present his wife. Lady Aston was alone in Utrecht. Mr. Brown[7] was invited to this dinner. He went at four o'clock, fearing that he was too late. But the dinner was put off to five. My Lady became very impatient. She asked Mr. Brown if he was not hungry. He confessed that he was. 'But,' said he, 'we must wait for Mr. Pye, for he said he would be a little late.' It was a very correct and sensible remark. However, it struck my Lady's giddy brain with some disproportionate emphasis, and brought into her mind the thought: 'On my word, these bourgeois are very impolite. They ought to conform to the hours of people of quality. I will not wait another minute.' Mr. Brown begged her not to take such hasty measures, but she was inexorable. She had the dinner brought in, and my Lady and Mr. Brown took their places at a table set for eighteen. They had hardly begun on their soup when the whole company arrived, and before all the honours were done the dinner was cold. They ate it, however, and my Lady gave herself tremendous airs.

"After dinner they sat down to cards. Mr. Brown and Mr. Pye did not play, but chatted in Dutch. 'Well,' said Pye, 'have you ever seen the like of that sister of mine? I think she is the greatest fool in the world.' 'But,' said Mr. Brown, 'why do you let these people travel about any more? They expose themselves wherever they go.' 'That is true,' replied Mr. Pye, 'but I let them travel because I want to keep them away from me.'

"Sir Willoughby used to stay in bed till one o'clock. He would

---

[7] Boswell is now telling the story in the third person, but as it is impossible to fix the point at which the construction changes, it seems better to continue the marks of direct quotation.

get up and place himself before the fire with the utmost indolence. He would shout to one of his daughters, 'Polly! My shoes—Aa—'[8]. She would bring them. 'Aa—' said he, 'shoes without buckles—Aa—'. He would grumble like that through the whole morning. He was very fond of drinking when he had company. He lived in Utrecht on a magnificent footing. He received a great many courtesies. But finally he bored everybody. Guiffardière and Hill, two young preachers who liked good living, were the only ones who remained faithful to the Aston family.

"The Knight had five daughters, the eldest of whom was very amiable and suffered sadly from the absurdity of her father and her mother. Young Willoughby was the most mischievous of imps without the least trace of manners. He came one Saturday into a good-sized party without invitation. He chattered and drank and ate their cracknels until Mr. Cochrane gave him a rap on the knuckles and chased him out of the room. Such was the Aston family.

"They had a Scotch servant whom they called 'Hume' or 'Humes.' Mr. Brown asked him, 'Where did you get that name?' 'Poh!' said he, 'my name is Hugh Macgregor, but her silly Ladyship has given me the name of Humes.'

"This famous family is now at Tours in France, where they are spending more money than they spent in England."

THURSDAY 22 MARCH. Yesterday you was better. Rose and you walked after dinner. He said he was very lazy. You owned nothing. He drank coffee with you and talked of suicide. . . . You grew well at night. This day show that you are Boswell, a true soldier. Take your post. Shake off sloth and spleen, and just proceed. Nobody knows your conflicts. Be fixed as Christian, and shun vice. Go not to Amsterdam.[9] Read more law. Write Father neat clear little letter. No metaphysics. Plain things. Be silent and

---

[8] A yawn.

[9] To a brothel. See p. 236. For the first time since coming to Utrecht he is beginning to consider seriously the possibility of patriarchal indulgence.

polite always. Just resume Utrecht and expel antipathies. Affleck, Broomholm, J. Bruce.[10]

THURSDAY 22 MARCH

> And must not I have speculations sad
> Who still am shudd'ring lest I should grow mad?
> Who think that sentence is against me pass'd
> And that my reason has not long to last?
> With an alarming consciousness I feel
> My wild ideas in confusion reel,
> And through my gloomy and tumult'ous brain
> With cruel rage successive horrors reign.
> I think that I (O height of dire despair!)
> Am a poor blasted tree that cannot bear.

FRIDAY 23 MARCH. Yesterday you got up bad. After dinner you grew better. At Society *chez* Peterson (Montesquieu's principle of honour),[1] you recovered quite. You came home quite well. ... You will make a man. Adore GOD and rejoice that you are virtuous. Reserve for wife except some Maintenon[2] occur. Be good to Rose. Get little box for journal. Be a true soldier. Read more French. Saturday, journal. To keep nerves firm, shave fine. Have good humour.

[Boswell to Temple]

Utrecht, 23 March 1764

MY DEAR TEMPLE,—For some time past our correspondence has been very irregular. You delayed for two months to answer my last. I have delayed to answer yours still longer.[3] I must

[10] The Broomholm was a farm at Auchinleck, and James Bruce was the overseer.   [1] The topic discussed at the Society.

[2] That is, a mistress of a very unusual and superior sort.

[3] Temple had delayed roughly two months, for Boswell had written to him on 4 December and he had replied on 7 February. But his letter was actually

however for my vindication inform you that I have at different
times this week written you two long letters. But they were so very
splenetic that I have not sent them. During our Christmas vacation
I went to The Hague, where I passed some weeks in brilliant dissipation. I received very great civilities from my Dutch relations
and other people of the first distinction. Upon my return to Utrecht
I found that my mind had been weakened. I had not the same vigour as before. I took a severe cold, which hurt my spirits, and some
posts ago I received accounts of the death of that child of whom
you have heard me talk so much. This is an affliction of an uncommon nature; for although I never saw him, believe me, I am not
a little distressed. I mourn for an idea. I mourn for one with respect
to whom I had formed many agreeable plans which must now be
dashed from my mind.

You see a concurrence of circumstances to bring back my melancholy. You may conceive what dreary thoughts have oppressed
me. You may conceive how I have extended the gloomy prospect. I
have indeed been so bad as almost to despair. I wrote yesterday
a letter to my worthy father and told him my situation. I am vexed
that I did so. For although I have talked with moderation, yet I am
afraid he will be uneasy. I have told him that I am weary of
Utrecht, and that I am anxious to know his scheme for my travels.
This day I am so much better as to see that I must not yield to slight
disgust, that I must follow out the plan upon which I came hither,
nor think of stirring till the Civil Law lectures are ended.

I see too that I am getting improvement here. I have read
Xenophon's *Anabasis*, his *Spartan and Athenian Republics*, and
his *Life of Agesilaus*. I am now reading Plutarch's *Lives*. I shall
select some of them only. I have advanced very well in French.
I am just about finishing Voltaire's *General History*. I have picked
up a little Dutch. I have not given such application to the Civil and
Scots law as I ought to have done; however, I have done tolerably.

I am now so sadly clouded that I cannot see the advantage of

---

dated 7 January; and it is this erroneous date that Boswell has in mind when
he says he has delayed still longer.

my studies. But this must pass. I have been tormenting myself with abstract questions concerning Liberty and Necessity, the attributes of the Deity, and the origin of Evil. I have truly a dark disposition. I must be patient. I may yet become quite clear. I have rather a hard task of it. I have no friend to whom I can disclose my anxieties and receive immediate relief.

Come, I will be firm. Excuse me, my friend, for writing in this insipid manner. I never felt such an absence of genius. I never was so lumpish.

The Countess of whom I talked so much turns out a very so-so *vrouw*. I have a woeful want of discernment. Witness the beauty to whom I paid my respects last summer under the gallant name of Sir Charles Boston. How ugly did we find her![4]

Paris must no doubt be delicious at present. But I imagine I shall first take a tour in Germany. I would choose to proceed through Switzerland, Italy, Spain, and return by France.

I have no relish at present for anything. But undoubtedly I shall have some by and by. You are used to splenetic complaints. You have heard them from Clarke and from Stockdale,[5] and often and often from Boswell.

I fear my father will wish to shorten my course as much as possible. He will wish to have me at home to set me fairly a-going as a man of business. I shall do my best to please him. I may yet be an useful and respected man.

I am at this moment so well that I despise myself for having been so subdued by gloom, and I will not allow myself the vanity of being melancholy. Thus it is, my dear friend. Forgive me. I shall give you a much better epistle soon. In the mean time, I beg to hear from you without delay. Encourage me, and bid me conceal

[4] Not a hint of this is entered in the London journal of the period, nor in the parallel memoranda. Could the lady have been Miss Floyer? See p. 36.

[5] "Stockdale" is Percival Stockdale, rake, wit, clergyman, editor—the man to whom Johnson said that living in a ship was worse than living in jail. "Clarke" became an officer in the Guards. Both were friends of Temple at Cambridge.

my distress. Indeed, I have been very prudent. People only observe that I am *un peu triste*. Bless me! how easy am I just now. I am with my Temple. I am happy. Have you yet determined for the priesthood? What is Bob about? Is Claxton well? I have had a long letter from Mr. Johnson. I correspond in French with Sir David Dalrymple. I have a great quantity of journal. Should I send it to you? I left some papers in chambers. My dear friend, yours ever,

JAMES BOSWELL.

I am infinitely better. My next shall be a more agreeable epistle. Pray write soon.

SATURDAY 24 MARCH. Yesterday you was very bad after dinner, and shuddered with dire ideas. You was incertain and confused and lazy, talked of going to bed, and could scarcely read Greek. You went to Assembly. You cleared up. You went to Brown's, was cheerful and content; came home happy and resolved to do well. This day recollect the dreadful conflict which you have had. Just a return of the black foe. You have behaved well. You have only written to Father and friends, and have owned it moderately to Brown. Journal all morning. . . . Tea, Amerongen at four; five, Zélide; eight, Hungarians. . . .

SUNDAY 25 MARCH. Yesterday you awaked in great disorder, thinking that you was dying, and exclaiming, "There's no more of it! 'Tis all over." Horrid idea! You had sat up till four, writing. You got up and found that your sitting up had made quite an alteration in your system. You was clear, active, pious in a clear and benevolent manner, which you may always be. Rose's departure being fixed pleased you. Brown said that spleen is distemper, and you must with time be quite free of it. You drank tea at Zélide's; walked with Des Essar; had fine Society, Hungarians, and translated Johnson's satire[6] in Latin. This day see how you can go on. At any time sit up to cure. . . .

MONDAY 26 MARCH. Yesterday you called on Grand Bailiff, where you are always filled with excellent ideas. He said a jaunt to The Hague deranged him quite. So are men. You was much

---

[6] *London* or *The Vanity of Human Wishes*, probably the latter.

diseased, for you had during the day perhaps seven or eight different minds. . . . After you came home, you was sound: neither
high nor low. This day recollect. You've only owned a little melancholy; that's all. You have maintained character. . . . Lose no time.
But be always busy or gay. See *la Veuve*. Command tongue. Eat
moderate.

TUESDAY 27 MARCH. Yesterday, though bad in the morning,
you was well all day. You have resolved neither to own misery
nor weakness for ten days. Send to see how Zélide is. . . . At night
you was clear and happy and in humour to write. But, by reason,
you went to bed not to risk night damp. Fix law hours, and write
a page [of] Erskine as regular as ten lines; also journal, so much
each morning. Tonight mild with *la Veuve*. Write Johnston soon
. . . At all events, *retenue*. If joy comes, well. Mem. Demosthenes.[7]

[*c.* 27 MARCH. FRENCH THEME] [Indolence] attacks me
especially in the morning. I go to bed at night with the most determined resolutions to get up early. François, my faithful servant,
wakes me at half-past six. But when I open my eyes and see day-
light again, a crowd of disagreeable ideas comes into my mind.
I think gloomily of the vanity and misery of human life. I think
that it is not worth while to do anything. Everything is insipid
or everything is dark. Either my feelings will be numbed, or I shall
feel pain; and I can only solace myself with a little present ease.
Happy is the man who can forget that he exists. That is the doctrine
of Monsieur Maupertuis, who, in order to maintain his thesis that
men are desperately unhappy, observes that they try by all possible
means to escape from themselves: by sleep, by amusements, and
even by work. But this flighty philosopher has explained the
nature of man very falsely. The truth is that man is made for
action. When he is busy, he fulfils the intention of his Creator,

[7] Probably the following passage from Plutarch's *Parallel Lives:* "Demosthenes . . . regarded other points in the character of Pericles to be unsuited to
him; but his reserve and his sustained manner, and his forbearing to speak on
the sudden, or upon every occasion, as being the things to which principally
he owed his greatness, these he followed . . . " (Translation by Dryden).

and he is happy. Sleep and amusement serve to refresh his body and his mind and qualify him to continue his course of action. How is it then that I feel so gloomy every morning, and that these convincing arguments have not the least influence on my conduct? I believe the explanation is some physical disorder. My nerves at that time are relaxed, the vapours have risen to my head. If I get up and move about a little, I am happy and brisk. But it is with the utmost difficulty that I can get up. I have thought of having my bed constructed in a curious fashion. I would have it so that when I pulled a cord, the middle of the bed would be immediately raised and me raised with it and gradually set up on the floor. Thus I should be gently forced into what is good for me.[8]

TUESDAY 27 MARCH

> And must I now heroic lines compose,
> I, who fatigu'd with various thinking, doze?
> Who, by a kind of lethargy oppress'd,
> Maintain that man was only made for rest;
> Whose lazy blood is stirr'd by no desire,
> In whose fat frame there is no spark of fire,

[8] "I talked of the difficulty of rising in the morning. [Dr. Johnson told him of a home-made alarm devised by Mrs. Elizabeth Carter; when she was roused from sleep, she had no difficulty in getting up.] But I said *that* was my difficulty; and wished there could be some medicine invented which would make one rise without pain, which I never did, unless after lying in bed a very long time. Perhaps there may be something in the stores of Nature which could do this. I have thought of a pulley to raise me gradually; but that would give me pain, as it would counteract my internal inclination. I would have something that can dissipate the *vis inertiae* and give elasticity to the muscles. As I imagine that the human body may be put, by the operation of other substances, into any state in which it has ever been, and as I have experienced a state in which rising from bed was not disagreeable but easy, nay, sometimes agreeable, I suppose that this state may be produced if we knew by what. We can heat the body, we can cool it; we can give it tension or relaxation; and surely it is possible to bring it into a state in which rising from bed will not be a pain" (*Life of Johnson,* 19 September 1777).

Who the warm chimney-corner would not quit
For all the brilliant charms of lively Wit;
Nor by the voice of Glory or the Fair
Be tempted to forsake an easy-chair.

WEDNESDAY 28 MARCH. Yesterday you was still gloomy; but you read Civil and Scots law and found that they are only bugbears, and grew well. At Assembly *chez* Mademoiselles Bottestein you saw *la Veuve* and was charming, but had not time to talk fully. Hardenbroek said to her, "You are the loadstone." You said, "I am the steel." ... At night you was clear and resolved to go on manly. This day write ... Madame Spaen ...

[Boswell to Madame de Spaen. Original in French][9]

Utrecht, 28 March 1764

MADAME:—You had the goodness to tell me that you would permit me to correspond with you when my travels should have carried me to greater distance. In saying this, did you have a scheme of testing my love for your country? Did you wish to see if I could resist so great a temptation to leave it? But, Madame, is it not possible for me to enjoy so flattering a favour while I remain in Holland? This letter comes to ask it; rather to beg it.

My French is still very imperfect, but I dare risk it. I hope that you will understand me for the greater part, and when you meet phrases that are absolutely unintelligible, you have only to invite a few scholars to dinner. It will give them something to do to decipher them, and you will be pleasantly diverted. It is, however, a consolation to know that my French will all the time be improving. ...

Mademoiselle de Zuylen and I are very good friends. I find her charming, in spite of the simile of the *battalion* which amused me

[9] This, the first of several long letters to Madame de Spaen, consists mainly of compliments which I have ventured to excise. But the portion about Belle de Zuylen is interesting.

so much.[1] But granting the battalion, would one not be happy to be
its colonel? If it is "badly drilled," that must be remedied. Mademoiselle de Zuylen deserves a great deal more fame and love than
she gets. She has quite superior parts and the best heart in the
world. If I boast of her friendship, I shall be accused of tacitly
boasting that I possess wit myself. I confess that I do sometimes
pretend to a little. I fear, however, that you will say only that my
esprit resembles those other *esprits* of which we are so frightened,
those that never show themselves in company. Excuse a play on
words.[2] To tell the truth I do not make the figure in company
which I imagine in my closet. I have not yet enough breeding in
society so that I can always show uniform cheerfulness. And sometimes a proud bashfulness makes me remain in gloomy silence.

My letter is already too long. I hardly dare detain you further
to beg you to pay my respects to all those who were so kind to me at
The Hague. I have the honour to be, with the most distinguished
consideration, Madame, your most obliged and very humble
servant,

BOSWELL D'AUCHINLECK.

WEDNESDAY 28 MARCH[3]

> That life is changeful, all who live allow,
> But none e'er felt it more than I feel now.
> Last night my verses were in rueful tone,
> I tried to sing, but I could only groan.
> The blackest clouds of melancholy hung
> Upon my mind, unwieldy was my tongue.

[1] Madame de Spaen (or her husband—he was a colonel) had probably said
that Belle was as alarming as a badly drilled battalion of troops.
[2] A rather clumsy one on two meanings of the French word *esprit*: "wit" and
"ghost."
[3] The reader needs constantly to remind himself that the memoranda were
written in the morning, reviewing the events of the preceding day, while
the ten-line verses were written at night, generally with reference to events
of the day just concluding. In this instance the relief which Boswell records
came *after* the frantic gesture recorded in the memorandum dated 29 March.

And yet (what changes can produce one day!)
I now am easy, vigorous, and gay;
And am a bold and generous soldier found
Resolv'd at all events to stand my ground.

THURSDAY 29 MARCH. Yesterday you was bad in the morning, but at one you talked to Trotz of new scheme for Scots law which put you in spirits.[4] You went out to fields, and in view of the tower, drew your sword glittering in the sun,[5] and on your knee swore that if there is a Fatality, then that was also ordained; but if you had free will, as you believed, you swore and called the Great G— to witness that, although you're melancholy, you'll stand it, and for the time before you go to Hague, not own it. After dinner you mounted tower.[6] Tea, Zélide, fine; *la Veuve* there. ... This day, books to Trotz; Greek at nine. Be busy; no love, firm. You may have women as well as live full. But only fine ones.

FRIDAY 30 MARCH. Yesterday you was very well. You was, however, pretty idle except geography and Greek. You see what

[4] A proposal to translate Erskine's *Principles* into Latin. See p. 245.
[5] The "tower" is the great tower of the mediaeval cathedral. Boswell is swearing on the hilt of his sword, like his knightly ancestors.
[6] "The only substantial remains of the cathedral are one aisle, in which divine service is performed, and a lofty, magnificent Gothic tower [then 364 feet high, now 338], that stands apart from it. ... A stone staircase, steep, narrow, and winding, after passing several grated doors, leads into a floor which you hope is the top, but which is little more than half way up. Here the family of the belfry-man fill several decently furnished apartments and show the great bell, with several others, the noise of which it might be supposed no human ears could bear, as these people must at only the distance of a few yards.—After resting some minutes in a room the windows of which command perhaps a more extended land-view than any other inhabited apartment in Europe, you begin the second ascent by a staircase still narrower and steeper, and when you seem to be so weary as to be incapable of another step, half the horizon suddenly bursts upon the view, and all your complaints are overborne by expressions of admiration. ... A circle of probably more than sixty miles diameter strains the sight from this tremendous steeple" (Charles Campbell, *The Traveller's Complete Guide through Belgium, Holland, and Germany*, 1815, pp. 95–96).

fixed hours do. The Society was *chez* Rham, who gave discourse on passions and their being confused. . . . When you came home, you read a very little. You fell asleep almost on your chair, which you never knew till you came to Holland. This day at nine, Brown's, and see Wallace's Scots law, so as not to be anxious with Trotz, to whom you must only offer six ducats.[7] At half eleven, let blood, and after this no more lethargy. Go on; be firm. Home at five and journal hard; 'twill please you much hence. Never be rash.

FRIDAY 30 MARCH

> Illustrious Johnson! When of thee I think,
> Into my little self I timid shrink.
> With all my soul thy genius I admire:
> Thy vig'rous judgment, thy poetic fire,
> Thy knowledge vast, thy excellence of mirth,
> And all thy moral and religious worth.
> The noble dignity of man I see,
> But fear it cannot be attain'd by me.
> Yet I resolve the gen'rous path to try:
> Though less than thee, I may be very high.

SATURDAY 31 MARCH. Yesterday you was better. You let blood. You was resolute. Your blood was thick and black.[8] You

---

[7] George Wallace, advocate, had published in 1760 *A System of the Principles of the Law of Scotland;* Boswell may be referring to this book or (perhaps less likely, since he seems to expect to see "Wallace's Scots law" at Brown's) to notes he had taken on the lectures of William Wallace, Professor of Scots Law in the University of Edinburgh. In either case, the object of the memorandum seems to have been to assure himself that he would not be completely dependent on Trotz for "illustrations" (see p. 245). Six ducats (thirty-three guilders, something less than £3) was probably the monthly honorarium he planned to suggest, not the total that he expected to pay. See the entries for 1 and 8 April. His expense account shows that he gave Trotz only forty guilders (£3-12-9) for the entire course of lectures in Civil Law, but in that course there were several other students besides himself.

[8] "30 March, For having blood drawn, 1 guilder 10 stivers" (Expense Account). Boswell was constitutionally timid and submitted himself to bloodletting much less frequently than the majority of people of his time.

walked with Grand Bailiff. You read Greek and chased laziness.
You was at home all evening and grew bold by reading Johnson's
satires. You brought up a sweep of journal. You now know where
you are. This day, French theme. At ten, Trotz. Show specimen of
translation. Give at most ten ducats. . . .

[*c*. 31 MARCH. FRENCH THEME] . . . Des Essar is a true
pedant, a fop in learning, and sometimes he is very much mistaken.[9] He was once a Capuchin. He ran away twice from his mon-
astery, and the second time he escaped to Brussels, where he lived
for some time. He taught mathematics to people of the first rank.
He had an affair which did not go very far, but in which he behaved
like a man of honour who had noble blood, for Monsieur des Essar
is assuredly of a distinguished family, though of a rather distant
branch of it. It was discovered, however, that he had been a Capuchin, and he had to decamp. Poor man! He came into Holland like
other good Huguenots. He established himself at Amsterdam. He
had there pupils of the right sort. He belonged to a literary society
composed of men of wit and amiable women. . . . Finally Monsieur
des Essar married a young Hollandized Englishwoman. He came
to Utrecht, where he has remained for some time. He still teaches
mathematics, and he conducts the *Gazette Française*. He is extravagantly French. He is vain, he makes compliments. He gets bored,
and his misery makes the rest of us ashamed of ours, because in him
it appears so contemptible.

SUNDAY 1 APRIL. Yesterday you was fine. You lay too long
indulging. You sat long with Trotz and found him to be *avarus*.[1]
Yet you was fond of the *scheme*. You walked with Rose. After dinner Brown advised you to *scheme*, if you can labour it enough. You
thought yourself weak and not grand enough. You have always
complaints. You wrote some of *scheme*, but found it very tedious.
This day, Scots law till ten, and then eclipse,[2] and at twelve, Trotz:

[9] He had corrected Boswell's French rather rudely at the meeting of the
Literary Society on Thursday evening.

[1] "Greedy." (Boswell thinks in Latin when he thinks of Trotz.)

[2] An almost total eclipse of the sun, beginning at London at 9.14 A.M. and

tell fear that you could not write five hours a day. Advise; make bargain: for month thirty-three, or four months in all. But *think.* . . .

SUNDAY 1 APRIL

No more I'll fret because the time is long,
No more I'll call the world's great system wrong,
No more on good and evil will debate,
And walk the wilds of Liberty and Fate.
No more on wings of speculation fly:
Blind goes man's reason when it soars too high.
To solid studies I my time will give,
And as a decent worthy fellow live.
I'll be the honest Laird of Auchinleck,[3]
And from my friends and neighbours have respect.

MONDAY 2 APRIL. Yesterday you was tolerable. You went to the Observatory, but could see nothing. You called on Trotz, who was clear for *scheme,* "Si tu pensam tuam prestare possis."[4] You laboured six hours at it, and did much. At night you supped. Nothing to mark, only you speak too little, nor keep Brown enough in order. You are *retenu.* Keep to it. . . . This day see if you can go

---

reaching the maximum of eclipse at 10.42. In the manuscript of *Boswelliana* appears the following anecdote, not included in Rogers's edition and now printed with the kind permission of the owners of the manuscript, Mr. and Mrs. Donald F. Hyde: "Boswell said to Rham, a short-sighted German who had mounted the Utrecht observatory to see the eclipse, April, 1764, 'You ought to look at the ladies of the town with your telescope.' 'Sir,' said Rham, 'that would have been to look at them *de haut en bas.*'" (Literally, "from top to bottom," but in a common figurative sense, "haughtily, contemptuously": our "to look down on a person." Rham, I suppose, meant, "That would *really* be looking down on them." I am informed that a pun on *bas,* "stockings," would be impossible in good French, and would hardly have been ventured even by a German addressing a Scotsman.)
[3] Boswell here treats *Auchinleck* as a word of three syllables by the same kind of poetic license that permits Shakespeare occasionally to give three syllables to *Gloucester.*   [4] "If you can perform your daily stint."

on: seven to eight; quarter after nine to eleven; two. At night talk to Brown. But be prudent, and O think! Temple, Johnson. The Scheme will be certain, noble, and cost only cure of *lues*.[5]

TUESDAY 3 APRIL. Yesterday nothing happened, but only you was better, though still hesitating as to Scheme. This day, see how you can make it out. At one, talk again to Trotz, and perhaps begin it. *Consider:* it is a plan that may be of use to you for a whole life. It is to take a *privatissimum*[6] on the law of your country with one of the ablest lawyers in Europe, who, by comparing it with the Civil and Dutch, will give you a complete knowledge of law. It is only remaining here a month longer. At night be fine with *la Veuve* and say you're *changeant*.[7] Be more *retenu*, and have *tranquillitatem animi*.[8]

TUESDAY 3 APRIL

This night, ye gods! can I to rhyme pretend,
The night when Utrecht's dear assemblies end?
Where I again, ah! never shall appear?
Can I think thus, nor shed a gloomy tear?
Around the room my doleful eyes I cast,
And sadly mutter'd, "Is it then the last?"
At *trente-et-un* (forbidden game!) I play'd,[9]
And to take leave some small diversion made;
I made the power of British luck be felt,
And snapp'd up fourteen guilders of their *geld*.[1]

WEDNESDAY 4 APRIL. Yesterday you was pretty well, but confused and changed and desperate. After dinner you said to Rose,

[5] "Cost only as much as you would pay a surgeon for curing a venereal infection."
[6] A lecture or course of lectures given by a professor at his home to a select few, in this case to Boswell as sole student.   [7] "Changeable."
[8] "Calm of mind."
[9] "Forbidden" presumably because, having been lent by Thomas Sheridan money to pay some embarrassing card debts, he had promised never to lose more than three guineas at a sitting, and *trente-et-un* was a game in which he could easily lose more.   [1] "Money" (pronounced *gelt*).

"I have passed a very disagreeable winter of it, with little enjoyment." You was truly splenetic. You said to him after, "When I recollect, 'twas not so." You *are* imbecile. You are made by company. This day, Trotz at nine, and sign no paction but trust mutually. At dinner be easy and say as wonder, "Oh, how complaisant I was to say of Utrecht that, &c.," and swear that you're content, and that Rose *must* report so in England.² Let this be lesson of prudent silence till fit goes off. Home at five ... Mem., ... you cannot be complete all at once. Make a study of constant good humour.

WEDNESDAY 4 APRIL

> The cruel Spleen torments me now again,
> And its foul vapours sheds upon my brain.
> It comes and goes inconstant as the wind,
> And makes a sport of my unhappy mind.
> Three hours ago I was entir'ly sound:
> All was complacent, all was smiling found;
> Hearty I supped and sung a jolly song,
> And thought the time ran cheerfully along.
> But now, alas! I feel a weight of woe,
> And all confus'd and wild to bed I go.

THURSDAY 5 APRIL. Yesterday you began hour with Trotz. You was not a little gloomy. You was distressed about the Scheme. Your mind was distracted. At last a lucky hint occurred. You wrote to Maclaine, and will have his advice. You walked with Rose for last time, and had him and Carron at coffee. You supped Brown's, but was galled with his rude mirth. He is quite Scotch. He grows too free. You owned your change of ideas; 'twas wrong. Swear never own more. Go on with Scheme this week. You went to bed to see if ideas change.

² Rose had probably started the conversation of the previous day by complaining that he did not like Utrecht. Boswell's self-direction here means, "Open the subject again, and say that you made your unkind remarks about Utrecht merely out of kindness for Rose."

THURSDAY 5 APRIL

> In tepid water now I hold my feet
> And all the comfort feel of genial heat.
> Down from my head the noxious vapours flow,
> And to my heels without obstruction go.
> Last night I little slept, so that today
> The drowsy god I indolent obey.
> I scarce retain the consciousness of thought,
> And like great Homer I am nodding caught.
> One night I surely shall not be distress'd;
> One night I shall enjoy luxurious rest.

FRIDAY 6 APRIL. Yesterday after four hours' confused sleep you bounced up, went to Carron's, and according to usual form, had warm English breakfast. Then went in coach and convoyed poor Rose out of *Porte* and took leave of him. You was dreadful, but it could not be perceived. Brown told you of Limier's being vain yet timorous, and thinking people despised him; talking of his scheme to acquaintances, and at last, though a polite, pretty man——. Horrid. You shuddered. Swear drive off [such] thoughts.[3] Society was *chez vous* for last time. This day, Greek, one; Trotz, three. Resolve; recollect winter, and just go on clear. See what Maclaine says. Determine tomorrow.

SATURDAY 7 APRIL. Yesterday you was still gloomy. You began Greek at one with Brown, and did it well. You're much better of some active, springy man along with you. Suffer no antipathies to rise at Brown. He is a generous and clever little man. *Think*, talk of him as he deserves. . . . Run through *ville* to drink tea, found none, was uneasy; resolved so no more. Played two games at billiards at each coffee-house. . . . You must *this* day fix finally law Scots. Perhaps send to Professor [Trotz], not today but tomorrow. . . .

[3] "Limier" or "Limiers" is not certainly identified, but the point is clear enough: Brown told of a man much like Boswell who finally committed suicide.

[Received 7 April, the Reverend Archibald Maclaine to Boswell]

[The Hague, 6 April 1764]

My dear Sir,—You will no doubt be surprised at having received no answer to your first letter, and still more so at my letting a post pass without answering your second. Your first letter gave me inexpressible pleasure, as it confirmed me in the agreeable persuasion of my having a share in your friendship and esteem; and could the principle of self-love have conquered that unspeakable antipathy I have to writing letters, the following post would have brought you the warm expressions of that gratitude I shall ever feel when I think of your partial goodness to me.

Your second letter demands a speedy answer; and to speak frankly, that answer might be contained in two words, *nosce teipsum.*[4] Five hundred hours in one hundred days, employed upon an object where neither wit, genius, nor imagination can have the smallest exercise, and going cheek by jowl with a heavy recluse, called *privatissimum;*[5] and this labour to be undertaken by the sprightly, brilliant, amiable philosopher whom I know and you, *at present,* know not—and this work to be done at a fixed time by a man that hates restraint, and that in conjunction with a sublime Professor who talks of guilders, *rascal counters,*[6] profits, &c.—and by a man who loves change, wants often relaxation, and is subject to low spirits!—Surely you joke—or dream—or are inspired with a portion of the spirits of Cujas,[7] who has appeared to you in a vision

---

[4] "Know thyself": the Latin equivalent of Boswell's favourite Greek tag γνῶθι σεαυτόν.

[5] The sentence would be more intelligible if these two words had followed "object." The "heavy recluse" is Professor Trotz.

[6] Debased coin, quoting Shakespeare's *Julius Caesar*, IV. ii. 79–80: "When Marcus Brutus grows so covetous To lock such rascal counters from his friends." In Holland at this time all coins except the local ones were accepted at the intrinsic value of the metal they contained (Thomas Nugent, *The Grand Tour*, 3d ed., 1778, i. 51).

[7] Jacques Cujas (1522–1590), French jurist, exponent of the historical method in the teaching of law.

and taken the advantage of some foggy night, when the atmosphere loaded with heavy vapours has damped the wings of fancy, &c., &c., &c., &c.

Merriment aside, I should mightily approve of your plan were it to be executed with ease, liberty, and a proper mixture of amusement, polite literature, and *light summer reading*. The plan is good, must be useful and highly so to yourself, and *when executed*, will be a valuable present to the Republic of Letters; but if you thus measure your daily labour, as a weaver, by the yard, I will venture to foretell that before twenty days of the hundred are past, you will be wearied, *ennuyé*, you will begin to yawn, to grow drowsy, to curse plans, fixed time, measured tasks, ells of Civil Law, hundred guilders, profits of the edition; and tell Mr. Trotz that you are out of order, that your nerves are weak, your spirits low, and bid him (silently) go to the D———. My dear Boswell, the post will not wait. A hundred things prevented me from writing sooner. If this letter does not make impression, I shall send you another written at more leisure. In the mean time I am, with the warmest heart and the truest affection and esteem, ever yours,

A. MACLAINE.

SUNDAY 8 APRIL. Yesterday you awaked bad. You lay abed till nine. You sent apology to Trotz. You was uneasy. You received Maclaine's letter. It gave you pleasure. You read Greek well and did geography. You walked in Mall and played billiards. *Do so no more.* You called on Trotz; you said, "Sollicitudinem mihi dedit dubitatio." You told him, "Desinam."[8] You was well with Hungarians. . . . See objects as they really are. Be pious and constant. Once for all, *think.* You may give Trotz one hundred guilders for his assistance till the end of June, and more if it be published. 'Twill hold you firm. Be silent. You can finish the rest after. Determine to stay at Utrecht till you're in good humour and learn moral discipline. Amen. . . .

MONDAY 9 APRIL. Yesterday you awaked very bad. You got

---

[8] "My irresolution has made me nervous. . . . I shall discontinue the scheme."

up as dreary as a dromedary.... Supped Hahn's; grew well. This day, send to Brown: Greek three. Say to Trotz you'll go on by degrees, and so be content and easy. Mem., you're a man....

[Boswell to Johnston]

Utrecht, 9 April 1764

My dear Friend,—On the eight of March I received your last letter, which contained the melancholy news of my poor boy's death. It has affected me more than you could have imagined. I had cherished a fond idea. I had warmed my heart with parental affection. I had formed many agreeable plans for the young Charles. All is now wrapped in darkness. All is gone. My dear Sir! let me repeat my sincere sentiments of friendship. Let me again assure you that you are ever dear to me. Your care of my child while he lived was always tender. It showed your attachment to his father. I much approve of your having given him a decent interment and of the company that you selected. Cairnie is a worthy fellow. I have been very much obliged to him. I retain a very grateful sense of his kindness, and wish much for an opportunity of being of use to him. I have not written to him since I came abroad. I did not choose to put him to the expense of postage. Pray assure him fully of my sentiments towards him. Let me know what his schemes are, and find out if my writing to him is expected....[9]

My jaunt during the Christmas vacation produced some alteration on my mind. When I returned to Utrecht, I had not the same internal firmness that I had carried from it. I began to think that my resolute philosophy was a mere imagination which I had formed in the sober retreat of a provincial town; that I had indeed acted from this imagination and might have continued to do so, had I remained in the same uniform circumstances as when I first

[9] Cairnie was a doctor who had transmitted to Charles's mother the sums Boswell allowed her, and had delivered the child; he had also put him to nurse, and had a general oversight of his health. Boswell was attracted to him because he had been an active Jacobite, and had had many interesting adventures.

framed the idea. But, alas! a short change, a transient view of the brilliant Hague, a little tumble in the real world, shook off the fascination and showed me that I was still the same weak-minded being as ever.

I fell desperately in love with a young, beautiful, amiable, and rich widow. This passion tore and hurt my mind. I was seized with a severe cold. My nerves were relaxed, my blood was thickened. Low spirits approached. I heard of Charles's death. It shocked me. It filled me with gloomy reflections on the uncertainty of life, and that every post might bring me accounts of the departure of those whom I most regarded. I saw all things as so precarious and vain that I had no relish of them, no views to fill my mind, no motives to incite me to action. I groaned under those dismal truths which nothing but a lucky oblivion prevents from weighing down the most vivacious souls. Black melancholy again took dominion over me. All my old dreary and fretful feelings recurred. I was much worse on this account, that after my first severe fit on coming to Utrecht, I really believed that I had conquered spleen for ever, and that I should never again be overcome by it. I lived in this persuasion for four months. I had my dull hours. But I considered myself as a soldier. I endured such hardships; but I kept my post.

You may conceive what I felt on the sad conviction that my hopes were fanciful. Oh, how I was galled! Oh, how did I despise myself! I must mention one circumstance which is very hard. When I am attacked by melancholy, I seldom enjoy the comforts of religion. A future state seems so clouded, and my attempts towards devotion are so unsuitable, that I often withdraw my mind from divine subjects lest I should communicate to the most sublime and cheering doctrines my own imbecility and sadness. In short, for some weeks past I have suffered much. . . .

I shall be here till July or August. My route after that is not yet fixed. You shall hear it particularly. Come, my friend, let us both determine to be manly; let us "resist the devil and he will flee far from us."[1] Here is my plan. I am to travel. I am to return to

---

[1] James, 4. 7.

Scotland, put on the gown, remain advocate or get into Parliament, and at last be comfortably settled in a good office. I hope also to do good at Auchinleck. The great point is to be always employed, as my worthy father says. Upon this principle he has always been happy. Long may he be so.

I have now proper ideas of religion. That is the most important article indeed. I am determined to act my part with vigour, and I doubt not to have a reward. My mind will go always stronger by discipline. Even this last attack has not been unrepelled by me. I really believe that these grievous complaints should not be vented; they should be considered as absurd chimeras, whose reality should not be allowed in words. One thing I am sure of, that if a man can believe himself well, he will be really so. The dignity of human nature is a noble preservative of the soul. Let us consider ourselves as immortal beings, who though now in a state inferior to our faculties, may one day hope to exult in the regions of light and glory. My dear Johnston, let us retain this splendid sentiment. Let us take all opportunities of elevating our minds by devotion, and let us indulge the expectation of meeting in heaven. But, at the same time, let us do our best in the state where GOD has placed us. Let us imitate the amiable Pitfour. Who is a better member of society? Yet who is a greater saint?

Write to me very fully. I will disdain to own that the melancholy fiend can get the better of me. I even hesitated if I should inform *you* of this last conflict. But to my friend I will own every weakness. My great loss[2] is an inconstancy of mind. I never view things in the same light for a month together. Are you so? . . . This letter carries its own apology. Write soon and give me full advices, and put my future life in Britain in agreeable colours. I have need of your assistance. May GOD bless you, my dear friend, prays yours ever,

JAMES BOSWELL.

TUESDAY 10 APRIL. Yesterday you was dreary. You could read none but hour of Greek. . . . You told *la Veuve*, "I could not bring

[2] "Lack"—a usage that seems very old-fashioned for 1764.

myself to confess the truth, and here it is.[3] I adore you, but I would not marry you for anything in the world. My feelings have changed." MME GEELVINCK. "You are very frank." BOSWELL. "But I can see you sometimes?" MME GEELVINCK. "Yes." In short, *perdidi diem*.[4] I did nothing. This day, rouse up: two or three hours Erskine, French version, journal. Swear yield not to idle spleen. . . .

[*c.* 10 APRIL. FRENCH THEME] I believe there have been very few Englishmen who have wanted so much to learn French as I, and I believe too that there have been very few of them who have made more rapid progress in that language than I have. It is not necessary to recapitulate the means by which I have advanced to the point where I now stand. One would find it very tiresome to hear me tell of my themes every morning, of the two hours a day that I have read French books, and of the foreign companies in which I have tried to profit all I could. I confess, however, that I do not speak French correctly. It is the common fault of all my countrymen. Mademoiselle de Zuylen once said to me, "You Englishmen never respect the tenses or the genders, or any distinctions of that sort, although you have learned them in Latin." I laughed and tried to turn the matter into a jest. All the same, I could not but feel that I was very much in the wrong, and that I was almost in the same case as an old Englishwoman who breaks all the rules of grammar and makes a ludicrous hodge-podge of crippled sentences. I must therefore apply myself sedulously to the *minutiae,* so to speak, of the French language. I must not give in to my indolent and negligent humour. No, I will not give in. I am resolved to write two pages carefully every day, and for each mistake that I make in grammar, I bind myself to pay a fine of a sou to the poor. . . .

WEDNESDAY 11 APRIL. Yesterday you got up as miserable as a being could be. All was insipid and dreary. But, blockhead that you are, have you not experienced this five hundred times? And can you not, as Sir William Temple says, "let such fits pass and return to yourself?"[5] Remember this. Do no follies. Do the duties

[3] "Je ne pouvois pas me confier et voici."
[4] "I lost a day," a famous remark of the Emperor Titus.   [5] See p. 123 *n.* 3.

of a Man. Keep your affairs in a good creditable situation, and so have comfort, and joy when well. Swear this and *retenue,* and you may defy the fiend. You read Greek well. You played billiards ... You grew quite well. But you laboured not enough. This day, French version[6] and two hours translation, morning; Greek, geography; Zélide, four; home six and translation and Voltaire till nine. You'll leave Utrecht with character. Monday and Tuesday, journal. Wednesday, Hague. Rise early to brace nerves. Think not to whore except very ——[7]

WEDNESDAY 11 APRIL

> Sure, of all clubs that ever yet were seen,
> The strangest club is that where I have been.
> It was indeed a truly precious sight
> To me who in rich ridicule delight.
> Say, is it possible to laugh too much
> At twelve or fourteen young untoward Dutch,
> Who come together duly once a week
> The English language horridly to speak,
> Mount on a stove a bowl of punch and rum,
> And British airs without compassion hum?

THURSDAY 12 APRIL. Yesterday you was still disordered. You had many changes. You received letter from Madame Spaen. That roused you and put you in mind that you are "Boswell of Auchinleck." You read your Greek well. You drank tea with Peterson; *do so no more; 'tis low.*[8] You passed the evening at home till nine, and by writing kept off dreary thoughts. You supped English Society.[9]

[6] As a matter of fact, the "French version" had almost ceased. Between 30 March and 20 April he wrote only seven pages, most of which are printed above.

[7] He did not finish the phrase, and struck out the qualification, probably as soon as he had written it.

[8] Peterson (presumably a Scandinavian) was a member of the Literary Society. Why Boswell thought his company "low" does not appear.

[9] The club of "young untoward Dutch" described above.

You had no pleasure in life, and your religion was dark. Yet you was gay, and sung. You are a fine fellow. You fight bravely. This day, much Erskine and Voltaire. Mem. Sir David [Dalrymple], nor be idle. Mem. *retenue,* and even softly with Maclaine.[1] No dire devotion.

[Received 11 April, Madame de Spaen to Boswell. Original in French]

The Hague, 10 April 1764

SIR:—Was it not a little through pride that you honoured me with a letter? Was it not to show me the great progress which you have made in the French language? Truly, I was astonished at it; and if I had been so indiscreet as to show your letter to scholars or to men of fashion, it would certainly not have been to get it deciphered nor to laugh at it. No, Sir, it would have been to get you admired for having mastered the language in so short a time, even to its delicacy and energy. This phrase "proud bashfulness"[2] is a good proof of what I have just been saying. I agree also with you in thinking well of the "battalion," &c.

Whatever may have been your motive, the result has given me much pleasure, since it has caused you to begin a correspondence, the wit of which I foresee, Sir, will all be on your side. I do not wish to deceive you and so confess candidly that I feel sure my scribbling will bore you. I have neither a lively imagination nor the gift of expressing myself well. One or the other is necessary for making a literary correspondence amusing and interesting. After what I have just said, you will decide whether you want my replies; but as for *your* letters, I demand them of you, even with eagerness, having a lively desire to see the remarks you will make on each country and people. If you have made any on my countrymen, you would oblige me greatly if you would let me see them. I believe they would be very judicious and even impartial. Nothing gives

---

[1] "Go slow in opening your mind even to Maclaine."
[2] "De la modestie orgueilleuse."

me greater pleasure than to see the people of Holland judged in this fashion.

I congratulate Mademoiselle de Zuylen and you, Sir, for being good friends; neither of you can fail to profit by the relationship. That amiable young lady proves that wit and beauty adorn each other reciprocally; and that there is no truth in the accusation that all pretty women neglect the former so as to occupy themselves solely with their faces. I am not surprised at all you say concerning her. A great many people think as you do. But what does surprise me is that you do not say a single word concerning a certain charming widow. I am, however, assured that she has found favour in your eyes, that she has even made a very lively impression on you. Might that not make you stay longer in Holland? Certain attachments sometimes upset many a project: witness Lord Fordwich, who in spite of all his promises and the anxious desires of his family to have him home, cannot resolve to quit Florence. Something, however, has just happened which may change his way of thinking a little. It is said that the Duke of York has taken a fancy to the lady who has bound my Lord in such strong chains. If he is sacrificed, anger perhaps will accomplish what reason could not. I heartily hope so.[3]

I hope, Sir, that you will not expect me to reply to all the kind and obliging things you have said to prove that you enjoyed your visit to The Hague. If our house contributed to your pleasure, be persuaded that we thought the advantage was all on our side, in

[3] Lord Fordwich was son and heir to Earl Cowper. "The third Earl Cowper, who had gone to travel in his father's life, fell in love at Florence with a married lady, and could not be prevailed on by the most earnest entreaties of his dying father to come to England. He continued there for many years after the death of his father and the extinction of his own passion; married an English young gentlewoman there, and in the year 1781 sent his children by her to England, without coming himself." (Note by Horace Walpole on a letter to Sir Horace Mann, 13 November 1765. Mann's letter, which Walpole is answering, identifies the married lady as Maria Maddalena de' Medici, Marchesa Corsi. Information kindly furnished by Dr. George Lam of the editorial staff of the Yale Edition of Horace Walpole's Correspondence.)

your having been willing to give us the pleasure of your company. If your plan to tour Germany still holds, I hope you will come and see us at Cleves. I shall repeat the invitation two weeks hence in Utrecht, through which I plan to pass on the way to Bellevue. In the mean time I have one favour to ask of you, and that is not to show my letters to any one whatsoever. My self-respect demands that absolutely; and by granting it you will oblige infinitely her who has the honour to be, Sir, your most humble and obedient servant,

B. DE SPAEN, NÉE C. DE NASSAU.

I have said nothing concerning Monsieur de Spaen. He is at his garrison, and is in excellent health.

FRIDAY 13 APRIL. Yesterday you awaked shocked, having dreamt you was condemned to be hanged. You lay dozing long. You was so sad that old Cirkz bid you not *take thought*. You was weak and mean and childish and infidel. At dinner you was disgusted. After it, you could not bear Brown's saying, "Give my service to General." You must fortify against these little rubs. You *can* do it. You saw Miss Stewart's marriage in news. It galled you.[4] You walked, just as at worst at Auchinleck. Oh! Oh! You supped General Tuyll's, fine. . . . This day, rouse. Mem., you've not owned. If so, you do no harm. You'll be strong. Be on guard.

SATURDAY 14 APRIL. Yesterday you was still amazingly gloomy. However, you said nothing. You played at billiards with Carron, and had him at coffee. But owned nothing. You went at seven to Monsieur de Zuylen's. You played *partie*, you grew well. You supped between Zélide and Madame Geelvinck. You talked of misery, but kept secret. You tried to sit up. But it won't do in Holland. This day, several pages of Erskine and some journal. Resolve: be busy and recover mind. Take no step, and nought appears.

[4] "Edinburgh, March 30. Monday Sir William Maxwell, of Springkell, in Scotland, Bart., was married to Miss Stewart, only daughter of Sir Michael Stewart, of Blackhall, Bart." (*London Chronicle*, 3 April 1764). Sir William was a cousin of Boswell's.

[Received 14 April, Lord Auchinleck to Boswell]

Auchinleck, 2 April 1764

MY DEAR SON,—Yours of the 20th of March came to hand on Friday. I looked for it with impatience, as I had not heard from you for a month. I entreat you not to let again so great an interval be between your letters, as we are, you may be sure, anxious to hear from you. There is no necessity among friends to wait till materials cast up for a long letter. Cicero, whose *Epistles* surpass anything of that kind yet published, has sometimes to his friend no more than, "Si tu vales, bene est; ego valeo."[5]

Your letter gave me great concern when it came, though I must find fault with you for concealing from me so long the distress you was under. Be assured you have no friend can sympathize so much with you as I do. GOD ALMIGHTY describes his pity for mankind by comparing it to that of an earthly father; and my experience in the world puts it in my power to suggest things may be of use to you under every distress. I have the greatest feeling for you under these melancholy fits you are sometimes attacked with, but for your comfort know that numbers who have been subject to this distress in a much greater degree have made a good and an useful figure in life. You are not therefore to despond or despair; on the contrary, you must arm yourself doubly against them, as the poet directs: "Tu ne cede malis, sed contra audentior ito."[6] Neither are you to imagine that variety of company and of diversions is the proper cure. I can assure you from the authority of severals[7] very sensible people who were subject to this disorder that it is just the reverse. It is like an opiate which allays the trouble for a little, but that is all; the trouble bursts out afterwards with double force. The only certain cure is to acquire the knowledge of as many things that you may constantly command as possible, for this is clear: that idleness to those who have a vicious turn is the mother of all manner of vice,

[5] "If you are well, good; I am well."
[6] "Do not succumb to misfortunes, but march the more boldly against them" (Virgil, *Aeneid*, VI. 95).   [7] A Scotticism.

and to those who have a virtuous turn, it commonly produces melancholy and gloom. The point therefore is still to be busy at something, and then melancholy cannot find a lodging.

My worthy father, whom you justly notice had a melancholic turn, was never troubled with it in Session time. Business drove it away. In the vacation, indeed, as he had not acquired tastes for amusing himself to fill up the vacancies in his mind, melancholy frequently got hold of him. My constitution, blessed be GOD, is good, but when I happen to be from home and ill set,[8] I am as unhappy as anybody indeed. When I am at home, whether in town or country, the case is different, for when in Edinburgh the Session business and now and then at a spare hour Horace, Anacreon, *Fingal,* Lady Mary Wortley, and the like come readily in to amuse. And on Sunday good old Erasmus and Bishop Latimer are my entertainment and instructors.

As for your modern polemic writers, essayers, &c., I know nothing of them. When I was young, I read sundry of these performances, and observed that, prompted by vanity, they endeavoured to strike out no path not tending to make men more useful or giving them any desire to be so.[9] I therefore returned to the good old stagers who had stood the test of ages, and considered the modern authors (a very few excepted) to be like almanacs, which go out of request when they lose their new face.

When I come to the country, my understanding planting gives me a taste for it that is my business; and in bad days, such as we have had mostly since we came out here, I go up to the library, sort my books, look at my medals and natural curiosities, and am quite happy. I have always recommended to you to acquire a taste for planting and gardening, and you'll find it of the greatest use. In short, the more of these tastes you acquire, so much the better. And it is in vain to say that a taste is natural and not to be acquired. The last is undoubtedly the case: practice and habit is all.

[8] "Out of sorts."
[9] Lord Auchinleck has got in an extra negative. Read "to strike out no path tending," &c.

The same post that brought yours brought me a most obliging
letter from Monsieur Sommelsdyck, who, I am glad to find, writes
of you with regard. I have got his great-grandfather's charter of
naturalisation in Scotland elegantly wrote by Mr. George Frazer,
and have got it signed by the Deputy Director of the Chancery, so
that it bears faith as much as the principal.¹⁰ It goes to you to the
care of Mr. Davidson by the first ship, and along with it Erskine's
Institutes. . . . You may open up the box which is addressed for
Mr. Sommelsdyck and read over the paper and then put it up
again. He is anxious to have it, as he writes me. In the little box
with Erskine's *Institutes* are two or three Session papers, one wrote
by your friend H. Dundas.¹

If you incline to go to The Hague for two-three days at Easter,
it won't be amiss; and as you have clothes, the expense can be but
a trifle.

As to news in this country, I shall mention three marriages:
Mr. Fraser (young Strichen) to Miss Menzies, a niece of Culdares;
Sir William Maxwell (Springkell) to Miss Stewart, Sir Michael's
daughter (both these are over); and Sir R. Mackenzie to Miss
Colquhoun, which I formerly mentioned, but it is not to be for
some days yet. Your Dutch wit and Dutch widow are not so easily
catched as our Scots lasses.²

I go the North Circuit this season. Lord Prestongrange is my
colleague; but, poor man, he is gone for Bath in a very declining

¹⁰ "So that it has as much legal force as the original document."
¹ To spur Boswell on, Lord Auchinleck reminds him that his younger contemporary and classmate in college, Henry Dundas, has already been admitted to the bar and is in practice. As a matter of fact, he was not a "friend";
Boswell and Temple had always disliked him for what they considered his
coarse ambition. He was appointed Solicitor General at twenty-four, Lord
Advocate for Scotland at thirty-three, and in middle age established himself
as the political dictator of all Scotland.
² Lord Auchinleck had wished Boswell to marry Miss Colquhoun; and, as
we have seen, Boswell had himself entertained the thought of marrying Miss
Stewart.

state. Johnny goes with me, and I leave him with the regiment, which is at Fort Augustus.

As to the course you should steer when the college is over, and when I hope you shall emulate Sir David in reputation, I am at some loss what to advise. In general, I must tell you that travelling is a very useless thing, further than for one to say they have travelled; and therefore think you should spend very little time that way. You may think and advise whether it would be best to go through some of the German courts or go through Flanders and see Paris. The Prince of Brunswick, the Prince of Baden-Durlach, and the King of Prussia Lord Marischal recommends; and I can get him (whom I am to see at Aberdeen) to recommend to them all; and Mr. Mitchell, my friend at Berlin, will treat you kindly.[3] I could wish to see you 'gainst winter at home. I shall be at this place till the 5th of May, at Perth from the 9th to the 15, at Aberdeen from the 18 to the 24, and then go to Inverness. Pray write me directly on receipt of this. Your mother is some better since she came out. She and Johnny salute you. I am your affectionate father,

ALEXR. BOSWEL.

SUNDAY 15 APRIL. Yesterday, after late sitting up, you rose with blood changed: all well, all gay. . . . You received excellent letter from worthy father, who sympathized with your distress and gave you noble ideas. His mention of *return* roused you. You read Greek fine. You was cheerful at dinner, and after it told one or two stories and heard plan of travel, which mark. . . . Brown said you'd be better of travelling, and he'd mention some things. Then you was at concert (Hahnus), and had Hungarians,[4] fine.

[3] Lord Marischal is characterized below, p. 268. Andrew Mitchell (knighted in 1765) was British envoy to Frederick the Great. He had studied at both Edinburgh and Leyden.

[4] Possibly "Hungarian": the manuscript has merely *Hung.* See p. 172 *n.* 8. But as this was a night when the society for Latin conversation was supposed to meet, he probably here means the entire group.

This day copy Zélide, or write some journal and Erskine. Lose not Plan. Mem. your fine situation here ... Think if GOD really forbids girls. Dine not this week. Apply French.

MONDAY 16 APRIL. Yesterday you was so-so. You passed the day in reading and writing. At church you was dismal. After it, bad, and played at billiards. Resolve no more of that. You wrote letter to Temple, and grew quite well. This day send to Brown that you'll read Greek at twelve. Tell him you was really not well. Besides, 'tis Holy Week. Be grave. Journal neat. . . .

[Boswell to Temple]

Utrecht, 17 April 1764

MY DEAR TEMPLE,—My last letter has no doubt given you some uneasiness, as it contained accounts of a return of that gloomy distress from which I had flattered myself that I should for the rest of my life be free. But, alas! I have sadly felt that my hopes were vain. I have been almost as miserable as ever. I wrote a folio page and a half last night, relating the dismal thoughts which disturbed my mind. But I found myself gravely rounding most solemn periods of the wildest absurdity. . . .⁵ I am now employing an hour in which "Boswell is himself" to write to my dear Temple; and I please myself by thinking that what I write may be of service to us both. . . .

You tell me you fear you shall not have a competency. Think, my dear Temple! how these words must affect me. And yet, will you believe that upon reflection, I cannot feel much pain on that account? I am almost certain of having a handsome fortune, and have no notion that you should not share it with me. Be assured that I am sincere when I talk thus. You must remember our conversation in the Temple garden. True disinterested, celestial friendship is rarely found. But that it really exists you and I afford a

⁵ He destroyed this letter, wrote another shortly after midnight (that is, very early on the morning of 17 April), and a third later in the day.

certain proof. Believe me, my dearest Temple—I wish you saw the generous tear which now fills my eye—believe me, my friend, that I have an entire confidence in *you*, and that the sacred flame is never extinguished in *my* breast. I have not words to express my feelings. I fear not to write to you in this strong incorrect manner. My heart speaks. . . .

Pray, are you subject to this mutability which ruins me? Give me your advice how I may cure it; or must Time do it by gradual operation? My ideas alter above all with respect to my own character. Sometimes I think myself good for nothing, and sometimes the finest fellow in the world. You know I went abroad determined to attain a composed, learned, and virtuous character. I have supported this character to admiration. No Briton since Sir David Dalrymple ever met with such a reception at Utrecht. I wish only that you could have my character from the people here. Certain it is that I have for seven months conducted myself in a manly and genteel manner. "All is well, then," one would say. It is so in all appearance. But I, who am conscious of changes and waverings and weaknesses and horrors, can I look upon myself as a man of dignity?

I have kept my mind to myself. I have only owned that I was a little low-spirited, but uttered none of the distracted reveries which tormented my brain. Rouse me to ardour, my friend. Impart to me a portion of your calm firmness.

I ask you this. If I persist in study, and never mention my splenetic chimeras, am I not then a man? Can I not review my life with pride? Counsel me. I will swear to observe the precepts of my friend. Tomorrow I go to The Hague for a week. Let us correspond frequently. I am ever yours,

JAMES BOSWELL.

I am vexed that my paper is filled up. I could talk to you this hour yet. I shall probably write again from The Hague.

Give me your impartial opinion of your friend, and your best counsel.

Read this letter first.⁶

Remember me in the kindest manner to Nicholls, to Claxton, and to Bob, when you write to him.

My dear Temple! what a friend have you got in me! Write fully and furnish me with agreeable ideas. If I can preserve an external uniformity, it is much. I am anxious to hear from you.

[Boswell to Temple]

Utrecht, 17 April 1764

My dearest Temple,—You must not grudge a shilling extraordinary this post. Were I now in London, you should be put to much more expense. I would hurry you away to Drury Lane or to Covent Garden, to Ranelagh or to the tavern. Perhaps a chariot might be ordered to the Temple Gate, and we might drive with gay velocity to Richmond or to Windsor. You see my foreign airs. Nothing will serve me but a chariot. It is so long since I have seen a post-chaise that I have almost forgot there is such a machine.

Could I but see my worthy friend at this moment! Could I but behold the wonder and pleasure which spreads over his countenance! But sea and land conspire to separate us. It is impossible for me to talk to you. I therefore sit down to write. My letter of last night, which is enclosed in this, is the sedate production of a man just recovered from a severe fit of melancholy. The letter which you are now reading is the spontaneous effusion of a man fully restored to life and to joy, whose blood is bounding through his veins, and whose spirits are at the highest pitch of elevation. Good heaven! what is Boswell? Last night he was himself. Today he is more than himself.

Let me think. Am I indeed the same being who was lately so wretched, to whom all things appeared so dismal, who imagined himself of no manner of value? Now I am happy. All things appear cheerful. I am a worthy, an amiable, and a brilliant man. I am

⁶ This and the two following postscripts were added after the letter following this had been written, or at least after Boswell had decided to write it.

at a foreign university town. I am advancing in knowledge. I am received upon the very best footing by the people of rank in this country. My days of dissipation and absurdity are past. I am now pursuing the road of propriety. I am acting as well as my friends could wish. I am forming into a character which may do honour to the ancient family which I am born to represent.

But, my dear friend! I feel something more. I feel a glow of delight. I feel a real ecstasy. You have seen me thus. At times we have both been so. Our souls have mingled in exalted friendship, in transport divine. Let us recall such splendid moments. Let us hope for many such in a future world. The frame which I am now in is to me a convincing evidence of the immortality of the soul.— Infinite Deity, from whom I derived my being! I doubt not that this ethereal spirit shall ever live, shall be more and more refined, and shall at last arrive at a state of supreme felicity.

What think you of me now, Temple? Was there ever such a change? Two days ago, I should have considered it as absolutely impossible. All I expected was to be tolerably patient. I dreamt not of the least glimpse of joy. I have an entire new set of ideas. I look back with astonishment on my history since I came abroad, and cannot conceive how it has happened.

Thus I explain it. I have constitutionally a tender and a gloomy mind. After being convinced that idleness and folly rendered me unhappy, I determined to alter my conduct. But my enthusiasm determined too much. I proposed to myself a plan so very severe that my feeble powers were crushed in attempting to put it in execution. Hence was I thrown into that deplorable state which my dismal letter from Rotterdam informed you of. You know how I picked up resolution and returned to Utrecht. You know how I have struggled, and how much I have been able to do. But still a black cloud hung over me. Still I was but a distempered creature, who strove to make the best he could of a wretched existence. I had great merit in this. I stood the most grievous shocks.

Now the cloud is removed. All is clear around me. Upon a retrospective view of that time which I have passed with so much anxiety and so much horror, it looks like a dream. What had I to fear? What cause of terror existed then which does not equally exist at present? Yet let me remember this truth: I am subject to melancholy, and of the operations of melancholy, reason can give no account. Ah! Temple! is it not morally certain that I shall ere long be as much depressed as ever? Shall I not again groan beneath a weight of woe? Shall I not despise this very letter which conveys to you the accounts of my exceeding elevation? Perhaps not. Perhaps I shall never again be melancholy. This is possible; much more so than those chimeras which I have shuddered to think of. Formerly I have had vivacious days. But I had no solid cause to hope for their continuance. My mind had no stable principles. I was the mere slave of caprice. Now I can calmly revolve my plan of conduct. I can "know myself a Man!"[7]

My dearest friend! let this letter give you pleasure. Am I not acting properly in writing to you an account of this prodigious change? I have acquired a degree of reserve. During my season of darkness, I was able to conceal my complaints. I find it more difficult to conceal my joy. To you, my friend, I can freely disclose both.

Now when I am clear and happy, let me renew my good resolutions. Let me above all maintain an uniformity of behaviour. It is certain that I am subject to melancholy. It is the distemper of our family. I am equally subject to excessive high spirits. Such is my constitution. Let me study it, and let me maintain an equality of mind. You have this post a variety of circumstances laid before you. Consider them, my friend, and send me a long letter of kind advice.

I wrote to my father an account of my late dreary state of mind. ... Worthy man! I hope to give him satisfaction. He is perhaps too anxiously devoted to utility. He tells me that he thinks little time

> Teach me to love and to forgive,
> Exact my own defects to scan,
> What others are, to feel, and know myself a Man.
> Thomas Gray, *Hymn to Adversity*, conclusion.

should be spent in travelling; and that he would have me make a tour through some of the German courts, or through Flanders and part of France, and return to Scotland against winter. You will agree with me in thinking this scheme greatly too confined. I laid my account with travelling for at least a couple of years after leaving this. I must however compound matters. I shall insist upon being abroad another winter, and so may pursue the following plan.

I shall set out from Utrecht about the middle of June. I shall make the tour of The Netherlands, from thence proceed to Germany, where I shall visit the Courts of Brunswick and Lüneburg, and about the end of August arrive at Berlin. I shall pass a month there. In the end of September I shall go to the Court of Baden-Durlach, from thence through Switzerland to Geneva. I shall visit Rousseau and Voltaire, and about the middle of November shall cross the Alps and get fairly into Italy. I shall there pass a delicious winter, and in April shall pass the Pyrenees and get into Spain, remain there a couple of months, and at last come to Paris. Upon this plan, I cannot expect to be in Britain before the autumn of 1765. Pray give me your opinion of it. I think it is an excellent plan. Perhaps I allow myself too little time for it. However, I may perhaps prevail with my father to allow me more time. When a son is at a distance, he can have great influence upon an affectionate parent. I would by no means be extravagant; I would only travel genteelly.

Miss Stewart is now Lady Maxwell. So much for that scheme, which I consulted you upon some months ago. There are two ladies here, a young, handsome, amiable widow with £4000 a year, and Mademoiselle de Zuylen, who has only a fortune of £20,000. She is a charming creature. But she is a *savante* and a *bel esprit,* and has published some things. She is much my superior. One does not like that. One does not like a widow, neither. You won't allow me to yoke myself here? You *will* have me married to an Englishwoman?

I have now written my most intimate thoughts. Tomorrow I

go to The Hague for a week. God bless you.—Write soon. I ever
remain, your most affectionate friend,

JAMES BOSWELL.

WEDNESDAY 18 APRIL. Yesterday you continued in a kind of
delirium. You wrote all day. At night you was at Monsieur de
Zuylen's. You said one might trace resemblance in a young child
as in a piece of wood, or a cinder, or the head of a staff.[8] Zélide
was *nervish*. You saw she would make a sad wife and propagate
wretches. You reflected when you came home that you have not
made enough use of your time. You have not been active enough,
learned enough Dutch, enough of manners. The months which
remain, employ with more vigour. *Last night* you did not write
lines.[9] You are only to do so when in humour. *Swear* this morning
to keep Plan. Have a care. You may grow idle. Stop. Resolve copy
one or two pages [of] Erskine each day, besides reading and writing French. Shun indolence. At Leyden make out plan for Hague.
Only be *retenu*. . . .

THURSDAY 19 APRIL. Yesterday you got up with much reluc-
tance. You was dreary in bark with Mademoiselle Vernett, who
told stories of religious melancholy. . . . You came to Leyden in
good time. At five, went to Monsieur Gronovius; had coffee, fine;
walked to Garden.[1] Ideas altered; was calmly happy, yet remembered melancholy. . . . You went and drank wine with him. Came
to inn, wrote Erskine, was quite clear, lively, ambitious. Forgot
all your spleen. See today how you do. Johnson. Plan. Maclaine
to sup neat. Yet be on guard.

FRIDAY 20 APRIL. (Good Friday. Be holy and fine, English
———— .[2]) Yesterday, after sleeping with clothes on and having a
night all glowing with fiery vivacious blood, you got up well,
breakfasted with Gordon, and was equal to him in vivacity, and far
above him in force. . . . You visited Abraham Gronovius once more,
and was fine; promised white port, and to see him again. You was

[8] That is, one may *imagine* a resemblance.
[9] Nor a memorandum in the morning, either. The ten-line verses were not
resumed until 1 October 1764.   [1] The Botanic Garden.   [2] English Chapel.

rather too high and looked with astonishment at Leyden, where
you had been so horrid, and loved it for Father's sake. Came pleasant to Hague; quite new ideas; entered Maréchal as young man of
fashion. Sent to Maclaine; had him and Richardson both to wait on
you. Quite man of respect. O noble! In delicious spirits. This day,
cards. At ten, Yorke, fine. After, Sommelsdyck, Spaen, Maasdam,
De Wilhem ... Have a care. Don't seem altered. Have Temple's
uniformity; and if you're clear, girl ...[3]

[20 APRIL. FRENCH THEME] This is the first of the days
that I plan to spend at The Hague during the Easter vacation. I
find this beautiful city more charming than the first time I was
here. It was then Christmas, the most severe weather of the entire
year. The trees were all leafless. The fields were all brown. But
now the trees are well leafed out and the fields are vividly green.
As for the air, I cannot say much. The month of April is always uncertain, and this year it is more uncertain than usual. However, I
imagine that we shall have fairly settled weather, if one may
judge from Monsieur Gronovius's cat at Leyden, which (as they
say) washed its face, and that is a certain sign of good weather.
Besides, the sky appears clear, and there is a remarkable softness
in the air which flatters us with the promise of fair weather. It
is now Holy Week, so every one is in seclusion and the city does not
have the same brilliance that it had in the winter. There are no
plays. There are almost no assemblies. Moreover, The Hague does
not have the charms of novelty that it had when I was here for the
first time.

I have dressed myself. I have gone out. I have left cards for
many people. I have been at the Society. I was received at the
house of Captain Reynst. I found him in undress, seated in a very
handsome room adorned with elegant pictures. He said to me, "Sir,
I love to be well lodged. When one is comfortable at home, one
stays all morning in one's lodgings. One reads, one never gets bored,
and that is much." "Yes, Sir," I replied. "In that way one is inde-

[3] About seven words following this have been heavily deleted by Boswell
himself.

pendent. One has no need of others to be amused." He continued, "I am not on good terms with Mademoiselle de Zuylen. I supped with her at Madame Degenfeld's, and we had a little dispute. We were speaking of a certain person, and I said in passing that there was a story about that person that was not so pretty; however, I had no wish to say more. Mademoiselle de Zuylen said to me eagerly, 'Please tell me that story.' I did so. But when I had finished, she said to me, 'Sir, I knew that story as well as you. But one ought not always to repeat everything people say.' I was a little piqued, and I replied, 'Mademoiselle, it was by your orders that I did it, and I did it in good faith. I thought you were as candid as I. I have been the dupe of my own civility.' That was not at all pleasant. But really, though Mademoiselle de Zuylen has a great deal of wit, she tries too hard to be subtle. She was brought up at Geneva, where certainly there is unlimited wit among the ladies. But they lack good principles. They sometimes sacrifice probity to brilliance."

Really, Monsieur Reynst gave me a far from favourable idea of my dear Zélide. I would give a great deal to cure myself of my weakness of being too much affected by the opinions of others. Reynst changed to some extent my idea of Zélide. However, I fought like her champion. I said, "That young lady makes me feel very humble, when I find her so much above me in wit, in knowledge, in good sense." "Excuse me," said Reynst. "She lacks good sense and consequently she goes wrong; and a man who has not half her wit and knowledge may still be above her." I made no reply to that. I thought it very true, and I thought it was a good thing. For if it were not for that lack, Zélide would have an absolute power. She would have unlimited dominion over men, and would overthrow the dignity of the male sex.

SATURDAY 21 APRIL. Yesterday you waked so-so; got up and breakfasted in fine spirits and dressed elegant and went to Yorke's; found Richardson pulling on surplice; was struck with Cambridge ideas. In chapel, had a group of fine circumstances: Hague; Ambassador's chapel; Baron Winn; Hon. Charles Gordon; Richardson,

son of Cambridge head.[4] Yorke was elegant, and told stories of Lady Findlater, who went with Duke's secretary to see Culloden, and mounted box; but going back made pull up blinds. "I love to see them killed, but not dead." Noble. My Lord, &c.: "He's my *baastard*."[5] ... This day, rouse, recollect. You have done no harm. . . .

SUNDAY 22 APRIL. Yesterday you called on Maclaine. He said he had not for twelve years altered his sentiments in important matters. . . . You was dreary, but had not time to talk of spirits. . . . This day (*Easter*) rouse. Be Johnson. You've done no harm. Be *retenu*, &c. *What* am I? Oho! is it so? I'll marry English lady. At all events, be *manly*, and Sir David, &c.

MONDAY 23 APRIL. Yesterday though *Easter*, you got up quite gloomy and confused. However, you cleared and went to Chapel. Confess, even in Ambassador's elegant Church-of-England chapel, you was gloomy and fretful. Yet a good sermon and prayers raised your devotion, and you received sacrament seriously. Afterwards walked with Caldwell[6] and Richardson, who was quite Cambridge and happy. Dined inn, and had Caldwell, &c., at tea, and was for *contingents*.[7] ... This day, physic; resolve new resuscitation. . . . Mem. Johnson. Think. Maintain character gained at Utrecht, nor ever rave. Mem. Father. If you whore, all ideas change.

[4] George Winn (later Lord Headley) was one of the barons of the Court of Exchequer in Scotland. The Reverend Robert Richardson's father, William Richardson, was Master of Emmanuel College, Cambridge.
[5] The "Duke" is the Duke of Cumberland, Commander-in-Chief of the Government forces at Culloden. "My Lord" is presumably James Ogilvy (?1714–1770), sixth Earl of Findlater. If I understand Boswell's note of Yorke's story, Lord Findlater had the habit of introducing an illegitimate son in the singularly blunt fashion here recorded.
[6] The Reverend Samuel Caldwell, an Anglican Irishman from County Derry, appears to have been assistant priest in the Ambassador's chapel at The Hague. Boswell met him on 21 April, took to him, and ended by telling him all his secrets. See p. 267.
[7] That is, opposed the doctrine of necessity or predestination.

TUESDAY 24 APRIL. Yesterday after physic, you was better. You went to Maclaine and talked to him. He said he had the spleen now and then. But that he always preserved himself, and knew 'twould pass. You owned your wavering notions. He said 'twas vapours, and bid you read Gaubius's *De morbis mentis, quoad medicin.,*[8] &c.; exercise, and rhubarb. But he was too rough. Then dined Monsieur Spaen, but a little off guard. Then multitudes of visits. Then Monsieur Spaen, fine. This day, jaunt. Mem. uniformity, Church of England, *retenue.* No marriage till English; whore not for fear of change. Talk still more to Maclaine, and bid him give you directions. But be sober. Mem., your winter at Utrecht is so much fixed; go on.

WEDNESDAY 25 APRIL. Yesterday Reynst called and carried you to bark. You convoyed Madame Spaen to Leidschendam. You was dreary and thought the journey just like a *Scots* journey. Took leave. Then Reynst and you saw Prince's *Place:*[9] pheasants, &c.; then breakfasted with him elegant; then Maclaine, and owned changes of mind and *Roman Catholic,*[1] after he had said, "You may be a Methodist, but philosophical." You read Ramsay[2] and was clear against Prescience; keep to this. Dined hearty Maclaine. ... Bid him not mention spleen, and asked if he did not think worse.[3] He said, "Indeed, no"; for he had known so many so and never a bad man—always good hearts and well-turned heads.

[8] The correct title is *Sermo academicus alter de regimine mentis quod medicorum est habitus,* which a contemporary translation by J. Taprell, M.D. gives as *On the Passions: or a Philosophical Discourse concerning the Duty and Office of Physicians in the Management and Cure of the Disorders of the Mind.* Boswell's own copy of this translation is in the Yale University Library.

[9] House and surrounding grounds. The "Prince" is the Prince of Orange; the "Place" probably the House in the Woods.

[1] That is, "that you had once been a Roman Catholic."

[2] Andrew Michael Ramsay, *Philosophical Principles of Natural and Revealed Religion,* 1749. Ramsay (an Ayrshireman) was a Jacobite and Roman Catholic. He had served as tutor to Prince Charles Edward.

[3] Think worse of you now that he knew you were subject to melancholy.

Then you walked to Scheveningen[4] with Richardson, who laughed at metaphysics and put you fine; then home. . . .

FRIDAY 27 APRIL. Yesterday you strolled in Wood with Caldwell, fine morning; then sauntered, paying visits, and found yourself sadly unhinged. Dined ordinary, after being at Mr. Houston's— grievous Scots. At four saw *Gardes hollandais.* Home all evening; a little *Candide.* . . . This day . . . exert vigour; yield not to low spleen. . . . Talk of white port and servant to Maclaine, also bid him advise studies. Swear *retenu* and manly, &c. If you're silent, you're well. Spirit and activity.

SATURDAY 28 APRIL. . . . At nine you went with young Reede, Lord Athlone's brother, and waited on Comte de Rhoon, who was polite; great man of business in Dutch affairs. Said, "I shall be charmed to know you better," &c. You see you have acquaintance with the first people here. Maclaine dined with you at inn, fine, lively; grew well. Coffee. (*Pay this or you're not gentleman.*)[5] You told him case. Said he, " 'Tis.much you know it, so just consider it as imagination, and time and reason will take it away." . . . Walked with Maclaine: stars, religion, future life, &c. Said he, "Everybody thinks well of you." This day, journal all forenoon. Engage not servant. You saw with Maclaine that chimeras vanish.

[Received 28 April, Lord Auchinleck to Boswell]

Auchinleck, 15 April 1764

MY DEAR SON,—I have received yours of the 23d of March and commend your care and attention in writing it so speedily after your former, as you were under the apprehension that what you had wrote before would give me a desponding view of your situation; but the answer I made to your first letter would show you that I had no such apprehension from what you had wrote. It gave me in-

---

[4] A fishing-village two and a half miles from The Hague, now a great seashore resort. Boswell, like other eighteenth-century Englishmen, always uses the form *Scheveling* or *Schevling.*

[5] Boswell (as he freely admitted) had a lifelong tendency to narrowness.

deed concern to find that you had been in distress, but that did not appear to me strange; the change from an idle dissipated life to a life of application and study was so great that it could not but affect your spirits. Any change we make as to our course of life naturally has that effect.

I remember to hear Lord Newhall tell that Dr. Cheyne, who was Physician at the Bath, having, by too full living, brought himself to that degree of corpulency that he had his coach made to open wholly on the side and was really become a burden to himself, came to the resolution to live abstemiously, and reduced his body thereby so much that he was obliged to be swaddled to make his loose skin clasp to his body. By this operation his intellectuals were reduced prodigiously and his spirits sunk to the greatest degree. However, as he had given a strict charge to his friends to keep him still in that abstemious way though he should alter his mind from the lowness of his spirits, they kept him at it; and the consequence was that by degrees he became inured to the new method of living and all his faculties, with his spirits, returned to him and he came out a clever agile man, and continued so with a high reputation and in great business till his death.

And therefore, as I said formerly, your point is to persevere and by keeping your mind constantly employed, to leave no room for gloomy thoughts entering your mind. Be *totus in hoc;*[6] think of the thing you are about and of nothing else, and when you find your mind like to wander, write notes that will fix your attention, and if you be attentive to the thing you are about, there is no fear that anything will get access to disturb you. This is the only possible method to make you easy and to keep free from these splenetic fits. You are made with a mind fit for study, and by no means fit to have any ease in a dissipated idle course. The pleasures of this last are so unworthy of a rational thinking creature that they pall; and when the round of them is over, if the person have reflection, he is ashamed of the course he has been in and sees that there is no

[6] Horace, *Satires,* I. ix. 2 ("totus in illis").

proper enjoyment in it for a rational man. A person whose abilities are small—of which the greatest part of mankind is composed— can go the routine of trifling as a turnspit dog does. But you are not cut out for that; and it was chiefly from that reason that I opposed with such earnestness your Guard schemes, as I was sure you would soon have wearied of them and been vexed and distressed that, when God had given you faculties fit for making you useful in life, you had rendered yourself useless. It is our duty as well as our interest to improve the talents God gives us, in order that we may make a figure and be serviceable to mankind, to our friends, and our families. You have great natural abilities, and it is in your power to be useful by improving them properly. But all depends upon the improvement. Your being a good speaker is of no import if you have nothing useful to say; your having a great memory is nought unless it be stored with proper materials; and your acute- ness is nought unless it be accustomed to things of moment. I have in this and my last suggested all that occurs to me on this subject. *Hoc age* is the point, I do assure you. When you are at Utrecht, think of Utrecht and of the people of Utrecht, and wherever you are, let that be your rule. "I have learnt," says the inspired author,[7] "in whatever state I am in, therewith to be content." You say you have not the *animus aequus,* but you should strive to get it and make the best of all situations.[8]

As to the course you are to follow after leaving Utrecht, I hinted my notion in my last. Travelling about from place to place is a thing extremely little improving except where one needs to rub off bashfulness, which is not your case; but to make a little tour through some of the German courts may be amusing, and a stranger

[7] St. Paul, Phil. 4. 11.

[8] With reference to the motto from Horace which Lord Auchinleck had caused to be displayed prominently on the front of the new house he had just com- pleted at Auchinleck: "Quod petis hic est, Est Ulubris, animus si te non deficit aequus." It may be freely translated, "All you seek is here, here in the remoteness and quiet of Auchinleck, if you have fitted yourself with a good steady mind."

is more noticed in them than at the great courts. Before you set out, it would not be amiss you passed some little time to improve your connections with your Dutch relations. The paper for Mynheer Sommelsdyck and Erskine's *Institutes* I suppose will be with you before or as soon as this. Your mother and Johnny remember you with affection. I am your affectionate father,

ALEXR. BOSWEL.

SUNDAY 29 APRIL. Yesterday the Hibernians[9] breakfasted with you. You dined together at Yorke's; all was noble and elegant. You was pretty easy and grave, though miserably distressed. You got letter from worthy father. You was a little hurt at not being in right frame. You passed the evening at Madame de Wilhem's and grew well. This day be cool. Mem., you've owned gloom, but you have maintained character, as Temple. Return Maclaine's books. Chapel: swear anew conduct, and never to act in gloom. . . . Be active, &c. *Retenue* and all's well. Whore not except fine; Amsterdam, private.[1]

WEDNESDAY 2 MAY.[2] Yesterday (1 May) after night boat (*roovers*—patience—fine girl, risk of sensual[ity] and adventures)[3] you arrived at Utrecht at seven. You breakfasted. At ten Baron Winn came and surprised you. You had chocolate, carried him . . . to Tower and Mall; was fine and polite. Dined well; after it, maintained soul different, &c. Hungarian at tea. Brown said, "Veteres avias,"[4] and said you was new ale working. This day,

[9] Caldwell, Rowley (see below, 12 May) and at least one other not certainly identified by Boswell.

[1] "And at Amsterdam, where you will not be observed."

[2] Boswell wrote no memoranda on 30 April and 1 May.

[3] The words within the parenthesis have been heavily scored out in a recent ink, but the reading here given is practically certain. *Roovers* is Dutch for "robbers." Since Boswell is being deliberately cryptic, the meaning is anybody's guess. My own expansion would be, "You were afraid that certain rough-looking passengers were *robbers*, but bore your fear with *patience*. You fondled a *fine girl* and ran the *risk of sensuality and* low *adventures*."

[4] "Old wives' tales" (Persius, *Satires*, V. 92). Brown told him that he was bothered by superstition and the fermentation of youth.

resume Plan; be Temple. Prepare Hague.[5] Shun dissipation. Persist *retenue*. Bravo!

THURSDAY 3 MAY. Yesterday after twelve hours sleep you rose unrelaxed and refreshed and content. You read Greek, but that's all. At *five* you went . . . to Zélide. She sang and repeated verses, but was too *forced-meat*.[6] She would never make wife. After dinner, Brown argued that Society is happiest by marriage and knowing that we have real descendants, &c., and all contrary practices are bad. You are to be husband to English lady, so keep yourself healthy. Concubinage is no dire sin, but never do it unless some very extraordinary opportunity of fresh girl that can do no harm; and such a case is impossible.[7] This day, swear *retenue*, and to pursue Father's plan, and to be a resolute man.

FRIDAY 4 MAY. Yesterday you got up well. You fenced well. But you was bad. You called on Brown, who was warm for rational Christianity. But you was weak and stayed too long. You read Greek well. At four you walked in Mall with Zélide and *la Veuve*, charming; then with Hennert, who said, "The English are hypochondriacs." Then on Observatory: saw moon, Venus, &c. . . . This day, mem., you *must* stand fast. Don't be idle. Letters Father, Mother, Pringle, Lieutenant John.[8] Pay Brown six guilders for dinner. Compose mind and take *Marie*[9] at eight. But do no harm. Be prudent. If you have *retenue*, all is safe, even follies, and joy comes.

[5] He plans to go back to The Hague for the *kermis* or fair, but it is not clear why he bothered to return to Utrecht for four days.

[6] Too artificial, too sophisticated. "Force-meat" is (for example) sausage meat, meat whose original nature is concealed by mincing and spicing.

[7] This entire sentence has been scored out in a recent ink. "Dire" is not altogether certain and "concubinage" is a guess, but there is no doubt as to the general sense.

[8] "Pringle" is Dr. (later Sir) John Pringle, physician and scientist in London, a close friend of Lord Auchinleck who had been kind to Boswell on his London jaunts; "Lieutenant John" is Boswell's brother. It is odd that though Boswell loved his mother tenderly, he very seldom wrote to her or she to him. Lord Auchinleck wrote the letters for the family at home.

[9] The name of the boat for The Hague?

[Boswell to Jerome David Gaubius, M.D.][1]

[Leyden] 4 May 1764

AUDIVI, PROFESSOR SPECTATISSIME! te linguam Anglicam in-
telligere; attamen quia de hoc non satis certus sum, latinitatem in-
accuratam tibi offero. Spero errores candide excuses; nam vix un-
quam sic scribere occasionem habui.

Autumno praecedente ad portam tuam famulae tradidi prae-
parationem quandam chymicam quam patruus meus, M. D. Edin-
burgi, tibi per me misit. Professorem eo tempore videre non potui.
Hyemem Ultratrajecti transegi. Nunc quando iterum Leydae sum,

---

[1] It is difficult to fit together satisfactorily the evidence of Boswell's memoranda and of his correspondence with Gaubius. If one had the letters alone
to go by, one would conclude that Boswell was in Leyden on the morning of
Friday 4 May and saw Gaubius at Leyden at twelve noon that same day.
But according to the memoranda, he left Utrecht on the evening of Friday
4 May, arrived at The Hague at nine the next morning (Saturday 5 May)
and saw Gaubius there (at The Hague) about noon. But he certainly saw
Gaubius in Leyden. The only possible solution appears to be that his letter
to Gaubius—it is a draft—is misdated: that he went directly from Utrecht
to The Hague Friday night, went back to Leyden (ten miles) in the middle
of the forenoon of Saturday 5 May, sent his letter to Gaubius, got a reply,
saw Gaubius, and returned to The Hague in time to see the performance
of a play, say six o'clock. The letter may be translated as follows: "I have
heard, most excellent Professor, that you understand English, but as I am not
quite sure of it, I offer you inaccurate Latin. I hope you will be candid
enough to excuse my mistakes, for I have scarcely ever had an occasion for
writing thus.—Last autumn I left at your door with the maid a certain
chemical preparation which my uncle, a Doctor of Medicine at Edinburgh,
sent you through me. At that time I was unable to see you. I have spent the
winter in Utrecht. Now, when I am again in Leyden, I greatly desire the
honour of calling on you. Such a meeting will be both useful and pleasant to
a foreigner. For since I suffer from a delicate constitution, I am very eager to
have the advice of so celebrated a physician, whose lectures *De regimine
mentis quod medicorum est* I have recently read with the greatest admiration.—I shall remain here only during this day. I therefore beg that you will
let me know by a written reply at what hour I may have an appointment with
you. I am, with the greatest regard and obligation, J. BOSWELL."

honorem te adeundi magnopere cupio. Tale consortium utilissi-
mum aeque ac jucundissimum peregrino erit. Quia etiam consti-
tutione parum firma laboro, medici tam celebris cujus sermones
De regimine mentis quod medicorum est, summa cum admiratione
nuper perlegi, consilium habere valde sollicitus sum.

Per hunc diem tantum hic maneo; precor igitur ut per respon-
sionem scriptam mihi dicas quota hora tecum colloqui possim. Sum
tibi summa observantia obstrictus,

J. Boswell.[2]

SATURDAY 5 MAY. Yesterday you was pretty well, and set out
at night for Hague.

SUNDAY 6 MAY. Yesterday after sound sleep in *roef,* you
came to Hague at nine; found good Hibernians at breakfast; saw
Richardson, who was clear for Scripture accounts; then Maclaine,
kind and hearty. Then Gaubius, who said, "You will be cured by
thirty." Lost dinner, and strolled, as in London; went in coach to
Scheveningen; then *Mahomet,*[3] fine, quite gay; was sceptical and
wild, but silent. Supped Count Bentinck's.[4] Library, lemonade;
saw E. and B.'s letters;[5] convinced all things are as usual. This day,
Chapel, clear and generous, no narrow views. . . . Be vigorous. Be
Temple. Return Tuesday or Wednesday. Be uniform. Write Dr.
Pringle and Lieutenant John. *Think.*

MONDAY 7 MAY. Yesterday you got up well. Had the Irish to
breakfast in *Great Room.* Was fine at Chapel and calm; good sermon on leaving us an example. Then walked with Richardson in

[2] Gaubius returned a brief note in Latin saying that he would expect him
at twelve o'clock.   [3] Voltaire's tragedy.

[4] Christian Frederick Anthony, Count Bentinck de Varel (1734–1768), grandson of the first Earl of Portland by a second marriage, a Captain in the British
Navy. Boswell had met him during the Easter vacation. His wife was a Van
Tuyll, a first cousin of Belle de Zuylen. He had served as intermediary in
the clandestine correspondence between Belle and D'Hermenches, and was to
perform the same function for Belle and Boswell. See p. 305.

[5] That is, he saw a copy of the *Letters Between the Honourable Andrew
Erskine and James Boswell, Esq.,* which he and Erskine had published the
previous year.

Wood; disputed Athanasian Creed, which he said *might* be left out. But he took the Scripture account of GOD. Was pleased to find him quite Cambridge. He was not for Clarke's arguments *a priori,* but from Nature. . . . This day, think. Be uniform. Be *retenu* and manly and pursue Plan with unperceived relaxation. Return soon and recover habits [of] study. Be upon honour to continue Christian, as Johnson. Church of England. At all events, firm; nor yield, nor own.

TUESDAY 8 MAY. Yesterday Monsieur de Sommelsdyck waited on you in morning. You breakfasted at Yorke's with a grand multitude. You was well. You met Chais, who said twenty years ago he had consulted Gaubius for low spirits, who bid him amuse and be his own physician; not study too much nor too little. "Sometimes I fast, sometimes take rhubarb," &c. He said well, "I may shorten my life some years. But in the mean time I have health and spirits to do my duties." Told story of Voltaire and fatality. Said between forty and sixty were the best years. "You think too much, but you will be a very active man." Strolled with Maclaine in fair;[6] dined Sommelsdyck. Yorke's ball, all fine, impossible to resist it. Home fine, &c.

WEDNESDAY 9 MAY. Yesterday at ten you went to Monsieur de Sommelsdyck's in fine, grand humour; a noble breakfast. Told him you heard of his family as of the Patriarchs, &c. Saw bourgeois pass, ludicrous. Viewed house, splendid picture at Culross; fine ideas.[7] Dined Count Bentinck; behaved well and checked him from

[6] "The month of May is distinguished at The Hague by the *kermis* or fair, which is held at this time and lasts a week. The *beau monde* used to go in masquerade about the streets on this occasion, and to divert themselves several other ways, as is done during the carnival at Venice. But the principal diversion now is walking about the fair and buying sundry commodities, or riding out in chaises, which from their lightness are properly called phaetons: common people divert themselves in playhouses which are erected at that time on purpose; some of them deserve to be seen for their drollery" (Thomas Nugent, *The Grand Tour,* 3d ed., 1778, i. 116).
[7] Not clear to me. Boswell's mother had grown up at Culross, and, like his

being too free. Well with Comte Boufflers[8] and Jesuit governor.
... Then rope-dancing; then home. ... This day be mild, think;
get character of *Grison,* and engage manly as self.[9] You'll breed
him. Breakfast Maasdam; then Richardson. Give him a ducat for
kermis.[1] Be pleased, you're forming fast. Your travels will please
after. Only be *retenu,* and fear not, and purge.

THURSDAY 10 MAY. Yesterday you breakfasted at Maasdam's,
charming and calm, and was well with him and with Sommelsdyck; then strolled in fair, and waited on Maclaine. Dined ordinary, and then with Richardson went to Scheveningen; passed the
evening at Maasdam's well. Had Maclaine and Richardson at
supper, quite gay and well. You said, "Miss Maasdam black as
chimney." MACLAINE: "Her husband chimney sweeper." This day,
recollect. Pay supper. See Swiss, but think to take Hercules. Write
journal till eleven, and French, to show you've not lost power; and
acquire strength of mind. Call Chais at one or Maclaine, and dine
with him. Be Christian truly. You're at Hague. Make use of time.
Despair not.

[Received 10 May 1764, Dalrymple to Boswell]

Edinburgh, 11 April 1764

MY DEAR SIR,—I am much to blame in having delayed so long
to answer your letter. It gives me pleasure to see that you are so well
employed, and that you have made such proficiency in French. As

father, was a Sommelsdyck descendant. It may be that the words should be
differently divided: "Viewed house, splendid; [thought of] picture at Culross
[of Veronica van Sommelsdyck, Lady Kincardine]."

[8] Born 1746, son of the Countess of Boufflers-Rouverel, famous bluestocking
and friend of Hume. See p. 272.

[9] Boswell is looking for a servant to accompany him on the Grand Tour, and
has had a Swiss ("Grison") recommended to him.

[1] The manuscript actually reads, "Give him a *kermis* for ducat," probably by
inadvertent transposition. But it could mean, "Take him through the fair and
spend a ducat [ten shillings] on him."

you have such a facility in learning languages, you will do well to fill up your hours with learning others besides French. I do not despair of seeing you an ambassador; you have a prodigious wise face at times and an *air imposant qui sied bien au maniement des affaires.*[2]

You tell me people observe that you are of a melancholy turn. This is owing to your not understanding the language of the country. By "melancholy" my honest old friends mean thoughtful. There is no people in the universe so free from low spirits or the affectation of them as the Dutch. They cannot endure anything that looks being pensive without a cause; and as for low spirits, they laugh at them. . . .

When you write to me about Utrecht, *vous me faites rajeunir.*[3] I reflect with pleasure on the easy days which I passed there, and I am proud of being remembered by so many persons who honoured me with their friendship. Let me entreat you to make my best compliments to all my friends. . . . Madame Sichterman, my old friend—an expression more tender than polite—does she remember me? . . .

I remember the young lady that you mention. Her taste for poetry is elegant. She was an infant when I knew her. Her little brother Reynold, is he alive? He used to speak Dutch and French together; "*Je ne saurais singen,*"[4] said he, when asked to sing. . . .

Did Count Nassau's son by the first marriage live? He was a poor weakly child. Adieu, dear Sir; may you be happy. Believe me ever yours,

DAV. DALRYMPLE.

FRIDAY 11 MAY. Yesterday after going to bed perfectly well, you got up gloomy and desponding. You dressed and grew well, but sauntered idly in *kermis,* yet you was easy. You maintained to

[2] "An imposing air which goes well with the handling of affairs."
[3] "You bring back my youth."
[4] "I can't sing." Reinout Gerard, Belle de Zuylen's oldest brother, was drowned in 1759, at the age of eighteen.

Maclaine that a wild fellow may be happy, &c., which is true. You breakfasted at Yorke's. Dined ordinary at four. Disputed with Caldwell on Contentment and on Happiness. . . . At nine in Sommelsdyck's coach, fine and cordial, to Yorke's. You was in too high spirits, though you had *retenue* and showed it not. But you played, and lost in all *nine ducats*.⁵ You was stunned. You recollected. You saw you might be ruined. Indeed, you have a turn to play. Oh, guard! You really forgot Sheridan's three guineas, but you lost it not *at a sitting*.⁶ However, swear, and think not to win back; 'tis mad. This day . . . be in all morning and compose mind, and write journal and to Johnny and Sheridan. Think on worthy father and on being calm; Pitfour, and uniform.

SATURDAY 12 MAY. Yesterday you breakfasted Rowley, &c., but talked too bold on Inquisition, &c., though you want knowledge. Then Maclaine's, but was idle and insipid. Then Richardson, fine; had walk, and advantage of the universities explained. He owned that young men were bad, not from want of knowing good and evil, but from want of moral principles. Dined Maasdam's and passed evening, but lost sadly. Pray take care. At night Maclaine was with Hibernians. You had literary conversation. Maclaine bid you read Jones on authenticity,⁷ and by discipline expel *veteres avias*. You sat up late with Caldwell, who made it clear that irregular love was wrong. This day, breakfast in room. Journal a little, and try to compose. Visit Perponcher,⁸ Chais, Maclaine, Bentinck, and dine not Sunday, as you must go. Pray lose only two ducats at time. *Retenue,* and none know your faults.

SUNDAY 13 MAY. Yesterday at eleven, after card, you waited on Chais, who . . . advised you to natural knowledge, and said if he were with you, he'd keep you always alive. Said occupation was quite necessary, &c. Then Maclaine, who said if you did not turn

⁵ About £4-6-0.   ⁶ See p. 205 *n.* 9.
⁷ Probably *A New and Full Method of Settling the Canonical Authority of the New Testament*, 1726, by Jeremiah Jones.
⁸ Husband of Belle de Zuylen's younger sister Johanna Maria.

out a sensible, clever, active man, he'd be surprised. Dined Sommelsdyck's, fine; went to *Comédie: Tancred* and *Anglais à Bordeaux.*[9] ... Was as well and gay as ever. Home, and grew fretful;
owned this to Caldwell; 'twas rather too easy. Supped Hibernians
and disputed *fornication,* and lost it, and saw you wanted firm
principles of good of society, which are certain, and death is only
a little interstice—no dreadful distinction. Went to bed clear, active, sound; resolved to clear up journal, as 'twill be very pleasing
yet. ... Set out bold, and determined to go on as Sir David.

MONDAY 14 MAY. Yesterday you rose all confused. But you
cleared. You went to Chapel and was well, and heard sermon on
truth of Christian religion: "He that hath ears to hear," &c. But
still you was backward with Yorke. No matter. Then you saw Maclaine, but was dreary. Dined Count Rhoon; Greffier Fagel[1] there,
who seemed pleased with you. You really behaved well, and
though sad, to your own satisfaction. Then a moment Richardson,
who was too free, as you had been uncertain, but promised visit
at five. Burgundy and Caldwell, to whom you had owned, and
appointed meeting. Said he had known many so, and Dr. Mead[2]
said at twenty-five it went off from young. Said all were in same
way, and thought others dreary. ... Then in coach; then Maasdam's and lost sadly. But peace![3] Then home, and long conversation with Caldwell, who inspired new views. This day, firm but
gay; resolve four weeks well.

TUESDAY 15 MAY. Yesterday at five, you left Hague, passed
the day at Leyden, &c., &c., took night boat to Utrecht.

WEDNESDAY 16 MAY. Yesterday you arrived at Utrecht unhinged; you grew better and began to think. You was glad to see
family. You was however too free with Brown. Take care. Be firm

[9] By Voltaire and C. S. Favart, respectively.

[1] Hendrik Fagel (1706–1790), Secretary of State for the States General. His
daughter Johanna married Belle de Zuylen's brother Willem in 1771.

[2] A famous English physician who died in 1754.

[3] According to the "Livre de Jeu" he lost seventy-two guilders at The Hague
during the Christmas vacation and one hundred and twelve during the
kermis (in all, £16-14-9).

and shun falling back to Houston Stewart.[4] You passed the evening at home. But as you had not yet taken *trempe*[5] since *kermis*, you took sleep in dear bed to refresh. This day, Carron at six; hour *Gil Blas. You* read, not he, and speak some. Swear for three weeks spring up at six. See review; home; theme; compose and depart calm.

[*c*. 1 6 MAY. FRENCH THEME][6] The plan I have spoken of, that is, to translate the *Institutes of the Law of Scotland,* is certainly an exercise which might do me much good. It will fix in my memory the laws of my country. It will teach me to write Latin fluently. And the illustrations of so able a scholar as Mr. Trotz could not but make me a complete *juris consultus.* Since the plan is so useful, I am sadly mortified that I did not think of it until it was too late; for my weakness of mind is such that it gives me a sort of horror to think that I should be obliged to stay four months more in this country. Besides, the plan is not an absolutely necessary one. I can forgo it without blame. Yet when I lay my hand on my heart, I confess that it would be inexcusable in me not to put it into practice.

This, then, is how I have arranged the matter. I do not bind myself to make this translation in a certain time. I have already begun it, and am advancing at a reasonable rate. While I stay here, I shall show my versions to Mr. Trotz, and afterwards, when I am travelling, I can easily send them. He will add his notes, and in time I shall have a very respectable work. Mr. Trotz proposes that I publish it. Perhaps I shall. Will it not seem odd to appear before the Republic of Letters as translator of the law into Latin, in collaboration with a true German, and especially to appear as an author of that sort at Amsterdam itself, the capital of boorish Holland?

[4] Archibald Stewart's older brother; to Boswell always a sobering example of lack of *retenue.*
[5] "Been hardened [literally, "tempered"] to your Utrecht regimen."
[6] This series of four pages (two joined leaves) was placed by Boswell himself at the end of the entire series, but as he has changed his original numbering, it may perhaps be doubted whether it really belongs there. It is impossible to assign a certain date to any theme after that for 20 April.

Well, then, the plan is settled. I can with a great deal of justice make use of these words of Virgil, "Hoc opus, hic labor est." But only think, those of you who know me! think of the labour that I shall have before the work is complete. Five hundred hours! What a thing to look forward to! But, courage! It is a certain truth that the harder I work the happier I am. When I am busy, melancholy has no chance to enter. Yet it is almost miraculous how little effect that consideration has on the very people who have experienced it. You will find thousands and thousands who complain bitterly. "O GOD," they say, "how gloomy life is! How wretched I am!" and all that. But all the same, they do not budge an inch to escape their woes. They fold their arms, they remain idle. Their blood becomes thick, their brains heavy, their thoughts dark. What a horrible situation! Dr. Armstrong, in his poem *On the Art of Preserving Health*, gives a description of that state which I have just described. He says,

> The prostrate soul beneath
> A load of huge Imagination heaves.

It is impossible to translate into French his force of style, a force remarkable even in English. Rouse yourselves, wretched mortals! Remember that you have the honour to be men. Act forthwith, and be happy!

THURSDAY 17 MAY. Yesterday Carron called you at seven. You sprung up and was well. If you do this, you'll awake always at regular hour. You saw horse-review. You was relaxed and bad. You talked with Brown on immortality. He was pretty clear. You walked Mall, and was well. You came home, and at eight went to bed, merely for one summer night to indulge and see if you rise clear at six. This day . . . repeat Ovid; French theme. Swear labour. Write Mother. Keep doubts to self.

FRIDAY 18 MAY. Yesterday after ten hours' sleep you went to bed again two hours. O fie! You passed the day so-so. But better. At night Brown called on you and said you'd come to stability. So just be patient and silent till that comes. How much better are you now than formerly! This day, spring up, rouse. Think for these four

weeks have fixed hours; above all for Scots law, perhaps with
Brown; and see to regain firm tone, and leave Utrecht clear and
bold. Have enlarged notions of GOD, and mem. Basil Cochrane.[7]
But be prudent.

SATURDAY 19 MAY. Yesterday you got up and drank whey.
You was better. You was, however, changeful. After dinner you
talked to Brown on Christian religion, and if one might not only
take Christ's sayings, and take Epistles according to conscience.
'Tis true, this. Be generous. Be liberal. Be firm. You and he drank
tea with Hennert. You was well; went to Brown's; supped with
ladies; talked of *ennui*, ghosts, religious horrors. Walked home in
dark, all solemn, all changed. Swore two hours a day Erskine, and
to write to Father to take your obligation, &c. Be *retenu*.

[Received 19 May, the Reverend Samuel Caldwell to Boswell]

The Hague, 18 May 1764

MY DEAR SIR,—I thank you for your exact and curious journal;
it was so laconic and sententious that had I not been too well convinced of the reality of your complaint, I should certainly have
taken it for an ingenious essay upon what a man *may* feel in that
unaccountable malady. I assure you your puns pleased me; why did
you not give us some at The Hague? You say you acted a part, pray
continue to do so; I know you are very capable of doing so. Until
the last day I had the pleasure of conversing with you, I thought
your mind was as serene and tranquil as my own. I find, then, you
have much more in your own power than I imagined. It rejoices me
much; continue the actor, and let your part be applauded on this
great stage. Some old philosopher says that the gods are pleased
with nothing more than to see a virtuous man bravely opposing
every misfortune and preserving his integrity and serenity amidst
all the storms of human life.

[7] His mother's uncle, brother to the Earl of Dundonald, Commissioner of
Excise in Scotland. A model of manly industry and regularity without narrowness.

But stop, I am beginning to moralize where there is no occasion; I am inadvertently speaking to a man of evils that cannot clearly delineate any that have the appearance of such. Did not an hour's conversation dispel these gloomy clouds last Sunday evening? When they returned, why did you not recall the same reasonings and apply the rules we proposed?

The learned professor you mention[8] gave you most excellent advice; pursue it immediately. Were it not presumptuous in me to add anything to the directions of so great a man, I would earnestly recommend the cold bath every morning the instant you get out of bed. It will wonderfully brace all the nerves and limbs. When the microcosm is once rectified, all the parts of the macrocosm will quickly appear in their true light and genuine beauty. You will then see a pleasing harmony everywhere, and a reasonable happiness diffused through all the species of being. You will then be pleased with yourself and everything will smile around you.

I, Samuel, do prophesy this will be your case; my predictions, as I told you before, have been happily accomplished to others who were plunged in a deeper abyss of gloom, and who by exerting themselves strenuously, and following advice and proper rules, have gloriously emerged and chased away these grim demons of imagination.

Our friend Maclaine is very well. I saw him today: always sensible, lively, and gay; always busy. Mr. Rowley uneven like some others. I hope to receive a good account of you very soon from your own hands. Adieu. Be happy. I am, dear Boswell, yours with much affection,

SAML. CALDWELL.

I should have answered your letter sooner, but having been more abroad this week than usual, I was obliged to defer it until this evening.

SUNDAY 20 MAY. Yesterday you got up and read *Gil Blas*, and was better.... You was bad at Greek. Brown said, "You're tired

[8] Gaubius.

here. You're out of your element." He said you'd understand Greek
ere you leave this. You and he walked. He said Christian religion
was that GOD has declared himself propitious through Christ and
immortality, and allowed to interpret by conscience. You was
dreary, and said weak and gloomy mind must be recompensed. At
night, Hungarian; shocked at orthodoxy. This day, journal till
one. Be Gray. Be *retenu* and worship GOD. Think.

MONDAY 21 MAY. Yesterday you lay till eleven. You was dismal. At dinner you was better. Brown gave good sermon on Sunday. You walked with Carron, and had him at coffee. You supped
well Brown's, and told stories gravely. This day, rouse. Swear
fixed hours. Write Mother and Johnny, and Father that nought is
certain, but he may tie you down. Also go to Amsterdam and try
Dutch girl Friday, and see what moderate Venus will do.

TUESDAY 22 MAY. Yesterday you rose ill and walked on ramparts in despair. You called on Brown, who freely interpreted
Scriptures. He said, "You're not well." You owned. You was, however, meanly scrupulous. Let Reason reign. You saw Hahn at five,
who told stories of Rücker's forgetting law, and officer hearing
voices blaspheming. You drank Tokay with Hungarians[9] and
walked fine. This day swear resume. Bring up journal. No Amsterdam yet. *Retenue.* Have Hahn soon. Tree of kings.[10] Johnson.

[Received 22 May, Temple to Boswell]

Inner Temple [London] 15 May 1764
MY DEAR FRIEND,— ... What can possess you that you are so
fond of visiting courts one never heard of? Who but yourself would
think of going to the Court of Baden-Durlach to see mankind and
learn politeness? I dare say you saw more of both here in England
at Lady Northumberland's and Carlisle House than you will see in

[9] Possibly "Hungarian." See the entries for 2 and 20 May; also p. 172 *n.* 8
above. The manuscript has merely *Hungar.*
[10] A "Jesse tree" (the royal descent of Jesus Christ, according to Matthew and
Luke)? Or a list of the kings of England? See the memorandum for 23 May.

all the courts of Germany, except that of Berlin. But perhaps I am mistaken; I am only solicitous lest you should neglect places worthy your curiosity for others that one would hardly go a mile to look at.

So the Countess turns out a jilt. I am already in love with Mademoiselle de Zuylen. Charming creature! young and handsome, *une savante et bel esprit*. Tell her an Englishman adores her and would think it the greatest happiness of his life to have it in his power to prostrate himself at her feet.[1] You shall have the widow. Don't be angry.

My dear Boswell, how sincere is your friendship for me! I know you love me, and you may be assured that you have the first place in my heart of all men in the world; but GOD forbid that I should ever be a burden to you or to any of my friends. No, I flatter myself I shall still have enough to support me as a gentleman, but though I should not, I hope I shall always be able to act in some sphere that may place me above dependence. . . .

Pray what does Mr. Johnson write to you about? I should like much to see your journal, but how can you convey it to me, for it will be too expensive to send it by the post? Do contrive to let me read it some way or other. I have long expected characters of your principal foreign acquaintance, especially of those at The Hague, and particularly of the ladies you admire most, and an account of the present manners and taste of the Dutch. Pray let me have a letter on this subject. . . .

Adieu, my dear friend, and believe me, with the most tender affection, yours entirely,

W. J. TEMPLE.

P.S. Pray write soon. I shall be more punctual for the future. Churchill published a new poem the other day entitled *The Candidate*. The first part of it is admirable. The last part of it is a severe invective against Lord Sandwich. Churchill is undoubtedly a gen-

[1] See p. 259. Belle de Zuylen's letters to Constant d'Hermenches show that Boswell at some time shortly after this seriously suggested to her that she should marry "his best friend," though he seems not to have given her Temple's name.

ius. His name will illustrate this age. Helvétius[2] is here, and much
caressed by the nobility. Are we to expect nothing more from Mr.
Johnson? Let us have his Shakespeare at least.

[Boswell to Temple]

Utrecht, 22 May 1764

MY DEAR TEMPLE,—This morning I had the pleasure to receive
your last. Your postscript has that natural expression of a friend:
"Pray write soon." How much in unison are our inclinations! Before the sun goes down, I shall have finished my answer. Long may
we be thus. Why do I say long? Amidst all the clouds with which
my mind is overcast, I have one incessant beam of joy. Yes—our
friendship must be immortal a̔s our souls. Infinite Author of Virtue
and Felicity! I thank thee for this. . . .

Since the high flow of spirits which I wrote to you of, I have
endured many a dreary hour. I read two discourses by Professor
Gaubius of Leyden: *De regimine mentis quod medicorum est.* I
was greatly pleased with them, and thought I would do well to consult this famous physician. I waited upon him a fortnight ago and
told him very fully my uneasy situation. He bid me be assured that
my distemper was owing to bad nerves, advised me to live temperate, to take a great deal of exercise, and never to want occupation.
He said he could prescribe no immediate cure, but that he was certain that in a few years I should be firm and happy. This consultation was really curious. I have it at length in my journal. You will
be much entertained with it. Yet, my friend! is it not hard to think
that we depend so much on our bodies, those ἐργασταλα, those

---

[2] Claude Adrien Helvétius, French philosopher and littérateur, had caused
great scandal in France by publishing *De l'esprit* (1758), a work reducing
all human faculties to sensation. The Sorbonne had condemned it, and it
had been publicly burned. Though such doctrines were by no means generally approved in England, they were less shocking there than in France
because of the well established English tradition of philosophical empiricism.
From England Helvétius went to Berlin on the invitation of Frederick the
Great.

earthy cases which the Stoics despised so much? What think you of the idea that it was a brawny frame which gave to Anacharsis the fortitude of despising it?[3] Is this possible? Such speculations suit not our lofty sentiments of the dignity of human nature. I hope Mr. Gray is never sick; at least never splenetic. Long live the Bard of Sublimity.

You moralize on the *ennui*.[4] You are certainly right. It reminds us that we are not yet in the state of felicity. But, alas! my gloomy imagination will not allow me to think of felicity. Voltaire observes that wickedness does not so often suffer in this world as some would imagine. But weakness is sure to suffer. My feeble mind affords a strong proof of this. What variety of woe have I not endured! Above all, what have I not endured from dismal notions of religion! I need not remind you of the several changes which I have undergone in that respect. I will never disguise my fluctuations of sentiment. I will freely own to you my wildest inconsistencies. I thought myself an unshaken Christian. I thought my system was fixed for life. And yet, my friend, what shall I say? I find myself perplexed with doubts. Rousseau's Curate has suggested to me some objections which I cannot get rid of. Pray look at the Savoyard's Creed in *Émile*. I have a sceptical disposition. I would impute it to a disordered fancy; for I see strong proofs that Jesus Christ had a divine commission. My misery is that, like my friend Dempster, I am convinced by the last book which I have read. I have a horror at myself for doubting thus. I think of death, and I shudder. You know how sadly I was educated. The meanest and most frightful Presbyterian notions at times recur upon me.

My dear friend! write to me by the first post. Tell me, can the Supreme Being be offended at my waverings? Counsel me, I pray you. I have committed many offences. What am I to think on

[3] A favourite Boswellian illustration of Stoicism. The philosopher Anaxarchus (not Anacharsis), when he was beaten in a mortar, said, "You beat only the shell of Anaxarchus." Ἐργασταλα ("workhouses," "penitentiaries") does not deserve the Greek characters. It is a Latin word made from a Greek stem, and is properly spelled *ergastula*.

[4] In a passage in his letter of 15 May, omitted in this edition.

that head? My ideas of virtue and vice are not fixed. Shall I ever
be a solid, uniform, and happy man? Pray write soon. You shall
have a long epistle next post. God bless you, my ever dear Temple.
JAMES BOSWELL.

WEDNESDAY 23 MAY. Yesterday you got up better. At eight
you went with Hungarians[5] and heard Bonnet, and when you came
out, said, "An vel un. verb, &c.?"[6] It was a scene next to Newgate.
At dinner you seemed fretful. Madame said, "You are tired of
everything." You made tree of kings. You came home and laboured
some hours and grew quite well. This is an infallible cure. This
day, write to Lieutenant John and bring up journal; read Scots
law; recollect cool. Put books in order. *Rebegin* on new plan. Swear
Locke's Christianity,[7] and *retenue*, and speak each morn. At four,
Goens.[8]

THURSDAY 24 MAY. Yesterday you was much better. You
fenced noble; by not owning spleen at dinner you was pretty well.
At three you had Hungarian and famous Van Goens, pretty boy,
lively though very learned. See him often. . . . Then fields, quite delicious; read Guiffardière's letter. Resolved thus: "I believe Christ
sent from God to atone for offences and give morality. I keep to
this, and all the load of accessories I leave." You went to bed fine.
This day, resume. Swear to get into good humour, and be manly.

[Received 24 May, De Guiffardière to Boswell. Original in French]

Tilburg, 20 May 1764

IT WAS NOT AT ALL for any of the reasons you have imagined
that I have been so long silent. No, my dear Sir, be more just to my

[5] See p. 249 *n*. 9.

[6] Possibly, "An vel unum verbum [intellexistis]?" ("Did you understand a
single word of it?") Bonnet, it will be remembered, was the Professor of
Divinity.

[7] The system outlined in John Locke's *Reasonableness of Christianity*, 1695.
It accepts revelation but makes little account of it.

[8] Ryklof Michael van Goens (1748–1810), a prodigy of learning. He was at
this time sixteen years old. Four years later (1766) he was appointed Professor Extraordinary of Ancient Literature at the University of Utrecht.

candour. I read with avidity your lessons in virtue[9] (lessons from a Cato! a Cato only twenty years old!), and readily grant your experience in all the counsels you gave me. A friend who on returning from a ball or some other public diversion reads me a sermon of sublime morality, a morality worthy of the gods, is a friend to be treasured; besides, I respect your virtue as much as I honour your talents. Nor is it because you have changed your tone that I hasten to reply to you. The book which you ask me for and which I have a chance to send you tomorrow by the messenger; the approaching departure with which you threaten me; my wish to communicate all the flattering things I heard concerning you from people who saw you at The Hague—these are my real reasons for writing.

But to come to your letter. I do not understand why you thought the suggestions I made in my last so libertine. You must have been in a very bad humour when you read it. Or can you really be so depraved as to prefer to have me utter fine sentimental sentences set off by austere maxims? *You*, my friend, running after that chimera called Prudence, Reason? At twenty to take futile pains to be what one cannot be even at sixty without doing violence to one's nature? That is funny enough.

But, seeing you are a philosopher, tell me, I beg you, if it is not highly philosophic to follow Nature? I am a man and I want to be a man: *homo sum, nihil humani a me alienum puto.*[10] So do not tell me to make myself into an angel or a hog. Leave me my foibles, my passions, my caprices. I am no more to be blamed for being as I am than Monsieur Bart[1] is for having pouting lips and bandy legs. I do not love vice, far from it, but I seek pleasure in everything, just like you, just like every one else. Now, to give myself pleasure, I want to enjoy life with all my senses. I want to feast my eyes on a young beauty whose sparkling eyes bear to the

---

[9] Above, p. 92.

[10] "I am a man, and think nothing human foreign to my interests" (Terence, *Heauton Timorumenos*, I. i. 25).

[1] Boswell's landlord.

depths of my heart that benign heat which melts the ice even of old age; I want to smell the sweet scent of the most brilliant flowers, intoxicate myself with the most exquisite perfumes; I want to melt in ecstasy at a fine voice, at the thrilling sound of a flute; I want to savour the most succulent foods and touch with my hands the smoothness and softness of a beautiful skin.

As for the pleasures of the soul, I exclude them only as they are above me. Poetry will enchant me, Eloquence with its fiery masculine strokes will elevate me, Philosophy will console me. I hold these tranquil pleasures in reserve for a time when my soul is calm and has subsided into itself. But when Pleasure, that strong spring of my being, moves me, I fly into the arms of sensual delight without consulting Reason or Philosophy. Either of them at that time would only embarrass me. I even say to myself, "Lucky mortal! You are made for pleasure: enjoy yourself and let life end when pleasure ends."

There, my friend, is the system which I should like to get you to try. What? You frown? What means that look severe? Fie! It disfigures your face. It shows the baneful effects of study, of books, and of all those learned vapidities with which the best days of our lives are made wearisome. Believe me, my dear Boswell, the man who reasons is a depraved animal, and the man who reflects a madman who strangles himself with his own hands. *Caton t'a trop séduit, mon fils; prends d'autres sentiments.*[2] Drop your Johnson and all those fine writers on morality. Have the courage to analyze them, and you will see that they are a tissue of meannesses, of vanities, of trifles dressed up with the fine name of Philosophy. Remove all the borrowed finery, and what remains? A man, made like other men.

> Le masque tombe, l'homme reste,
> Et le sage s'évanouit.[3]

[2] "Cato has captivated you too much, my son; adopt other opinions" (parts of two lines from Voltaire's *La Mort de César*, III. iv).

[3] "The mask falls, the man remains, and the sage vanishes" (J. B. Rousseau, *Odes*, II. vi, 12th strophe, *sage* for *héros*).

Ha! ha! ha! ha! What extravagance! How indignant you will be! I beg you, write me quickly some touching bits to strengthen me. However hideous you may think this country, there are a small number of pretty women here who make my virtue totter. Come to my relief, powerful and sublime wisdom! Confirm my trembling steps, and lead the way with your torch down all the crooked and slippery paths of the labyrinth of life.

By now, you have perhaps twelve thousand hexameters ready to print, with two volumes of *haircloth and bees*.[4] You cannot possibly have wanted matter since you began frequenting the *beau monde* of Utrecht and The Hague. Speaking of The Hague, some one who saw you at Madame de Sommelsdyck's has sung your praises to me. He said you were a very likable man who needed only to be trained by some woman of quality in the jargon of fashion (that is, in good French); that you must form an attachment, must seek a mistress among women of fashion who will take it upon herself to teach you how to behave so as to turn women's heads. You are going shortly, I believe, to Berlin. Provided you are six feet tall, have a proud look, wear a little gold lace on your coat, and have little or no religion, you will be abundantly equipped to please. But if you go to France, it is quite otherwise. There the women rule, it is they who set the fashion; and you must give all your thought to making your court to them, to diverting them, to making them laugh. Otherwise you will see nothing but cabarets and *filles de joie*. I well know that many of your countrymen are reduced to that, but you have too much delicacy and taste to plunge into that kind of debauchery.

Always prefer the society of well bred people. If their pleasures are not always innocent, they are at least always decent; and vice

---

[4] The italicized words are in English in the original. By "twelve thousand hexameters" Guiffardière means, I think, to say that Boswell will vie with Virgil, who, besides his great epic poem (*The Aeneid*), wrote pastoral and amatory poems (*Eclogues*) and didactic poems on farming (*Georgics*). The fourth book of *The Georgics* deals with bee-culture. But Boswell, Guiffardière implies, will substitute ascetic for amatory verses.

that is concealed loses half its viciousness. I think already that I see you nonchalantly stretched out in an armchair in the midst of a circle of women, playing with your snuffbox, smiling at one, whispering endearments into the ear of another, making a rendez-vous with a third, hearing a thousand flattering remarks on your air, your dress, your taste, your wit—I say, I think I see you flying away to the opera in a chariot blazing with gold, to frolic with the prettiest of actresses behind the scenes, to decide the fate of a comedy, the talent of an actor, the reputation of women—that is how I see my dear Mr. Boswell at Paris.

Forgive my nonsense; it is not meant seriously.

Pay my respects to Mr. Brown and his family; tell him that as he lent Vernet[5] to me to read, he will wish me to finish it, and that he can count on having it this summer. *Addison's Travels* accompanies this. I read them with pleasure and send my thanks. I have the honour to be, with true esteem, Sir, your most humble and devoted

DE GUIFFARDIÈRE.

Give my regards to La Roche if you write to him.

I[6] intended to send you Addisson along with this letter, but unluckily the Man was gone. Just as I got this news, comes young M. de Zeulen from Bois-le-Duc to see me; as he is going within eight days back again to Utrecht, I desired him to deliver you the Book, which he did promise.

FRIDAY 25 MAY. Yesterday Brown said you reasoned exactly contrary to probability, for although you was well each day ere night, you imagined each morn you could never be well. He said

[5] Probably *Lettres critiques d'un voyageur anglais sur l'article Genève*, by Jacob Vernet, a Swiss pastor, at one time the friend of Rousseau, later his bitter enemy. This pamphlet attacked Voltaire. Brown had edited it and had written the preface. See p. 23 *n.* 7.

[6] This last paragraph is in English in the original. I have made a few changes in punctuation, but have otherwise left it as Guiffardière wrote it. Though he makes one slip in idiom, he clearly had a good command of English, as Boswell maintained (above, p. 49 *n.* 5). His spelling is remarkably accurate for a French-speaking foreigner.

Helvétius never mentioned our reasoning from probability, which is the greatest faculty of the mind and source of knowledge. Hahn was with you at six. You told him case. He pronounced gravely: bad nerves, acrimonious juices, lax solids. Sweeten, fortify, amuse. No metaphysics, plain common sense. No claps. Women are necessary when one has been accustomed, or retention will influence the brain. Nicely disputed. Eglinton's interpretations. Milk with ladies. Wine Lombach. This day, think. Be fine. Hahn said he saw something in eyes; mark this.

[THURSDAY 24 MAY. JOURNAL][7] ... break it, and shall set Reason upon the throne which is his due; and indeed till that happens, I cannot expect settled satisfaction. I went to a cottage near Utrecht, where Brown entertained our ladies with milk. I went home with Lombach, a genteel Swiss, and over a bit of bread and glass of wine we were very well.

FRIDAY 25 MAY. Brown bid me judge of precepts about fornication as my reason directed; I saw then that irregular coition was not commendable but that it was no dreadful crime, and that as society is now constituted I did little or no harm in taking a girl, especially as my health required it. Bless me! Were Dempster or any other of my old gay friends to find me hesitating thus, how would they laugh! Yet they are worthy fellows; ay, and sensible dogs, too. I should have mentioned that Dr. Tissot was with me this morning at six. He is a true original, a shrewd, lively little fellow of sixty. He said a hypochondriac should not be cured by medicines, but by a regular employment of all the hours of the four and twenty. Little knew he that I was a grievous sufferer. He talks well the modern languages. I found he was a great sceptic. No help for that. He and I went and saw a review of the regiment

[7] From this point we recover Boswell's journal. See pp. ix, xv. The reason that the record of his last three weeks in Holland has survived is that he had fallen behind and wrote these pages up from his notes after he left Utrecht on 18 June for his tour of the German courts. All that he left behind (536 pages, if his own pagination was correct) has disappeared. The fragmentary first sentence records part of Dr. Hahn's diagnosis, or of Boswell's comment on it.

of infantry at Utrecht. I was much amused. But I was in undress, which looked odd amongst the Dutch, who were in full splendour. However, I was the easy man of fashion and well with dear Zélide, who asked me to come out to the country and see her after dinner. I determined to take a trip to Amsterdam, and have a girl.

At four Brown walked out with me to Zuylen and returned. I went to the General's[8] where I found all the Zuylen family and Count Bentinck. Zélide was too vivacious, abused system, and laughed at reason, saying that she was guided by a *sentiment intérieur*. I was lively in defence of wisdom and showed her[9] how wrong she was, for if she had no settled system one could never count on her. One could not say what she would do. I said to her also, "You must show a little decorum. You are among rational beings, who boast of their reason, and who do not like to hear it flouted." Old De Zuylen[1] and all the fifteen friends were delighted with me, as was Madame Geelvinck, who was there "as demure as ever." We went and walked in a sweet pretty wood. I delivered to Zélide the fine compliments which my friend Temple had charged me to deliver: that is to say, the warm sentiments of adoration. She was much pleased. I talked to her seriously and bid her marry a *bon baron* of good sense and amiable manners who would be her superior in common life, while he admired her fine genius and all that. She said she would marry such a man if she saw him. But still she would fain have something finer. I told her that she erred much in wishing for what could not last. I said she should never have a man of much sensibility. For instance, "I would not marry you if you would make me King of the Seven Provinces."[2] In this fine, gay, free conversation did the minutes fly. I don't remember the half of what we said.

[8] General van Tuyll's.

[9] From here to "flouted" the original is written in French. It may be assumed unless notice is given to the contrary that Boswell used French for both sides of dialogue with Hollanders in the journal as in the memoranda.

[1] Belle's father. He was actually only fifty-six years old.

[2] Boswell recorded (and probably spoke) this sentence in English.

At nine I went into the Amsterdam boat. The *roef* was hired, so I was all night amongst ragamuffins. Yet were my thoughts sweet and lively till the last two hours, when I sunk to gloom.

[SATURDAY 26 MAY] I came to Grub's, an English house. I was restless. I was fretful. I despised myself.³ At ten I waited on Longueville, one of the Scots ministers, a heavy, sulky dog, but born near Auchinleck.⁴ At eleven I went and called on Dr. Blinshall, the other Scots minister, a hearty, honest fellow, knowing and active, but Scotch to the very backbone. I next waited on Mr. James Boswell, glass-merchant, who has been here I believe forty years. He was very kind, and asked me to dinner next day. I strolled about very uneasy. I dined with Mr. Rich, merchant.

At five I went to a bawdy-house. I was shown upstairs, and had a bottle of claret and a *juffrouw*. But the girl was much fitter for being wrapped in the blankets of salivation than kissed between the sheets of love. I had no armour, so did not fight. It was truly ludicrous to talk in Dutch to a whore. This scene was to me a rarity as great as peas in February. Yet I was hurt to find myself in the sinks of gross debauchery. This was a proper way to consider the thing. But so sickly was my brain that I had the low scruples of an Edinburgh divine.

I went to Blinshall's at eight. He talked of religious melancholy like a good sound fellow. He pleased me by saying it was bodily. I

---

³ To use the terminology of his present enlightened state, he was having "low scruples": that is, he was having difficulty in persuading himself that what he proposed to do was not a sin. The journal, which is deliberately written in a libertine tone, does not do justice to the moral struggle which was really going on.

⁴ See Lord Auchinleck's letter, p. 53. Boswell is just getting around to make the calls his father suggested. It is a little odd that Holland's largest city (generally thought at the time to be the largest city in Christendom after London and Paris) should have meant so little to Boswell—nothing in fact except a place where he could go to a bawdy-house unobserved. Utrecht is nearer to Amsterdam than it is to The Hague, but Boswell had not been there once after the hasty and disconsolate tour of Holland which he made in August, 1763.

was so fretted as to be glad of any relief. I supped with Blinshall's landlord, Connal, an Irish peruke-maker who it seems was once a young fellow of fortune in London, and acquainted with Pope and many more men of genius. It was a queer evening. At six I had been so tired as to go to Farquhar's[5] and drink amongst blackguards a bottle of wine. I shall never forget that lowness; for low it was indeed. At eleven we parted. I resolved to go to a *speelhuis*[6] but had no guide. I therefore very madly sought for one myself and strolled up and down the Amsterdam streets, which are by all accounts very dangerous at night. I began to be frightened and to think of Belgic *knives*. At last I came to a *speelhuis*, where I entered boldly. I danced with a fine lady in laced riding-clothes, a true blackguard minuet. I had my pipe in my mouth and performed like any common sailor. I had near quarrelled with one of the musicians. But I was told to take care, which I wisely did. I spoke plenty of Dutch but could find no girl that elicited my inclinations. I was disgusted with this low confusion, came home and slept sound.

SUNDAY 27 MAY. I went to Chapel[7] and heard a good sermon from Mr. Charles, a very pretty man. I dined with honest Boswell whom I found just a plain, kind-hearted Scotsman. His wife was a hearty Englishwoman. One of his sons was at Surinam. I saw the other, a smart active lad, and a daughter. I went and heard Blinshall preach; but had all the old Scots gloomy ideas. I then strolled through mean brothels in dirty lanes. I was quite splenetic. I still wanted armour. I drank tea with Blinshall. At eight I got into

[5] Apparently a tavern kept by a Scotsman.
[6] "It is also customary for strangers to see something of the famous *speel* houses, or music houses in this city. These are a kind of taverns and halls where young people of the meaner sort, both men and women, meet two or three times a week for dancing. Here they only make their rendezvous, but the execution is done elsewhere. Those who choose to satisfy their curiosity in this respect should take care to behave civilly, and especially not to offer familiarities to any girl that is engaged with another man; otherwise the consequence might be dangerous, for the Dutch are very brutish in their quarrels" (Thomas Nugent, *The Grand Tour*, 3d ed., 1778, i. 83).
[7] The Church-of-England chapel.

the *roef* of the Utrecht boat. I had with me an Italian fiddler, a German officer, his wife and his child.

MONDAY 28 MAY. After a *schuit* sleep I arrived at five very nervous. I went to my naked bed. I rose at ten. I was changeful and uneasy all day.

[Received *c.* 28 May, Constant d'Hermenches[8] to Boswell. Original in French]

The Hague, Saturday [26 May 1764]

I AM DELIGHTED, SIR, to have it in my power to serve you in some way. Here is the letter you asked for.[9] If you had told me but one detail of your approaching journey, I could have mentioned it; however, persons like you are always sure to receive a kind reception from that remarkable man whose heart and mind deserve the homage and gratitude of every thinking being.

Though it may astonish you to hear it, I dare assure you that the admiration you feel for Mademoiselle de Zuylen will not be eclipsed by meeting him. I am told that she writes as well as he does, and perhaps she has more wit. Her beauty, her youth, her intelligence exert a fascination which is overpowering but very precious to any feeling heart.

Is it not true, my dear Sir? It is impossible that being in accord, as we are, in our opinions of her, we should not have other points in common: and I am proud of them so far as our slight acquaintance permits me to know them. As good men all have only one country, so an amiable woman is a benevolent star which draws together the most opposed characters and conditions and makes all the bonds of society precious.

[8] Constant d'Hermenches, a married man forty years old, was a Swiss nobleman in the military service of the States General. He was a man of many ambitions, but was perhaps best known for his amorous triumphs. Belle de Zuylen was carrying on a clandestine and extremely candid epistolary correspondence with him.

[9] A letter of introduction to Voltaire, with whom D'Hermenches was intimately acquainted.

I assure you a thousand times, Sir, of my wish to be helpful in all your concerns; and have the honour to be, without reservation, your most humble and obedient servant,

CONSTANT D'HERMENCHES.

The Hague, Saturday, in great haste.[1]

TUESDAY 29 MAY. Gordon came here last night. He lodged at Baron d'Ablaing's. I see him scarcely at all. At three Tissot carried me to the Utrecht Bedlam. The poor creatures were almost all silly. They were mostly going about loose. They called me the King of England. I was amused with this scene. Tissot said mankind were all mad and differed only in degree. At night I had Lombach with me. We talked politics.

WEDNESDAY 30 MAY. I had sat up all night. I was in an agreeable fever. But I must not repeat this often. I sent a card to Zélide that I would bring Gordon to see her.[2] In the afternoon I carried him to Zuylen, one league from town, in a cabriolet. We were politely received. I saw the old castle and all the family pictures.[3] Zélide was rather too vivacious. I was discontented.

[1] Boswell showed this letter to Belle, and she wrote to D'Hermenches, "If Boswell has not written to you, it is not because he was not very much pleased with you and with your letter: he showed it to me. Allow me the vanity of recalling word for word a compliment which, however exaggerated it is, could not fail to be very agreeable to me: 'I am told that Mademoiselle de Zuylen writes as well as Voltaire,' &c. I thought that 'I am told' very pretty, very delicate, but not exactly discreet. For if there had been no mystery, you would not have thought of making one: you would have based your judgment on *Le Noble,* the Portraits. But never mind, 'I am told' pleases me a good deal." (Nobody was supposed to know about her letters to D'Hermenches. Actually, every one did.)

[2] "Take Gordon to Zélide, and talk to her sweet" (Memorandum for 30 May).

[3] Apparently his first visit to the ancestral mansion of the Tuyll family. All through the winter they had lived in their town house in Utrecht, an imposing structure in the Kromme Nieuwe Gracht. The Castle was described by Philippe Godet in 1906 as follows: "A pleasant path following the right bank of the Vecht brings you after an hour's walk from Utrecht to Zuylen. In an old album ... which appears to be of the middle of the eighteenth century are shown various views of the castles and homes which this branch of

THURSDAY 31 MAY. Awaked as disordered as ever. I got a letter from Mr. William Nairne begging me to meet him and Andrew Stuart at The Hague, next day.[4] I had also an invitation from Sir Joseph Yorke to his ball on Monday, the King's birthday. I hesitated and fretted, but at last determined to go. From this I am sure that I am now much better. Formerly in such circumstances I would not have stirred. Now, whenever I am called upon, I go to my post. This being Ascension Day, I went to Brown's church. I heard sermon and prayers and all that makes me so dreary on Sundays. Today I did not feel the same effects. I looked around to see what on earth could make the gloom on Sundays.

the Old Rhine bathes before it goes to lose itself in the Zuider Zee. There, among others, may be seen the village of Zuilen, drawn out along the bank of the river, which here describes a gracious bend, its houses low, its farms neat and pleasant. Behind the village a bell-tower rises above a group of trees. . . . Not far from the church, imposing and haughty, stands the Castle of Zuylen. . . . In spite of certain reconstructions which Belle's father made in the Castle, it has kept its appearance of former days, or at least its general silhouette. Flanked by turrets at the four corners, it is, in the fashion of the country, surrounded on three sides by water. You cross a wide moat on a bridge of three arches, after having passed under a postern gate which must be of very ancient construction, where are carved, beside the arms of Utrecht and of Zuylen, those of the families of Tuyll and Weede. Not far from the main building are grouped its dependencies; its farms, barns, and carriage-houses. Through the curtain of century-old trees which frame the Castle, the eye embraces the vast perspectives of the plain of Holland; on the horizon to the west one discerns through the haze the lofty tower of the Cathedral of Utrecht. The impression of uncramped and ancient opulence which the visitor feels on approaching the manor-house is accentuated when he enters the spacious vestibule, from which rises a double staircase of marble. The corridor of the first floor [American: second floor], which runs the entire width of the main façade, is adorned with a glorious series of ancestral portraits, among whom one notices a kneeling Chevalier of Malta" (*Madame de Charrière et ses amis*, i. 1-3, translated).

[4] Andrew Stuart, an able Scottish solicitor, one of the guardians of the children of the sixth Duke of Hamilton, had come to Holland to collect evidence for his young ward, the seventh Duke, in the famous Douglas Cause. Nairne, an advocate or barrister, was also one of the Duke's lawyers.

I ordered a genteel flowered-silk suit, and at eight I set out in the Leyden *roef*. I had with me two Brussels lawyers. One of them wanted much to convert me to the Popish religion. He was a learned, lively, pretty man. He told me what tranquillity, what joy, his holy religion gave him by its many aids to the imperfections of human nature, and how he had no doubts, but reposed in the bosom of his sacred Mother, the Church. I owned to him that I envied his situation. But for my part, I was pretty enlarged in my notions and was not afraid of my Creator. He seemed to have no difficulty at all with regard to transubstantiation. I went this far with him: "Sir, allow me to ask you one question. If the Church should say to you, 'Two and three make ten,' what would you do?" "Sir," said he, "I should believe it, and I should count like this: one, two, three, four, *ten*." I was now fully satisfied. This conversation, however, made me calmly think that religion is a more universal thing than people imagine.

FRIDAY 1 JUNE. I arrived at The Hague at nine, after a good sleep. I had written to good Caldwell that I was very bad, and had begged him to come for a day to Utrecht. He received me with open arms and seemed quite happy to see me.[5] I told him—strange event!—that I was perfectly well. I went immediately to the Parliament of England, where I found Mr. Andrew Stuart, whom I had not seen for two years. He had a number of papers before him, quite the man of business, and he had the air of the Duke of Kingston.[6] I was altogether changed by seeing him. My best ideas of family and Major Cochrane and the Abbey returned.[7] I talked well

[5] He had sent Boswell two long and affectionate letters of advice dated 27 and 31 May.

[6] The Parliament of England was the principal inn of The Hague. The reference to the Duke of Kingston is probably a tribute to Stuart's fine features, the Duke being one of the handsomest men of his time. Boswell had not yet taken sides in the Douglas Cause; when later he became an ardent supporter of Douglas, he conceived a violent antipathy to Stuart.

[7] A complex of associations. Boswell's grand-uncle, Major Cochrane (by this time eighth Earl of Dundonald), was Stuart's brother-in-law, and as warm a partisan of the Hamilton claims as Stuart himself. Boswell's first published

and manly. After breakfast we went to the Parade. Nairne came from a jaunt to Amsterdam, just the old man, quiet, sensible, worthy. Also came Colonel Scott of the Guards, natural son to the late Duke of Buccleuch.

At twelve I went with them in a coach for Rotterdam. Stuart said he would not live in Holland for a great deal. I had a pride in having passed my winter here. We stopped at Delft and looked at the churches, and got to Rotterdam about four. I was in immense spirits and could not believe that I had been so bad here in winter last. It however galled me to recollect my hypochondria, especially when I knew not but it might return upon me this very night. Stuart talked to me in a very friendly way, and promised to get Basil Cochrane to advise my father to allow me a pretty handsome tour abroad. I called at Stewart's and saw Sally and Mr. Mollison, and wrote a line to Stewart.[8] At six we had a hearty dinner at our inn, the Maréchal de Turenne. Scott was a fine, gay, hearty fellow, quite English and happy. They insisted on my staying all night. I did so. I said I had almost lost my memory in Holland; and when they said, "Have you eat of this dish?" I answered, "Yes, to the best of my remembrance." Stuart and I called on Craufurd,[9] then returned to our inn. All went nobly.

SATURDAY 2 JUNE. Scott and I slept in the same room. I got up better than usual. I was amused to see Scott and Stuart and Nairne in their morning figures. How curious is a man with regard to times or circumstances which touch him nearly. Scott said the Guards were lazy dogs, and when Shafto was an officer there, he used to ask his servant who called him, "John, what's a clock?" "Two minutes from five, Sir." "Call me then, John, when those two

poem, *An Evening Walk in the Abbey Church of Holyroodhouse* (*Scots Magazine,* August, 1758) had praised Major Cochrane for causing the church to be re-roofed. The Abbey was also, and very directly, connected with the Douglas Cause by the fact that Lady Jane Douglas was buried there.

[8] See p. 131 *n.* 8.

[9] Patrick (later Sir Patrick) Craufurd, another Scots merchant settled in Rotterdam. Boswell applied to him for the wine he had promised Gronovius (above, p. 228).

minutes are run." I found real life relume me quite. I took leave of my good friends.

I went in the *schuit* to Delft and from thence took a chariot to The Hague; came just in time to breakfast with my good Hibernians. This forenoon, I took Caldwell out to the Wood and told him the whole story of my most extraordinary life. My external changes have been pretty well, but for internal ones, I think I may enter the lists with any living being. Caldwell was struck with wonder; his amiable mind appeared very plainly. He was pleased with Lord Eglinton's method of freeing me from the gloom of superstition, although it led me to the other extreme.[1] He spoke like a philosopher and said I must have had great strength of mind to struggle through so many conflicts, and a fine genius to have improved my mind so much although so hardly oppressed. He said my misery was now over; that now I should be a firm and a happy man provided I lived an active, temperate, agreeable life. He really gave me rational hopes of being yet a man.

Monsieur de Sommelsdyck paid me a visit this morning. I dined with him, and was very well. I then waited on Maclaine and put him in sweats by defending transubstantiation. He was a little splenetic.[2] I met Richardson and carried him to the inn, where I gave him a neat supper. I found his morality to be just the common sense of mankind. He said in his parish the young fellows got the girls with child first, without any idea of harm, and then married them.[3] He said this showed what couples loved each other, and he never blamed them. He said, too, that if three stout youths were cast upon a desert island with three old men who had young wives, that the youths ought surely to propagate with the young wives, although they were all Christians; so that the Doctor was of opinion that the sexes may unite just according as

[1] See p. 1.

[2] Boswell's unexpected emancipation from religious gloom shows itself in a malicious desire to tease the exponents of Calvinistic theology.

[3] His parish in England. He no doubt had more than one living besides the chaplaincy.

circumstances are. This is surely sound sense, and when I am clear and unclouded by the gloom of prejudice, I must think so too.

SUNDAY 3 JUNE. I rose as easy and well as mortal could be. The Hibernians breakfasted with me. I was fine at Chapel, then had a drive to Scheveningen. I dined at Maasdam's, and was quite cheerful. I drank tea at Colonel Houston's, then went to Maasdam's where I lost at cards, and was angry at myself therefor. At night I had some good conversation with Caldwell.

[Received *c.* 3 June, Patrick Craufurd to Boswell]

Rotterdam, 2 June 1764

DEAR SIR:—According as you desired, I have made inquiry about the port wine, an anker of which I have bought for you and is at your disposal. It costs *f*18. If you please to send me down a *briefje*,⁴ I shall send it where you please. I beg my compliments to Mrs. and Mr. Brown. I am, Sir, your most obedient humble servant,

PATRICK CRAUFURD.

MONDAY 4 JUNE. In a genteel suit of flowered silk, I went this morning and paid my respects at the English Ambassador's, where was a very great crowd, it being King George's birthday. This morning was indeed a morning of joy. I received a large packet of letters, one from my Lord Marischal, informing me that I was to accompany him to Berlin, one from my father to the same purpose, and letters from my Scots and London bankers with a credit upon Berlin of £30 a month. Never was man happier than I this morning. I was now to travel with a venerable Scots nobleman who had passed all his life abroad, had known intimately kings and great men of all kinds, and could introduce me with the greatest advantage at courts.⁵ A multitude of rich ideas filled my imagina-

---

⁴ An anker is eight and one third imperial gallons (ten gallons U.S.); eighteen guilders amounted to about £1-12-9; *briefje* means "a written order."

⁵ George Keith, tenth Earl Marischal of Scotland, had been attainted for his active participation in the Jacobite uprisings of 1715 and 1719, but because of later services to the Government, had received a full pardon in 1759. He was

tion. The Hibernians were pleased. Caldwell said it was the luckiest
event in the world for me. I was quite elevated. I despised my dull
plodding at Utrecht in the clay of metaphysical theology. "Ah,"
said I, "if Brown came to me now with a dispute about Necessity,
how would I laugh at him."

I dined at Maasdam's, quite the gay foreign cousin.[6] He has
taken a great liking to me. At night I went to the ball given by
Yorke. It was splendid, but his dry insolence was insupportable. I
danced one country-dance with a Mademoiselle Wassenaer. I was
in a glow of delicious spirits. I took my excellent Caldwell aside
and told him how very happy I was, but at the same time said that
I was a complete sceptic as to Christianity. He said I was wrong,
for its evidence was very convincing; and he owned that he himself
had been a sceptic. I was too feverish.

[Received 4 June, Lord Marischal to Boswell]

Allanbank, 25 May 1764

SIR:—I flatter myself with the hopes of your good company to
Lüneburg, and perhaps on to Berlin, as you will have heard from
my Lord, your father.

I shall want a *voiture* (a chaise) for three, if you go, as I hope,
otherwise only for two. Pray look out for one in Utrecht, and make
my compliments to Mrs. Brown, the Minister's wife (she is Kinloch
by birth) to know if she knows of a chaise. Inquire also of
Mademoiselle Maitland *chez le général* Sporken *à la Haye,* if she
has found one, as her father wrote to her. Excuse this liberty and
trouble.

---

one of the most trusted counsellors of Frederick the Great; had served as
Prussian Ambassador to France and to Spain, and as Governor of Neuchâtel.
He had been in Scotland arranging his affairs with the intention of settling
there, but had been recalled by an urgent letter from Frederick. Lord
Auchinleck had seized the opportunity to launch his son on the Grand Tour
under the most distinguished auspices. Lord Marischal was at this time past
seventy, a shrewd, stately, polished courtier of vast practical experience.
[6] The Baroness van Maasdam was a Sommelsdyck.

I suppose that, living a studious life at Leyden, your wardrobe will need some addition, now you are going to courts. A suit of summer clothes, fine camlet with a gold thread button but no lace; and against winter a complete suit of worked flowered velvet, the buttons of velvet; four pairs of laced ruffles. This I think will do, for cloth is to be had everywhere, and velvet, though this last not so cheap as in Holland.

I shall make no stay in London, but hasten to Holland, where perhaps I may be about the 8 or 10th June. I go from Hellevoet to Rotterdam; from thence straight to Utrecht; and if you and my *voiture* are ready, shall stay there only a day. I want only a *voiture* sufficient for my journey to Berlin, for I count it will be of little use to me there, and therefore want to lay out as little money as I can on it. Please write under cover of Mr. Craufurd in Rotterdam to, Sir, your most humble and obedient servant,

MARISCHAL.

[Received 4 June, Dempster to Boswell]

Manchester Buildings [London] 25 May 1764

MY DEAREST BOSWELL:—

I like your friend Rose well;
By your odd sort of talk
I thought him Kilra—k,
And took much pains and trouble
To amuse the *Rose noble;*[7]
But if the young man is possessed
Of solid head and candid breast,
What matters it to me or you
On how obscure a bush he grew?
The business of the Nation past,

[7] "From your very imperfect description, I concluded that your Utrecht friend Rose was Rose of Kilravock [pronounced Kilróck] and entertained him under the mistaken assumption that he was *the* Rose, the representative of the family." A rose noble was a mediaeval coin stamped with the English rose.

Sunshine and vacance come at last;
And Britain saddled for the year
With armies and excise on beer,
No hireling mean, no patriot sour,
Dempster to thee devotes an hour.
How can I, fetter'd thus in rhyme,
Inquire your news or give you mine?
Ask how you like Batavian air,
The men, the manners, and the Fair?
Whether your mind a firmer tone
Acquires, or is more fickle grown?
Whether you study hard at home,
Or (as you used in London) roam,
Full of spleen and mirth and glee,
'Tween Dash[8] and Eglinton and me?
 Pray, has the solid Dutchman's school
Proved every sceptic knave or fool,
Your doubts restrain'd within due bounds,
And fixed morality on solid grounds?
In Number 5, removed from noise and strife,
I jog as usual calmly on in life,
Sometimes partake in senates' high debate,
Unbias'd vote, by post or party heat.

Unfortunately for you, my dear Boswell, your last verses inspired me with the desire to undertake the arduous task of an answer in verse. Two months ago I came as far as you see; since that I have not found one moment fit for the Muses. East India faction, private business, private pleasure, and public diversions or public dulness, have occupied every second of my time. I often however think of you, and that with an affection unimpaired by length of time or absence. I thought you would have writ me ten letters for one. Friends should pay to friendship the tribute of correspondence as men do the taxes of a State, not an equal quantity each, but

[8] Andrew Erskine's nickname.

proportioned to their respective wealth and ability. You, Sir, inherit ten times more imagination, and have acquired ten times more leisure than me. I'd as soon pay pound for pound land-tax with the Duke of Bedford as page for page letter-tax with the Laird of Auchinleck.

Poor Jean,[9] who is at present with me, has enjoyed very indifferent health since you left us. She is grown a skeleton, and I have the most serious apprehensions about her. I have scarce seen Dash once since he went to Scotland. He published a piece of the dramatic farcical kind which was represented at Edinburgh. I asked Donaldson, the printer of it,[1] how it took. "Oh, very well, Sir, very well I can assure you; it was not damned till the second night."

What are you about? Where are you going? How do you like Utrecht after a summer and winter's trial?

Let me now, my dear friend, conclude, as all friends should do their letters, with a word of advice. Avoid all company in general, and all kinds of reading, whether law, history, morality, poetry, or politics. Never roger any woman, eat but once a day, and that of one dish. Tailors are thieves all Europe over, so make up no clothes. Avoid travelling, either by land or by water, but leave Utrecht as fast as possible. This is the Law and the Prophets. Farewell.[2]

TUESDAY 5 JUNE. I dined at the inn. After dinner Baron Beulwitz of the Duke of Brunswick's family waited upon me with great civility, and asked me to sup with the Duke. I went to the *Comédie*, then to the Duke's; played a party and supped. All was elegant and easy. I sat by a Mademoiselle de Starrenburg, who knew young Pitfour and talked to me of him. We had now at The Hague a good many English: Lord Holdernesse, Lord John Cavendish, &c.

WEDNESDAY 6 JUNE. I went with Count Boufflers and his Jesuit tutor to wait on Madame Boufflers,[3] who was now at The

[9] His sister and housekeeper. He was still a bachelor, though he afterwards married.   [1] Publisher to both Erskine and Boswell.   [2] No signature.
[3] The famous Countess of Boufflers-Rouverel, mistress of the Prince de Conti, at this time engaged in a sentimental correspondence with David Hume. She had called on Samuel Johnson in London the previous year.

Hague. She was at her toilet, quite the French fine lady. She was distant. I admired her much. I paid my visits of *congé partout*. I agreed with Monsieur de Sommelsdyck to have a correspondence. I shall have it too with Monsieur de Maasdam. I had a parting conversation with Caldwell. He disputed seriously with me against irregular love. I wavered between his opinion and my own. Weak I was, that is sure. But it must also be owned that the matter is somewhat difficult. Rowley and he took cordial leave of me.

I went in the *schuit* to Leyden. It was the *kermis* there, and all was gay. I found Monsieur Gronovius in his garden. I owned to him my melancholy. He bid me conceal it, and be always busy or amused. We passed this our last evening with much satisfaction. I took a hearty leave of him. I had engaged at The Hague a servant, his name Jacob Hänni, a *Bernois*, who spoke French and German. I took him with me, so that I had my two attendants. I own that I had little vanity enough to be pleased with this. One of my *schuit* companions asked me if my servant was German. "Sir," said I, "one of my servants is German and the other is French." My companion looked at me with a much more respectful eye.

At eight I went into the Utrecht *roef* with a French officer in the Prussian service who had been in Portugal and knew Captain Preston well.[4] He talked finely and gave me a share of his cold meat and wine. I slept well.

[Received *c.* 6 June, Count Bentinck to Boswell][5]

Hague, 5 June 1764

DEAR SIR:—I send you enclosed three letters for Brunswick, of which you will make use if you think proper. Messrs. Stainer and Feronce will introduce you to all the good company in that town.

[4] Boswell's cousin, Patrick Preston, eldest son of Sir George Preston of Valley-field, was a major in the British Army and a brigadier-general in the service of Portugal.

[5] Original in English, which Bentinck handles like a native. He had probably spoken it from childhood.

The former is an honest, good, worthy man as ever breathed, and a great friend of mine. He is plain and good-naturedly civil. Feronce is very sensible, quick, and sprightly; knows a great deal, writes very good prose and pretty poetry; a little wicked, but good company. I have sent you another letter for the Abbé Jerusalem, a worthy man who has all the good nature, the affability, and the modesty of a child, with the most deep and sublime study and the most refined taste. The first sight you will find him backward, but if you talk with him, I am sure you will love him.

Be so kind, dear Sir, to spend now and then a few minutes of your leisure hours in writing to me. You will oblige him vastly who professes himself to be always your faithful friend and obedient humble servant,

BENTINCK, SEIGNEUR DE VAREL.

P.S. On second thoughts I have not sent you any letter for Berlin, as Lord Marischal will certainly give you opportunities of getting enough acquainted with everybody. However, if desired you shall have it. When you write to me, tell me where I am to direct.

THURSDAY 7 JUNE. Once more I returned to Utrecht. To my surprise I found that Trotzius had concluded his college. I was very, very gay at Brown's. I drank tea *chez* Mademoiselle Tuyll, aunt to Zélide. I passed the evening at home.

[Boswell to Madame de Spaen. Original in French]

Utrecht, 7 June 1764

MADAME:—Although I had an opportunity to thank you by word of mouth for the obliging letter with which you honoured me before your departure for Germany, I still feel guilty for not having written to you since then. Fresh courtesies call for fresh acknowledgments. The reception you recently gave me in the Prinsesse Gracht is another proof of your goodness to me. Accept my thanks and believe that I feel what I say. Indeed, I was treated as a friend; I had the privilege of supping with you the last evening and of accompanying you to Leidschendam. Could an acquaintance of fifteen years do more? Am I not very fortunate? Such worthy Scots as I ought to travel.

I have been twice more to The Hague, first to see their *kermis*, which I found very amusing, perhaps too amusing to last ten days in a row. A mob of that size upsets most people, even the most steady. I was there also to celebrate our King's birthday. Sir Joseph Yorke gave a superb ball. There were ten or twelve of us English there. Everything was gay and brilliant. I had the honour to sup on the following evening with the Duke,[6] whom I cannot praise enough. The world has never seen a prince who succeeded better in adding amiable virtues to strength of character. He receives one with true politeness, a politeness that comes from the heart.

I have taken leave of my friends at The Hague. I expect to leave this country soon. I have the best possible opportunity for going into Germany. My Lord Marischal, who has been some time in Scotland, is on his way back to Berlin. He is good enough to take me with him.

We shall go to Lüneburg, to Brunswick, and finally to the Court of Prussia. Nothing could be more fortunate for a young man than to make this tour with a nobleman who has seen so much of the world and is held everywhere in such esteem. I shall certainly have extraordinary advantages. I have no doubt, Madame, that you and Monsieur Spaen will be pleased when I inform you of a circumstance so lucky for a stranger to whom you have shown so much goodness.

I expect my Lord here every day. I do not know whether he has the honour to be known to Monsieur Spaen. I imagine, however, that he will be charmed to accompany me when I pay my respects to you at your paradise of Bellevue. I flatter myself that I shall have that pleasure by the middle of this week.

This letter will be carried by our excellent friend Reynst, who has promised me the pleasure of his good company at supper at my house when he passes through Utrecht.

[6] Of Brunswick.

I am very busy in putting my affairs in order before leaving. What formality! I confess it, Madame. But you must know that I draw highly flattering hopes from it. It seems to me that some day I shall occupy a distinguished post because I naturally feel myself to be a man of so much importance. Nature is wise. She always has designs when she grants qualities. It depends on us, however, to turn these qualities to good use. Be good enough, Madame, to excuse my jesting. I write to you as I speak, without ceremony.

Perhaps you ask me, Madame, if I am leaving Utrecht with perfect indifference, if I feel no tender regrets on being separated from ————. O Baroness! do not ask me. Yes, yes. I feel regrets indeed. Charming Zélide! May heaven grant her the happiness she deserves. To hear that Zélide is happy will rejoice my soul.

I beg you to pay my affectionate respects to Monsieur de Spaen, to assure my young Baron of my friendship, and to present my compliments to his governor.

I am always, Madame, your most obliged and humble servant,
                                BOSWELL D'AUCHINLECK.

FRIDAY 8 JUNE. I kept the house with a cold. Hahn visited me for the last time, advised me against taking drugs, and bid me not consult physicians, as people distressed as I was were timorous and obedient, and might be imposed upon. This was very honest. He assured me that time, attention, and regularity would make me quite well. Brown came and smoked a pipe with me, and said that we must take the Christian religion liberally, according to reason.

[Received *c.* 8 June, Count Bentinck to Boswell]

                                Hague, 7 June 1764

DEAR BOSWELL,—In great hurry I send you the letter you have desired. I hope it will answer your ends, and that the dear black philosopher will meet everywhere with the good reception he so well deserves; and with a sirloin every Sunday, a leek and some oatmeal on other days, in order to partake of every part of the rights of a *great* Briton—saving *brimstone,* however, in every kind and shape.[7] GOD bless you; remember me often, and don't forget that you have promised to show me Dempster's letter.—Adieu. Ever yours,

BENTINCK.

SATURDAY 9 JUNE. After dinner I had a long conversation with Brown, who told me that I judged too hardly of myself, for that I never had discovered much melancholy. He said I should never own it at all. He said I might very probably be an envoy, and so rise in foreign employment. I found that I might be something. He said he could trust me with any business. I passed the evening with Jánosi, my Hungarian friend, and was very vivacious.

[Received *c.* 9 June, Craufurd to Boswell]

Rotterdam, 8 June 1764

DEAR SIR:—I duly received both your letters, the first inclosing your bill for ƒ18. on Mr. Davidson, and the last a *briefje* for the anker port, which shall be sent tomorrow to Leyden with the address you desire.[8] I see you are going to Berlin with Lord Marischal, who won't be here before Sunday or Monday, as the wind is contrary. I am afraid I won't have the pleasure of seeing you before your journey, as some unforeseen business has prevented our jaunt tomorrow, which is put off to the Saturday following. I beg you will make compliments to Mr. and Mrs. Brown, and believe me, Sir, your most obedient humble servant,

PATRICK CRAUFURD.

P.S. Your letter shall be delivered to Lord M.

SUNDAY 10 JUNE. I sat in all forenoon. At one I had a handsome chaise and drove myself to Zuylen. I was in solid spirits in the old *château,* but rather too odd was I; for I talked of my pride, and

[7] The sirloin for England, the leek for Wales, the oatmeal for Scotland. By brimstone Bentinck perhaps refers to the British devotion to brimstone and treacle (sulphur and molasses) as medicine, and to hell-fire as subject-matter for sermons.   [8] The port was a present to Gronovius. See pp. 228, 268.

wishing to be a king. Zélide and I were left alone. She owned to me that she was hypochondriac, and that she had no religion other than that of the adoration of one God. In short, she discovered an unhinged mind; yet I loved her.[9] I supped at Brown's.

[Received *c.* 10 June, Abraham Gronovius to Boswell. Original in Latin][1]

Leyden, 9 June 1764

MOST NOBLE FRIEND,—I profess myself, of course, indebted in the highest degree to the singular thoughtfulness which prompted you, though short of time, to honour me last Wednesday in my garden with your most agreeable company; I hope that you arrived safely at Utrecht. But I blush at the excess of your generosity even while I acknowledge my obligation to you; I mean of course the forty-five bottles of port which, by your order and through the attention of Mr. Craufurd at Rotterdam, were delivered today. What return I can make for this gift, what thanks I can utter for this ready liberality of yours, I hardly know. In the mean time I hope that the journey into Germany, which you are about to undertake in the company of that famous hero the Earl Marischal, will be happy and auspicious; and when it has been prosperously concluded, I shall congratulate myself heartily if it is my lot again to enjoy the pleasure of your friendly conversation, and to admire those virtues with which you have adorned an ingenuous heart. Continue therefore to press your father's footsteps: to do so is to cultivate piety, virtue, and learning, and thus to aggrandize the glory of the name of Boswell to your country's profit: I predict that it will one day resound with gratitude for your services. May GOD ALMIGHTY in his goodness grant it. Farewell, my pride and glory; keep a place in your heart for your

ABRAHAM GRONOVIUS.

[9] "You would be miserable with her. Yet she is to write, and loves you" (Memorandum for 11 June).

[1] Gronovius's original (an elegant bit of classical Latinity quite different in style from the workaday Latin of Trotz and Gaubius) is printed on p. 393.

MONDAY 11 JUNE. I had sat up all night. Reynst of The Hague met me, and carried me to Oblet's,[2] where I found Monsieur and Madame Hasselaer, whom I have an antipathy against, and my dear Zélide, whom I have a sympathy with. My imbecility will never leave me. Zélide was in a fever of spirits.[3] I drove about with her and Madame Hasselaer and had curious reflections to myself. In August last I was a gloomy, deplorable wretch in this dull city. Now I am a fine, gay gentleman, the gallant of fine, gay ladies. After dinner I went about and paid my visits *pour prendre congé*. I was as happy as a prince. At seven Trotzius was with me. Over a glass of cordial Malaga, we vowed everlasting friendship, as a German professor understands *Amicitia*. We parted upon excellent terms. At eight Reynst came to me, and from many circumstances well interpreted, he persuaded me that Zélide was really in love with me. I believed it. But I was mild and *retenu*. Richardson also arrived. I had Reynst and him at supper.

[Boswell to Johnston]

Utrecht, 11 June 1764

MY DEAR FRIEND,—More than two months ago, I sent you a long letter to the care of Provost Graham. If it has been lost or miscarried, I am very sorry. Yet I think at any rate you might have written to me again before this time. I hope you are well, at least in your ordinary state.

Since I received your last, I have had most dreadful returns of the blackest melancholy. I have endured more than I ever did. To tell you my sufferings from a horrid imagination is scarcely possible; for I have had ideas of which to describe the frightful

---

[2] An inn.

[3] "Yesterday, after sitting up all night, you went with Reynst to Oblet's and met Zélide. She sent you play. . . . She was *échauffée* but sweet. . . . This day read her play. At eleven go to her" (Memorandum for 12 June). Belle's comedy was never printed, and Godet, her biographer, makes no mention of having seen it in manuscript.

effects, no language has words sufficient. GOD preserve me from
returns of the dire distemper, for indeed of late it had almost
crushed me. My mind was tortured in a thousand ways. I really
was not myself. O Johnston, how unfortunate am I to have such
a mind! However, let me console myself. Let me view the agreeable
side. I have bright parts. I have generous sentiments. I have warm
affections. When I am well, I am supremely blessed.

No more of this. 'Tis all chimera. Let me talk plain matter of
fact, plain common sense. I have now completed my winter at
Utrecht, have improved in knowledge, and have made the most of
the company here. I have been several times at the brilliant Hague,
and have established a friendship with my Dutch relations, and
obtained the acquaintance of other people of distinction. In short,
I have passed nine months in Holland to rational purpose, and to
the satisfaction of my worthy father.

And now, Johnston, as a reward for my behaviour, behold me
enjoying uncommon good fortune. My Lord Marischal is so good
as to take me with him to Germany. I expect him here every day.
We are to go to Lüneburg, to Brunswick, and at last to Berlin. My
father is highly pleased with the scheme, and has given me a
genteel credit. All is well; and if I am not happy, it must be owing
to a disturbed mind. This unexpected felicity has made me quite
a new man, has given new life to me. Not three weeks ago the
whole Creation and all the events of life seemed equal and indifferent. All was jumbled in one dreary chaos. You have no notion
how bad I was. However, I have had such a conduct here as to leave
a character which will always do me honour. Think only of my
happiness now to travel with the ancient Scottish nobleman who
has seen so much of the world in all its grandeur and all its
pleasure; who is at courts as I am in the houses of Ayrshire lairds,
and who is with all this a friendly, easy man. Such a change as I
now feel makes me more and more convinced of immortality, for
I see how a man can be quite extinguished and yet can revive. Go,
my friend, by yourself to Arthur Seat; think of me in distant
regions. Love me ever, and let us hope for many, many happy days

together. God bless and preserve you, my worthy Sir. I ever remain, your most affectionate friend,

JAMES BOSWELL.

Pray recollect the conversations which we have had on travelling. I shall, while abroad, lay up a store of pleasing ideas. I shall return composed and put on the gown and be a useful member of society as well as an agreeable private friend. Be as happy as you can, and think that you contribute to make me so; as indeed you certainly will when you relate to me your complacent days during my absence. Remember me kindly to Cairnie and to our other good common acquaintances. Farewell.

[Boswell to Temple]

[Utrecht, *c.* 11 June 1764]

MY DEAR FRIEND,— . . . I am now surprisingly well. I look back to my late situation with fearful amazement, and scarcely can believe that it has been.

What is the human mind? Let us calm our restless curiosity, for in this life we shall never know. While I have been crushed with a load of gloom, I have strove with severe intenseness of thought to find out the "Spirit of Man." But all my thinking has been in vain. It has increased my disorder and turned my speculations inwards upon my own mind, concerning which distempered imagination has formed the most wild and dreary conjectures. I have been so cruelly dejected as seriously to dread annihilation. I have found my faculties decaying gradually, and have imagined that in a very little time the last spark of celestial fire would be totally extinguished. Demon no less absurd than malevolent! why torment me thus? *Can* celestial fire be extinguished? No, it cannot. I have thought, if my mind is a collection of springs, these springs are all unhinged, and the machine is all destroyed; or if my mind is a waxen table, the wax is melted by the furnace of sorrow, and all my ideas and all my principles are dissolved, are run into one dead mass. Good God, my friend, what horrid chimeras! Where was

manly Reason at such seasons? Reason existed, but was over-
powered. Yet have I felt the generous resolve swelling in my bosom.
I have said to the Demon of Hypochondria, as the bold Highlander
in *Fingal* says to his Deity of fanciful conjecture, "Show thyself to
me, and I will search thee with my spear."

Take it not ill, Temple, that I have once more rehearsed my
sufferings. It is Boswell who suffered. Ah! Temple! what a strange
friend have you got! Behold him at one time an abject, perhaps an
offensive, being; at another time the most spirited, the most agreeable of the sons of men. Love him, for he ever loves you. His friendship is proof against wretchedness and against felicity. In that he is
invariable. After all, let us hope for many years of serene happiness
here, and for permanent felicity hereafter.

In my last I was doubting the truth of Christianity. Shall I tell
you why? Spleen brought back upon my mind the Christianity of
my nurse, and of that could I *not* doubt? You know how miserably
I was educated with respect to religion. I am now again at rest. I
view Deity as I ought to do, and I am convinced that Jesus Christ
had a divine commission, that through him the justice of GOD is
satisfied; and that he has given us the most exalted morality: "To
love GOD with all our heart, and our neighbour as ourselves." There
is enough. As to the accessory doctrines which have been disputed
about with holy zeal, I let them alone.

My dear Temple, how great is the force of early impressions!
Is it not incredible that we should think worse of the character of
God than of that of a sensible worthy *man?* And yet I have done
so, and shuddered with horror to think of my benevolent Creator.
You have always had clear and elevated sentiments of religion.
After all my struggles I am in the same happy situation. "Father
of light and life," grant that I may continue so!

And now, Temple, let me rejoice thee, for the joy of thy friend
is fully thine. In a day or two I am to set out for Berlin. . . . I shall
be presented at the different courts upon the very best footing. I
shall acquire real knowledge as well as elegance of behaviour in the

company of a politician and a courtier. My father is highly pleased with this scheme and has given me a handsome credit. In short, all things are as I could wish.

Well, my friend, what think you? Am I not now myself? Farewell—GOD bless you. Think of me with your usual affection. I shall write to you henceforth in a style that will give you pleasure. I leave my friendly compliments to Bob, to Nicholls, and to Claxton; and I ever remain your most affectionate friend,

JAMES BOSWELL.

TUESDAY 12 JUNE. I had a room in the opposite side of my *Cour de l'Empereur* where I had Richardson lodged. At eleven I met Zélide at her music master's, where she played delightfully. I then walked with her and Bernard. I was touched with regret at the thoughts of parting with her. Yet she rattled so much that she really vexed me.

I gave a plain dinner to Richardson, Brown, and Carron, after which we went and saw the old library of the canons of Utrecht. We drank tea at Brown's, where was Hahn, who said that Zélide would be always *une malheureuse demoiselle*, as she was quite governed by fancy. Richardson and I walked. He said he was surprised to find a physician talk so of his patient, for that from Hahn's manner of talking, Mademoiselle de Zuylen seemed to be crazy. I was vexed at this. Richardson's sound, hard knowledge entertained me well. We supped *tête à tête*.

[Received *c.* 12 June 1764, Lord Marischal to Boswell]

Rotterdam, 11 June [1764]

LORD MARISCHAL's compliments to Mr. Boswell, whom he hopes to have the pleasure to see the 13th at Utrecht, and shall stay two nights, to wait on Mrs. Brown and give her a day to *jobeler avec son amie*,[4] Madame de Froment.

[4] "To frolic with her friend." *Jobeler* (which I find recorded only with the spelling *jobler*) is slang.

WEDNESDAY 13 JUNE.[5] I carried Richardson to dine at the
Plaats Royaal, my old eating table. I was lumpish and dreary. I
wished to be rid of Richardson. I thought my being obliged to entertain him a most laborious task. So discontented a mortal am I.
My fancy forms plans. I execute them. They prove insipid. He and
I walked. I complained to him of black ideas of religion. He said,
"You think too much." At eight Lord Marischal arrived. I immediately waited upon him, and found him the plain old Scots nobleman. He had with him Madame de Froment, a Turkish lady who
was taken prisoner by Marshal Keith at the siege of Otchakov in
the year 1733. My Lord has educated her just as his own daughter,
and has married her to a French gentleman.[6] I introduced to his
Lordship Richardson and Brown. They supped with me.

THURSDAY 14 JUNE. At ten Lord Marischal honoured me
with a visit, as did Monsieur de Zuylen, whom I had promised to
present to my Lord. Was I not well? I then again met Zélide at her
music master's. I was proud and solemn. She gave me her confession of faith, which I found elegant but slight. She threw out the
common objections against revelation. She was a poetical sceptic.
One great objection was that Christ says of his Gospel, "They that
believe shall be saved; but they that believe not shall be damned."
Richardson said people did not know what was meant by damna-
tion. For his part, he considered that those who believe not shall be
damned in no other sense but that they shall be as those who never

[5] "This day, get up soon. *Think.* Pay all. Ducat, Marion. Books, Carron and
Bonnet" (Memorandum for this day. Marion was Mrs. Brown's maid).
[6] Lord Marischal's younger brother, James Keith, after the failure of the
Jacobite uprising of 1715, held high commands successively in the Spanish and Russian services, then became a field-marshal in the Prussian Army
and Frederick the Great's most trusted general. He was killed in 1758 at
the battle of Hochkirch. The siege of Otchakov occurred in 1737, not 1733;
in it Keith was seriously wounded. Emet-Ulla (at this time thirty-nine
years old) was the daughter of a Turkish chief-janissary. In 1763 she had been
converted to Protestant Christianity, and had married Denis-Daniel de
Froment, a lieutenant-colonel in the Sardinian service. They were later
divorced.

had the happiness to hear of Christ. "For," said he, "Christ has diffused salvation 'to all men.' 'This is the light which lighteth every man that cometh into the world.' " In short, I find every man has his own Christianity.

At two I had a chaise and drove Richardson out to Zuylen, where we dined. Zélide and I had a long conversation. She said she did not care for respect. She liked to have everybody free with her, and that they should tell her her faults. I told her that this was very wrong; for she would hardly find a husband of merit who had not some pride, and who would not be hurt at finding people so free with his wife.[7] I owned to her that I was very sorry to leave her. She gave me many a tender look. We took a kind farewell, as I did of all the family. Monsieur de Zuylen and I talked a long time. I am sure he liked me. He has been exceedingly civil to me. Richardson could not well understand Zélide and me. "It is lucky," said Mr. Chaplain to me, "that you are to be no longer together; for you would learn her nonsense, and she would learn yours." He was right. Our airy speculating is not thinking.

Richardson left me this evening. I went to Brown's, where I found my good Lord Marischal, who told us many good stories of miracles in Spain, from whence I could well see that his lordship was none of the most orthodox. Madame de Froment was indisposed, which kept my Lord still at Utrecht.

FRIDAY 15 JUNE. I took cordial farewell of old Fencer Cirx and bid him live till he was past one hundred. After breakfast I waited on Lord Marischal, who told us many stories with a calm, cheerful vivacity that pleased me immensely. Hahn was charmed. He and I walked together. He said Zélide had no use of her reasoning powers. That she had no pleasure in realities. All must be ideal,

[7] The memorandum shows that Boswell was actually not so abstract: "After dinner, talked fully to Zélide, who owned she wanted not respect. But you said, 'A husband—*I*, for instance—would be miserable to have people snub his wife.' " Belle reported this conversation—or probably summarized many similar conversations—in one of her letters to Constant d'Hermenches. See p. 381.

all visionary. She was not a bit amused with the most ingenious chemical experiments.[8] In short, my fair friend is an unhappy existence. I dined with Brown. Madame Brown is now lying in. Lord Marischal drank coffee with us, and was as entertaining as ever.

SATURDAY 16 JUNE. I dined *tête à tête* with Brown. I had heard that Madame de Froment had got no agreeable character of me, and imagined me a misanthrope. She wanted to make acquaintance with me before we set out on our long journey. I went with her and Mademoiselle Kinloch to Van Mollem's Gardens,[9] and then returned to Brown's, walked, and went to Oblet's, where I wished the Turk a good night, leaving her possessed with different sentiments of me, her fellow-traveller. At night I found myself hurried, having journal to bring up, accounts to settle, letters to write. I intended to sit up. But my nerves failed me. I lay naked on the hard floor with a coverlet above me. Was not this madness? At last I went to bed.

SUNDAY 17 JUNE. Brown's child was baptized in the English church. Lord Marischal was the *parrain*. I was sour and gloomy. I was just in a Scots country kirk.[1] We all drank coffee at Madame Brown's. It was agreeable to see a family happy on the increase of the species, &c. But it gave no pleasure to me.

At six Lord Marischal, Madame de Froment, Mademoiselle Kinloch, and I drove to Zuylen, where we drank tea before the gate in the open air. Zélide said to me, "Are you back again? We made a touching adieu." She gave me a letter which she had written to me, on my departure, and bid me not read it till I was just going. She and I and Madame de Froment in one coach, Madame de Zuylen, Lord Marischal, and Mademoiselle Kinloch

[8] Boswell remembered this and put it (with a not very decent comment of his own) into the draft of a letter to Belle, though he appears to have deleted it in the letter actually sent. See p. 317.

[9] On the Vecht, the gardens of a prosperous silk manufacturer. Then one of the sights of Utrecht.

[1] So sour and gloomy that he preferred not to mention the fact that he was joint godfather. See p. 376. The child was a girl.

in another, went and saw a beautiful *campagne*[2] on the way to Amsterdam. Zélide seemed much agitated, said she had never been in love, but said that *one* might meet with *un homme aimable*, &c., &c., &c., for whom *one* might feel a strong affection, which would probably be lasting, *but* this amiable man might not have the same affection for *one*. In short she spoke too plain to leave me in doubt that she *really* loved me. But then away she went with her wild fancy, saying that she thought only of the present moment. "I had rather feel than think. I should like to have a husband who would let me go away sometimes to amuse myself." In short, she seemed a frantic libertine. She said to me, "Sir, if you see the Count of Anhalt, don't speak to him of me. He may some day be my husband."[3] She gave me her hand at parting, and the tender tear stood crystal in her eye. Poor Zélide! I took hearty leave at Brown's. I was sorry to leave the scene of much internal exercise. I sat up all night.

[Boswell to Temple]

Utrecht, 17 June 1764

MY DEAR TEMPLE,— . . . I now sit down a very happy man. I am neither high nor low. I am quite free from hypochondria. I have a fine gentle flow of spirits. I hope to show you this by my manner of writing. You have asked me for a letter on the present state of the Dutch, which I can only make out by giving you some detached observations, from which, however, you may form a tolerable idea of what you wish to know.

The Dutch, like all other republican states, have never con-

---

[2] That is, a *maison de campagne*, a country-house with a garden.

[3] Friedrich Count of Anhalt, the son by a morganatic marriage of the Hereditary Prince of Anhalt-Dessau, was in the Prussian service; he was at this time Frederick's *aide-de-camp* and later became his Adjutant General. He had never seen Belle de Zuylen, but Henri Alexandre de Catt, a Swiss who had been tutor to her brothers and then had gone to Potsdam as reader to Frederick, had sung her praises so effectively that the Count had made overtures of marriage and was proposing a trip to Utrecht.

tinued long in the same situation as to riches and felicity. But, besides the usual disadvantages of having the supreme power in a
great many hands, this nation has been remarkably precarious on
account of its subsisting entirely by trade, which renders it absolutely dependent on foreign states. Formerly their trade was exceedingly extensive. Not only had they the sole market for several
sorts of Indian merchandise, but they furnished many of the most
necessary manufactures to the greatest part of Europe. Hence was
the spirit of industry so universally diffused amongst this people.
Hence they became so rich and so powerful. Now the case is very
much altered. The English share with them the Indian trade, and
the other nations manufacture for themselves. While the Dutch
had the universal trade, the States loaded with exorbitant taxes the
necessaries of life, knowing that the manufacturers would propor-
tionably heighten the price of their labour, so that the nations who
purchased their goods should in reality furnish the public money.
When those nations began to work themselves, the States should
undoubtedly have lowered their taxes, and by selling at a moderate
price have prevented the progress of manufactures in other countries. But the griping disposition of the Batavian government was
greater than their wisdom. The taxes continued the same, so that
in a little time the other nations, where living was not so dear, were
able to undersell the Dutch in some of their principal commodities.
Nay, so great is the difference that French, but particularly English, cloth is sold cheaper here than cloth made in the country,
although the imposts upon foreign cloth are very high. Several of
the Dutch regiments are clothed with English manufacture.

In such circumstances this trading nation must be in a very bad
way. Most of their principal towns are sadly decayed, and instead
of finding every mortal employed, you meet with multitudes of
poor creatures who are starving in idleness. Utrecht is remarkably
ruined. There are whole lanes of wretches who have no other sub-
sistence than potatoes, gin, and stuff which they call tea and coffee;
and what is worst of all, I believe they are so habituated to this life
that they would not take work if it should be offered to them. The

Hague is a beautiful and elegant place. It is, however, by no means a Dutch town; the simplicity and plain honesty of the old Hollanders has given way to the show and politeness of the French, with this difference, that a Frenchman is <truly at> ease, whereas the Dutchman is <as y>et but a painful imitator. Luxury prevails much both at The Hague and among the rich merchants at Amsterdam.

You see, then, that things are very different here from what most people in England imagine. Were Sir William Temple to revisit these Provinces, he would scarcely believe the amazing alteration which they have undergone. The Magistrates' places in most of the towns, which in his time were filled up by worthy, substantial citizens who were burgomasters for honour and not for profit, are now filled up by hungry fellows who take them for bread and squeeze as much as they can from the inhabitants. The contests with respect to the Stadtholder are now over. Almost all the men of weight have acceded to the Court, except the citizens of Amsterdam, who must always wish to be free from any superior power. The present Prince of Orange will be of age two years hence. What changes he may produce, I cannot say. But surely he has it in his power to do a great deal. The universities here are much fallen. In short, the Seven Provinces would require the powers of all the politicians that they ever had to set them right again.

After politics what say you to the fair? I delivered your respects with all due enthusiasm to Mademoiselle de Zuylen. She was much pleased. I gave her a sketch of your character, which I believe she will not easily forget. It struck her not a little; and my expressions of friendship pleased her because they seemed romantic. Temple, be assured that I could have this angelic creature for my wife. But she has such an imagination that I pity the man who puts his head in her power. For my part, I choose to be safe. I shall write you more of her.

18 June, four in the morning. Two hours hence, my friend, away I go. Farewell once more, my dear Temple. Yours ever,

JAMES BOSWELL.

MONDAY 18 JUNE. My wakeful night well past, I was in glow of spirits. Zélide's letter was long and warm. She imagined me in love with her, and with much romantic delicacy talked of this having rendered her *distraite*. I was honest or simple enough to leave her a short letter, assuring her that I was not *amoureux*, but would always be her *fidèle ami.*[4]

I had all my affairs in order. Honest Carron came and took leave of me. And next comes a most flagrant whim. Some days ago I called to me François, told him that he had served me honestly and well, and that I could give him a good character as a servant. I said I hoped that I had been a good master. To know this certainly, I ordered him to write out a full character of me, since he entered to my service, and charged him to mark equally the bad and the good which he had observed, and to give it me carefully sealed up. I accordingly received it this morning.

I took leave of my house in which I have had such an infinity of ideas. At seven we set out in a coach and four. . . .

[Received 18 June 1764, François Mazerac to Boswell.
Original in French][5]

Utrecht, 17 June 1764

MONSIEUR:—My small ability makes it almost impossible for me to comply with your orders, and I hope that Monsieur will take my remarks kindly and regard them as coming from a person who is only trying to obey you.

First: I have found that Monsieur is extremely negligent about his money, his watch, and other effects, in leaving them on the table, or in leaving the key on the bureau, and going out of the room leaving the door open, as happened several times at The Hague. If it should ever happen that you have the misfortune to lose something in this way, you might entertain suspicions of your

---

[4] The entire correspondence with Zélide is collected below, pp. 293–385.
[5] François's spelling and punctuation are so amusing that I have ventured to print his letter below, p. 394, without editing.

servant or some other innocent person. There is a saying, "Opportunity makes the thief."

Secondly: I have found that Monsieur has a good heart, in doing good to the poor: a virtue which is dictated by humanity and prescribed by religion.

Thirdly: Monsieur is not at all given to backbiting, a vice very common among great minds.

Fourthly:[6] Very punctual in performing the duties of your religion, by going to church, not swearing, and above all by saying your prayers every morning.

Fifthly: I have found that when Monsieur has invited company, the guests always arrived before you, which might expose you to some reproach, especially in another country where they care more for social formalities than they do here.

Sixthly: I have found that Monsieur applies himself too much to study, which is noble in itself but ruinous to health if not done judiciously.

Seventhly: I find that Monsieur goes to bed too late, which, with the study, will make you lose your health, which Monsieur will regret when it is too late and there is no help for it.

Eighthly and last item: I have found in Monsieur a really Christian and noble heart, especially towards me, which I shall never forget. May the Father of fathers take you under His holy protection, and keep His eye on you, guarding you as a beloved child. May He guide your steps and direct your thoughts, so that no harm may come to you, and that when you have returned home safe and sound, you will bless Him therefor eternally.

I end by thanking Monsieur again for all his goodness, begging him to think of me sometimes. As for me, I believe I shall never forget Monsieur.—Permit me to beg you, Monsieur, that, should you ever have a chance, you will let me know how you are. Your very grieved and faithful servant,

FRANÇOIS MAZERAC.

---

[6] François's original has two "Thirdlys."

*Belle de Zuylen (Zélide) about 1766, from a drawing
by Maurice Quentin de La Tour, in the Louvre.*

Correspondence with
Belle de Zuylen (Zélide) and Others
1764–1769.

INTRODUCTION.[1] Isabella Agneta Elisabeth van Tuyll, Belle de Zuylen, or "Zélide," belonged to one of the oldest families in Holland. For six hundred years the Van Tuylls had upheld their noble rank with a conscious rectitude. Her father, Diederik Jacob van Tuyll van Serooskerken, Lord of Zuylen and Westbroek, Marshal of Montfoort, owned estates a few miles from Utrecht. He was one of the governors of the Province, a man remarkable, even in his own scrupulous world, for integrity and service of the state. In his moated castle on the Vecht, and in his sedate town-house, Zélide grew up, chastened by the decorum and restraint of the seventeenth century which still lingered there, unmodified by the lapse of generations. Family pride, the deeper for a provincial simplicity, enclosed her in its distinguished prison. At the time of Boswell's arrival she was twenty-three years of age. Society at Utrecht and The Hague was perplexed, ruffled, or entertained by the unconventionality of Monsieur de Zuylen's daughter. She had just written and printed *Le Noble,* an anonymous satire on the prejudices of caste.[2] Heraldically minded seigneurs could find no precedent

[1] By the late Geoffrey Scott, slightly revised by Frederick A. Pottle. This essay was first published in 1928 in Colonel Isham's privately printed *Private Papers of James Boswell.* The notes that follow are all by Frederick A. Pottle unless Mr. Scott's name is attached.

[2] Perhaps "was just writing and was about to print." *Le Noble* bears the

in their experience for a young lady writing, still less publishing, a *conte* in the style of Voltaire's *Candide,* particularly if its irony was at their expense. Her conversation, though respectful in tone and even deferential when addressed to themselves (for Zélide was willing to please) took distressing turns; orthodoxy was ignored and flouted; rank made light of; religion—chastity even—treated as an open question; she talked inappropriately for her sex and years and she talked too fast and too much. She carried on clandestine correspondences, and, owing to the transparency of her character, she seldom erred without being found out. "Une demoiselle—cela!"[3] was the protest of offended dowagers. Yet frankness and good nature were assigned to her credit and she was a Van Tuyll: as such she could be neither accounted for nor condoned; still less could she be ignored.

Belle de Zuylen, exasperated by the tedium of Dutch still-life ("Ici," she complained, "l'on est vif tout seul"),[4] scanned the horizon of Utrecht for any object that might be moving, animated, or odd. In the autumn of 1763 she could not fail to recognize that such an object had appeared. Boswell had arrived, dressed in silver and

imprint Amsterdam, 1763, but I do not know that the exact date of its publication has been fixed. The first reference to it in Belle's correspondence with Constant d'Hermenches occurs in a letter dated 10 January 1764. It seems to me more likely that *Le Noble* appeared *after* Boswell's arrival in Utrecht than before, and that he was witness to the scandal it caused. The story runs as follows: Julie, daughter of the Baron d'Arnonville, a stiff and stupid representative of the *ancienne noblesse,* is in love with young Valaincourt, a recent noble, his father having received his title for distinguished services to the state. Knowing that the Baron d'Arnonville will never listen to her lover's suit unless he believes him to be descended from an ancient family, Julie, a level-headed girl, arranges matters satisfactorily for a time by announcing airily that Valaincourt is descended from Rinaldo, the legendary foe of Charlemagne. When this genealogy explodes and she is locked up, she escapes out of the window to her lover, after throwing down several of the family portraits to fill a mud hole underneath. "She had never believed that one could get so much support from one's grandfathers. . . . She was happy, and her sons were not chevaliers."   [3] "*That* a young lady!"
[4] "Here one has to be lively all by one's self."

green; an introduction from Sir David Dalrymple to Count Nassau had placed him in the circle of Zélide's friends and relations. He commended himself to her at once by his originality. "J'étais prévenue pour vous," she later confessed. "Mais moi pas pour vous," he had replied, with the frankness in which she delighted.[5] The interplay of the two characters is clear. Boswell had come to Utrecht full of plans and circumspection. The new influence of Johnson was in its earliest force; he must be serious, and be taken seriously; he pictured himself as the future Laird of Auchinleck, propping the established order of things. He was determined to cut a dignified figure, to commend himself on terms of equality to the best society of Holland. He found in that society a general verdict that Zélide was unmaidenly and unbalanced. He assumed from the start an attitude of reproof. Zélide was, in any case, not of the type he favoured. He desired society ladies to be conspicuously *grandes dames,* stimulating in his mind a feudal "group of ideas"; Zélide laughed at all such pretensions. Or else they should pay a visibly palpitating tribute to his sex. Irony put him at a disadvantage; he mistrusted it deeply; as for metaphysics, "speculations of that kind in a woman are more ridiculous than I choose to express."

For the first months at Utrecht the acquaintance was indifferently pursued. The occasional comments in Boswell's casual memoranda are cautious or disparaging. "You passed three hours at Brown's with Miss de Zuylen. You was too much off guard" (12 November 1763).... "Miss de Zuylen. You was shocked or rather offended with her unlimited vivacity. You was on your guard" (28 November 1763). Zélide, on her side, was tolerably well occupied with a number of suitors, a clandestine epistolary intimacy with Constant d'Hermenches, and an elaborate plot to marry his friend, the Marquis de Bellegarde. The sententious young Scotchman, awkwardly masking his native drollery by what he conceived to be a demeanour of Spanish pride, afforded her friendly amusement and no more.

Nevertheless, if Zélide shocked Boswell's conventional preju-

[5] See p. 128.

dices, the Van Tuylls as a family were everything he approved; they very worthily held their part in the Great Scheme of Subordination which was Boswell's philosophy, and Zélide was a considerable heiress. Finding himself well received, and observing that Zélide had, after all, some devoted friends and could occasionally be quiet and "retenue," he placed her tentatively on his probationary list of wives. Here he had many misgivings: "Zélide was *nervish*. You saw she would make a sad wife, and propagate wretches" (Memorandum, 18 April). In any case Madame Geelvinck, a young, soft, rich widow, was to be preferred. An inconclusive courtship of *la Veuve* filled the last weeks of his Dutch residence; but this tended rather to give his friendship with Belle de Zuylen a romantic colour, since the two ladies were friends and frequently found together. Such was the situation when Boswell drove out to the castle on 14 June 1764 to pay his farewell visit. Belle de Zuylen saw one more of her few human amusements on the point of vanishing. Boswell, dressed up for his *visite de congé*, comical and warm-hearted, bows himself away from the portcullis. The "odd and lovable" could not in her narrow world be lost without a pang.[6]

At this point, on 14 June 1764, four days before Boswell's actual departure from Utrecht, begins the correspondence here printed; it continued over a period of four years. From Utrecht Boswell went in Lord Marischal's company to Berlin, where he spent the summer. He then made a tour of several of the German courts, and visited Switzerland, where he obtained interviews with both Rousseau and Voltaire. Early in January, 1765, he crossed into Italy, remaining there, with a momentous excursion into Corsica, almost a year. In December, 1765, he turned his steps towards Scotland, reaching Paris in January, 1766. He had intended to stay there some time and then to go home by way of Holland, so as to see Zélide again, but abandoned these plans upon receiving news of his mother's death and a plea from his father to come home at once. By March, 1766, he was again in Scotland, from which he had been absent more than three years. The correspondence with Zélide

[6] The remainder of the Introduction is by Frederick A. Pottle.

lapsed for some time. He was admitted a member of the Scottish bar in July, 1766, and after that date, for the next twenty years, was kept busy in Edinburgh by his legal practice during the terms of the courts. Zélide visited London in the autumn and winter of 1766–1767, at a period of the year when Boswell, even if he had known in time of her being there, could have paid her no more than a flying visit, but she did not write to him. It was he who took the first step towards re-opening the correspondence. The Reverend Mr. Brown of Utrecht made a visit to Scotland in the summer of 1767, and when he returned, Boswell gave him a letter to Zélide proposing that they should write to each other. Boswell was at this time committed to a scheme of marrying a Scots heiress, Miss Blair. But Miss Blair refused him, and his appealing and very successful book on Corsica, published early in 1768, revived Zélide's affection and respect. The comedy ended in a flurry of letters exchanged in the spring of 1768, while Boswell was in London, whither he had gone to savour the success of the *Account of Corsica*. But there remained an epilogue: a letter from Mr. Brown, written more than a year later, giving him news of Zélide and his old servant, François.

[1. Belle de Zuylen to Boswell. Original in French][7]

[Zuylen] Thursday 14 June [1764] 11 o'clock
IN SPITE OF ALL YOUR PHILOSOPHY, you are singularly curious, my friend, to find out what my feelings are about you. It would perhaps be more dignified in you not to *say so;* but I have no regard for dignity, and I despise the art which you revere so much. I am ready to afford you this pleasure because I desire your happiness; and pleasure is a part of happiness. Besides, it is natural to me to say what I feel and what I think.

Well, then, I should tell you that there is a man[8] in the world

[7] Translation by Geoffrey Scott, who also translated letters Nos. 2, 3, 5, 9, 12, 13, 15, 17, and 19 below. These translations originally appeared in the second volume of Colonel Isham's privately printed *Private Papers of James Boswell*.
[8] The Marquis de Bellegarde, a man much older than herself, whom she had

(I do not think that you know him) of whom I usually think at night, in the morning, and sometimes during the day. For three or four days past I have thought of him less often. Do you guess why? It is because you, my philosophical friend, appeared to me to be experiencing the agitation of a lover. Had you always shown your-self a cold and grave mortal such as you require my husband to be, you would not have caused me a single minute's distraction. I am affected by your departure; I have thought of you all the evening. I find you odd and lovable. I have a higher regard for you than for any one, and I am proud of being your friend. Are you not satisfied?

What I find *less* admirable in you is to have so quickly rid your-self of those generous scruples for which you took so much credit to yourself the other day.[9] The circumstances were the same today: my father showed you the same friendship; why did you not reason as you did before? Admit that it is only a question of *degree:* our inclinations only require a certain degree of force to get the better of our principles and to make us forget our duty; or else they seduce our minds, and then we alter our ideas. It would be a much finer plan to address yourself to my father, adding to each of your letters to him a letter for me, unsealed, in which you shall preach morality and religion. *I* would not reply to you, because that would not be correct; but you could always go on preaching and it is possible that the improvement you desire might be effected.

Good-bye, I am going to bed.

If you do not like my plan, and I am to go on writing to you, I shall write with the utmost freedom. With libertines I am rigid and reserved, but I can afford to be free with a discreet friend, with a prudent man—so *prudent* that he would refuse supreme happi-ness if it were offered to him, out of fear of not being equally happy all the days of his life. For my own part, I dare not flatter myself

---

determined to marry, though she had actually seen very little of him and was finding him a very sluggish suitor.

[9] Boswell had said that he would not correspond with her surreptitiously because of his respect for her father.

that Providence has such riches of felicity in store for me that I have only to choose between them; I think I shall take hold of the first happiness that may present itself. My thought will perhaps be, "If this one does not last, well, after this, . . . another."

Good-bye.

Friday morning

You believe that out of mere goodness, out of compassion, a woman, such as I am, might be weak; I believe you are mistaken. To sympathize with the pains of love, you must share in its feelings. If a man should say, "I love you and I suffer," it would not excite much sympathy in me unless my heart suffered like his and felt the same desires. Even supposing a keen feeling of pity, a woman who understands what love means would not, out of pity alone, accord the last of the gifts which love has to bestow: the lover one merely pities will not obtain what is hardly obtained by the lover whom one loves. We are inclined to get the most we can out of our weaknesses: we forgive ourselves more readily for our lapses in proportion as they make us happy. I could say many other things on this head; for, though one's conduct may be irreproachable, one knows a great deal about the subject when the senses teach the soul all the feelings of which they are capable, and the imagination lets no one of them pass without extending it to the full.

In my present humour I do not regard the advice of selecting a cold husband as the wisest of your propositions. If I am much in love with my husband, and he with me, it is at least possible that I shall not fall in love with another; if we were but little in love, I would certainly love some one else. My spirit is formed to have strong feelings, and will assuredly not escape its destiny. If I had neither father nor mother, as I said to you the other day, I would not get married. You explained to me the wickedness of such a course; but I should run the risk of doing much more harm by taking any other. Besides, to make up for this smallest injury in the world, I would do all the good in my power: I would restrict the harm within the narrowest limits and extend the good to my utmost. I should send my daughters away from me, if I had any, lest they should resemble me; my sons would be less ill-advised in resembling me, and I would make them my chief care. Nothing, nothing, would be neglected in their education which could make them useful and happy members of society; I would do so much for them that no one could reproach them with their birth, and the world would be forced to thank me for it. But I have a father and a mother whom I do not wish to bring to the grave and whose life I do not wish to render miserable.

What course should I take? I do not know. One must live from day to day, be guided by one's heart and by circumstances; not reason too much; sleep peacefully; amuse oneself, and follow one's inclinations when they do not lead straight into crime. Some weeks ago, when I was with Madame Hasselaer[1] and Monsieur Rendorp (he is one of my best friends and her best friend, and the most decent man I know), I said much that was wild, in my usual way, blended with much that was reasonable. I was dressing, and the point came when they had to leave. Madame Hasselaer's last words were that I was the strangest creature she had ever seen, and that if I ended by being worthless after all I had received from heaven, I should be a thousand times more culpable than another woman. "Not at all," said Monsieur Rendorp; "GOD has surely excused her. In this world it would work out very badly; but I assure you in the next world it can all be arranged."

I should be well pleased with a husband who would take me as his mistress: I should say to him, "Do not look on faithfulness as a duty: so long as I have more charm, more wit, more gaiety than another, so long as I am ready to act plays, to sing and play the harpsichord better than another, in order to please you, you will prefer me out of inclination; that is all I desire; and you on your side should have none but the rights and jealousies of a lover. If you wish me to love you always, the only way is to be always lovable."

[1] Cousin of "*la Veuve*" (Madame Geelvinck), and one of Belle de Zuylen's most intimate friends. Boswell did not like her.

You are now well up in my ideas on this subject. What would D'Hermenches and his like say if such a letter as this were to fall into their hands! What advantage they would expect to take of it! But I am writing to Cato. Cato's friend is very unlike him, but loves him much.

Sunday

You are still in Utrecht: that makes something of a difference. This letter is more suited to be posted than given into your hands. But no matter. On my first page I expressed myself rather badly when I said that my heart had been distracted from its usual inclination because I noticed in you the agitation of a lover. Not all agitations, thank God, are infectious. One must have some disposition of sympathy for that to happen. If between two good friends one remembers he is a man, the other naturally enough remembers she is a woman: a few days' absence should be sufficient to enable both to forget it.

Write to me, not often, but write long letters; and address them to Spruyt, the bookseller. I will send every fortnight to him to ask if there is anything for me. It will not matter if the end of your letters contradicts the beginning: when one knows human nature, one is not surprised to see contradictions in what is unstudied. Write your rapid thoughts in English; when you wish to make grave reflections, the dictionary will do less harm, and you may write in French. I will do the same; that is to say, the opposite. Give me always your exact address for towns where you intend a long visit. Be very careful, and remember that all my peace of mind depends on it. Do not ever be so absent-minded as to send your letters to my father's house. But would you not do well to write to him from Berlin that you have seen Monsieur Catt,[2] &c.? and you will tell him to give me your respects.

Good-bye, I have said everything; or at least I have said much.

[2] Henri Alexandre de Catt had been domestic tutor to Belle's brothers. Frederick the Great of Prussia, travelling *incognito* in Holland, had met him on a canal boat, and had been so much pleased with him that he had invited him to Potsdam as French reader. See also p. 287 *n.* 8.

[2. Boswell to Belle de Zuylen. Original in French][3]

Utrecht, 18 June 1764

YOU MAY WELL BELIEVE, my dear Zélide, that I am very much flattered by your interesting letter. But I must admit that you have given me some anxiety. You say that I "appear to you to have the agitation of a lover." I am extremely sorry for this. My sincerity, or perhaps my extreme simplicity, prevents me from leaving Utrecht without frankly enlightening you on this subject.

I have told you several times what my sentiments are towards you. I admire your mind. I love your goodness. But I am not in love with you. I swear to you I am not. I speak strongly because you have given me reason to think that your peace of mind may be involved. In such circumstances one must not stand on ceremony.

I am your faithful friend. I shall always be, if you allow me. If I can be of the least use to you, you will have a proof of how much I am yours. To be in correspondence with Zélide will be a great pleasure to me. Good-bye.[4]

[3. Belle de Zuylen to Boswell. Original in French]

[Zuylen] Monday evening, 18 June 1764

SO MUCH THE BETTER MY FRIEND; all the better if I made a mistake. I am not the least mortified by having remained in error for three days. Nor am I the least annoyed to have thought less, dur-

---

[3] All the letters by Boswell in this series, except Nos. 4 and 19, are drafts or copies.

[4] Among the memoranda is the following, headed "Nymwegen Memorandum," consequently written on the same day as this letter: "In sweet fine spirits you saw all well. You adored GOD. You resolved to have uniform command of passions; to keep up the character which Zélide has; to suffer in silence and never to own; never to be too strict; to judge by reason always, but get command of self. Habit is much. Now form above all *retenue*. Be fine with Zélide; love her." The "character which Zélide has" probably means "the character which Zélide believes you to have."

ing three days, of the man I love. Your friendship is more worth having than love. You are to be esteemed all the more that you are able to feel as you describe; I on my side am more flattered that you should feel towards me in that way. As for your peace of mind and my own (as I understood the matter), these were never in danger. What I wrote on Thursday evening was perfectly true when I wrote it: on Friday it appeared to me less true. I had slept well; I was no longer clear whether I had believed you to be in love with me, whether I had believed myself to be a little inclined to love you: all that appeared to me more or less a dream. On Sunday it appeared to me more or less an untruth. I felt some scruple in giving you my letter: I would have liked to have torn off the first page. But that would have been to destroy it all. I thought, "The date is my justification: what I wrote at evening on Thursday is what I thought at evening on Thursday. With Monsieur Boswell, there is no need for prudence. Give him the letter; it is an act of frankness, it is the diary of the heart of a live and feeling woman." I told you that two or three days' absence would make us forget the difference that Nature creates between friends of different sexes. *You* did not need to forget, since you had never remembered. In my case it is already entirely forgotten, but I shall always remember the excellent advice that your pure and disinterested affection prompted.

My friendship is yours for ever: count on it, however much you may think me fickle. I count on the stability of your feelings as on that of the rocks which God placed on the surface of the earth when he created the world. On my side I will be a little more tender one day than another, but every day you will be dear to me; every day I shall think as you said yesterday, "I am amusing myself, but if Monsieur Boswell were here it would be better still." On Thursday I was much touched by your going away. When you had left me, I remained alone for some time in a deep reverie; then I went for a turn in the carriage, and I spoke to my brother of nothing but you. Yesterday there was no reverie: I played comet,[5] and told stories to

[5] A card game.

my father. Yet I was not less fond of you than on Thursday; I was not less inclined to sacrifice a part of my happiness to yours; my heart was not less regretful of your departure.

Where, then, comes in the difference? I beg you not to accuse my heart: it is, I fancy, an affair of temperament; it depends on the wind or on the sun, and perhaps on the stomach. Why did Caesar neglect to conquer your islands? "Perhaps," says Pope, "he had not dined." Whether I have dined or not, I promise you that the bottom of my heart will always be the same towards you. I hope, all your life, you will be glad of it and it will never be an enigma to you. I am unwilling your ideas about it should depend on the false penetration of a Monsieur Reynst.[6] I am very glad to have told you everything and I will always be equally frank with you.

And now I must go to bed. I hope to sleep as peacefully as last night. It would be a very pleasant thing for once to think of no one, at least for a few days. But this wretched man that I love does not leave me in calm for long. He soon resumes his full rights. What I told you yesterday is not a fiction. Every word of it is truth; but no, I told you that you did not know him, and *that* is not at all certain. In fact it is very clear you have seen him; but fearing that his appearance is not of a kind to please you, I was unwilling either to describe him or to name him to you. He is a Roman Catholic, and my parents are Calvinists. I have loved him for two years, and I love him much. He has less imagination than I: he has not the same flight of passion, but he has a delicacy of taste, a cultivated, subtle, and just mind, a tender heart, a quiet and indolent vanity. How happy it makes me when I write verses to think he will read them! When he reads them he is very happy that I love him. But I am mad not to go to bed. Good-bye, good-bye.

19 June

I forgot yesterday to thank you for your letter, though these thanks should have been the very first words of mine. Your letter, you now see, was not in point of fact quite so *necessary;* but the

⁶ See p. 279.

motive which prompted it is worthy of you; that is to say, it was dictated by a most perfect and generous honesty. Not to fall short of you, I will not keep you waiting for this reply, which ought to put your mind completely at ease. I will send it to Bentinck, so that you may get it quickly. I shall not write to you again for some time; clandestine letters keep me up too late. I look to your guidance to cure me of this libertine habit. But you must write to me by day-light everything that comes into your head; thoughts born in England and thoughts born in France, I shall understand them all, for they will all be fellow citizens of my thoughts. Mine belong to every country.

Put what you write into a first envelope addressed to me, and enclose that in a cover where my name must not appear, made out *To Monsieur Spruyt, Bookseller in the Koor Straat, Utrecht.* Allow yourself no imprudence. It is in *that* sense that my peace of mind is in your hands. Do not forget to write to my father from Berlin. He likes you and will appreciate the attention. Once more, let your letters be long and infrequent. Give me your views on everything interesting you come across. I venture to say that your essays could not be better addressed, nor your confidence better placed, than they are: in the matter of honesty, my fickle head has never wavered for a moment. Good-bye. I shall be your faithful friend so long as I have a head and a heart.

P.S. Send a line of thanks to D'Hermenches. He complains of having had no sign of life from you. But don't let it slip out that I have told you so.

You are very right to say that I should be worth nothing as your wife. We are entirely in agreement on that head. I have no sub-altern talents.

P.P.S. Why did you say, the day before yesterday, that you regretted your role of Mentor? It did you much credit in my eyes. I saw at one flash your sense, your goodness, and the extent of your friendship for me; and it has given me a great friendship for you. Perhaps you feel your labours have been wasted, but they are not entirely lost. Even if an argument fails to touch the heart or persuade the brain, it lives at least in the memory. It may lead one, some day in the future, to think anew. Some day when one is hesitating in a decision, the argument may be thrown into the balance and tilt it to the better side.

As I would like you to carry away a right idea of me on one essential point, I will hastily fill a spare moment to make you understand what manner of doubts I have on the subject of religion. Everything tells me that there is a GOD, an eternal, perfect, and all-powerful being. What my heart approves as being good, what all men in spite of themselves approve, is good certainly; and actions which all consciences condemn, are bad. Since there is no limit either to the soul's desire or faculty of perfection, so I am persuaded is there no limit to its existence; the horror we feel at the thought of falling back into the void persuades me no less. Why should GOD inspire us with repugnance for a destiny we cannot avoid, or with desires for what we are incapable of attaining? Why, too, should he implant in us illusory feelings? I believe our actions are free, because all our thoughts, all our calculations, spring from that hypothesis; because the most specious argument on that head can create in us no more than a speculative doubt or an intellectual conviction, without ever destroying our awareness of being free. Far from thinking it indifferent whether we employ that freedom ill or well, I believe that every good habit formed by the soul in this life is a further step towards happiness in the next, and every bad habit will delay us on that path. This penalty is no more than natural logic, for a vicious soul would be incapable of deriving happiness from what will make a virtuous one happy. The knowledge of GOD and the contemplation of Nature will only provide joy to such a soul after a very long interval, and it will long be tortured by the lack of all which made its happiness in this world. That this torture will be endless, I am neither able nor willing to believe. To me the thought would be a more cruel torture than you can invent.

Revelation has qualities of grandeur, goodness, and mercy which are infinitely entitled to our respect; if I understood it better, I should perhaps recognize the marks of divinity in it throughout; but I am held back by much that is obscure, and by what appear to me contradictions. I doubt, and I keep my doubts to myself; I should think it a crime to destroy the belief of others when I can replace it only by an anxious doubt. But I am incapable of forcing my mind to believe what it does not understand, or of compelling my heart to subscribe to a religion which I can never love so long as I find it denies its promised happiness to part of God's creatures. I cannot separate my lot from that of others. I shall never be content to say, "It is enough that my faith procures me salvation; what matter that an infinite number of creatures, children of the same God as myself, will be lost by their incredulity." The problem as between Deism and Christianity is no doubt interesting enough to deserve our most careful study, but too much so for my health, my peace, or my happiness. Rather than go astray, I steer clear. I wait, modestly and peacefully doubting, for truth to come and enlighten my eyes. There you have my ideas. I hope they will not lose me a friend's esteem. I hope I shall seem to you, in all this, less blameworthy and less unhappy than you thought.

[4. Boswell to Belle de Zuylen][7]

Berlin, 9 July 1764

MY DEAR ZÉLIDE,—Be not angry with me for not writing to my fair friend before now. You know I am a man of form, a man who says to himself, "Thus will I act," and acts accordingly. In short, a man subjected to discipline, who has his *orders* for his conduct during the day with as much exactness as any soldier in any service.[8] And who gives these orders? I give them. Boswell when cool

---

[7] This letter (except for certain quotations from Belle, here given in translation) was written in English. No copy has been found among Boswell's papers (he was no doubt intimidated by its length), but Belle kept the original, and it is now preserved, with others of her papers, in the Public Library of Neuchâtel. It is here reprinted from Professor Tinker's edition of the letters of Boswell, i. 45–54.

[8] Literally true, but he exaggerates the extent to which he *follows* his orders. Though he had relaxed somewhat on leaving Utrecht, he was still addressing

and sedate fixes rules for Boswell to live by in the common course
of life, when perhaps Boswell might be dissipated and forget the
distinctions between right and wrong, between propriety and impropriety.

I own to you that this method of living according to a plan may
sometimes be inconvenient and may even cause me to err. When
such a man as I am employs his great judgment to regulate small
matters, methinks he resembles a giant washing teacups or thread-
ing a needle, both of which operations would be much better performed by a pretty little miss. There now is a pompous affectation
of dignity; you must expect a good deal of this from me. But you
have indeed seen me often enough not to be surprised at it. Is it not,
however, a great deal in favour of my candour that I own that plans
may sometimes make one go wrong? Mr. Smith, whose *Moral
Sentiments* you admire so much, wrote to me some time ago, "Your
great fault is acting upon system." What a curious reproof to a
young man from a grave philosopher! It is, however, a just one,
and but too well founded with respect to me. For a proof of its
justness I need go no farther than the letter which you are now
reading. It was part of my system not to write to Zélide till my
journey should be over. By my following that system, you must be
almost four weeks without hearing a word from me. I will not
pretend to doubt of your being sorry at this. I have even vanity
enough to make me view you in tender attitudes of anxiety, such,
however, as become a friend. Love is a passion which you and I
have no thought of, at least for each other.

I received your kind letter enclosed to Count Bentinck, from
his friend at Brunswick. It gave me great pleasure. It was much
more to my mind than the first was. You discover in it the same
amiable dispositions, the same brilliant imagination, the same regard for me that you discovered in the first, with more consistency

---

much the same sort of memoranda to himself. Here, for example, are his
"orders" for 5 July 1764: "This day be alive, be manly. Fear not censure. If
pleasure be a deception, so is pain. Enter Berlin content. Pursue Plan. Forget
dreary ideas and sensual Turkish ones. Be Johnson."

and more cordiality. I really must ask your pardon for being so free with you. It is not treating you with the politeness which I ought to do. But you are good enough to believe me your sincere friend, and you know a sincere friend is never ceremonious, but, on the contrary, speaks his mind without reserve. I have observed, too, that a sincere friend, in the warmth of his concern, will speak of our faults with a degree of severity which shows that he is pained by them.

I remember an officer of the British Army, whom I had a regard for, ruined himself by extravagance. I was happy enough to save him from prison and get him sent home to his friends. I was not rich, but I had money enough to relieve him. At the very time that I was talking with his creditors, did he propose some fanciful party of pleasure. This hurt me most severely, so that I cried out with tears in my eyes, "Was there ever such a good-for-nothing fellow?" This officer, Zélide, was a pretty man, a man of genius, who wrote a comedy and who wrote verses. He had a fine figure; he was a good player of tragedy. He was generous, he was lively. Had he been at Utrecht, you would have liked him much. You would have corresponded with him after he left you. And yet, Zélide, this officer is an unhappy being and a bad member of society, merely from the want of that sober quality *prudence,* a quality which you laugh at, although it is of all qualities the most essential.[9] It makes the most of every circumstance; if we have distinguished parts, it en-

[9] Boswell's own records are otherwise completely silent about this transaction. One naturally thinks of Andrew Erskine. The only time when Boswell could have saved Erskine from prison and sent him home to his friends would have been in July, 1763, when Erskine, whose regiment had been disbanded in April, and who certainly had been associating with riotous company, went home to Scotland. But the *London Journal, 1762–1763* makes no mention of aid asked or received by Erskine; and the matter does not seem of the sort that Boswell would have felt it improper to record. Furthermore, though Erskine wrote verses and by 1764 had written a farce, it is hard to believe that he was "a good player of tragedy." Lord Auchinleck's assertion (above, p. 26) that Boswell had been cheated of his money by a friend he did not know sufficiently well, may refer to this affair.

ables us to make a great figure. If our talents are moderate, it en-
ables us to make a good figure, and even very weak people under
its protection, have passed decently through life. Thou favourite of
Nature, listen to thy friend. Let Prudence be thy counsellor. Learn
to be mistress of thyself. Learn to live, and pray despise not Art.
Art has taught thee to play so divinely on the harpsichord. Let her
teach thee to modulate the powers of thy mind with equal harmony.

> Talk not to me of Nature's charming ease
> By which alone a woman ought to please;
> Nature shoots forth rank weeds as well as flowers,
> And oft the nettle o'er the lily towers.
> The buxom lass whom you may always see
> So mighty nat'ral and so mighty free,
> A vulgar bosom may with love inspire,
> But Art must form the woman I admire;
> Art which usurps not beauteous Nature's place,
> But adds to Nature's dignity and grace.

You see I am in high spirits, for I give you heroic verses.[1]

I heartily wish I could do you any real service. You will tell me,
"You give me pleasure, Sir, and that is to me a very great service."
My dear Zélide! let me prevail with you to give up your attachment to pleasure and to court the mild happiness. Believe me, GOD
does not intend that we should have much pleasure in this world.
But he has been kind enough to place us so that we may attain to
a pleasing serenity, what one of our poets calls

> The soul's calm sunshine and the heartfelt joy.[2]

To be thus is, truly, to follow Nature. They who seek for exquisite
joy were always deceived. If they obtain it, it is but for a moment.
Their powers are destroyed by excess, and they languish in a state
of tedious infirmity. If they do not obtain it, they are wretched and

[1] His ten-line verses for 3 October 1763.   [2] Pope, *An Essay on Man*, IV. 168.

fretful; they swear that there is no happiness in life, because they
have not experienced the fancied happiness which life denies. You
will now say that I am preaching, and perhaps you will be heartily
tired. However, you must have a little more of it. I shall try to
enliven my discourse. I shall just give you hints of good advice.
It will amuse you to enlarge upon these hints.

Religion is the noblest employment of the mind. Believe me,
this is no prejudice. Is it not noble to adore the Supreme Lord
of the Universe, and to aim at rendering our souls divine? I own
to you that mankind have confounded and perplexed religion.
One thing, however, I am absolutely sure of, and that is devotion,
the adoration of one great and good GOD. As to systems of faith, I
am no bigot. I think I see a very great probability that Jesus Christ
had a divine commission to reveal to mankind a certainty of immortality and an amiable collection of precepts for their conduct
in this life; and that by His death He atoned for the offences of the
world, which GOD's justice required satisfaction for. I am happy to
believe this. It makes me live in cheerful hope. I do not believe that
a few only shall be made happy in another world. My notions of
GOD's benevolence are grand and extensive. I puzzle not myself
with texts here and texts here, with the interpretation of a gloomy
priest or with the interpretation of a gay priest. I worship my
Creator and I fear no evil. You see, my dear Zélide, that your
friend is very happy as to the great article of religion. Be you the
same. Pray make a firm resolution never to think of metaphysics.
Speculations of that kind are absurd in a man, but in a woman are
more absurd than I choose to express.

You may say perhaps that you cannot prevent your mind from
soaring into the regions of perplexity. Allow me to deny this. Suppose you should be seized with a strange inclination to touch the
ceiling of your bedchamber while you stood upon the floor. You
would in that case stretch your arm till it was very sore without
coming much nearer your aim. You would tell me that you had got
such a habit of doing this that you really could not help it, although
you owned it to be very ridiculous. I would answer, "My dear

Zélide, while your arms are unemployed, no doubt they will take
their usual curious direction, but if you will sit quietly down and
embroider a waistcoat for your brother, I defy your hands to mount,
and I assure you that by degrees they will forget their bad habit
and rest as peaceable as the charming Comtesse d'Aumale's."[3]
Just so is your mind to be managed. Study history, plain and certain parts of knowledge, and above all endeavour to relish the
common affairs of life. David Hume, who has thought as much as
any man who has been tortured on the metaphysical rack, who has
walked the wilds of speculation, wisely and calmly concludes that
the business of ordinary life is the proper employment of man.

Consider, my dear Zélide, your many *real* advantages. You are
a daughter of one of the first families in the Seven Provinces; you
have a number of relations of rank. You have a very handsome
fortune, and I must tell you too that Zélide herself is handsome.
You have a title to expect a distinguished marriage. You may support a respected and an amiable character in life. Your genius and
your many accomplishments may do you great honour. But take
care. If those enchanting qualities are not governed by prudence,
they may do you a great deal of harm. You have confessed to me
that you are subject to hypochondria. I well believe it. You have a
delicate constitution and a strong imagination. In order to be free
from a distemper which renders you miserable, you must not act
like one in despair. You must be careful of your health by living
regularly, and careful of your mind by employing it moderately. If
you act thus, you may expect to be happy; if you resign yourself to
fancy, you will have now and then a little feverish joy but no permanent satisfaction. I should think you should believe me. I am no
clergyman. I am no physician. I am not even a lover. I am just a
gentleman upon his travels who has taken an attachment to you
and who has your happiness at heart. I may add, a gentleman
whom you honour with your esteem. My dear Zélide! You are very

[3] There were at least four Countesses d'Aumale, none of whom receives prominent mention in Boswell's records. Belle appears never to have mentioned the
name in her correspondence with Constant d'Hermenches.

good, you are very candid. Pray forgive me for begging you to be less vain. You have fine talents of one kind, but are you not deficient in others? Do you think your *reason* is as distinguished as your imagination? Believe me, Zélide, it is not. Believe me, and endeavour to improve.

After all this serious counsel, I think my conscience cannot reproach me for writing to you. I am sure that your worthy father could not be offended at it. I am sure that I intend to do you service if I can.

Now, Zélide, give me leave to reprove you for your libertine sentiments, of which your letters to me furnish several examples. You say if your husband and you loved each other only a little, "I would certainly love some one else. My spirit is formed to have strong feelings, and will assuredly not escape its destiny." I hope this love of yours for another is not *destined* like that of many a fine lady. "If I had neither father nor mother, I would not get married." And yet you would have your tender connections. Ah, poor Zélide! Do you not see that you would reduce yourself to the most despicable of all situations? No, Zélide, whatever men may do, a woman without virtue is terrible. Excuse me for talking so freely. I know you mean no harm; you gave way to your fancy. You see, however, whither it leads you. "I should be well pleased with a husband who would take me as his mistress: I should say to him, 'Do not look on faithfulness as a duty. You should have none but the rights and jealousies of a lover.' " Fie, my Zélide, what fancies are these? Is a mistress half so agreeable a name as a wife? Is a connection of love merely, equal to a connection strengthened by a variety of circumstances which have a pleasing influence on a sound mind? I beseech you, never indulge such ideas. Respect mankind. Respect the institutions of society. If imagination presents gay caprice, be amused with it. But let reason reign. Conceal such ideas. Act with wisdom.

I have had a most agreeable journey. My Lord Marischal was most entertaining company, and the Turkish lady talked extremely well when indolence did not keep her in silence. We were very happy at Brunswick. I have been only two days at Berlin. But I see that much happiness awaits me in this beautiful capital. The German formality and state pleases me much, for I am the true old Scots Baron. I found Monsieur Catt very polite. I shall write to Monsieur de Zuylen very soon. I esteem and love him. I had the honour of being presented to the Comte d'Anhalt. You may be sure I considered him with some attention. He appears to be a sensible, polite, spirited man, with a manner very *prévenant*.[4] I saw him only a very short time, so cannot say much. From what I have seen of him and from what I have heard, it would make me very happy to see him the husband of my fair friend. But she must be upon honour to behave with propriety.

As you and I, Zélide, are perfectly easy with each other, I must tell you that I am vain enough to read your letters in such a manner as to imagine that you really was in love with me, as much as you can be with any man. I say *was*, because I am much mistaken if it is not over before now. Reynst had not judged so ill. You have no command of yourself. You can conceal nothing. You seemed uneasy. You had a forced merriment. The Sunday evening that I left you, I could perceive you touched. But I took no notice of it. From your conversation I saw very well that I had a place in your heart, that you regarded me with a warmth more than friendly. Your letters showed me that you was pleasing yourself with having at last met with the man for whom you could have a strong and a lasting passion. But I am too generous not to undeceive you. You are sensible that I am a man of strict probity. You have told me so. I thank you. I hope you shall always find me so. Is it not, however, a little hard that I have not a better opinion of you? Own, Zélide, that your ungoverned vivacity *may* be of disservice to you. It renders you less esteemed by the man whose esteem you value. You tell me, "I should be worth nothing as your wife. I have no subaltern talents." If by these talents you mean the domestic virtues, you will find them necessary for the wife of every sensible man. But there are many stronger reasons against your being my wife;

---

[4] "Prepossessing."

so strong that, as I said to you formerly, I would not be married to
you to be a king. I know myself and I know you. And from all probability of reasoning, I am very certain that if we were married together, it would not be long before we should be both very miserable. My wife must be a character directly opposite to my dear
Zélide, except in affection, in honesty, and in good humour. You
may depend upon me as a friend. It vexes me to think what a number of friends you have. I know, Zélide, of several people that you
correspond with. I am therefore not so vain of your corresponding
with me. But I love you and would wish to contribute to your happiness.

You bid me write whatever I think. I ask your pardon for not
complying with that request. I shall write nothing that I do *not*
think. But you are not the person to whom I could without reserve
write *all* that I think. After this, I shall write in French. Your correspondence will improve me much in that language. You write
it charmingly. Am I not very obedient to your orders of writing
des grandes lettres? You must do the same. While I remain at Berlin, my address is *Chez Messieurs Splitgerber et Daum, Berlin.*
Adieu. Think and be happy. Pray write soon and continue to show
me all your *heart.* I fear all your *fancy.* I fear that the heart of
Zélide is not to be found. It has been consumed by the fire of an
excessive imagination.

Forgive me for talking to you with such an air of authority. I
have assumed the person of Mentor. I must keep it up. Perhaps I
judge too hardly of you. I think you have no cordiality, and yet
you are much attached to your father and to your brothers. Defend
yourself. Tell me that I am the severe Cato. Tell me that you will
make a very good wife. Let me ask you then, Zélide, could you
submit your inclinations to the opinion, perhaps the *caprice* of a
husband? Could you do this with cheerfulness, without losing any
of your sweet good humour, without boasting of it? Could you live
quietly in the country six months in the year? Could you make
yourself agreeable to plain honest neighbours? Could you talk
like any other woman, and have your fancy as much at command

as your harpsichord? Could you pass the other six months in a city
where there is very good society, though not the high mode?
Could you live thus and be content, could you have a great deal
of amusement in your own family? Could you give spirits to your
husband when he is melancholy? I have known such wives, Zélide.
What think you? Could you be such a one? If you can, you may be
happy with the sort of man that I once described to you.[5] Adieu.

Let not religion make you unhappy. Think of God as he really
is, and all will appear cheerful. I hope you shall be a Christian. But
my dear Zélide! worship the sun rather than be a Calvinist. You
know what I mean.

I had sealed this letter. I must break it up and write a little
more. This is somewhat like you. I charge you, once for all, be
strictly honest with me. If you love me, own it. I can give you the
best advice. If you change, tell me. If you love another, tell me. I
don't understand a word of your mystery about a certain gentleman whom you think of three times a day. What do you mean by
it?—Berlin is a most delightful city.—I am quite happy. I love you
more than ever. I would do more than ever to serve you. I
would kneel and kiss your hand if I saw you married to the man
that could make you happy. Answer me this one question: If I had
pretended a passion for you (which I might easily have done, for
it is not difficult to make us believe what we are already pleased
to imagine)— answer me: would you not have gone with me to the
world's end? Supposing even that I had been disinherited by my
father, would you not have said, "Sir, here is my portion. It is yours.
We may live genteelly upon it." Zélide, Zélide, excuse my vanity.
But I tell you you do not know yourself if you say that you would
not have done thus. You see how freely I write, and how proudly.
Write you with all freedom, but with your enchanting humility!
"I am proud of being your friend." That is the style. Is not this
a long letter? You must not expect me to write regularly. Farewell,

[5] Belle supposed that the hypothetical husband of this paragraph was Temple. (See p. 381.) It is clear, however, that though Boswell may have intended
her to think this, he is really talking about himself. It is very characteristic of
him to assume a firm position and then retreat from it in the same letter.

my dear Zélide. Heaven bless you and make you rationally happy. Farewell.

[5. Boswell to Belle de Zuylen]

[Fragment: undated][6]

PRAY BE NOT OFFENDED at my way of writing, but answer me calmly and perhaps I may be convinced. I am afraid you are not made to be happy. You have no taste for the ordinary satisfactions of life. You have no taste for realities. Monsieur Hahn told me once that he had shown you some of the most beautiful experiments in Natural Philosophy and you was not a bit pleased. I was wicked enough to say, "Perhaps, Sir, she would not be pleased with the great experiment of all."[7] You don't like pictures, you don't like gardens.

[6. Boswell to Monsieur de Zuylen. Original in French]

Berlin, 30 July 1764

ALLOW ME, MY DEAR SIR, to recall to your memory a stranger who left you with sincere regret, and to assure you that that stranger will always preserve a deep sense of gratitude for all the civilities—dare I say acts of friendship? which he was shown by Monsieur de Zuylen.

Indeed, Sir, you had the goodness to treat me, I shall not say as though you were my father, but—as though you were my father-in-law. I make use of a weaker expression instead of the common one because I do not like to say just what every one else has said a thousand times. But I beg you not to communicate this sentiment to my friend[8] Zélide. She would make a very different application of it from the one that I intended. I like to seek novelty only in things which depend on taste, on imagination. But I am afraid that Zélide would seek novelty in serious matters, those con-

[6] In English. Mr. Scott has argued convincingly that this scrap found among the Boswell Papers was a rejected portion of the preceding letter.
[7] See p. 286.
[8] Boswell wrote "charming friend" and then struck out the adjective.

cerning which we have judgment, judgment which has given us fixed rules. I said, "You treated me like a father-in-law" because every one else has said, "You treated me like a father." But I am afraid that Zélide would say, "Two and three make six and prudence amounts to nothing" because every one else has said that two and three make five and that prudence is worth almost as much as all the other good qualities put together. My dear Sir, excuse this jocularity. I have often taken the liberty to run on with you in this fashion, and you have never taken it amiss.

I had a very pleasant trip, although mingled with discomforts, as philosophers say of life. We encountered very sandy roads and very bad inns. I have been mounted on tables covered with straw instead of reposing in a good bed. I have had nothing for dinner but eggs, and I have had to eat bread that was black and sour. In a word, I have suffered discomforts which would have made some Englishmen cry out against Providence. But as for me, I do not have an exquisite sensibility. I was very well satisfied. I enjoyed the fine season. I enjoyed the pretty countryside: the mountains which I love delighted me after having been almost a year in the level plains of Holland. Forgive, Sir, a good Scot born in a romantic land and nourished by prejudices for which he will always preserve an agreeable veneration.

My Lord Marischal told me an infinity of amusing anecdotes. Is it not to the honour of the human race to see a nobleman like him preserving all his faculties entire to the age of seventy-five? Madame Turk is extremely listless, but when she is willing to give herself the trouble, she can display liveliness of mind. Sometimes we sat under the trees in the fashion of her country, and she was gay and witty.

I remained two or three days at Brunswick, where the Court is very gracious to strangers. I would willingly have stayed there several weeks, but I did not wish to quit my worthy guide. However, I shall return there next month. At Potsdam I presented the letter which you had the goodness to give me for Monsieur Catt. He was indisposed and could not leave the house, but he very politely arranged for me to see everything at Potsdam and Sans Souci.

I am much pleased with Berlin. It is a handsome city, and the Germans have a frankness and a gaiety which pleases me much. I have the good fortune to be lodged in the house of the President of Police, where there is a very amiable family. His daughter is young and pretty and lively enough to make time pass agreeably for so serious a man as I am. She plays for me on the harpsichord. She makes me laugh with pleasant, natural sallies. She is always the same, and when she thinks me too pensive, she says to me, "Heavens! You have the *spleen,*" with so animated an air that I rouse from it immediately. Up to now she has had a surprising influence on me. I am very curious to see how long it can last.[1]

My route is not yet entirely fixed. But I hope to be at Rome before Christmas. I wish to see some of the courts of Germany and to visit Switzerland before I pass over into Italy. I have been presented to all the princes and princesses here, excepting the King. You could not believe how eager I am to speak with that famous man; and I shall speak with him if it is possible. You shall hear the adventure.

I beg you to present my respects to Madame de Zuylen, and my affectionate duty to Mademoiselle. Might I have the vanity to believe that she will not completely forget my sage counsels? She does not know how much I admire her. Perhaps she ought not to know. If my friend Captain Vincent is at Zuylen, embrace him for me. I recall with pleasure a long walk we made together one Sunday.[2] If you honour me with your correspondence, you will give me a very lively pleasure. I have the honour to be your most humble and most cordial servant,

BOSWELL D'AUCHINLECK.

[7. Monsieur de Zuylen to Boswell. Original in French]

Zuylen, 17 August 1764

YOUR LETTER, MY DEAR SIR, came most opportunely to furnish me diversion from ideas that were troubling me. The question was

---

[1] Her name was Caroline Kirkheisen. In the Bodleian manuscript of Boswell's poems there is a poem in French addressed to her.   [2] See p. 183.

one of the marriage of a young lady for whom I ought to feel concern; and I was pondering the matter when your letter gave me, at least while I remained in its mood, a detachment, a diminution of care which was good for me. Furthermore, I see with pleasure that you are well pleased with the fashion in which I received and treated you. I felt an inclination to treat you as a friend when I saw your good sense, your gaiety, and your cordiality.

I am sorry that Monsieur Catt was indisposed when you were at Potsdam and that you did not see him. I hope you do see him and are able to talk to him about us. Your trip must have been fairly agreeable in spite of the bad lodgings and the bad meals. My Lord Marischal's anecdotes, Madame Turk's conversation, and the fertility of your imagination, must have cast on those discomforts a picturesque, even a romantic colouring which you will have found amusing. *Et meminisse juvabit.*[3] You will have been presented to the King. You say nothing about Professor Castillon. I beg you to pay him my compliments. You will give me pleasure by writing again. I am curious to know also how long the influence (as you call it) of the young lady of Berlin will last. I hope she is making an agreeable diversion from the excessively serious thoughts you might be having.

Madame de Zuylen sends you her compliments. My daughter also sends hers. She says she will not forget your counsels, but to follow them is another matter.

I originally intended to send you the beginning of the translation of a poem I once mentioned to you and you seemed curious about, but it would swell the packet too much. Apropos of that, the French of your letter is much better than I expected. You will improve a great deal more at Berlin.

My son Vincent salutes you humbly. We continue to read Caesar's *Commentaries* together. I have to recall all my Latin to be of any help to him. He is now making a tour in Zeeland. I beg you to salute for us my Lord Marischal, the Turkish lady, Monsieur

[3] "*It will be a pleasure* one day *to recall* even these hardships" (Virgil, *Aeneid*, I. 203).

Catt, Monsieur Castillon. I have the honour to be cordially, Sir, your most humble and most obedient servant,

D. J. VAN TUYLL VAN SEROOSKERKEN.

[8. Boswell to Monsieur de Zuylen. Original in French]

Potsdam, 18 September 1764

DEAR SIR:—I am very much flattered by the compliments which you have been good enough to pay me. If my last letter really sweetened a moment of your life, I congratulate myself for it, I glory in it. You may well believe that I sincerely wish to share in your perplexities.

But, my dear Sir, allow me to speak frankly to you. Why so much caution? Why so many mysterious expressions? "The question was one of the marriage of a young lady for whom I ought to feel concern"—why not name Mademoiselle de Zuylen and Baron *Brömbsen* (if I am not mistaken)? "I am sorry that you did not see Monsieur Catt. I hope you do see him and are able to talk to him about us," instead of saying, "I wish to have news of the Comte d'Anhalt." "You say nothing about Professor Castillon": that is to say, "Has the Professor heard nothing of the Count?" You will excuse me, Sir, if my commentary is mistaken, if I find in your letter ideas which you never thought of. I imagine, however, that I am right in my conjectures; and I am not quite happy that you have not treated me with greater frankness, for I should like to be reckoned a true friend and a friend in whom you can have confidence. I admit that it would look a little odd to write gravely to a young man and to discuss soberly with him, as with an uncle, the marriage of a charming young lady whom he had deeply admired. But you know, Sir, that I put myself on the footing of a mentor *vis-à-vis* our dear Zélide, and your great philosophers are a little eccentric; perhaps also by dint of preaching on the defects of their pupils, they believe them greater than they are, they fear them more than they have reason to. You see, Sir, that I am more *au fait* than you think in all that concerns my friend. Believe me when I say that I wish her happiness. I hope she will be happy one day. But my first hope is that she will be able to change her ideas a little, for I dare not hope that the world will completely change its own in order to please her.

I am charmed to hear of your noble conduct with regard to Monsieur Vincent. I see you occupied in forming the mind of a young warrior who perhaps will bring great honour to his family.

I quit Berlin today to go to Geneva; but as I shall stop at a number of courts, I do not count on being on the shores of Lake Leman before the end of November.

I beg you to present my best compliments to Madame de Zuylen, to Mademoiselle, and to Monsieur Vincent. I embrace you, my dear Sir, and I beg you to believe me always your most humble and most cordial servant,

BOSWELL D'AUCHINLECK.

I beg you to write to me in care of Messieurs Cazenove, Clavière, et fils at Geneva. I hope always to be honoured with your correspondence.

The young lady of Berlin continued to exert the influence I spoke to you about. I left her with regret. She is very amiable. But alas! Sir, I shall never see her again. A traveller ought to have a great deal of friendliness, but no susceptibility.

[9. Boswell to Belle de Zuylen. Original in French]

Anhalt-Dessau, 1 October 1764

NEARLY THREE MONTHS HAVE PASSED, my dear Zélide, since I wrote to you from Berlin, and so far I have had no reply. What can be the reason? It is possible my letter did not reach you. Yet it was addressed according to your directions, and I cannot believe you have not received it. One must therefore guess at some other reason. It requires no long search to find it. You were displeased with the manner of my letter. But, my friend, you are perhaps too severe. You know as well as I that it is very difficult to give advice, particularly on so delicate a matter as that which then concerned us. Do not attempt, my dear friend, to disguise your true feelings; and do not give me reason to believe that this frankness you boast of so much is only a weakness which you are well able to correct when your vanity is sufficiently piqued to teach you a little prudence.

No, Zélide; do not tell me you have never experienced feelings for me more lively and tender than those of friendship. Say it as much as you please, I shall not believe you. You have already done me one honour of which you can never remove the flattering recollection.

Had I been like several others who are perhaps more agreeable to you than I, I would have told you many pretty things which I did not believe. But I will always preserve that probity which is a mark of my character. I wrote to you with the completest honesty of intention, as to the daughter of a man I esteem, and as to a friend whose happiness I had sincerely at heart. If I employed expressions of too unsparing a character, I am sincerely sorry and ask your pardon. What more would you exact?

If this letter has the good fortune to fall under the eyes of Mademoiselle de Zuylen, pray believe that it comes from an honest Scot who still feels for her what he felt at Utrecht. He begs her to be good enough to write, as soon as she has a moment to spare for him. Write, if it were only to say, "I shall never write to you again." GOD bless you.

BOSWELL.

[10. Monsieur de Zuylen to Boswell. Original in French]

Utrecht, 11 December 1764

I ASSUME, MY DEAR SIR, from your letter of 18 September that you will have been able to reach Geneva when this letter arrives. I have no doubt that you have continued your tour with satisfaction. You will have added to your knowledge, found both resemblances and differences between countries and men, explored the causes, exercised your appetite for speculation, and reasoned like a philosopher.

In my last, in an overflow of my heart, I told you of the situation I was in when I received yours and of the good it did me. I thought it would not be disagreeable to you if I did so, and I see that I was not deceived. You thought I did not say enough: that it would·have been better to name my daughter and the Baron de Brömbsen without reserve, and say that I hoped you had picked up news of the Comte d'Anhalt from Monsieur Catt and Monsieur Castillon. But supposing that I had thought all that, what would have been the good of making it explicit? As it was, at least I gave you something on which to form conjectures; I furnished you with a subject of conversation. It is, however, true that similar matters had been occupying my thoughts, but not those. The case was not entirely as you thought it. The Baron de Brömbsen was no longer a subject of deliberation. I had had news touching the Comte d'Anhalt, and my daughter had begged him no longer to entertain the project he had formed, nor to think of making the trip which had been postponed because of various obstacles. But why tell you all that now? To satisfy you by showing you less reserve, to show you that your conjecture was only partly true: out of love for the truth and a little out of love of myself. Furthermore, if I had any doubt, it would not be lack of confidence in your intelligence and in your prudence that would have prevented me from telling you more of the matter and asking your advice. I believe also that as a good friend you would have been willing to give it.

One of our regents is dead, at the age of ninety-four. Professor Wesseling is dead also at an advanced age. Madame de Maarseveen, my niece, was very ill during her pregnancy; she has just been brought to bed and is doing well. All that is quite in the ordinary course of events. What is less so is that Comte Dönhof, in our Service, a Pole and a Roman Catholic, who had suffered for a long time from a dangerous debility, having kept his bed at Aix for three weeks, got up, ran off with an English Protestant young lady named Tankerville, and married her before a priest; at the end of two or three weeks he died, which is not to be wondered at. Friends of the deceased came to the assistance of the disconsolate widow, and wrote to his Polish relations. She went to stay with a relation of her own at Rotterdam. Her mother came from England and offered her the choice of a prison room at home or a convent; besides that, the mother took away from her the little money that she had and then went back home. The daughter had not made her choice. A Princess Czartoryski, a relation of the deceased, saw that she was supplied with money, wrote to her, and made her the most humane and generous offers. In the first days after the elopement and the marriage, some people were discussing its validity. "Well," said a lady by way of comment, "they will certainly have married themselves as firmly as *they* are able"—so much so that she is said to be with child. Do you not find in all this a great deal that is out of the ordinary?

Would you have heard in Germany or Switzerland of an able professor of Public Law? If you have, I beg you to let me know as soon as possible—but he must be of our religion.

I end by assuring you, my dear Sir, that I am, with cordial regard, your most humble and most obedient servant,

D. J. van Tuyll van Serooskerken.

Madame de Zuylen sends you her regards. My daughter is at The Hague, at her sister's.[4]

[11. Boswell to Monsieur de Zuylen. Original in French]

Geneva, 25 December 1764

You will not be able to believe, my dear and respectable Sir, how much your last letter rejoiced my heart. You do not know me, Sir. You know only some of the more attractive traits of a singular character, of a character so composite that you would need a great deal of time and many opportunities to study it. You would never think I had a gloomy mind, and you would be far from suspecting that I am diffident. Yet it is certain that both those things are true. Is it possible otherwise to explain the uneasiness that I have experienced with regard to you? You delayed a little

4 Madame de Perponcher, Belle's junior by six years.

in writing to me, and I could not help fearing that you had taken offence at the frankness of my letter on the subject of that marriage to which you have devoted so much thought and I so many conjectures.

I imagined I know not how many disagreeable things. My imagination was rendered gloomy by dismal chimeras. O Sir! that kind of imagination can give me bitter days. That kind of imagination can make me a jealous husband. Your letter has calmed me so far as concerns the fear I had on your account. But one can never completely calm a melancholy soul torn by suspicions.

And you have confidence in me. Be assured that you make no mistake in having it. No, Sir, if ever probity has existed on earth, it exists in the heart of Boswell. You have not yet said enough to me about this mysterious marriage. Really you have not. I beg you tell me more. Tell me everything. Must I ask you questions? "Is it so-and-so?" "Is it so-and-so?" No. Although I am not in the least timid, I should blush to tell you what I am thinking in spite of myself. My dear Sir! hide nothing. Whatever you reveal, your honour will be safe.

I do not cease to please myself with the recollection of Mademoiselle de Zuylen. She has for some time had at least a sincere friendship for me. I find her more and more charming. I begin to retreat from some of my prejudices towards her. Some time ago I gave her character to my most intimate friend, on whose judgment I count more than on my own. He replied, "O adorable Zélide! &c., &c.[5] Your objections are nothing. She will remain metaphysician and mathematician only until she is married." My friend, Sir, is an Englishman, a man of good sense, sensitive and generous. Advance then, haughty counts! Advance, bold barons! Throw yourself at the feet of an angel worthy of all your vows! After all I have said, I swear to you that I cannot decide how I stand with regard to Zélide. But you are a man of honour. I entrust you with a letter

[5] The "&c., &c." stand for other expressions of Temple's which Boswell does not bother to transcribe into his copy. Unfortunately Temple's letter which contained them is not among those that have been recovered.

for her. I repeat, you are a man of honour. If you think your daughter should not receive a letter from me, burn it, but do not open it.

I have made the tour of Germany that I planned. I have spent a month in Switzerland. I have been to see the illustrious Rousseau. I have been much at his house. Will you believe it? He has granted me his friendship. My record of that occasion is extraordinary: romantic and noble. I promise that you shall see it. I have been very well received at the home of Monsieur de Voltaire. I am going back there tomorrow, and Madame Denis has been good enough to say that I shall spend the night in his *château*. I am the most fortunate of men. I have already had letters from the worthy reigning Margrave of Baden-Durlach, and from Rousseau. On Monday I leave for Turin. You can well believe that my soul is filled with enthusiasm when I think of making the tour of Italy. My dear and respectable Sir, may God bless you.

BOSWELL D'AUCHINLECK.

P.S. The learned world has lost a very great man by the death of Monsieur Wesseling. I have heard of no Professor of Public Law in Switzerland or in Germany.

The story of Miss Tankerville is extraordinary. It was a truly English caprice to marry a foreigner at the point of death. I am enough of a stoic to regard her misfortunes as the natural consequence of her bad behaviour. If a daughter is so lacking in respect for her parents and in confidence in them as to engage in the most important of contracts without consulting them, ought she to be surprised if her parents lose a little of their affection for her? I am sorry when such a marriage succeeds. It gives encouragement to girls of impressionable hearts and light heads to forget the weakness of their sex, to scorn the sage maxims of prudence, and to disturb the settled order of Society. The parents of Miss Tankerville are more to be pitied than she is. The heroine has her imagination heated by an adventure. But her parents are obliged to consider her sad folly cool-headedly. I hope people will have pity on her up to a certain point. But she ought to suffer.

I beg you, Sir, to pay my respects to your wife, to General Tuyll and his lady, to the worthy Grand Bailiff of Amersfoort, and to his brother (I think) in *die breed Straat*.⁶ Your assemblies no doubt are following their ordinary course. I kiss the hands of the Misses d'Averhoult.

Do not forget the translation of the Dutch poem you promised me. You will give it to me when I have the honour to see you again.

[12. Boswell to Belle de Zuylen. Original in French]

Geneva, 25 December 1764

MADEMOISELLE:—I send you but a few words; for I know not if you want more of me. Some time ago you displayed towards me the appearances, at least, of sincere friendship. Allow me to recall to you a few expressions which you will recognize.

"I have a higher regard for you than for any one, &c."⁷

Mademoiselle, I think a man could not but be flattered by such words as these from a charming woman.

And what have I done since those days? I wrote you a long letter from Berlin. I gave you such advice as I imagined would assist you to be happy. You made me no reply. I feared I had spoken of your conduct in terms which were too wounding. I wrote to you from Dessau to tender you my excuses. Once more you did not write.

Mademoiselle, I am proud, and I shall be proud always. You ought to be flattered by my attachment. I know not if I ought to have been equally flattered by yours. A man who has a mind and a heart like mine is rare. A woman with many talents is not so rare. Perhaps I blame you unreasonably. Perhaps you are able to give me an explanation of your conduct towards me. O Zélide! I believed you to be without the weaknesses of your sex. I had almost come to count upon your heart. I had almost—

⁶ Monsieur de Natewisch and Monsieur d'Amerongen.
⁷ "It is evident from Letter No. 13 that Boswell at this point inserted a whole catalogue of Zélide's flattering expressions. In the manuscript copy which he retained these are represented by '&c.' "—GEOFFREY SCOTT.

My friend, have I been mistaken? Tell me the simple truth without reserve. I am capable of admiring the candour of a woman who makes acknowledgment of her inconstancy; if she owns it to me without lightness, if she owns it with regret.

I have entrusted this letter to your father. I am confident he is a man of honour. I wish to be sure of your receiving it. If this is an indiscretion, you are the cause of it.

I ask a reply. You owe me that, at least. Zélide, good-bye. I have the honour to remain your faithful friend and very humble servant,

BOSWELL.

[13. Belle de Zuylen to Boswell. Original in French]

Utrecht, 27 January 1765

MY FATHER'S ACTION JUSTIFIED YOUR HOPES. He did not open your letter; he gave it me; I received it with joy and read it with gratitude. I am completely alone and perfectly free for an hour: let us make the most of it.

I will tell you the truth, and you will not think the worse of me. I would begin by assuring you that all those expressions of friendship and all those promises of eternal regard and of constantly tender recollection which you have collected, are acknowledged and renewed by my heart at this moment.

Now, Sir, let us review my conduct and consider my silence which you make a ground of reproach. I had spent one extraordinary day this summer, a day that might have counted as an event in my life, when, on coming to my room in the evening I found your long letter.[8] I read it with eagerness, and found in it qualities which filled me with delight, noble flights prompted by a generous nature and warmed by the liveliest friendship. Since then I have

[8] She wrote to D'Hermenches in the night of 21–22 July: "Am I not the unluckiest of beings? I was terribly in need of sleep, and I thought I should sleep soundly; I complained of being sleepy and hurried through supper, but I found in my room an English letter from Boswell seventeen pages long. I read it; I went to bed. The seventeen thousand thoughts of my friend Boswell ... revolved in my head with such violence that I have not been able to stay in bed more than a quarter of an hour."

re-read the earlier pages; I made D'Hermenches read and admire them;[9] I intend to read them again.

After all this fineness came your reproaches, and I found passages copied from my letters, passages which had been suggested by my libertine imagination and written to you (as I thought I might safely do) in thoughtless confidence. These were sent back to me and severely refuted, so that each was made the excuse of some wounding admonishment which you heaped upon me without choosing your words, and needlessly. For what need was there to copy out my sentences and put me to the blush, if your object was to give me useful advice and to correct my mistaken views, if you thought them mistaken?

But that is not all. You went on repeating, ringing all the changes possible on the words, that I was in love with you, or that I had been in love with you, that my feelings were those of love. You would have me admit this, you were determined to hear me say it and say it again. I find this a very strange whim in a man who does not love me and thinks it incumbent on him (from motives of delicacy) to tell me so in the most express and vigorous terms. I was going to answer your letter the following day; I remember even I made a beginning, in English; but at that point I was interrupted by receiving the strangest possible proposal of marriage,[1] and since that moment I have had nothing but worries, fears, anxieties, hopes, problems that needed thinking out; I have had no more tranquillity; I have never again had the leisure and peace of mind I needed to answer your letter properly.

[9] He wrote on 24 July: "The English letter charms me. I find in it things that take hold of me and make me overlook its pedantry. Now, one would like to see how he reduces all those respectable principles to everyday practice. That's the reef on which your moralizers commonly split. If they do not take refuge in cynicism, they condemn only those things that are not in the line of their own ruling passion" (Translated).

[1] From Bellegarde, in a letter written by D'Hermenches. The "strangeness" of the proposal seems to have been due to certain extremely blunt questions which D'Hermenches put on the part of his friend: What was the size of her dowry? What likelihood was there of her remaining faithful?

I was blaming myself, none the less, for my silence, when, towards the middle of October I got your second letter. Once more
I found myself commanded by you to confess that I had felt a passionate desire for you. I was shocked and saddened to find, in a
friend whom I had conceived of as a young and sensible man, the
puerile vanity of a fatuous fool, coupled with the arrogant rigidity
of an old Cato. I would none the less have answered you, for I
wished to lay it down as a condition of our correspondence that
you should burn all my previous letters. With my habitual frankness I wished to tell you that it showed a poor knowledge of the
human heart to attribute a momentary instinct, that springs from
no perceivable source, and passes, leaving no discernible trace, to
any clear, recognized or established sentiment in our nature. The
heart is less consistent; and the senses, too, count for something.
Whatever a prude may object, Nature intended them to have a
say in the matter. With an old friend, they say nothing; it is pure
friendship. If the friend be young, they may at some moment utter
a word. But that word is not love. The moment passes and friendship is once more peaceful, generous, and reasonable as before.
There is no question of love's anxieties, its suspicions, its jealousies
or its transports.

My dear Boswell, I will not answer for it that never at any
moment may my talk, my tone, or my look have kindled with you.
If it happened, forget it. I have written letters to you with the
vivacity and freedom of a headlong imagination, which, with a
trustworthy friend, shakes off the yoke of constraint that is laid
upon our sex; burn them. But never lose the memory of so many
talks when each in our own fashion was reasonable, and both were
sincere; when the pair of us were equally light-hearted: I, well-
content in the flattery of your attachment, and you as happy to
count me your friend *as if there were something rare about a
woman with many talents*. Keep that memory, I say, and be sure
that my tenderness, my esteem, I would even say my respect, are
yours, always.

But in talking like this I have lost track of some sentence I left incomplete. Ah, yes, I was telling you that I intended an answer; I would have sent it, I would have sent you a few lines at least, in spite of new worries and complications, had you given me your address at Geneva. But you never gave it.

If I saw my own situation more clearly, if I saw any certain future for myself, I would tell you of it; but possibilities would be too long and are too little interesting to explain. Burn my old letters if you wish to deserve new ones. Keep nothing in your desk but what is creditable to me. I am not inconstant. I dissimulate nothing, I have not ceased to be your friend, and I shall be your friend always.

BELLE DE ZUYLEN.

[14. Monsieur de Zuylen to Boswell. Original in French]

Utrecht, 8 February 1765

I WAS SORRY TO LEARN, MY DEAR SIR, from your letter of the 25th of last month[2] that you had been uneasy about the effect which your former letter might have produced; and I am sorry that my delay in replying to you prolonged your uneasiness for some time. But the joy which my reply caused you has almost consoled me. I cannot evaluate precisely the two opposed sentiments which you have felt, so as to regulate my own accordingly. But it is certain that I should like to inspire in you only agreeable ones, the more so if the part of your portrait which you give me is not exaggerated. I mean, if you are easily disturbed, it is all the more proper to treat you tactfully and spare you subjects that are disturbing. But you know how to divert yourself, and you have at present the finest of opportunities: travel in general, and travel in Italy particularly, ought not only to dissipate present melancholy but also to efface the tendency towards that state that you might have for the future.

So your mind is at peace so far as I personally am concerned, but you urge me to confide to you what I could not tell you in my last. I do have confidence in you, and I should like to be able to give you this proof of it, but the secret in question is not my own.

[2] Actually of 25 December 1764.

Of course I did not read the letter which you sent to me for my daughter; you had sent it to me in confidence that I would not. But I doubted whether I should burn it or give it to her. The confidence I have in you made me decide to deliver it to her. Just now I asked her if she had anything to say to you. Concerning your friend's prediction that her appetite for metaphysics would pass off, she begged me to reply that so far as it was excessive, she hoped it would, but as for all exercise of it, no. I love her enough to hope that she will establish herself in this country or in a neighbouring one, and that I can see her often. . . .³ Adieu . . . my dear Sir. I have paid your compliments to the persons you named, and they have been gratefully received. . . . May the Lord guide you.

D. J. van Tuyll van Serooskerken.

[15. Boswell to Belle de Zuylen. Original in French]

[Probably Rome, 3 April 1765]⁴

P.S. Forgive me for having written in English.

Allow me to add one word more. Our letters are truly *mysterious*, as you said at the outset of our correspondence. Know then, my dear friend, that I am prepared to make you a recital which will surprise you; and though I shall speak *without choosing my*

³ Monsieur de Zuylen was so courtly and also so fond of Boswell that it is hard to decide how he really felt about the prospect of having him for a son-in-law. But this sentence is, I think, completely sincere. To Belle's father the disqualification of living in Scotland was about as great as that of being a Roman Catholic.—I have omitted, following this sentence, a long and sensible criticism of the religious tendency of Rousseau's writings. It is worth publishing, but not in this series.

⁴ The Register of Letters shows that Boswell received No. 13 on 15 March 1765 and replied to it on 3 April; we know also from Belle's letter of 25 May 1765 (No. 17) that the reply was a long one and that it was probably in English. Boswell seems to have kept no copy. The Boswell Papers do, however, contain the present fragment, which looks like a discarded postscript of the missing letter. After hinting at a proposal of marriage, Boswell no doubt decided that caution was the wiser course.

words,[5] this time you will not blame me. Next time I have the honour to be in your company, my friend will have to admit that I understand the human heart very well. Believe me, Zélide, it is you who have not sufficiently entered into the singular character of your amiable and proud Scot. You have advanced many steps on the path. That was fine; and I know but one man who could have withstood you. If for that "one man" you had gone some steps further, if you had trusted him *fully* and spoken everything out . . .[6]

[16. Boswell to Monsieur de Zuylen. Original in French]

Rome, 23 April 1765

THERE ARE HOURS, MY DEAR SIR, when a man feels that he is worth ten times as much as in the ordinary course of his existence: hours when he finds himself in perfect health, finds his mind gay and at peace with itself, finds his soul strong and virtuous; hours when he is not perplexed by the question why GOD has created him, because he sees the system of the universe as the work of an All-powerful and All-good Father. As I write, I have the good fortune to enjoy one of these delicious hours. I wish to share it with Monsieur de Zuylen.

How beautiful your conduct toward me is, Sir. I am touched by it to the bottom of my heart. You have delivered to your daughter the letter which I took the liberty to put in your charge. What a proof of the confidence you have in a stranger! I flatter myself exceedingly because you did so, but I respect you for it still more. May it be a bond between us for the rest of our lives! I am perfectly satisfied with what you tell me concerning my friend. I hope that the days of secrets, of conjectures, and of discreet dealings are over, and that she is established in a fashion that will satisfy all of us. I shall always take a most sincere interest in her happiness.

I know you, my respectable friend, too well to fear that you

---

[5] A quotation from Belle's letter of 27 January 1765. See p. 330.

[6] The writing ends here at the bottom of a full page, but as the reverse is blank, it may be doubted whether Boswell ever completed his sentence.

have been offended because I have delayed so long in answering the last letter you honoured me with. If you had made me wait in that fashion, how uneasy I should have been! But I know the difference there is between us, and I am persuaded that you will excuse me when you remember that I am both busied with and dissipated by the antiquities, the arts, and the pleasures of Italy. I must tell you besides that I have been putting off writing because of something that will amuse you. For some time now I have had almost no occasion to speak French; and I assure you that in jabbering Italian I have lost part of the tongue I learned at Utrecht. On my honour, I began a letter to you two weeks ago and could not continue it. This evening I am taking advantage of a fine moment, and I think I shall be able to express myself passably well. It is humiliating to find that one forgets so quickly. What is the memory? There is a question to which the most profound, the most subtle, metaphysicians can give no answer. I know not if there is any question more curious.

My tour of Italy comes up to the exquisite ideas which I had formed of it. It is true that I had sometimes imagined that I should find more agreeable people there than I have found. That apart, all my hopes are realized. The fine climate, the variety of objects, the exercise which I take every day, have so completely dissipated my melancholy that I hardly know myself. I am quite another man. My perceptions are clear, my judgments firm. Every day I increase in knowledge. Every day I improve in taste. My mind is so full of gay ideas that it has no room for gloomy ones. I am completely content with this world. I have elevated hopes for the future. I adore my GOD with gratitude and with joy. Oh, why cannot I remain in these sentiments? I do not know. But the recollection of this happiness will sustain me in the shades, the doubts, and the sadnesses into which a baleful malady casts my troubled mind. I know that I can be made happy. My idea of the Divine Nature makes me believe that in the end I shall be happy always.

I have read with attention and pleasure your remarks on the works of Monsieur Rousseau. You criticize them as a sound politician, as a man of fixed faith, but with the candour and delicacy of a true philosopher. I had not seen his *Lettres de la montagne* when I was with him, and he did not speak of them. We did, however, discuss religion, and especially the Christian religion, at great length. He repeated to me what was practically the doctrine of the Savoyard Vicar. I asked him boldly if he was truly a Christian. He replied with a piercing and noble glance, "Yes. I pique myself on being one. All the objections make no difference to me. But do not trouble me with your proofs of the Gospel. I have it here. It speaks in my heart. It must be divine." Such is the enthusiasm of a soul like his, and I believe that he is very happy in it. He appeared to me full of goodness and devotion. Perhaps he would have done better to keep the "Profession of Faith" for a few particular friends. But he has formerly suffered himself from black ideas of his Creator, and he has set himself to alleviate the sufferings of others, without considering that there are very, very few people who think enough about religion to be tormented by it, and a great many people who are delighted to have excuses for not performing their religious duties.

And finally, my dear Sir, the most enlightened people do not see everything. As for me, who am not one of those vigorous spirits capable of acquiring wide and profound knowledge, I do not disturb myself in useless efforts to raise myself higher than Nature intended me to rise. It seems to me that I act philosophically when I fit myself to the rank where I am placed. My imagination presents me with a thousand lots in life above mine. I try to admire them all without envying them, and I keep myself as much from the greed of fame as from the greed of money.

I could wish that my intellectual friend Zélide had a little of this philosophy. She would be happier for it, and (if I may say so in simple frankness of heart) she would be still more amiable. I should like to fulfil the real duties of my station, and yet make myself little by little better, in the hope that my capacity will be enlarged in the other world. Doomed to suffer, I cultivate especially the virtue of patience; and although I am changeable in matters of religion, I never lose an entire confidence in the Being of Beings.

My dear Sir, continue to hold me in esteem. I put great store in your friendship, and when all is said, I am not unworthy of it. When I was saying good-bye to Monsieur Rousseau, he embraced me cordially and said to me, "Always remember that there are points at which our souls are bound together." Such a sentiment from such a philosopher is enough to nourish my pride for ever. Believe me, Sir, that those who are proud in the way that I am are the men on whom one can count; and if one takes a little pains to treat them with the respect which they deserve, they are the most amiable portion of any society. It is with calm and satisfying pleasure that I recall the hours I had the honour to spend in your home. I shall be highly charmed to see you again. The prospect of doing so delights me. But I am already saddened at the thought of saying an eternal farewell to you. That is too painful for me. I do not wish to believe it.

I hope you have received good accounts of your son who is at Paris. Perhaps I shall find him there. In that case, our acquaintance shall proceed with no detours of ceremony. I believe the young baron will not be sorry to see some one who was received as a friend at Zuylen. I shall be curious to observe how much he resembles you, and how much he prides himself on being destined to preserve the memory of the bold Van Tuylls whose portraits I saw in your castle. Without doubt you have inspired him with an affectionate respect for his family. My worthy father has brought me up much in these sentiments, and I shall be obliged to him for it for the rest of my life. The honour of an ancient family is a noble principle; and I know nothing which has contributed more towards giving a true grandeur to humanity. It is well known how much the Romans owed their success to it. Their *imagines majorum*[7] incited them to glory as much as did their most sublime orators. Let us pay no attention to the ridiculous abuse which weak men have poured on this principle.

The honour of my family is perhaps a species of self-love. I do

[7] Ancestral images, portrait-masks of the ancestors of a family. The tag is from Cicero.

not care to perplex myself with pedantic distinctions which spring from restless minds. I know only that to be attached to my family has in it something less selfish,[8] something more generous, than to pride myself on my wealth, my talents; I venture to say, even my virtues. Develop this sentiment, Sir, and you will see that it is romantic but that it is not false. Self-love rules in this age; and the philosophers and *beaux esprits* would like to destroy principles fortified by the general suffrage of civilized peoples and conse- crated by the most remote antiquity. One of them wishes to degrade the nobility because he knows mathematics; another because he has had his head turned with metaphysics; another because he has the gift of saying amusing things from morning to night; and a fourth because of pride and singularity. Can one conceive any prejudice more foolish than that of these luminaries of the world? Monsieur d'Alembert has written a discourse to prove how difficult com- merce between the Great and the Learned is. If Monsieur d'Alem- bert had a little more common sense, he would see that rank and power of mind are things so different that they ought never to be put in comparison, and that a duke and an *encyclopédiste* can very well pass the day together, each keeping his place, each showing for the other the respect due to him.

I tire you, my dear Sir. But my intention was to try to amuse you. I send my respect to all your family, and I remain always, with sincere cordiality, yours, &c.[9]

[17. Belle de Zuylen to Boswell. Original in French]

Utrecht, 25 May 1765
I HAVE JUST HAD an agitation and am still upset. My father entered suddenly; I had begun a letter to you in English. Your long

---

[8] The manuscript reads "less unselfish" (*moins désintéressé*). Boswell got confused between his "more" and his "less."

[9] Our manuscript, as explained above, is a draft or copy. The "&c." here stands for the formal conclusion and signature of the letter actually sent.

letter was laid out over my table, your writing can be recognized
a mile off; I spread my elbows as far as they would reach to cover
our correspondence. I do not think he saw any of it. I was mad, of
course,,to have put off writing to you till Saturday, the day on
which my father, having nothing to do at his government office,
runs to and fro like a man with nothing to do. That means there is
no safety and no peace in my room. I put your letter and my own
English writing into my pocket in fear of some new mishap. *This*
can be passed off, if I wish it, as a letter to some cousin or other. I
will reply to you today a little unmethodically: moreover I have
not enough time, and another day will be better.

I could put off writing but I do not wish to, for I want you to
find a letter from me at Genoa; it will please you and I am too fond
of you to make you wait in future longer than is necessary for a
thing which you require of me. I have indeed much feeling for you,
and now that you exempt me from saying or believing that I am in
love with you, all will go well between us. As you say very rightly,
our best times lie ahead. You were good enough to promise me that
you will read me my letters, those letters of mine in which you find
so many things to blame, and which should cause me to blush; that
is the treat you propose to me when you visit here on your return. I
am indeed most grateful to you. Your letters I will keep and return
to you, since that pleases you;[1] but mine can go on the fire and be
turned to ashes and smoke without causing me the smallest regret.

I shall play no game of long apologies. It is a matter of taste.
You are delighted that I blame you for being too systematic; you
are very well content to have, at twenty-five, the faults of a man of
fifty. For my part, I am not clever enough to understand your
felicity in this. Fault for fault, I like those of my own age, those
which are natural to me, as well as any others. At the same time I
must beg you to believe that in speaking of those "pleasures" which
I wished to enjoy successively, I meant nothing you need have

[1] Boswell did not get back to Utrecht to claim the letters in person, but it is
somewhat remarkable that he did not secure them later through Mr. Brown.

understood in a vulgar sense, nothing which might not enter "a virgin mind."[2] You never tire of repeating my own phrases to me; I have no recollection of this one: "after one happiness, another";[3] but once again I cannot possibly have meant anything by that which need have scandalized you: and if in this instance one of our two imaginations is in any way to blame, it is not mine.

I forgive you readily for having fallen short of your principles, especially as you have admitted it with regret. But profit by this and be more indulgent, and do not make so great a difference in your estimate between the man who is always reasoning and sinning against his reason, and the man who reasons less and sins just the same. Both have their passions and their weaknesses, but one of them is always aware of the fact and does not make a display of a futile code of wisdom. The other forgets it; imagines himself to be strong; makes rules when he has no motive for violating them; and takes advantage of the intervals between his passions to preach against them with self-satisfaction.

My sister has just been delivered of a son, my mother is at The Hague, and I am looking after the household. Today I am giving an elegant dinner to Monsieur Bicker, who received his doctor's degree yesterday with much applause. He is a young man of whom much may be hoped, both for literature and the State.

Bentinck is very well; he has been in England. I do not know why he has ceased writing to you, but I know it is not a great misfortune for you. Leave that vast mass to occupy itself with all the nothings in the world. You act as I used to: my vanity used to put up with anything and require praise from everybody. It caused me to extend my correspondence without rhyme or reason. Why write to Madame Spaen? What is she but an immense collection of pretensions, of which her talk is the catalogue? Your letters to my father, on the contrary, are the most tactful in the world. He is, as you say, very reserved; what a pity that I have not a little more of the quality he has to excess!

[2] The quoted words are in English in the original.
[3] But she wrote it all the same: see p. 299.

Shall I tell you everything? But do not repeat a word—nothing is yet certain. I shall perhaps marry early next winter the Marquis de Bellegarde, colonel in our Service, with fine estates in Savoy and a house at Chambéry; a Roman Catholic whose children must be Catholics, a man of forty, a man with brains, kind and good-natured. I have seen little of him but I shall see more. I shall see whether my parents' objections are such as to force me to abandon a scheme in which I expect to find my happiness; then I shall make up my mind. Do not accuse me and do not condemn me. My heart has no self-reproach: I love my parents and I am not forgetful of religion. If one day you want further explanations and justifications you shall have them. Good-bye, my dear Boswell. I am your friend for always.[4]

[18. Monsieur de Zuylen to Boswell. Original in French]

[Utrecht, *c.* 1 January 1766]

No, MY VERY DEAR SIR, I am not at all angry with you and never have been. I replied to your letter from Rome at the address you had given me at Genoa, a little later, but only a few days later, than the time which you had indicated to me. But that could not have prevented your receiving my letter, for you have been there since. I hasten now to write to you at Paris, not merely because you asked me to, but also in order that you may perhaps still see my eldest son there. You can get his address from Messrs. Thellusson and Necker, bankers.

My daughter has received proposals of marriage from a gentle-

[4] At least three, and possibly more than three, letters are missing from the series at this point: (1) To Belle, in reply to No. 17, sent 13 September 1765 (Register of Letters); (2) From Monsieur de Zuylen, in answer to No. 16, sent to Genoa but never received (mentioned in No. 18; see also p. 343); (3) To Monsieur de Zuylen, probably from Genoa, early December, 1765 (not entered in Register of Letters but implied in No. 18). Besides these, there may have been another letter from Belle to Boswell which was lost in the post, like her father's, and a letter from Boswell to her complaining of her silence.

man of distinguished family of Savoy, a colonel in the service of
the States General. She would not be averse to it, but as he is a
Roman Catholic, we have some repugnance to the match. However,
before stating our position positively, we have asked for firm as-
surances that such a marriage would be valid in Savoy, and we are
waiting for the reply. I am thus explicit with you because of the
interest which you take in the matter, and because I count on your
discretion and your friendship.

Your father's dangerous illness is a circumstance which must
distress you and fill you with concern.[5] I sympathize sincerely with
you. I had the same experience, being in France at the time, and I
returned to Utrecht to see my father and care for him, with my
brother. It was a great consolation to him, as he testified to us a
hundred times in the most tender manner. But you know what
your duty is better than I do. However, I am by no means without
personal regret, for this will lessen the chances of your return by
way of Holland, and I shall always be very happy to see you, quite
apart from any other motive than that of conversing with you.

Adieu, my very dear Sir. Try to recall the happy balance of
your spirits in Italy; and count on the sincerity of my sentiments of
esteem, of consideration, and of friendship for you.

D. J. van Tuyll van Serooskerken.

My son is just on the point of setting out for home. You will be
lucky if you find him still there by looking him up at once.

[19. Boswell to Monsieur de Zuylen. Original in French][6]

Paris, 16 January 1766

Your affectionate letter, dear and respectable Sir, which I
have just received here, relieves and rejoices my heart. Thousands

[5] On arriving at Genoa, 29 November 1765, after his tour of Corsica, Boswell
found an accumulation of letters from his father telling him that he had
been at death's door with a suppression of urine and requesting him to come
home at once. Lord Auchinleck suffered from this complaint (probably an
enlarged prostate) for the rest of his life.

[6] The manuscript in the Boswell Papers is not a copy but the original document, which was returned at Boswell's request. See pp. 351, 359.

of times do I curse the posts of Italy for having caused me so great uneasiness. I have lost by their means many letters from my friends; and my imagination, ever ready to lend its black colours, has led me to form many disagreeable suspicions. I had the good fortune to find your son at Paris. You shall see what course I took:

To Monsieur de Tuyll

Will you, Sir, be pleased to allow a man you have never seen to address you on the footing of an old friend, or of a relation? I have enjoyed so much kindness from the family of Zuylen, and am so much the friend of your worthy and respectable father, that I look on you already with sincere affection. Today I am indisposed, and confined to the house.[7] *If you could visit me here, you will oblige me infinitely. If you have an engagement elsewhere, I will call on you tomorrow to pay you my respects. Most sincerely yours,*

BOSWELL.

What is your opinion, Sir, of this note? I have given it you, I believe, in its actual terms, for I have the best memory in the world for minutiae. Monsieur de Tuyll called on me that evening. We formed an immediate attachment. He is a man formed for me. He has principles. He has even prejudices. You are to be congratulated. We conversed, with the confidence of true friends, on Mademoiselle de Zuylen. We said every unfavourable thing that could possibly be said of her, and concluded always by contemplating her with admiration and affection. I spoke to Monsieur de Tuyll with a perfect candour, and it is after listening to his sentiments and benefiting by his advice that I am about to write to you, without reserve, on a most delicate subject.

During my stay at Utrecht, I studied the character of your daughter with close attention; for I must admit to you that I could not help thinking of her as in every respect a noble match for your humble servant, providing always that the faults in her character were not such as to be incompatible with married happiness. I

---

[7] 13 January 1766. He was laid up with a painful case of ingrowing toenails which he had acquired by tramping the trails of Corsica in riding boots.

swear to you that I was never in love with Mademoiselle. That is to say, I never felt for her that madness of passion which is unaccountable to reason. I formed a true friendship with her. I saw so clearly the mistaken and—dare I say it?—licentious ideas of her imagination that, to tell the truth, I believed she would make her husband unhappy.

Before my departure with Lord Marischal I had sufficiently strong proofs that she would look on me with preference over all others on whom she was then thinking to bestow her hand, and over Monsieur de B——— among the rest. In a word, I am as sure as one can be of such a thing when there has been no exchange of yes and no, that I had the honour, at that time at least, to be the possessor of the affections of Zélide. Like a man of the most perfect and most scrupulous probity, I assured Mademoiselle that I was not in love with her, that I was simply her true friend, and that I should be charmed to see her married to some worthy man with whom she could be happy. She praised my honesty, but rallied me not a little, assuring me that I had no need to make use of it in her case.

Well and good, my dear Sir; my sensitive conscience was the guide of my conduct; and, believe me, I was not wrong. I confess to you that I always had a leaning towards a marriage with my friend. But, in the first place, her faults filled me with alarm. In the second, I was still darkened by clouds of the blackest melancholy, and dared make no promises for myself. I saw Mademoiselle was of an age to marry; I was assured that several satisfactory alliances were open to her. I therefore resolved (and I assure you it was at a cost to myself)—I resolved, I say, to do nothing that might hinder the success of others in a matter as to which I was wholly undecided. And I swear to you that in so acting I had the pride of an heroic soul. None the less my inclination was unaffected, and in truth I suffered not a little from my heroism. I calmed myself by the consciousness of having done what appeared to me an honest man's duty in such circumstances. I thought that I ought not to place too much reliance upon a preference felt by a mind so light as my friend's. I resolved to allow her the time of my absence on my travels to conclude if this preference of hers was durable; and, should she remain in the same frame of ideas, I believed this would render me the happiest man in the world.

During my travels, I never ceased to think very seriously of her, in spite of changes, of life in prodigious variety, and (let me admit) in spite of acts of licence. I said nothing; but it was always a satisfaction to me to learn that the projects of marriage which were on foot for her were still unrealized. When I learnt of the latest of these (and for some time I have had no very reliable news on the subject), I was at first put out; but, after a little reflection, I was very happy that my friend was at last to be well established. But, after talking with Monsieur de Tuyll, my views underwent some change. For he assured me that, in his opinion, Mademoiselle would enter into marriage with Monsieur de B——— with considerable indifference, and only because she has decided that the time is come for her to marry, and that Monsieur de B——— is a *suitable* match. Your phrase, "She would not be averse to it,"[8] does not indicate a strong attachment; and, as I find there are many objections to such a choice, I cannot yet lose sight of my brilliant friend.

I told Monsieur de Tuyll all that I have here written you, and in his opinion it would be a pity to conceal it. Said I, "Perhaps your sister has not continued to feel that preference for me, because of the express terms in which I assured her that such a preference would be misplaced; perhaps she would still prefer me to all the men of her acquaintance; perhaps she would be overjoyed to know my sentiments in regard to her." He thinks it likely enough. May I venture to say that he seems very much my friend in this matter.

My dear and respectable Sir, here is my proposal. My confidence in your wisdom and honour is such that I give you full authority to decide for me. You can easily discover whether Mademoiselle de Zuylen would still give me her preference. If that is so no longer, say nothing to her on the topic of which I have written

[8] Above, p. 342.

you, for only her preference could engage me firmly in her favour, and without it I would banish the idea. Secondly, should there be any kind of promise or any engagement, however slight, with Monsieur de B———, let it be cleared up before you mention my name. And if there be any means of fulfilling that engagement, let the blood of De Tuyll be ever fired for the sentiment of honour. Thirdly, if you, my dear and respectable Sir, should not accord me your own preference in the proposal I am minded to make, I renounce it.

Do not accuse me of being a cold and indifferent lover. I am not the lover of Mademoiselle de Zuylen. Had I that fever in my soul, I would not be thinking of a calm, conjugal engagement. No. I am the heir of an ancient family, and think myself under obligation to prolong it, to lead an ordered and hospitable life like my ancestors before me. I see a person who would suit me more than any I have found, or even can well hope to find. That person is my friend.

I beseech you, Sir, to advise me. I consider I am too young to marry; but a wife such as Zélide might prove is well worth some years of freedom. Were she to feel a true affection for me, she has force enough to adapt herself in every respect.

I should marry her, no doubt, by the forms of the Church. But that would not be enough for me. I should require a clear and express agreement. I should require an oath, taken in your presence, Sir, and before two of her brothers, that she would always remain faithful, that she would never design to see, or have any exchange of letters with, any one of whom her husband and her brothers disapproved; and that without their approbation she would neither publish nor cause to be acted any of her literary compositions; and in conclusion she must promise never to speak against the established religion or customs of the country she might find herself in.

If she would promise all that for my sake, I would marry her tomorrow, and thank heaven for it, supposing my father were to give his consent; for I have given him my word of honour not to marry without it; and, indeed, it is my belief that the eldest son of a noble family should never do otherwise. I have no doubts about obtaining my father's consent. He has written to me, "Tempus est spargere nuces," and when he learns of my friend's family and fortune, he will certainly say, "Sparge, marite."[9] The great question is that of Mademoiselle's attachment to me. If I could be sure of that, I have no doubt I can arrange all else. I am quite in the dark; but I can allow myself the agreeable fancy of her learning with delightful astonishment that it is in her power to have her friend for a husband on certain conditions. And I picture with the most heartfelt satisfaction an alliance between the family of De Tuyll and that of Auchinleck.

And you, my dear and respectable Sir, perhaps will see it in the same light. You will embrace me as your son, and my children would call you grandfather, and Madame de Zuylen would possess an authority over me, and would be well pleased with her dear daughter, and my friends would become my brothers-in-law, and all of you would come and visit us in Scotland, and every two or three years we would come to Utrecht. There you have true ideas of durable happiness: the sweet simplicity of a family affection.

Although I did not have good health in Holland, although I have spoken and written in strong terms against your country, nevertheless at the bottom of my heart I always love it. I know not by what association of ideas the rich pastures where your cows graze appear to me like the fields of the pious patriarchs. The amiable Belle would be my Rebecca. But she has not enough feeling for nature. To speak the truth, she has not enough feeling for anything solid or real. She would rather read fictions than facts. She is more concerned with words than with the things they represent. To speak clearly, her heart is more precious to me than her mind, and it is rather what I hope she will become than what she actually is that I desire to marry.

As for me, I am the eldest son of an excellent family, which is not one of the wealthiest but nevertheless well-off, having a rental

[9] "It is time to scatter nuts. . . . Scatter, bridegroom!" (Alluding to the Roman custom of scattering nuts at a wedding; tags from Catullus and Virgil.)

of £1000 sterling a year. My father is one of the Scots judges, and his profession brings him in as much again; he will consequently be in a position to make me a very respectable settlement if I decide to marry. I have studied the law, and my plan is to practise as an advocate at our Scottish bar; and after a certain number of years I hope to obtain a position similar to my father's. It is not impossible that I may become a Member of Parliament. But in these days of political corruption, my mind is not set on it. I need not, I am sure, tell you that the profession of advocate in Scotland is in no sense degrading, as, by an absurd fashion, it has come to be looked upon in some other European countries. In Holland, I believe, it is held in the same esteem as with us. I know, at any rate, that the advocates attached to the court at Brabant are drawn from the noblest families. Monsieur Perponcher is a gentleman of most ancient stock. If I may allow myself a passing pleasantry, would it not be excessive on your part to marry both your two daughters to advocates?

There is excellent society at Edinburgh. That is to say, there are persons of good sense and instruction. We make no boast of brilliancy, *ton*, &c. But as far as that goes, my friend has no undue leanings to that species of extravagance. We would spend half the year in the country, where we should find sufficient diversion. I fancy a very happy life could be spent in that manner; for I am supposing that my wife and I will experience ever-increasing pleasure in each other's society, and I am persuaded that once we were well accustomed to each other, Zélide and I would be very, very happy. I am singular and romantic, and such a character is made to give her infinite pleasure. But I will enter into an agreement with her to maintain a decent composure, a certain reserve even, before the world. In private, *vive la bagatelle,* let us give full rein to our fantasy, as the most illustrious of the ancients have done. Sir, I am proud, very proud, and it is perhaps to my pride that I owe my best virtues. What a pride is this which makes me refuse to petition for a young lady's hand until I have the certainty that she prefers me to all the world! But in this case the motives of prudence and, on my honour, of disinterested friendship, are associated in great measure with that of pride.

I have visited the island of Corsica with a letter of recommendation from Monsieur Rousseau. There I saw realized for the first time what I had read of with admiration. I saw a whole people animated with the spirit of liberty and patriotic fire. I saw Romans and Spartans. I saw the illustrious Paoli, a man brave, wise, enlightened, owning the hearts of all his countrymen: a Numa, a Lycurgus. It will give me infinite pleasure to render you a full account of my Corsican tour and to tell you how, in crossing to Genoa, I was compelled by rough weather to put in for seven days at the little island of Capraja, where I led the most curious existence in a convent of poor Franciscan monks.

Sir, since being in Corsica, since making such proof of my talents and address, I am more proud than ever. I have a right to look to a distinguished career; I am worthy to make one of the best matches in England. Do not therefore find fault that I take so high a tone in speaking of Zélide. Would it not be a pity if so fortunate an alliance were unrealized for lack of speaking of it? And, in speaking, I could use no other terms.

I still flatter myself with hopes of soon seeing you again. My father's health is better and he has granted me permission to remain a month in Paris. I wrote to him this morning begging him to allow me, on my way back to England, to cross from Holland; pointing out that by this means, I should see Flanders, and give my tour great completeness.[1] It is two years since I wrote to him from Utrecht of my ideas in regard to Mademoiselle de Zuylen, as to which he has never given me any answer. Today I indicate to him my intention of seeing this young lady once more and of coming to a decision in the matter. I have told him that my impatience to see this affair concluded may perhaps cause me to travel to Holland before receiving his reply. But I should do better

---

[1] Lord Auchinleck's letter has not been recovered. As has been mentioned above, not one of the many letters which Boswell wrote to his father is known to exist.

to await it. I have the liveliest desire to be with you. I am worth ten times what I was when I left you. Mademoiselle will be the judge of that.

But it must not be forgotten that I am a hypochondriac, as she is, and that it might be a grave error to unite two victims of that malady. Mademoiselle is, I think, in fair health, and, as for me, give me a horse and Epictetus and I fear nothing. Nevertheless, I must in all seriousness admit to you that these attacks of melancholy are sometimes so strong that it is well nigh impossible to support them, and at such times I am truly out of temper. To conclude, I have many faults; on my word, I mean what I say. My knowledge is very restricted. I have an excess of self-esteem. I cannot apply myself to study. I can nevertheless maintain my energy where my attention is interested. I have no sufficient zest for life. I have the greatest imaginable difficulty in overcoming avarice. I am not *alieni cupidus sui profusus,*[2] for I do not covet riches; I have only the low weakness of wishing to make little savings. I should require a prudent wife, a good housekeeper who would attend to everything and leave me in peace. Judge, my worthy friend, if Zélide is capable of ever becoming such an one? Judge, I beg you, if she would not be happier with Monsieur de B———, who makes no such fastidious scrutiny, than with me who already have formed so severe a judgment of her.

I have at least this one consolation, that if my marriage with her were to prove unhappy, it could not be worse than I *fear*. It is equally true that matrimony is incapable of supplying greater felicity than I *hope* for from our union, which I sometimes contemplate with transports. I picture Zélide pious, prudent, kind, and tender, while retaining all her charms. I picture her giving complete satisfaction to all her relations, and triumphing over those mean and envious minds who have concluded that she can never possibly become a good woman. Ah! Sir, if only all this could come to pass!

[2] "Covetous of the riches of others, lavish of his own" (Sallust, *Catilina,* V. 4; *cupidus* for *appetens*).

Listen. You know Mademoiselle, you know me, and all the circumstances of the case. As a man of honour, I ask you to decide for us. I have set forth all my thoughts before you in a manner which I am confident will obtain your praise. Whatever happens, our friendship will be maintained, and I trust you will look on this letter as a sure token of my respect for yourself and of my attachment to your family. I beg for the earliest possible reply. If *jacta est alea,*[3] and I may no longer indulge the thought of our marriage, I beg you to return me this letter. If you are of opinion that the alliance might be brought about, keep the letter, and, when I pay my visit, you will give it me or allow me to take a copy of it; for I shall always be curious to recall how I expressed myself in an affair of this consequence.

You will forgive the tedious length of this epistle. I think I have said everything; and I hope you will be enabled to understand accurately my singular sentiments. I tender my best respects to Madame de Zuylen; and I embrace my dearest friend with all my heart. If I could be but two days with her, we should reach a satisfactory decision. All I ask of you, Sir, is to answer me frankly. I deserve it. And I swear to you I shall take offence at nothing you may say. Will you confess to me if, during my absence, you have entertained thoughts of such an alliance? When you say that "you will be very happy to see me, quite apart from any other motive than that of conversing with me," this "other motive" strikes me as being precisely the question now at issue; and this, too, is the conclusion drawn by my worthy brother-in-law, Monsieur de Tuyll.

Ah, Sir, cherish him; treat him like a man! He has genuine good sense of which one never tires. He believes his sister will make an excellent wife. He believes I would make a good husband for her. But he would make no decision for me. "I am acquainted," said he, "with your way of thinking, but not with your character." Wisely said! Sir, you have in your hands an important trust. I lean confidently upon your goodness.

[3] "The die is cast."

I ever am, dear and respectable Sir, with the most perfect consideration and sincere cordiality, most truly yours,

BOSWELL D'AUCHINLECK.

Postscript.   17 January. Morning

I ought perhaps to ask your pardon for the boldness of my letter; but I thought I was doing right in painting you a precise picture of my character, both good and bad. If you give me encouragement to risk my happiness with my friend, I will step forward with feelings of glory. If the event disprove your wisdom, there will be nothing to be said. We shall have acted for the best. Be an impartial judge. Do not bind a worthy Scot in the chains of a melancholy regret. If you cannot pronounce for the probability of our happiness, do not cast us together. You understand my views. The thought of marriage affects me with fear. Nothing could make me think of it but the unusual merits of my friend, coupled with my heartfelt attachment to your family. My tranquillity, I should tell you, is somewhat disturbed at this moment. I am sensible of more agitation than a philosopher ought to experience, and all this has come about as a result of my conversation with your son. I await your answer with impatience. Once for all, I implore you to take this letter in good part.

B.[4]

[20. Monsieur de Zuylen to Boswell. Original in French]

Utrecht, 30 January 1766

MY DEAR SIR,—I have received your letter of the 16–17th of this month: it affected me exactly as you wished it to.

[4] On 27 January 1766, at Paris, Boswell received a letter from Lord Auchinleck telling him that his mother had died on the 11th, and begging him not to postpone his return. On receiving this letter, Boswell wrote at once to Monsieur de Zuylen informing him of Lady Auchinleck's death and telling him that he would not now be able to come to Holland. This letter has not been recovered. It crossed one from Monsieur de Zuylen, replying to No. 19. Boswell left Paris on 30 January, remained briefly in London, and was in Scotland about the first of March.

In the first place, I am very much pleased that you hunted up my son at Paris, treated him with the confidence of a friend, and made yourself known to him in your true character. Nothing is more useful for a young man in an age and in a country where relaxation of morals reigns than the example of a man of birth and intellectual distinction who remains attached to his good principles of religion and virtue; who dares declare his position with firmness, and conducts himself accordingly. And you did make a strong impression on him. I know it from his own lips: he arrived yesterday.

I have admired the thoroughness, the ingenuity, and the energy with which you paint for me your character, your situation, and your project of marriage. You give me at the same time a very strong proof of your confidence, of which I am very sensible; and that fact itself ought to make me so much the more circumspect. It would be necessary to compare your situation and your character with my daughter's and decide if it is probable that you would both be happy together. A difficult decision. But we have not yet reached the point at which it can be faced. Monsieur de B.'s case is not settled. The investigations which I mentioned to you into the possibility of a marriage with him have revealed this much: that he absolutely must have a dispensation; that he is not sure he can get one; but that if he consents to what we demanded in our last letter, he will proceed to try to get one. You see then that though there certainly is no engagement, she does have a disposition to say yes if the marriage is feasible. So I could not make your proposal for that reason alone; and it was only in the case that the other match could not take place and you still persisted in your scheme that there would be any question of my assuming the dignity of impartial arbiter which you had conferred on me and which I consider an honour.

I rejoice to hear that your father is better, both for your own sake and because of the respect for him which you have inspired me with. Besides, this makes me hope to see you again. If you remain where you are some time yet, and if you have anything to communicate to me of what you see, it will give me pleasure. The autobiography in your letter, as in the preceding ones, has pleased me a good deal. I shall preserve the letter because it richly deserves it, and also so that you can re-read it here.

Farewell, my very dear Sir. Count always on the true esteem and the sincere friendship of your servant,

D. J. VAN TUYLL VAN SEROOSKERKEN.

[21. Lord Auchinleck to Boswell][5]

Edinburgh, 30 January 1766

UPON THE 11 OF THIS MONTH I wrote you the account of the death of your excellent mother, who was no *bel esprit,* no wit, no genius, but one who endeavoured to make her husband, children, friends, and all round her happy; who lived the life of a true practical Christian, exerting herself with diligence in doing her duty without intermission to GOD and her fellow creatures, and whose end was peace. Her exit, which she made with the greatest satisfaction, as my former particularly mentioned, has left me in a most desolate state; and as I therein desired you might come home speedily, as I needed all the aid and comfort an affectionate son can give, I have been counting with impatience when I may expect to see you here and flatter myself that it will be in a few days. For although I had a letter from Dr. Pringle acquainting me of some proposals you had bid him mention to me from Lyons, and a letter from yourself from Paris containing another very strange proposal, I have reason, I think, to hope that the melancholy news I wrote you would immediately put an end to that fermentation, and make you think seriously what you owe to duty, to gratitude, and to interest.

If that be so, all is well. But if contrary to expectation you shall be unmoved, and go on in pursuit of a scheme which you in your unstayed state are absolutely unfit for at present, and a scheme,

[5] Endorsed by Boswell, "This letter arrived at Paris after I had left it, and lay at Foley's [Boswell's banker's] until July, 1766, when I got it over to Scotland."

which, abstracting from that, is improper and would be ruinous—
a foreigner, a *bel esprit* and one who even in your own opinion has
not solidity enough for this country—what can you expect from
me? All that I need say further is that as I gave you a full allowance
to answer your expenses in every place you were in and you have
got all that advanced and considerably more; and as I ordered you
one hundred pounds at Paris, which was to defray your expense
the few days you stayed there and bring you over to London; if
you shall employ that money for other purposes, it is what I cannot prevent, but I acquaint you that I am to answer no more of
your bills, either for one purpose or another. I hope there will be
no occasion for this last *caveat*, as I hope you will show yourself a
dutiful and affectionate son, as I have been, and wish to continue,
your affectionate father,

                                        ALEXR. BOSWEL.[6]

[22. Willem de Tuyll to Boswell. Original in French]

                              Utrecht, 11 November 1766
    I TAKE TOO MUCH PLEASURE, SIR, in receiving a mark of friend-
ship and remembrance from a friend not to reply promptly. I received your letter this instant and have hardly finished reading it.
I congratulate you with all my heart on the state of mind which
you now enjoy. It delights me to re-read your remark, "I think I
shall be able to pass through this life tolerably well." The hope is a
sure guarantee of it.
    You speak of your long silence. It is very easy to make peace
with me on that score: one letter puts all to rights. Letters are one of
the pleasures of friendship, but they are not its essential feature.
After a long silence say only, "I have often thought of my friend,"

[6] I here omit letters of condolence from Monsieur de Zuylen and his eldest
son, Willem: they are both very friendly but say about what one would expect. I have ventured, however, to include nearly the whole of a letter from
Willem de Tuyll written nearly a year later. He was then about twenty-three.

and I shall hold you released from the debt of all that you could
have said to me in the interval. But I fear that this rule does not
augur well for the future. Remember then, Sir, I beg you, that it is
to be invoked only with reference to the past.

You mention what I told you at Paris concerning my father.
You guessed the truth as accurately as any mortal could. We are, I
believe, as well with each other as it is possible to be. I profit as
much as I can from his knowledge. I did not know him well until
after my return. I wish I could have retained all his instructive
conversations in my memory; they are very instructive indeed.

My sister is nearer you than you imagine: she is in London.
She went there almost a month ago. My brother accompanied
her there and left her, having business here. He has been promoted
and is now commanding a vessel.[7] He is thinking of marrying, and
has asked the hand of Mademoiselle de Reede, sister to Lord
Athlone. She has not refused him, but she absolutely insists that he
quit the Service, having invincible prejudices against it. That puts
my brother in a serious quandary. My father would be displeased if
he left the Service. He is very much torn this way and that. I do
not know yet how it will come out.

But before going further, I ought to warn you, Sir, that today
is the 4th of December. I was obliged to break off our conversation
of the 11th of November, and I have been unable to resume it until
today. I have spent a great deal of time hunting.[8] Now that the
hunting season is over, I am entirely at the service of my friends,
and I have no regrets for the forests. How far we are from each
other! I marvel how our ideas brave the elements, leap over seas

[7] "Commandeur de Vaisseau." I do not know what this is technically; hardly,
I should suppose, "Captain." Diederik van Tuyll was at this time about
twenty-two.

[8] "Willem ... is always hunting, provided he is not ill from having hunted
too much" (Belle de Zuylen to Constant d'Hermenches, 2 November 1769).
Godet reproduces a handsome full-length portrait of Willem in hunting cos-
tume, holding a gun, a heap of dead game at his feet (*Madame de Charrière
et ses amis*, i. 65).

and mountains, and arrive in each other's presence without having lost anything in so strange a journey. . . .[9]

I am better than I was in Paris, much better. I had to confess my illness to my father. You saw the beginning of it in Paris. I have been obliged to undergo heroic treatment. I was very ill. I was always hoping to cure myself without going that length, but I grew worse daily. I thought of you when my mother and my sister were near my bed, pitying me and little suspecting the cause of my sufferings. I was much impressed by the way in which my father conducted himself in that affair: not a word of reproach, not a moment of ill humour, always giving the best advice and managing my confidential concerns without entering into them except indirectly. For a long time I was uneasy about my condition. I took the cure at Aix-la-Chapelle, but I did not meet good doctors. I consulted far and wide: Monsieur Tissot of Switzerland and another Dr. Tissot here. For a long time I thought I was not going to be cured, but finally I was. And I am better in mind and in body.

What more can I say that will interest you? I am sitting at the moment with my father and mother; the one is writing and the other is working. I have carried on long conversations with my father. I spend a great deal of time in the company of both of them. I read Hume's *History* in French to my mother. I should be happy if I did not have an imagination that runs about the fields without asking my permission. But every one must seek his own amusements.

I have not given up hope of seeing you one day in your own country. It is one of the countries where it pleases me to let my ideas wander. But I am not yet there for all that: I am farther from Scotland at Utrecht than I was in Paris or in Switzerland.

Adieu, Sir; continue to be happy, and let me hear sometimes of your happiness; it will. contribute to mine. Your old friends at Utrecht are well. The *Dom* is still the most venerable, the most

[9] A paragraph dealing with the quarrel between Rousseau and Hume is omitted.

melancholy, and the most vaunting of all possible buildings; I forgot to say the most Gothic, which would have been to say everything in one word. Mr. Brown and his household are also very well. I say very well in general, but I am wrong. Mr. Brown is often badly indisposed and his health is precarious. He is indeed a most estimable man. Monsieur de Guiffardière is asking to be third minister with Messieurs Rambonnet and Huet.[1] Do you know those wearisome and mournful personages? Their church is no longer anything but a *church-yard*, I mean a cemetery.[2]

[23. The Reverend Robert Brown to Boswell]

Utrecht, 27 January 1767

DEAR SIR:—Yours of the 5th of January I received last post, and from it understand you have not had my last dated about three months ago. 'Twas wrong in me not to have sent it by the post, at least not to have wrote you by that conveyance soon after; for my letter was rather a volume than a missive, and concluded with a long shred of an old sermon. I sent it, with several others, in a box to a friend, who I suppose was gone for America before the box arrived; for by what I find, not one of my letters have been forwarded.

I'm extremely sorry for this, because it has put you in pain with respect to your books, papers, &c., which are all very safe and entire at this present moment, being still in my hands. The death of my worthy friend Mr. James Craufurd at Rotterdam having for some time (viz., till his son was settled) deprived me of the opportunities I formerly had, and now again have, of getting things sent to Scotland by shipmasters to be absolutely depended on, I thought 'twas better to delay sending your papers for some time after I was favoured with yours. Last autumn I fell into a lingering distemper which held me for some months and disabled me from thinking of anything but my daily and necessary occupations,

---

[1] In what Boswell calls "the French Meeting."

[2] "Church-yard" is in English. There is no signature, but the sheet is full.

which are at present very numerous. On my recovery I wrote you the letter above alluded to, in which I informed you that I would keep the papers till the spring, unless some sure hand should cast up sooner for carrying them over. Such an opportunity now actually offers. A son of Mr. Kinloch of Gilmerton[3] who has lived with me these two winters past is recalled to join his regiment; sets out tomorrow, and takes your papers in his cloakbag, together with a letter from you to Mr. de Zuylen, which he delivered me some time ago, to transmit to you.[4] As I could never expect to find a fitter occasion than this, unless I had delayed till July when I might have been the bearer myself, I embraced it with pleasure; and I hope all will arrive safe and to your satisfaction.[5]

As for the books, as soon as ever our canals are again open, I shall send them to Rotterdam to be forwarded by the first ship for Leith. Johnson's *Dictionary* will not, probably, be of the number; for Miss de Zuylen having some time ago applied to me for it, I made no scruple to let her have it, as knowing the proprietor would willingly homologate the deed. If that fair lady is returned before the books are sent off, it shall be sent likewise; if not, when she

[3] Lieutenant Archibald Kinloch, Mrs. Brown's first cousin. He later succeeded to the Kinloch baronetcy.

[4] No. 19. Boswell, it will be remembered, had asked to have this letter back: immediately if Monsieur de Zuylen considered his suit unwise or hopeless, ultimately in any case.

[5] Lieutenant Kinloch did not carry the papers beyond London, and I have found no certain evidence that he even brought them from Holland himself. The parcel was sent down from London to a Mr. Gall, banker in Edinburgh, in the private chaise of a Mr. Tod, merchant in London, by a Mr. Henderson, who asked that great care be taken of it because it had been particularly recommended to him by a friend in Holland. Boswell's brother David got it from Mr. Gall and forwarded it to Auchinleck. When Boswell opened it, he found the entire Dutch journal missing. He wrote letters to Brown and to Lieutenant Kinloch's father and asked David to institute inquiries, but the journal was never recovered. The present state of the evidence indicates that it was lost somewhere between Utrecht and London, but Boswell seems not to have been able to free himself completely of a suspicion that through Brown's carelessness it had been mislaid or destroyed before the parcel was made up.

does return. There is no getting at present all the Latin *Gazettes* of Cologne for the year 1763; but the editor has promised to send me by the first occasion what of them he has already been able to pick up, and to continue to do his best to get the remainder. Those of 1766 I shall have by the first opportunity, and shall send you with the books.

The old fencing master was sensibly touched with your remembrance of him, but died suddenly soon after I communicated the contents of your letter relative to him, so that I had no occasion of making him the present you mentioned; and indeed he stood in no need of it.

And where then, you'll ask me, is Miss de Zuylen gone to? Had you received my letter, you would have known that she has been in London these three months past. She is much pleased with the British capital, and as you will easily believe, much admired there. She's lodged at Lieutenant-General Eliott's.[6] Won't you think of making a trip to see her on your own side the water? Not a word more of the Marquis de Bellegarde. Mr. de Zuylen and his lady are perfectly well, and seem to remember you with particular regard. Mr. de Tuyll, the eldest son, is as you know returned long ago. The second, who is lately advanced in the Navy, is here also at present. Both very pretty young gentlemen. The third is at his regiment.

My family is indeed much more numerous than when you left us, but they are not of my begetting. I have had a house full of Dutch and English boarders, who have given me enough to do,

---

[6] Later Lord Heathfield, defender of Gibraltar, subject of one of Sir Joshua Reynolds's finest portraits. He and his lady had met Belle at Utrecht and had been so much taken with her that they had invited her to pay them an extended visit in London. General Eliott had received part of his education at Leyden.—Boswell wrote to Temple on 4 March: "Zélide has been in London this winter. I never hear from her. She is a strange creature. Sir John Pringle attended her as a physician. He wrote to my father, 'She has too much vivacity. She talks of your son without either resentment or attachment.' Her brothers and I correspond. But I am well rid of her" (*Letters of James Boswell*, ed. C. B. Tinker, i. 104).

though all very good lads. Their number is at present diminished, which I am not sorry for, as we had rather too many. As for off-spring, the child at whose birth you was present, has, thank GOD! been hitherto preserved with us; and she is still all our stock. Mrs. Brown and her sister desire their best compliments, always remembering Mr. Boswell in a very cordial manner, as do all your acquaintances here; hoping to have the pleasure of seeing you here again some time or other. Mrs. Geelvinck, the handsome rich widow of Amsterdam and the great companion of Miss de Zuylen, is to be married next month to the Marquis de Chatelaine, a nobleman of Lorraine, Chamberlain to Prince Charles, a widower with three children, and as you can well conceive, Roman Catholic. This marriage has astonished all the world.[7]

I had almost forgot to tell you that your obligation to Mr. Peterson, duly discharged, is in my hands, and shall be sent by Mr. Kinloch.

My paper is at an end, and I don't choose to make you pay double postage; therefore conclude with subscribing myself, with sincere regard, dear Sir, your most affectionate, obliged, humble servant,

ROBERT BROWN.

P.S. I hope to have the pleasure of paying you my respects in Scotland in July next. Mr. Wishart, who is still with me, sets out

---

[7] *La Veuve* was in fact married by April of this year to François Gabriel Joseph, Marquis du Chasteler et de Courcelles. Belle had a low opinion of him: "I should very much like to go to Paris. If Madame Geelvinck had not married a ridiculous and despotic fool, we could have gone there together ... They tell a thousand ridiculous stories of this husband and this marriage. It is said that he took no pains to conceal his interest [in her fortune]; stupidity rather than frankness causes him to publish his thousand failings in absurd behaviour and absurd speech. I am very sorry that my friend did not profit by the warnings which he gave her himself from morning to night. If he had given me the tenth part of them, I would have broken with him, even in the church, in the midst of the marriage service" (*Lettres à Constant d'Her-menches*, 1909, p. 310). *La Veuve* was married for the third time in 1790, to Count von Schlitz, and died in 1792.

from here in June to return by the way of Paris; and if nothing falls out to prevent it, I propose to accompany him.[8]

[24. Brown to Boswell]

Utrecht, 22 October 1767

DEAR SIR:—Honest François, as you term him, arrived safe, and with him your letter, for which receive my thanks.[9] I had a very agreeable journey home, not without some adventures really amusing; and to crown all found my dear concerns here in perfect health. I can hardly say that this is my own case at present. My stomatical complaints are indeed much abated; but the weakness I have had ever since last winter in my left side, and particularly in the thigh and leg, seems to increase daily. Patience, patience is my only resource. I am already reduced to walk, not only with, but upon a stick, as we say in our part of the world, and shall be very happy if I can keep at this pass; being afraid I shall be obliged ere long to cause myself be hurled about in a wheelbarrow.—But of this enough.

Your books are certainly arrived at Leith several weeks ago. They are in a small chest, and were addressed to Mr. Gilbert Mason at Leith, or to Mr. Alexander Ogilvy of the Ropework. The reason of this alternative, which will appear strange to you, is that a chest of books belonging to Mr. Wishart was sent at the same time with yours, addressed to Mr. Ogilvy, and I am not certain but Mr. Craufurd sent both to the same hand. Please therefore to cause make inquiry at both these gentlemen; nay, the shortest way will perhaps be to inquire at the Custom-house, where very likely the chests may still be lying. If they are, please make the smallest be broke open, and take out your own books, which are at the top, and distinguished from the others by a stratum of brown

---

[8] Brown did make his trip to Scotland. On his return to Utrecht in September or October, 1767, he carried with him a letter from Boswell to Belle proposing a renewal of correspondence. This has not been recovered.

[9] François Mazerac, Boswell's former servant, had been in Scotland. I have not as yet discovered the circumstances.

paper. Those below are for my brother at St. Andrews. Mr. Ogilvy, I hope, will be so good as either forward them by the St. Andrews carrier, or give them house room till called for. All expenses will be refunded by my brother, whom I have already advised on that head. Of your books, you will find wanting Johnson's *Dictionary,* which I lent with your approbation to Miss de Zuylen and could not get back before the others were sent to Rotterdam, which was in May last; Salmon's *Geographical Grammar* and Tooke's *Pantheon,* which not being to be had here, I made free to keep for the use of a young gentleman who lives with me, and shall give orders that they be immediately furnished you, for my account at Edinburgh; *L'Anglais à Bordeaux* was claimed by Mr. Wishart as his property, and as such seized upon by his two claws. If in this the Laird of Carsboddie was badly founded, you are a man of law, and a man of weight in the Parliament House, and so can bring him to account. But please remember that if you call me over to give evidence, you must bear my charges; and I can neither walk afoot nor ride ahorseback. *Le Comte de Warwick* I myself lost, and therefore in the place of it send *Tancrède.*

You'll find a copy of the *Letters* I foolishly published concerning Geneva, according to the third and last edition, bound. This volume contains several other pieces than those you have seen. Should any of your acquaintances who read French have the curiosity to desire to look into these *Letters*, &c., please indulge them with a loan of the book. Had I weighed all circumstances as maturely as I might have done, I would not have been the midwife of this performance; however there's certainly a number of very good things in it, and things that ought to be known. I sent a parcel of Cologne *Gazettes* in the chest. Those for the year 1763 'twas impossible to find; but my correspondent has promised to lose no opportunity of procuring them. Your orders shall be strictly followed with regard to these papers, as also to whatever pieces this country affords relative to Corsica. I have wrote to an intelligent and active bookseller at Amsterdam to make a collection of all such tracts, which he has promised to do. For the future I shall send whatever I have to transmit to you to your friend Mr. Stewart at Rotterdam, who I dare say will take particular care of it.

I made the strictest inquiry everywhere concerning the packet of papers lost by Captain Kinloch, but all to no purpose. I hope he will be able to recollect something about it himself, otherwise shall begin to fear it gone for ever. 'Tis extremely unlucky that I had not kept these things still a few months longer, and carried them over myself; but when Mr. Kinloch left Utrecht, I had very little view of being in Scotland last summer. . . .[1]

You flatter me with the hopes of seeing you here next summer. A visit from you will, I dare say, be highly acceptable to more of your acquaintances at Utrecht than those of my family. You must have received a letter lately from a very fair hand, in answer to one you sent by me; in which you will remember you propose and desire a renewal of correspondence. Such matters are too delicate for me to meddle in; however, without meddling, I believe one might say (in his private judgment) that a correspondence between you, and a very close one too, might be abundantly suitable to both parties. Should you push the question farther, and ask if it would be agreeable to the party on this side the water, I could make no answer but from pure conjecture. "And what, then, are your conjectures?" perhaps you'll ask. Why, Sir, maids, you know, are shy; and I have been so long out of the practice of unravelling female hearts (for, thanks to Providence! my wife whose heart is the only one I give a fig for, is as sincere as her infant offspring) that I may be mistaken; but if I am not egregiously so, the lady in question would be sufficiently disposed to follow good advice on the occasion. What mean else those particular and impatient inquiries concerning Mr. B———? Scotland is certainly a country, which, according to the description of it, and what one sees of the Scotch who come abroad, one might live much more *à son gré*[2] than in England; and Edinburgh by all accounts abounds with polite,

---

[1] A paragraph dealing with the Douglas Cause is omitted.
[2] "To one's liking." Brown's *which* is written over another word, perhaps the *where* that the sense demands.

clever, sensible people. A Scotch gentleman of character and fortune is greatly preferable to half a score of Savoyard marquises,
German counts, or Jutland barons. *Sed satis superque dixi; nam
verbum sapienti sat est.*[3]

Shall I beg the favour of you to offer my compliments to my
worthy friend Mr. Constable when you meet him in the Parliament
House with his load of hornings,[4] adjudications, and subpoenas
under his arm? I intend to write him next week, if possible, desiring among other things that he will take the trouble of sending
me by the first Leith ship for Rotterdam a barrel of Bell's best ale,
which of all the good creatures that have entered my poor stomach
these six months past, is, I think, the most comforting and delectable. In case an opportunity should cast up before I write him, I
beg he'll be so good as dispatch it without further advice. Mr. Constable is one of the worthiest men I know, and I have reason to
think very capable in his business. If it should fall in your way to
wish him to a good fat cause now and then, your doing so would
be extremely obliging to me.

We talk of nothing here at present but the grand parade we are
to make next Friday, on occasion of the Prince's return with his
royal consort.[5] Oh, what fine doings there are to be at The Hague!
When we Dutchmen take it into our heads to cut a figure, I can
assure you we cut a long one and a large one and a broad one. The
Princess is extremely well spoke of; and the Prince they say is
passionately fond of her, which I pray God may continue to their
latest breath.

Mrs. Brown and her sister join me in the very kindest compliments to you. We often remember and speak of you with pleasure.

[3] "But I have said enough and more than enough, for to a wise man a word is
sufficient."—Boswell wrote to Temple on 8 November: "Do you know I had
a letter from *Zélide* the other day, written in English, and showing that an
old flame is easily rekindled. But you will not hear of her" (*Letters of James
Boswell*, ed. C. B. Tinker, i. 136). Belle's letter has not been recovered.
[4] Executions charging a debtor to pay under penalties.
[5] The young Stadtholder, William V, had married the Princess Wilhelmina
of Prussia.

I long much to see your *History of Corsica.* 'Twill make its way here, I suppose, early in the spring. I propose to engage Miss de Z——— to translate it. What do you think of this project? I shall not fail to send you all the journals where mention is made of it; nor do I doubt but they will all concur in commending it to the public.

Shall I beg my most respectful compliments to my Lord your father? Believe me ever, with the truest regard, dear Sir, your most faithful, humble servant,

ROBERT BROWN.

[25. Brown to Boswell]

Utrecht, 15 January 1768

DEAR SIR:—Having had no return to the epistle I did myself the honour to endite to you some considerable time ago, I ought not by rights to trouble you with a second; however, be it by rights or by wrongs, I'm resolved to do it. . . .[6]

As I am informed Captain Kinloch has been at home for some time past, I make no doubt but you have seen him, and that he has himself explained to you the channel by which he forwarded your papers from London, so that by his information you have recovered what was lost, to be assured of which will give me great pleasure. I hope too you received your books. It gave me pain that there was so much confusion in the way of sending them, but this I could not possibly foresee; for had not one chest been mistaken for another, they must have arrived in Scotland before me, which I had in view, and in that case I would have set all to rights in a moment.

Your acquaintances here still very kindly remember you, and are happy in the small glimmering of hope I have given them that you will favour us with a visit next summer; particularly the family De Zuylen, who are all in perfect health. Apropos to these

[6] A long section is omitted dealing with a study of the Douglas Cause by the Reverend Dr. Richardson, of The Hague.

good people, you are a letter, if I mistake not, in the young lady's debt. How is this to be answered for or excused? When I was as young a man as you, I assure you I was more punctual; and yet must acknowledge my female correspondents were not equal to yours.[7] The lady in question honoured us last Sunday evening with her company at supper. We talked much of you. She had had pretty late accounts of you from one Mr. Bentinck, who passed some time lately at Edinburgh and lodged over head of you.

Our town is rather gayer this winter than usual. The Laird of Newbyth, a young East Lothian, recommended to Mr. de Zuylen, has his own share in these amusements. He lodges with me. If you are acquainted with any of his relations, you may assure them freely from me that the young gentleman is doing superlatively well here. Mrs. Brown, who is now happily recovered of an illness I thought last week should have cost her her life, joins her sister and me in best compliments. I am with great truth, Sir, your most obedient and faithful servant,

R. BROWN.

P.S. Shall I beg my compliments to Lord Auchinleck and your uncle, the Doctor?

[26. Belle de Zuylen to Boswell. Original in French][8]

Utrecht, 16 February 1768

WHAT SHALL I SAY TO YOU, MY FRIEND? Ought I to congratulate you or to send you condolences? Everything you tell me is so uncertain that I do not know which impression to fasten on. "You think seriously of marriage—a fine girl—an heiress—an admirable wife for you—but she does not like you—but she likes nobody else—but you hear a report—but you hope it is not true"[9]—

---

[7] Boswell had anticipated Brown's advice. On 10 January he had written to Belle making an outright profession of love, but still leaving room for retreat. The letter has not been recovered, but its contents are pretty well canvassed by Belle's reply, which follows.

[8] The French original of this letter is printed below, p. 397.

[9] The quoted phrases are in English in the original.

I wish for you everything that you wish yourself, but it would be rash to conclude anything from what you have written. The fact is you do not love conclusions; you love problems which can never be solved. The debate you have been conducting for so long concerning our fate if we were married is the proof of this taste of yours. I leave it to you to ponder, my dear Boswell. Aside from the fact that I am not clever enough to decide it, I take little pleasure in discussing so idle a question. I do not know your Scotland. On the map it appears to me a little out of the world. You call it "a sober country."[1] I have seen it produce decidedly despotic husbands and humble, simple wives who blushed and looked at their lords before opening their mouths. That is all I know about it, and with so little to go on one can decide nothing. But why should I decide? The problem must remain as it is, and I leave it to you for your amusement.

Allow me to remark that you certainly take your time for everything. You waited to fall in love with me until you were in the island of Corsica; and to tell me so, you waited until you were in love with another woman and had spoken to her of marriage. That, I repeat, that is certainly to take one's time. As for the question *how we would do together*,[2] that came into your mind at Zuylen, it accompanied you in your travels, and it has been presenting itself in season and out of season ever since. A strictly sensible person who read our letters would perhaps not find you too rational, but, as for me, I do not wish to put my friend under constraint. Everything his singularity prompts him to tell me shall be well received. Imagination is so mad a thing that when one permits one's self to say all it has suggested, one necessarily says foolish things, and what harm is there in that? I see none. I read your belated endearments with pleasure, with a smile.

Well! So you once loved me! I wish you all the more success and happiness in the choice your heart makes at present. It seems to me that you interest me and belong to me a little more because of that than if you had always been my cold and philosophic friend.

[1] Quoted words in English.   [2] Italicized words in English.

Let us speak of your works. I shall be charmed to translate your *Account of Corsica,* but you will have to send it to me first. Add to it *The Essence of the Douglas Cause.* I have as yet read nothing on that subject. I am to receive from London a publication of yours the title of which I have heard given as *Appeal to all the People.* I shall be glad to be able to give my own judgment on so famous and interesting a cause.

You plead very well the cause of marriage, but I could turn all your arguments in favour of celibacy. I have fortune enough so that I do not need a husband's; I have a sufficiently happy cast of mind and enough mental resources to be able to dispense with a husband, with a family, and what is called an establishment. I therefore make no vows, I take no resolutions; I let the days come and go, deciding always for the better among the things which Fate presents to me with some power of choice. I should be glad if time in its flow might carry away my thousand little faults of humour and character which I recognize and deplore. Often my progress does not come up to my good intentions.

You ask what my life is like. To answer you, I look about me. My room is pretty; people like to come there. My brother is chatting near me with Mr. Baird, a young Scotsman who lives with Mr. Brown. I have good books and I read little, but when I do read, it is the best things in all the *genres* and it is with a pleasure that makes me forget in turn my toilet and my tasks. I constantly forget the time, I write to my friends. I read this morning one of Clarke's sermons with Mr. Cudgil or de Horn, an exiled Englishman, who listens severely and corrects from time to time the pronunciation of a word or a syllable. Four times a week in the evening I go with my brothers to Monsieur Hahn's, who explains and demonstrates to us electrical fire and ordinary fire, and we learn about all of Nature that she permits us to know. That amuses me exceedingly. We have balls where I dance without much pleasure, because I do not have a lover. We have great assemblies: I learn to play cards. One needs a lover if one is to like dancing, one does not need a lover to like gaming.

Farewell, my friend, I am going to Mr. Brown's. We shall speak of you. He sends you many friendly regards. His wife and sister are amiable and good, his daughter is pretty as an angel. I am always well received by them all, and love them all. Depend on the sincere and faithful friendship of your most devoted

I. A. E. VAN TUYLL VAN SEROOSKERKEN.

[27. Boswell to Belle de Zuylen][3]

Edinburgh, 26 February 1768

MY DEAR FRIEND,—I had yesterday the pleasure of a charming letter from you, which shows me myself better than all the little philosophy which I have can do. You know me intimately, and I am sure whatever favour you show to me does not proceed from any mistake, as my faults have not escaped your penetration. But then the same genius which can discern my faults can also discern my good qualities, so that upon the whole I am happy in such a correspondent.

You rally me with inimitable pleasantry on my singular and fanciful conduct. But for all that I am not to blame. When I bid you adieu at Zuylen, I was really a stoical friend. I had then been for many months oppressed with melancholy, in short a very hypochondriac. I was still a slave to form and to system, and when all the circumstances of my situation are considered, was I to blame in imagining that I did not *love* you, and in putting on such airs of coldness? You would have regretted your friend had you known the truth. You would have seen that he acted with a kind of silent heroism, and who knows but you might have delivered him from all his distress and rendered him happy at once? I used to think, how can so wretched a being as I ever propose to a fine woman to pass her days with me? She will see me gloomy and discontented, and her charms will be lost.

[3] In English.

And yet, will you believe it, my amiable friend? I have had moments of felicity when I almost adored you and wished to throw myself at your feet. But before I could have time to write to you, the evil spirit again darkened my soul, and I saw that I need not hope for any permanent comfort. In this disconsolate state I pursued my travels, the variety of which amused my melancholy thoughts and gave me by degrees more relief and cheerfulness than I ever expected. I need not tell you again that, notwithstanding of that faith which I have ever preserved, my passions hurried me into many licentious scenes. Dare I own that perhaps these contributed in some measure towards the cure of my sickly mind? At Paris I told your brother how much I admired you, and I wrote a long letter to your father asking his candid advice if I should propose marriage to you. But the Marquis de ———— was then in the field. The death of my dear mother made me return to Britain without seeing you as I intended. I spoke of you to Sir John Pringle; I spoke of you to my father. They both were against my marrying a foreign lady and a *bel esprit*. Still, however, I admired you, though I could not think of having you for my wife. You came over to London, and Sir John Pringle admired you, but thought you had too much vivacity for being the spouse of a Scotch lawyer or sober country gentleman.

In the mean time, I supposed that I was quite indifferent to you. My mind became more composed and firm as I applied to the duties of my employment. I began to think of marriage in a rational way. Mr. Brown came to Scotland, and he talked to me of Mademoiselle de Zuylen till I began to exclaim against myself for neglecting any possibility of obtaining so superior a lady. But the safe and rational plan of taking a good home-bred heiress, with health and common sense instead of genius and accomplishments, swayed me much; yet I examined my heart, and I saw I could not possibly live with a woman who seemed indifferent. I therefore resolved to have some certainty that the Heiress really liked me. While I waited for certainty, up came a Knight, and being a very pretty man with a handsome fortune, he was a good match for the Heiress; he asked her, and she accepted of him, while I comforted myself on having lost a woman who, though an excellent girl, proved to be not what I wished.[4]

I am therefore a free man, and you cannot again tell me, "You certainly take your time." To be plain with you, my dear friend, I want your advice. I am now, I think, a very agreeable man to those who know my merit and excuse my faults. Whether do you think that you and I shall live happier: as distant correspondents, or as partners for life? Friends we shall always be at any rate. But I think it is worth our while to consider in what manner we may have the greatest share of felicity. If you say at once it would be a bad scheme for us to marry, your judgment shall be a rule to me. If you say that the scheme appears rather favourable for us, let us consider it in all lights, and contrive how we could possibly make the old people on each side of the water agree to it. If after all it cannot be, there will be no harm done.

My *Account of Corsica* will be with you very soon. The *Essence of the Douglas Cause* and the *Appeal to the People* are the same. Adieu, my dear, lively, amiable friend. I am much yours,

JAMES BOSWELL.

[EDITORIAL NOTE: At least six more letters, three by Belle and three by Boswell, appear to have followed within the next few months. None of them has come to light, but we know the nature of their contents, and can even recover a few sentences from them, from Boswell's diary and his reports to Temple. The pertinent passages follow.][5]

(To Temple, 24 March 1768) "Do you know, my charming Dutchwoman and I have renewed our correspondence; and upon

---

[4] "The Heiress" was Miss Catherine Blair of Adamtown, a ward of Lord Auchinleck's; "the Knight," Sir Alexander Gilmour. But Boswell spoke prematurely. Miss Blair turned down Sir Alexander too, and finally married Sir William Maxwell of Monreith.

[5] The extracts from the letters to Temple are taken from *The Letters of James Boswell*, ed. C. B. Tinker, 1924.

my soul, Temple, I must have her. She is so sensible, so accomplished, and knows me so well and likes me so much, that I do not see how I can be unhappy with her. Sir John Pringle is now for it; and this night I write to my father begging his permission to go over to Utrecht just now. She very properly writes that we should meet without any engagement, and if we like an union for life, good and well; if not, we are still to be friends. What think you of this, Temple?"

(To Temple, 26 April 1768) ". . . I have not yet given up with Zélide. Just after I wrote to you last,[6] I received a letter from her, full of good sense and of tenderness. 'My dear friend,' says she, 'it is prejudice that has kept you so much at a distance from me. If we meet, I am sure that prejudice will be removed.' The letter is in English. I have sent it to my father, and have earnestly begged his permission to go and see her. I promise upon honour not to engage myself, but only to bring a faithful report and let him decide. Be patient, Temple. Read the enclosed letters and return them to me. Both my father and you know Zélide only from me. May I not have taken a prejudice, considering the melancholy of my mind while I was at Utrecht? How do we know but she is an inestimable prize? Surely it is worth while to go to Holland to see a fair conclusion, one way or other, of what has hovered in my mind for years. I have written to her and told her all my perplexity. I have put in the plainest light what conduct I absolutely require of her, and what my father will require.[7] I have bid her be my wife at present[8] and comfort me with a letter in which she shall show at once her wisdom, her spirit, and her regard for me. You shall see it. I tell

[6] That is, just after 16 April 1768, a letter of that date having intervened between the present and the one quoted above.
[7] He also laid down the law in another matter close to his heart, though he does not think it necessary to say so to Temple. Belle, who was well along in her translation of his *Account of Corsica,* had asked him if she might omit certain passages and change others. He peremptorily forbade her to alter or abridge.
[8] "Pretend she is my wife already."

you, man, she knows me and values me as you do. After reading the enclosed letters, I am sure you will be better disposed towards my charming Zélide."

(Diary, 2 May 1768) "Letter from Zélide—termagant."

(To Temple, 14 May 1768) "So you are pleased with the writings of Zélide. Ah, my friend! had you but seen the tender and affectionate letter which she wrote to me and which I transmitted to my father. And can you still oppose my union with her? Yes, you can; and my dearest friend, you are much in the right. I told you what sort of letter I last wrote to her. It was candid, fair, conscientious. I told her of many difficulties. I told her my fears from her levity and infidel notions, at the same time admiring her and hoping she was altered for the better. How did she answer? Read her letter. Could any actress at any of the theatres attack one with a keener—what is the word? not *fury*, something softer. The lightning that flashes with so much brilliance may scorch. And does not her *esprit* do so? Is she not a termagant, or at least will she not be one by the time she is forty? And she is near thirty now. Indeed, Temple, *thou reasonest well.*[9] You may believe I was perfectly brought over to your opinion by this acid epistle. I was then afraid that my father, out of his great indulgence, might have consented to my going to Utrecht. But I send you his answer, which is admirable if you make allowance for his imagining that I am not dutiful towards him. I have written to him, ' "I will take the Ghost's word for a thousand pounds."'[1] How happy am I at having a friend at home of such wisdom and firmness. I was eager for the Guards. I was eager for Mademoiselle. But you have happily restrained me from both. Since, then, I have experienced your superior judgment in the two important articles of a profession and the choice of a wife, I shall henceforth do nothing without your advice.' Worthy man! this will be a solace to him upon his circuit. As for Zélide I

[9] Quoting the famous soliloquy from Addison's *Cato*.
[1] *Hamlet,* III. ii. 297. I suppose the point is that the Ghost was Hamlet's father.

have written to her that we are agreed. 'My pride,' say I, 'and your vanity would never agree. It would be like the scene in our burlesque comedy, *The Rehearsal.* "I am the bold thunder," cries one. "The quick lightning I," cries another. *Et voilà notre ménage.*' But she and I will always be good correspondents."[2]

[28. Brown to Boswell]

[Utrecht, *c.* 25 December 1769]

DEAR SIR,—I thank you very heartily for your last letter, which is certainly extremely obliging. A variety of reasons have induced me to put off making a return till now, of which this in particular was one—that I might not be called upon in any shape whatever to touch upon the circumstance which occasioned the interruption of our correspondence. That whole affair I desire to bury in oblivion, assuring you only in the sincerest manner that nothing can diminish the real regard and esteem I have all along entertained for you, and will to my latest breath entertain, founded on that intimate acquaintance I had the pleasure of making with you here.[3]

I suppose I may now give you joy of your marriage, which I pray GOD may be the source of every possible comfort both to you

[2] They appear never to have written to each other again. Belle attributed the breach as much to his stiffness about the *Account of Corsica* as to his determination to preserve the ascendancy of his sex. See p. 383.

[3] The cause of this interruption of correspondence is not certainly known. Boswell may have pressed Brown too hard in the matter of the lost journal, or he may have rebuked him for taking Belle's part too warmly. The first conjecture perhaps receives some support from a passage in Boswell's essay on diaries in *The Hypochondriack,* written many years later: "I left a large parcel of diary in Holland to be sent after me to Britain with other papers. . . . The packages having been loosened, some of the other papers were chafed and spoiled with water, but the diary was missing. I was sadly vexed, and felt as if a part of my vitals had been separated from me; and all the consolation I received from a very good friend to whom I wrote in the most earnest anxiety to make inquiry if it could be found anywhere, was that he could discover no trace of it, though he had made diligent search in all the little houses [privies], so trifling did it appear to him."

and the lady you have chosen for your partner.[4] I make no doubt of your being happy (that is, as happy as a reasonable and sober-minded man will expect to be in this world), considering the character of your female friend and the motives which have induced you to make this choice. I wish you as good a wife as I myself have, and that you may be able to declare with a safe conscience at the end of seven years, as I now do, that you can wish no greater blessing to your best friend.

My family now consists of two children, a son born last June and the girl at whose baptism you was pleased to act as joint godfather with my Lord Marischal. She has hitherto been the most thriving and prosperous child one could desire to see. As for her brother, he and I are as yet but too slightly acquainted for me to say much about him. His mother, who is at the same time his nurse, is positive he promises great things; and I am very willing to believe her.

Ever since my return from Britain in 1767, my health has been on a very sorry *footing*. Besides a weakness in my legs which renders me almost lame, I am much and often afflicted with bilious colics. I begin now to be sorry in some measure that I have rooted myself so deeply in this place that I must never think of moving; since the air and manner of living my character subjects me to, notwithstanding the heretical liberties I take to myself, does not at all agree with my constitution. There is no help for this. The interest of the good woman and her dear babies must go before everything else where life and a good conscience are not immediately concerned.

Your history has been translated both into French and Dutch. I am surprised you don't know this, as nothing is more natural than that you should have a copy in both languages; which if you have not already, I will send you. The French translation is thought to be much preferable to the Dutch. I had the honour of paying my

[4] Boswell had married his cousin Margaret Montgomerie on 25 November 1769.

respects to General Paoli[5] when he passed here. He received me with great affability; I found his conversation very sensible, and so passed half an hour with him very agreeably; but I must be sincere enough to say I discovered nothing in his countenance or behaviour which decisively announces the great man and the hero, or which strikes one with an enthusiastic veneration. To tell the truth, I am become much less sensible than formerly to all transports of that or any other kind. The longer I live, the more orthodox and the more stoical I become. . . .[6]

Your old servant, François Mazerac, has lived with me ever since his return from Scotland. His sight begins now to fail to such a degree that he is almost incapable of serving; and indeed for this twelvemonth past I have had very little use of him, though I have kept him at the rate of five guilders per week. He is desirous of returning either into Germany or Switzerland, where he will be at no loss to find a farmer who will find him in everything for eight pounds sterling a year. By next autumn he will be able to bring together ninety pounds sterling in all; and till next autumn I will keep him on the same footing as hitherto. He tells me that you was so good as once mention to him that you would be glad to do something for him, when or in case age or infirmity should incapacitate him for further service; and he has asked me to mention this to you, not as if he had acquired any claim to your assistance, but only to make his situation known. I have thought that perhaps, on the supposition of your being willing to interest yourself in behalf of this poor man, you might be prevailed upon to take his £90 and give him an annuity of ten per cent upon it during his life. This money, I suppose, you could lay out at five per cent interest; so that, was François to live twenty years after next September, you should be

[5] The General of the Corsicans and hero of Boswell's *Account.* The French had finally conquered his country, and he was on his way to England, which had offered him honourable asylum.

[6] A paragraph dealing with Dr. Richardson's labours in the Douglas Cause is omitted.

no loser. Besides this, he has nothing to propose; but would your Honour generously and charitably agree to supply him with a trifle annually (not inclining to enter with him into the contract above supposed), he will very devoutly pray for the prosperity of your Honour and your Honour's wife and your Honour's gentle bairns as long as he continues in the land of the living. This, my dear Sir, is what I could not refuse to lay before you, at the desire of the poor man; but I beg you will not imagine I mean to importune you in his favours. If you think proper to supply him with a guinea now and then, I will consider it as extremely good in you; if you think you are not called to any exercise of charity towards this particular object, I will not pretend to say you are.

Miss de Zuylen ever since the death of her mother has kept still more at home than before.[7] She has not been well of late, so that I have seen her but seldom for several weeks past. The last time however I had that pleasure, she desired me to make her best compliments to Mr. Boswell the first time I wrote him, and to wish him joy of his marriage in her name—I had almost said *stead*. The second brother, threatening a consumption, is gone to spend the winter at Montauban. The youngest is just returned from Germany. . . .[8]

I am, with great regard, dear Sir, your most affectionate humble servant,

R. BROWN.

[EDITORIAL NOTE: The reader who has immersed himself for long in the enormous subjectivism of Boswell's records feels strongly the need of some external ground of reference, of a candid evaluation by some one who knew Boswell well but who was *not* writing or speaking to Boswell himself. It would be hard to imagine better testimonies than the casual characterizations which occur in the clandestine correspondence between Belle de Zuylen

[7] Madame de Zuylen died following inoculation for the smallpox in December, 1768. She was only forty-four years old, having been married at the age of fifteen.

[8] The remainder of the letter deals with Brown's attempts to secure Corsican materials for Boswell, and gives a *précis* of the literary news of the Continent.

and Const

and Constant d'Hermenches. There is no reason whatever to suspect them of not being perfectly candid and outspoken. Belle was always frank (even *maligne*) in discussing her friends, and D'Hermenches did not know Boswell well enough to have an opinion of him one way or the other. The following extracts are all translated from *Lettres de Belle de Zuylen (Madame de Charrière) à Constant d'Hermenches,* edited by Philippe Godet, 1909.]

"When I go to the Assembly, I chat and play with a young Scotsman, full of good sense, wit, and naïveté" (February or March, 1764).

"Boswell saw you an instant at Madame de Maasdam's, and in that instant you were being very witty. I think I once told you about him. He is a very good friend of mine and much esteemed by my father and mother, so that he is always well received when he comes to see me. He came often while I was ill, and was so surprised to find me always in good humour that he almost scolded me for it; it seemed to him almost queer and out of place" (27 May 1764).

"I am waiting impatiently for Boswell in order to hear what you two said to each other. He told me the other day that although I was *a charming creature,* he would not marry me if I had the Seven United Provinces for my dowry; I agreed heartily" (8 June 1764).

"Mr. Boswell asked me for a letter of introduction to Voltaire, and I sent it to him. He told me he was going to see you that very day; I envied him greatly. Since then he has given no sign of life" (D'Hermenches, 12 June 1764).

"If Boswell did not write to you, it was not because he was not delighted with you and your letter; he showed it to me. May I be vain enough to recall word for word the compliment you paid me in it, a compliment that was very pleasing in spite of its exaggeration: 'I am told that Mademoiselle de Zuylen writes as well as Voltaire,' &c. That 'I am told' seemed to me pretty, delicate; but discreet? Hardly. If there had been no mystery in the matter, you would have made none, but would have based your judgment on *Le Noble*, the Portraits. But never mind, that 'I am told' pleases me greatly. Boswell left three weeks ago. He lectured me to the very end on morality, religion, and friendship. He is so good a man that he looks odd in this perverse age" (*c.* 9 July 1764).

"Am I not the unluckiest of beings? I was terribly in need of sleep and I thought I should sleep soundly; I complained of being sleepy and hurried through supper, but I found in my room an English letter from Boswell seventeen pages long: I read it, I went to bed. The seventeen thousand thoughts of my friend Boswell, a dim recollection of Monsieur d'Hermenches, what the Marquis said, and some English people—all that revolved in my head with such violence that I have not been able to stay in bed more than a quarter of an hour. Here I am, pen in hand; my pen will move at the command of a distracted brain. Don't expect what you read to be rational, don't think that I write to please you. I write because I cannot do anything else" ("In the night between Saturday and Sunday," 21–22 July 1764).

"I send you the mad things I wrote last night as though there had been no question of being serious since; and to amuse you after having made you work so hard, I enclose part of Boswell's letter. Send it back to me tomorrow." ("Sunday evening," 22 July 1764. D'Hermenches replied on 24 July: "The English letter charms me: I find in it things that take hold of me and make me overlook its pedantry. Now, one would like to see how he reduces all those respectable principles to everyday practice. That's the reef on which your moralizers commonly split. If they do not take refuge in cynicism, they condemn only those things that are not in the line of their own ruling passion.")

"At fourteen, I wanted to know everything, but I have re-nounced that ambition since. Boswell is wrong in thinking that I wear myself out with speculation. A sort of scepticism, very humble and rather peaceful—that is the state I have remained in. When I have more illumination and better health, I shall perhaps envision certitudes. For the present, I see at most probabilities, and I experience nothing but doubts" (27 July 1764).

"I went with my mother and father to Utrecht, where I had nothing to do, solely to be alone with them. In the carriage they spoke only of indifferent matters, and then of Boswell, who has written a letter full of admiration for me, of which he does not wish one word to be repeated to me. I related to them all his reasons for not marrying me. I grew merry, I told them stories (true ones). I told them that at the very most, if I became a great deal more reasonable, more prudent, more reserved, Boswell would try in time to marry me to his best friend in Scotland. We were in very good humour. . . . [She runs over the list of her suitors.] The Comte d'Anhalt is the slave of his king, or is disgusted with my reputation. Boswell will never marry me; if he did marry me, he would repent a thousand times, for he is convinced that I do not suit him, and I do not know whether I would be willing to live in Scotland. His friend—that is all foolishness; I would not begin on that litany of reforms for a man I never saw" (August, 1764).

"Yesterday evening we were talking about deference. I said that I repudiated it: that cold compliance was always of negative value to me as compared to the lively and animated attentions of affection. That is what I always in my heart believe. I never care about being respected; I want people to give me much without feeling that they owe me anything; I do not wish to impose a tax, I wish to please. Boswell thought that very wrong. He wanted to see me in a large hoop, in a long dress with hanging fringes, looking grave, waiting until he accosted me before I smiled, not in short skirts, looking careless and merry. 'How can you possibly,' he used to say to me, 'how can you possibly neglect making yourself respected when it would be so easy? Instead of trying always to be prepossessing, let people look forward to some time when you consent to be amiable, to please, to amuse, to give yourself up to company; and then, after a season of freedom, resume the tone of reserve. Save all those wild things which you say to any one who will listen, which are not understood, which are misinterpreted—save them for me, for your friend. Say them in English. You ought to manage the jealousies of friendship better; you ought to realize that friends want privileges and that they are offended when they see everybody getting the same treatment they do. Everybody is easy with you! It is terrible to see such unworthy people easy with you!'

"But I find he was partly right, and if I was not afraid of being ridiculed for affectation and still more afraid of the tortures of constraint, I might perhaps try his plan. You must see how his ideas fit his character. He 'respects mankind,' he wishes those who honour human nature to be set apart and have homage rendered to them; he wants virtue to announce itself by an imposing exterior, that whatever accompanies virtue shall assume an air of grandeur that will subdue the vulgar in advance. The austerity of his morality does not make him condemn the pleasures of a lively imagination, of free conversation, but he wants them taken in the form of recreation: he wants me to relax with *him,* to take my pleasure, as a prince among his favourites forgets the purple and the power. Obdam, on the contrary, said to me one day, 'Oh, drop that air of gravity which you are always assuming when you enter a room; don't give yourself so much trouble to spoil your expression even for an instant. Remember that if a person loves you a great deal, he will always respect you enough.'

"Aside from the fact that the difference between their characters makes what is an agreeable sentiment to one disagreeable to the other, it is a turn of self-love that makes their judgments so contrary. Boswell is pleased in advance by the respect he counts on winning some day; Obdam knows he has no pretensions beyond being amiable" (August, 1764).

"My friend Boswell has just sent me his book, *An Account of Corsica.* The heroism of the Corsicans, the great qualities of their chief, the genius of the author—all is interesting and admirable. I wish I could toss it to you, provided you would toss it back immediately, for I want to try to translate it. There are here and there singularities in it that you will think ridiculous, and which I do not think too highly of" (27 March 1768).

"I ought to have replied sooner to any letter so pleasing as yours, but I could not. I have been at Amsterdam and I have been translating. When one is busy, one waits for the post-day to write, and when it comes, some little unforeseen occupation obliges one to put off writing again. That is precisely what has always happened since the receipt of your last letter. . . .

"I had anticipated the advice to translate Boswell which you give me. Although your approval has encouraged me, I almost repent of my agreement with the publisher. But it must be kept. I would never have believed that it was so difficult and wearisome to translate" (28 April 1768).

"I will write with much pleasure what you ask of me: it will be a little extract from an interesting book which I am fond of but which I am no longer translating. I was far advanced in the task, but I wanted permission to change some things that were bad, and to abridge others which French impatience would have found unmercifully long-winded. The author, although he had at the moment *almost* made up his mind to marry me if I would have him, was not willing to sacrifice a syllable of his book to my taste. I wrote to him that I was firmly decided never to marry him, and I have abandoned the translation" (2 June 1768).

EDITORIAL NOTE[9]

Zélide entered the world nine days before James Boswell. She outlived him by ten years. For a brief moment their paths cross; he is illuminated for us in the clear light of her intelligence, and enacts

[9] By Geoffrey Scott, reprinted from the second volume of Colonel Isham's privately printed *Private Papers of James Boswell.*

for us one of his most engaging comedies. On the later and unwritten acts of this drama—Zélide in the circle of Johnson—the imagination may be left to dwell; but the union of Boswell and Zélide was hardly possible in human chemistry. Two characters, and two destinies, could scarcely be more diverse. Boswell entered a world of mirrors and reflections, dependent on others for a realization of himself, and for the exercise of his genius. Zélide, whose independent force declared itself in early rebellion against society, turned scornfully from whatever was tainted by human competition and narrowed her life to a tragic solitude. Fantastically, three years after the breach with Boswell, she married her brothers' former tutor, Monsieur de Charrière, to escape from the restraints of Zuylen. Thereafter she lived with him and his two sisters near Neuchâtel, hedging herself in a disdainful privacy and refusing to know even her neighbour, Voltaire. She relieved the tedium of her life by a rather tyrannical philanthropy, some unhappy love-affairs, the harpsichord, and literary composition. Her novel *Caliste* had much contemporary success, and was translated into English; it in some measure inspired the *Corinne* of Madame de Staël. To this early specimen of romantic fiction, modern taste will prefer her studies of provincial *genre,* which, at their rare best, foreshadow Miss Austen. But Zélide's sure literary talent is shown less in her books than in her correspondence. Her letters to Constant d'Hermenches, and, later, to Benjamin Constant, place her in the front rank even of eighteenth-century letter writers; their wit is never verbal; truth of feeling and fineness of thought sharpen the edge of their unfailing precision, and the gift of friendship is perilously allied with a surgical insight into character. Boswell, indeed, had fair reason for alarm. Her own emotions, naturally profound, were tortured by her intellect; she could enchant; but more often than enchantment she inspired fear, which she could not explain, and pity, which she scorned. She saw Benjamin Constant, after an intimacy of eight years, reft from her by Madame de Staël. She staked all on her intimate life, and, losing, preserved a stoical silence: a Van Tuyll after all, a stickler for old-fashioned good manners; and, to the end, intolerant as Johnson himself of cant, self-deception, loose-thinking and illogical speech.

When Boswell, with the plan of marrying Zélide shaping itself in his mind, wandered on his travels in 1764, he visited the old castle, once Lord Marischal's, at Colombier; and from its rampart looked down upon the tiled roof of the manor house under which Zélide was to live and die, and on the *potager* beyond which, for fifteen years on end, she never stepped.

APPENDIX I

Inviolable Plan
To be read over frequently

[See p. 47, the memorandum for 16 October 1763,
and the footnote on that entry.]

You have got an excellent heart and bright parts. You are born to a respectable station in life. You are bound to do the duties of a *Laird* of Auchinleck. For some years past you have been idle, dissipated, absurd, and unhappy. Let those years be thought of no more. You are now determined to form yourself into a man. Formerly all your resolutions were overturned by a fit of the spleen. You believed that you had a real distemper. On your first coming to Utrecht you yielded to that idea. You endured severe torment. You was pitiful and wretched. You was in danger of utter ruin. This severe shock has proved of the highest advantage. Your friend Temple showed you that idleness was your sole disease. The Rambler showed you that vacuity, gloom, and fretfulness were the causes of your woe, and that you was only afflicted as others are. He furnished you with principles of philosophy and piety to support the soul at all times. You returned to Utrecht determined. You studied with diligence. You grew quite well. This is a certain fact. You must never forget it. Nor attempt to plead a real incurable distemper; for you cured it, when it was at its very worst, merely by following a proper plan with diligence and activity. This is a great era in your life; for from this time you fairly set out upon solid principles to be a man.

Your worthy father has the greatest affection for you and has suffered much from your follies. You are now resolved to make reparation by a rational and prudent conduct. Your dear mother is anxious to see you do well. All your friends and relations expect

387

that you will be an honour to them and will be useful to them as a lawyer, and make them happy as an agreeable private gentleman.

You have been long without a fixed plan and have felt the misery of being unsettled. You are now come abroad at a distance from company with whom you lived as a frivolous and as a ludicrous fellow. You are to attain habits of study, so that you may have constant entertainment by yourself, nor be at the mercy of every company; and to attain propriety of conduct, that you may be respected. You are not to set yourself to work to become stiff and unnatural. You must avoid affectation. You must act as you ought to do in the general tenor of life, and that will establish your character. Lesser things will form of course.

Remember that idleness renders you quite unhappy. That then your imagination broods over dreary ideas of its own forming, and you become contemptible and wretched. Let this be no more. Let your mind be filled with nobler principles. Remember religion and morality. Remember the dignity of human nature. Remember everything may be endured.

Have a sense of piety ever on your mind, and be ever mindful that this is subject to no change, but will last you as long as life and support you at death. Elevate your soul by prayer and by contemplation without mystical enthusiasm. Preserve a just, clear, and agreeable idea of the divine Christian religion. It is very clearly proved. You cannot expect demonstration. There is virtue in faith: in giving a candid assent upon examination. Keep quite clear of gloomy notions which have nothing to do with the mild and elegant religion of Jesus as it is beautifully displayed in the New Testament. Have this faith always firm. Be steady to the Church of England, whose noble worship has always raised your mind to exalted devotion and meditation on the joys of heaven. Be firm to religion, and at all times show your displeasure to profanity, like a decent gentleman. But don't enter into disputes in riotous and ludicrous companies where sacred things cannot be properly weighed.

Without a real plan, life is insipid and uneasy. You have an admirable plan before you. You are to return to Scotland, be one of the

Faculty of Advocates, have constant occupation, and a prospect of being in Parliament, or having a gown. You can live quite independent and go to London every year; and you can pass some months at Auchinleck, doing good to your tenants and living hospitably with your neighbours, beautifying your estate, rearing a family, and piously preparing for immortal felicity. To have all these advantages, firmness is necessary. Have constant command of yourself. Restrain ludicrous talents and, by habit, talk always on some useful subject, or enliven conversation with moderate cheerfulness. Keep to study ever to improve. Have your own plan and don't be put out of it. Your friends Temple and Johnston will assist you to do well. Never talk of yourself, nor repeat what you hear in a company. Be firm, and persist like a philosopher.

Now remember what you have resolved. Keep firm to your plan. Life has much uneasiness; that is certain. Always remember that, and it will never surprise you. Remember also life has much happiness. *To bear* is the noble power of man. This gives true dignity. Trifles are more frequently the causes of our disturbance than great matters. Be prepared therefore for uneasy trifles. You have indulged antipathies to places and persons. That is the sign of a weak and diseased mind. A hysteric lady or a sickly peevish boy may be so swayed. But let not antipathies move a man. It is not sensibility. You can cure it and at all times do so.

Resolve to make constant experiments, and be more and more confirmed in your theory. A man has much the command of his ideas. Check little uneasy ones. Encourage little pleasing ones. He who has baseless antipathies is foolishly deprived of much pleasure. Your great loss is too much wildness of fancy and ludicrous imagination. These are fine if regulated and given out in moderation, as Mr. Addison has done and as Sir David Dalrymple does. The pleasure of laughing is great. But the pleasure of being a respected gentleman is greater.

You have a character to support. You have to keep up the family of Auchinleck. To do this, your mind must be settled and filled with knowledge, and with good plain ideas of common sense and the practice of mankind, although you may be a Church-of-England man and indulge any other favourite principles; only never talk at random. Every man should be the best judge how to regulate his own conduct; there are many minutiae particular to every character. For some time be excessively careful against rattling, though cheerful to listen to others. What may be innocent to others is a fault to you till you attain more command of yourself. Temperance is very necessary for you, so never indulge your appetites without restraint. Be assured that restraint is always safe and always gives strength to virtue. Exercise must never be neglected, for without that you cannot have health, and health contributes much to render you fit for every duty. Never indulge the sarcastical Scotch humour. Be not jocular and free, and then you will not be hurt by the jocularity and freedom of others. If you are polite, you will seldom meet with uneasy rubs in conversation.

Τίμα σεαυτόν: reverence thyself.[1] But at the same time be afraid for thyself. Ever keep in mind your firm resolutions. If you should at times forget them, don't be cast down. Return with redoubled vigour to the field of propriety. Upon the whole you will be an excellent character. You will have all advantages from the approbation of the World, in your rational plan, which may be enlarged as you see occasion. But yield not to whims, nor ever be rash.

[1] A personal variation of the famous γνῶθι σεαυτόν ("know thyself"), the inscription on the Temple at Delphi. Boswell was fond of it but never managed to get the Greek right. The manuscript here actually reads τιμν.

APPENDIX II

Boswell's French Theme on the Aston Family

[See pp. xvii and 190. Boswell's spelling and capitalization have been retained, but some liberties have been taken with his punctuation.]

Je veux tacher de raconter en assez bon françois la conversation de Monsieur Brown hier a dinér.—Nous avons eu, dit il, á Utrecht une famille angloise la plus exotique qu'on puisse concevoir. Le Chevalier Willoughby Aston avoit un bien de cinq mille livres par an, dans l'ouest d'Anglettérre. Il a depensé beaucoup d'argent pour gagner une election qu'il a pourtant perdu; et il a vecu sur un pied trop splendide. Il trouvoit ses affaires un peu embarrassées, et il fit resolution de passer quelques années dans des païs etrangers, afin qu'il epargneroit. Il etoit un gros cochon, un lourdaud immense. Il louchoit horriblement mais il ne lui manquoit pas une espece de rude sens commun, et comme il avoit eté Justice du paix pendant plusieurs années, il savoit tres bien *the poors rates,* les taux des pauvres. Sa femme etoit une etre la plus ridicule et la plus degoutante. Elle avoit pres de cinquant ans et elle s'habilloit comme une fille de seize. Elle etoit affectée et vaine et insipide et capriceuse. Son frere Monsieur Pie, Negociant á Amsterdam, la detestoit. Il a engagé de venir et diner chez elle, et la presenter son epouse. Madame d'Aston etoit seule á Utrecht. M. Brown etoit invité a cette diner. Il y alloit á quatre heures et il craignoit d'etre trop tard. Mais le diner etoit arrete jusque a cinque[2] heures. Milady devenoit tres impatiente. Elle demandoit de Monsieur Brown s'il n'avoit pas faim. Il l'avouoit. "Mais," dit il, "il faut attendre pour Monsieur Pie car il a dit qu'il seroit un peu tard." C'etoit une observation tres juste et tres sensee. Il a pourtant frappee en quelque mannierre outrée la tête vertigineuse de Milady. Il a fait la venir dans l'esprit: "Ma foy, ces Bourgeois sont tres impolis. Ils doivent ses conformer

[2] Boswell has struck out the final *e*. He probably meant to indicate the spelling *cinq*.

aux heures de Gens de qualité. Je n'attenderai pas un moment de plus." Monsieur Brown la prioit de ne prendre pas des telles mesures precipités. Mais elle etoit inexorable. Elle a fait venir le diner et Milady et Monsieur Brown se mettoient a table de dix huit plaats. Apeine avoient ils commencés a manger la soupe quand toute la Compagnie arrivoit, et avant que toutes les ceremonies fussent finis le diner fut froid. Ils l'ont mangés pourtant, et Miladi se donnoit des airs immenses. Apres diné ils ont ses mits aux Cartes. Monsieur Brown et Monsieur Pie ne jouoient pas mais causoient ensemble en Hollandois. "Eh bien," dit Pie, "avez vous jamais vu la pareille de ma Seure la? Je crois qu'elle est la plus grande folle dans le monde." "Mais," disoit M. Brown, "pourquoy est-ce que vous laissez ces Gens voyager plus? Ils s'exposeroient par tout." "Cela est vraye," repondit M. Pie, "mais Je les laisse voyager parce que Je veux qu'ils seroient loin de Moy." Sir Willoughby restoit au lit jusque á une heure. Il s'elevoit, et se mit devant le feu avec la dernierre Paresse. Il crioit á une de ces filles, "Polly! mes souliers—a a—." Elle les apportoit. "A—" dit Il, "souliers sans boucles—a a—." Il grommeloit ainsi toute la matinnée. Il aimoit beaucoup a boire quand il avoit de Compagnie. Il vivoit á Utrecht sur un pied magnifique. Il recevoit beaucoup de politesses; mais a la fin il a ennuié tout le Monde. Giffardierre et Hill, deux jeunes Predicants qui aimoient a vivre bien, etoient les seuls qui restoient firmes a la famille d'Aston. Le Chevalier avoient cinq filles dont l'ainée etoit extremement aimable et souffroit beaucoup de l'absurdité de son Pere et de sa mere. Le Jeune Willoughby etoit le drole le plus mechant san la moindre grain de Bienseance. Il a entré un Samedi chez une Societé nombreuse sans invitation. Il a jasé et bu et mangé leurs crackelins, jusque a ce que Monsieur Cochrane lui donnoit sur les doix et le chassé de la Chambre. Telle fut la famille d'Aston. Ils avoient un domestique ecossois qu'ils appelloient Hume et Humes. Monsieur Brown lui demandoit, "Comment est-ce que vous avez ce nom la?" "Poh!" dit Il, "mon nom est Hugh Mcgregor, mais cette folle Miladi m'a donné le nom de Humes." Cette celebre famille est á present á Tours en france, ou ils depensent plus d'argent qu'ils n'avoient depensés en Angletterre.

APPENDIX III

Letter of Abraham Gronovius to Boswell

[The spelling and punctuation are those of the manuscript; capitalization has been standardized. See translation on p. 278.]

NOBILISSIME AMICISSIMEQUE,—Plurimum equidem singulari humanitati tuae me debere profiteor, quod, etsi temporis angustiis inclusus, me praeterita Mercurii die in hortulo jucundissima praesentia tua dignatus fueris; speroque te salvum Ultrajectum pervenisse: at rubore suffundor ad eximiam liberalitatem tuam, cujus vinculo me tibi obstrictum agnosco; siquidem quinque et quadraginta lagenae falerni Lusitanici jussu tuo et opera Clarissimi Craufurdii Roteradamo hodie ad me perlatae sunt. Quid autem pro hoc munere tibi rependam, quas grates propensae huic voluntati tuae habeam, vix invenio. Interim iter in Germaniam, quod una cum illustrissimo heroë Comite Marshallino suscepturus es, tibi felix faustumque voveo; eoque prospere peracto, vehementer mihi gratulabor, si suavissimo adfabilis oris tui adloquio iterum frui, virtutesque tuas, quibus ingenuum pectus exornasti, admirari mihi contigerit. Perge itaque paterna vestigia premere, hoc est pietatem, virtutem atque eruditionem colere, et hoc pacto nominis Boswelliani gloriam ad commodum patriae tuae, quam etiam gratam tuis meritis aliquando responsuram auguror, amplificare. Quod det Deus O. M.[3] Vale meum decus et amare perge tuum

ABRAHAMUM GRONOVIUM.

Dabam Leidis,
A. D. V. Eid. Junii,
A. MDCCLXIV.

[3] "Optimus Maximus."

394

APPENDIX IV

Letter of François Mazerac to Boswell

[The spelling, capitalization, and punctuation of the manuscript
have been retained. See translation on p. 290.]

Monsieur

Mon peu de Capasité met[4] met presque hors d'etat de satisfaire a
vos ordre, jespere que Monsieur les Recevrá avec bonté comme
venant d'une personne qui ne cherche qua vous obeir

premierement jai trouvé que Monsieur est extremement negligent sur son argent montre es autres efet en les laisant sur la Table
au[5] la Clé sur le bureau es en sortant de la Chambre laisant la port
ouverte comme il met arivé plusieur foi a la Haye, si jamai il
arivoit, que vous usie[6] le Malleur de perdre quelque chosse de cette
Maniere vous pourié avoir soupsons sur votre Domestique ou autre
personne qui serait jnocent on dit pour proverbe l'ocation fait le
l'aron

secondement jai trouvé que Monsieur avéz le Coeur bon pour
faire du bien au pauvre vertu qui nous et dicté par l'humanité, et
ordoné par la Religions

troisiemement Monsieur net point médisant vice voor[7] comun
parmi les Grand espiti[8]

Droisiememement exact dans les devoir de votre Religion soit pour
aller a lEglice ne point jurer surtout a faire votre priere tous les
matin

quatriememement jai trouve que quand Monsieur avez priez
quelquun les Conviéz eté toujour ches vous avan vous ce qui vous
pourés faire des Reproche sur tous dans un autre pais ou il sont plus
sur leur point d'honneur quici

[4] Read *me*.　　[5] Read *ou*.　　[6] That is, *eussiez*.
[7] That is, *fort*. François gives the word a Dutch spelling. Notice also below
his substitutions of *t* for *d* and *d* for *t*: e.g., *dart* for *tard*.
[8] Read *esprits*.

Cinquiemement jai trouvé que Monsieur sapliqué trop a létude noble en elle meme Mai Ruinneuce pour la santé si elle ne se fait avec Menagement

sixiemement je trouve que Monsieur se Couche trop tart qui avec léttude, vous feront pertre la santé et dont Monsieur se Repentirá quand il sera trop dart et quil ni aura point de Remede

septiemement es pour dernié article jai trouvé en Monsieur un Coeur Veritablement Chretien es noble sur tout a Mon Egart et que je Noublierai jamai Veullié le pere des pere Vous prendre en sa sainte Garde avoir loeil sur Vous, vous Gardan comme son afant cheri, quil guide vos pas dirige vos pensée afin quil ne vous arive au'qun Malleur. et quétant de Redour ches vous saint et sauf vous l'en benissiés eternellement

je finit en Remerciant encore Monsieur pour doute ses bont et le l prie'nt de se Resouvenir quelque foi de Moi pour Moi je ne Croi pas que joublierai Monsieur jamai

Monsieur si jamai locasion se presente permeté moi de vous prié de savoir comment Monsieur se port

wotre tres afligés et fitelle Domestique

françois Mazerac.

Utrecht ce 17
juin 1764

[List by François Mazerac. Original in French]

Clothes and linens that I found on entering the service of Monsieur Boswell

1 coat, waistcoat, and breeches, with silver lace
1 red coat, waistcoat, and breeches, with gold lace
1 rose-coloured coat and waistcoat, with gold buttons
1 blue coat, waistcoat, and breeches, with white buttons
1 brown frock-coat
1 pair of black silk breeches
1 pair of buckskin breeches
1 hat with gold lace

1 sword with a silver hilt

5 pairs of shoes

1 pair of slippers

2 pairs of shoe-buckles

1 pair of garter-buckles

1 collar clasp[9]

1 pair of shirt buttons

15 ruffled shirts

3 night-shirts

14 collars

6 ditto, new

6 new silk handkerchiefs, white ground

5 ditto, cotton, red ground

1 ditto, old, white ground

4 night-caps

2 sets of lace ruffles

2 pairs black silk stockings, new

2 pairs white silk stockings, new

3 pairs ditto, old

7 pairs thread and cotton stockings

1 pair of boots

1 powdering jacket

[9] "Un Boucle de Col."

APPENDIX V

Letter of Belle de Zuylen to Boswell

[The spelling of the manuscript has been retained,
but a few marks of punctuation have been added to regularize its breathless
but fairly systematic punctuation. See pp. xvii and 367.]

QUE VOUS DIRAI-JE, MON AMI? Faut-il vous feliciter ou vous plaindre? Tout ce que vous me dites est si douteux que je ne sai a quelle impression m'arrêter. You think seriously of marriage, a fine girl, an heiress, an admirable wife for you, but she does not like you, but she likes no body else, but you hear a report, but you hope it is not true: moi, je vous souhaite tout ce que vous souhaitez, mais il seroit temeraire de rien conclure de tout ce que vous dites, aussi n'aimez vous pas les conclusions, vous aimez les problêmes qu'on ne peut jamais resoudre. Celui que vous proposez depuis si longtems sur notre sort si nous etions mariés est la preuve de ce gout: je vous le laisse à mediter, mon cher Boswell; outre que je ne suis pas assez habile pour decider, je trouve peu de plaisir à discuter une question aussi oiseuse. Je ne connois pas votre Ecosse, sur la carte elle me paroit un peu hors du monde. Vous l'apellez *a sober country*, j'en ai vu sortir des maris assez despotiques et d'humbles bonnes femmes qui rougissoient et regardoient leurs epoux avant que d'ouvrir la bouche, voilà tout ce que j'en sai et là dessus on ne peut rien decider, mais pourquoi deciderois-je? Il faut que ce probleme reste ce qu'il est, et je vous le laisse pour amusement.

Permettez moi de remarquer que vous prenez bien votre tems pour toutes choses. Vous avez attendu pour m'aimer que vous fussiez dans l'Ile de Corse, et pour me le dire vous avez attendu que vous en aimassiez un autre et que lui eussiez parlé de marriage: voilà encore une fois, voilà bien prendre son tems. Pour la question *how we would do together*, elle a pris naissance a Zuylen, elle vous a accompagné dans vos voyages, et elle se represente en tems et hors de tems. Une personne sensée qui liroit nos lettres ne vous trouveroit peut-être pas trop raisonnable, mais pour moi je ne veux pas gener mon ami, tout ce que sa singularité voudra me dire sera bien receu: l'imagination est si folle que quand on se permet de dire tout ce qu'elle dicte, il faut bien dire des folies, et quel mal a cela? Je n'en vois aucun. J'ai lu avec plaisir et en souriant vos tardives douceurs. Ah! vous m'aimiez donc! Je vous en souhaite d'autant plus de succés et de felicité dans le choix que fait à present votre coeur. Il me semble que vous m'interressez et m'apartenez un peu plus a cause de cela que si vous aviez toujours été mon froid et philosophique ami.

Parlons de vos ouvrages: je serois charmé de traduire votre histoire, mais il faut me l'envoyer. Joignez y *l'Essence de l'affaire des Douglas*. Je n'ai encore rien lu là dessus. On doit m'envoyer de Londres un écrit de vous qu' on m'a nommé *Appel a toute la nation*. Je serai bien aise de pouvoir juger par moi même d'une cause si fameuse et si interressante.

Vous plaidez assez bien celle du marriage, mais je pourois tourner tous vos argumens en faveur du celibat. J'ai assez de fortune pour n'avoir pas besoin de celle d'un mari. J'ai l'humeur assez heureuse et assez de ressources dans l'esprit pour me passer d'un mari, d'un menage, et de ce qu'on apelle un etablissement. Je ne fais donc point de voeu, je ne prens point de resolution; je laisse les jours venir et passer, me decidant toujours pour ce que le sort me presente de mieux parmi les choses dont il me laisse le choix: je voudrois que le tems en s'ecoulant emportât mille petits defauts d'humeur et de caractere que je reconnois et que je deplore. Souvent là dessus mes progrés ne repondent pas a mes bonnes intentions.

Vous demandez comment je vis. Pour vous repondre je regarde autour de moi. Ma chambre est jolie, on aime a y venir. Mon frere cause ici près de moi avec Mr Baird, jeune Ecossois qui demeure chez M. Brown; j'ai de bons livres et je lis peu, mais quand je lis ce sont les meilleures choses dans tous les genres, et c'est avec un plaisir qui me fait negliger tour a tour ma toilette et mes devoirs. J'oublie sans cesse les heures, j'ecris à mes amis. J'ai lu ce matin un sermon de Clarke avec Mr Cudgil ou de Horn, un Anglois exilé qui m'ecoute severement et corrige de tems en tems le son d'un mot ou d'une sillabe. Quatre fois par semaine je vai l'aprés diné avec mes freres chez M. Hahn qui nous dit et nous montre ce que c'est que le feu electrique et le feu ordinaire, et nous aprenons a connoitre de la Nature tout ce qu'elle permet qu'on en connoisse. Cela m'amuse extremement. Nous avons des bals où je danse sans beaucoup de plaisir parce que je n'ai point d'amant. Nous avons de grandes assemblées: j'aprens a jouer. Il faut un amant pour aimer la danse, il faut n'en avoir point pour aimer le jeu.

Adieu, mon ami, je vai chez M. Brown, nous parlerons de vous, il vous fait beaucoup d'amitiés. Sa femme et sa soeur sont aimables et bonnes, sa fille est jolie comme un ange. Je suis toujours bien receue de tous et les aime tous. Comptez sur l'amitié sincere et fidele de votre trés devouée

I. A. E. van Tuyll van Serooskerken.

Utrecht ce 16 Fevr. 1768

INDEX

This is for the greater part an index of proper names, but Part II of the article BOSWELL, JAMES provides general headings for Boswell's traits of character, opinions, and religious sentiments. Observations on persons and places are generally entered under the person or place in question; for example, Boswell's opinions of the Reverend Robert Brown should be looked for under Brown and not under Boswell. Churches, inns, streets, &c. in Dutch cities are grouped under the cities concerned; if outside of Holland, churches, inns, streets, counties, mountains, &c. are given separate articles in the main alphabet. When a city, town, or other territorial designation is given without further specification, it may be assumed that it is in Holland. Peers and peeresses, Lords of Session and their wives are indexed under titles rather than family names, the titles chosen being usually those proper to 1764, but this rule has been broken when a person is decidedly better known by a later title or a family name. Isabella Agneta Elisabeth van Tuyll van Serooskerken, later Mme de Charrière, is entered as ZUYLEN, BELLE DE. The following abbreviations are employed: D. (Duke), E. (Earl), M. (Marquess), V. (Viscount), JB (James Boswell).

Averhoult, Mlles d', at Utrecht, 71, 328
Ayrshire, Scotland, 1, 115 *n.*, 232 *n.*2, 280

Baden-Durlach, Karl Friedrich, Margrave of, 221, 327
Baden-Durlach, Court of, 227, 249
Baird, Robert, of Newbyth, 367, 369
Barbour, John, Scottish poet, 165 *n.*
Bart, proprietor of the Keiserhof at Utrecht, 156, 254
Bath, England, 234
Baxter, Andrew, Scottish philosopher, 146
Bayle, Pierre, French philosopher, 183
Bedford, John Russell, 7th D. of, 272
Bellamy, George Anne, actress, 176
Bellegarde, François-Eugène Robert, Comte de (*also* Marquis des Marches and de Cursinge), account of him, 297 *n.*8, 341, 342; characterized, 304; Belle de Zuylen considers herself in love with, plans to marry, 295, 297–298, 304, 341; makes a proposal of marriage to Belle, 330, 341–342; difficulties because of his religion, 304, 342, 353; JB thinks Belle would prefer himself to, 344–345; JB would defer suit till his is settled, 346; mentioned, 350, 360, 371
Bellenden, John, Scottish divine and poet, 165
Bellevue, near Cleves, Germany, estate of Baron von Spaen, 217, 275
Bennett, C. H., xix
Bennett, Lady Camilla Elizabeth, daughter of the Earl of Tankerville, married Count Dönhof, 324–325, 327
Bentinck, Major Rudolph, 367
Bentinck de Varel, Christian Frederick Anthony, Count, account of him, 239 *n.*4; his command of English, 273 *n.*5; characterized, 340; letters to JB, 273, 276; JB sups with, 239; JB checks him from being too free, 240–241; mem. to visit, 243; JB in his company at Zuylen, 259; serves as intermediary in correspondence between Belle and JB, 305, 308; visits England, 340; stops writing to JB, 340

Bentinck de Varel, Maria Catharina (van Tuyll), Countess, 239 *n.*4
Berkeley, Norborne, M.P., 72
Berlin, Germany, JB thinks of escaping to from Utrecht, 10; Lord Auchinleck assures JB of kind reception at, 221; JB plans to visit, 227, 277, 280, 282; De Guiffardière sets down qualities needed to please at, 256; JB to accompany Lord Marischal to, 268, 269; Lord Marischal expected to promote JB socially at, 274; JB spends summer at, 296; JB pleased with, 314, 316, 319; M. de Zuylen expects JB to improve his French at, 320; JB leaves, 322
Bernard, ?Jean-Étienne, at Utrecht, 141, 283
Beulwitz, Ludwig Friedrich von, 272
Biblical references. *See* James, St.; Job; Luke, St.; Matthew, St.; Paul, St.
Bicker, Jan Bernd, 340
Blair, Catherine ("the Heiress"), *later* wife of Sir William Maxwell of Monreith, 297, 367, 368, 371–372
Blinshall, James, D.D., Scottish minister at Amsterdam, 260, 261
Bodegraven, 119
Boene, "Widow," Lord Auchinleck's landlady at Leyden, 53, 149
Boetzelaer, Countess of, at Utrecht, 71
Boetzelaer, Mlle, at Utrecht (same as preceding?), 113
Bois-le-Duc (s'Hertogenbosch), 257
Bonnet, Gijsbertus, professor at Utrecht, 138, 139, 253, 284 *n.*5
Boorsch, Jean, xix
Boston, Sir Charles (JB's pseudonym), 195
Boswell, bookseller at Utrecht, 59
Boswell, Alexander. *See* Auchinleck (Alexander Boswell), Lord
Boswell, Charles, son of JB, 31, 124, 177–179, 194, 210, 211
Boswell, David, *later* Thomas David, brother of JB, 40 *n.*4, 124, 359 *n.*5
Boswell, Lady Elizabeth (Bruce), grandmother of JB, 53 *n.*
Boswell, James, 4th laird of Auchinleck, 65

tic, 146; fickle in love, 157; fond of
money, 157; likes to sleep with his
head high, 159–160; given to whims of
regularity, 169; has great difficulty in
rising, 198; plagued by narrowness,
233, 350; has a facility in learning
languages, 242; a man of form, 307–
308, 370; a man of strict probity, 314;
likes novelty only in matters of the
imagination, 317; believes in subordination, 336, 338; knowledge restricted, cannot apply to study, 350;
subject to low spirits: *see* Part I of this
article, *passim*; seeks greater reserve of
character: *see* Part I of this article,
references beginning with p. 24

b. *Opinions.* On nightcaps, 49–50;
the Sabbath, 51; English music, 51–52;
Scots music, 55, 168; learning French,
57–58, 213; breeches, 59–60; the Tories,
67; the Hanoverian line, 67; Groom of
the Stole, 68–69; republicanism and
monarchy, 79, 83; English authors as
compared to French, 83; too great subtlety, 87; his own themes, 87–88;
French morality, 93; fashion, 101; indolence, 126–127, 140–141, 197–198;
education of children, 128–129; the fast
on 30 January, 129–130; the Dutch
language, 133–134, 136; the proper
way to fold coats, 134; treatment of
servants, 134–135; the *optimus mundus*, 135; origin of dreams, 146; stockings and shoes, 152; fasting, 152–153;
poverty, 160–161; Scots language and
literature, 162–165; pride and emulation, 169; Tokay wine, 172; gaming,
181; meals, 189–190; rising in the
morning, 198; prudence, 309–310; metaphysics in women, 311; disobedient
daughters, 327; women with talents,
328

c. *Religious Sentiments and Beliefs.*
Prayers and ejaculations, 7, 9, 10, 18,
23, 29, 169, 280, 281; church attendance, 23, 44, 51, 88, 106, 114, 119,
169, 179, 222, 231, 239, 244, 249, 261,
264, 268, 286, 291; calls life a state of
probation, 33; dreads Sunday because

of gloomy associations, 50–51, 264; defends revelation, 50, 62 *n*.5; counsels
piety, 54, 61, 95, 103, 140, 152, 179,
190, 196, 249, 388; thinks he is too
strict with himself, 61; hopes to be
prepared for death by an Anglican
clergyman, 61; depreciates Calvinism,
73, 316; tortured by metaphysics of
fate, free-will, necessity, and origin of
evil, 90–91, 179, 182, 183, 192, 195,
201, 204, 231, 232, 240, 269; considers
himself committed to moral behaviour
as a Christian, 95, 107; takes the sacrament for first time in Church of England, 106–107, 122; depreciates religious training of his childhood, 129,
252, 282; meditates on problem of soul
and body, 140–141; asks Mme Geelvinck's religion, 147, 152, 155–156;
fasts, reads prayers, 153; convinced of
Christian miracles, 174; debates Christian morals, 174; finds relief in religion from grief at son's death, 178;
convinced of revelation, 183, 212; prays
for delivery from gloom, 189; loses
comforts of religion when melancholy,
211, 215, 284; counsels against austere
devotion, 215; suffers sceptical (infidel) thoughts, 217, 239, 246, 252,
269; questions if GOD forbids girls, 222;
owns having been Roman Catholic,
232, 267; talks about future life, 233;
disputes Athanasian Creed, 240; "continue Christian, as Johnson; Church of
England," 240, 241; discusses immortality, 246; reads Rousseau, embraces
enlarged notions of GOD and liberal
interpretation of Christianity, 247,
252–253, 265, 267, 282, 285, 311, 334,
335–336; teases Maclaine about transubstantiation, 267

III. a. *Writings in Holland.* 1. Memoranda in Holland, described, x, xii–
xiv; bibliography of, xviii–xix; selection printed in this volume, 4–258; JB
begins in French but soon shifts to
English, except for dialogue, 4, 20, 24,
85 *n*.; to be looked at first thing each
morning and reviewed on Saturday,

CORRECTIONS AND ADDITIONS

Some of these correct mechanical errors by editor, typist, or printer; some
present information I have acquired myself since the book was printed;
some—very pleasant ones—were sent in by correspondents unknown to
me; finally, a valuable lot has been extracted from the preliminary reports of my friend and collaborator, Professor Robert Warnock, who
spent February–August, 1952, in Germany and Holland searching the
public archives for materials with which to annotate the research edition
of the Boswell Papers.

F. A. P.

vi, l. 8: *read* T. B. SIMPSON, Q.C., LL.D., F.R.S.E., Sheriff of Perth and Angus
xvi n.2, l. 5: *for* convention *read* conventions
4, l. 19: *Dr. C. H. Bennett and Professor Robert Warnock have independently deci-*

phered this signature: JAS. CLEMENTS. *He was* "agent of the packet boats at Harwich" (*Obituary in "Gentleman's Magazine," May,* 1767, *p.* 280).

6 *n.*9 (also p. 12 *n.*9): trek schuits *is an Anglicized plural. As Dr. H. C. Stek points out to me, the correct Dutch form is* trekschuiten

10 *n.*3: *Morgan wrote to Sir Alexander Dick in Edinburgh, an acquaintance and later a close friend of Boswell's, that Boswell's spirited and agreeable conversation gave him more pleasure than any other he had met with in Holland.* (*Information from Morgan's biographer, Professor Whitefield J. Bell, Jr.*)

20 *n.*5: (*and elsewhere*): *for* Keiserhof *read* Keizershof

39 *n.*3: *The Reverend Robert Brown in a letter to Boswell dated* 11 *September* 1764, *which I overlooked in preparing "Boswell in Holland," reported that Rose was* "to be ordained a priest, Saturday come sennight [22 September] by the Archbishop of Canterbury, having got a curacy of about fifty pounds a year in Kent."

71, l. 18: *for* Roosmalen *read* Roosmale

96 *n.*6: *A memorandum which Boswell wrote on* 13 *or* 14 *December* 1764 *in preparation for his fourth conversation with Rousseau contains a direction to raise the question of concubinage, and then goes on,* "If clear against this, can abstain, can live as Templar in Malta."

100, l. 3 (*and elsewhere*): Captain Reynst *was not Pieter Hendrik Reynst,* 1723–1791, *the naval officer, but his younger brother* Jean Lucas Reynst, 1730–1792, *an officer in the Army* (*Information from Professor Warnock*).

101, l. 24: *insert is after* This

107 *n.*5: *It is probably more to the point that she was a niece of Monsieur de Sommelsdyck, and hence a cousin to Boswell himself.*

120 *n.*1: *Boswell's spelling* Brower *was right after all. Professor Warnock has found in the Utrecht archives a* Herman Brower, *of the English Church, who lived at Count Nassau Beverweerd's. He was probably the "governor" to the young Count of Nassau Ouwerkerke mentioned on p.* 69.

135, l. 12 (*and elsewhere*): *for* Des Essar *read* Des Essarts. *Professor Warnock, who sends this correction, says that his Christian names were* Alexandre Étienne. *His wife's name* (p. 203) *was* Anne Françoise du Moulin.

158 *n.*2: *The record cited by Dr. Breuning was wrong and Boswell was right. The old fencing-master's name was* Frans Sircksen; *he died on* 30 *March* 1766, *his age then being given as* 98. (*Information from Professor Warnock.*)

167 *n.*: *Major Douglas E. Wilson, Chemical Corps, U.S.A., has convinced me that the obscurity is due to excessive condensation, not to Boswell's having lost the thread of his argument. If fully expressed, the passage might run,* "Excuse me, I am in error [in implying that the omission of the definitions will save me anything but mechanical labour.] I should not have more [real] work [if I included them], for I could copy his definitions exactly ... " *Or perhaps Boswell meant that if his scheme had called for definitions, he could have left to the printer the labour of extracting them from Johnson. The phrase which I have translated* "the work of printing" *is actually* " the work of the printer."

169 *n.*9: *Professor Warnock thinks that* "the little Amerongen" *was more probably Madame van Amerongen's first son,* Gerard Arnout, *at this time nearly ten years old.*

177 *n.*5: *Miss Uretta Crighton Stuart suggests that* "I cut up well" *is somehow related to the phrase* "I cut a fine figure," *and has approximately the same meaning. Can*

any one produce trustworthy evidence for or against this? Another distinct possibility is, "I indulge successfully in severe criticism."

180 *n.*7: *Professor Warnock points out, what I should have noticed myself, that in the "Livre de Jeu" Boswell enters his losses and gains under the names of his hostesses, not under those of the persons he lost to or won from. Consequently, though in this case he won from the Countess of Nassau Beverweerd, the entry is properly* "chez Madll. de Zuylen."

184 *n.*1: *Miss Rosalie Colie writes,* "Since Mevrouw Geelvinck signed herself 'Veuve,' there would be no doubt that she was 'H. Veuve Geelvinck' (Hasselaer v. Geelvinck) and none other. The signature is not uncommon in Holland even today. There is usually but one widow who fits a combination of names. So no confusion arises."

207 *n.*: *Professor Warnock finds that* Henri François Limiers (*not* Limier) *was for many years editor and publisher of the "Gazette d'Utrecht." He suffered a serious illness in* 1754 *and died in* 1758, *but Professor Warnock finds no confirmation of my guess that he was a suicide. Perhaps he had* attempted *suicide.*

214 *n.*8: Henry Peterson, *an American from Pennsylvania, was book-keeper of Abraham Renaud, a merchant dealing in woollens and silks, and at about the time of this entry took over half of Renaud's business under his own name. In* 1774 *he married as his second wife* Henrietta Louisa Vernet, *who may have been the very* Mademoiselle "Vernett" *who made Boswell so dreary in the bark between Utrecht and Leyden (see* p. 228). *Peterson later sold his business and went to live in Wakefield, Yorkshire. (Information from Professor Warnock.)*

216 *n.*: *add* Lord Fordwich was related both to Madame de Spaen and to Boswell, his mother being the daughter of Henry de Nassau, Heer van Ouwerkerke, whom William III made Earl of Grantham in the English peerage, and his great-grandmother (the Earl of Grantham's mother) being Frances van Aerssen van Sommelsdyck, daughter of the Cornelius mentioned by Lord Auchinleck on p. 66. Boswell undoubtedly knew of this relationship and had probably discussed it with Madame de Spaen.

226 *n.*: *add the footnote reference number,* 7

232 *n.*9: *for* House in the Woods. *read* House in the Wood.

ibid., *n.*2: *Mrs. Katharine Day Little points out that it is misleading to characterize* Andrew Michael Ramsay *simply as a Roman Catholic when the reference is to his theological writing. He submitted to the Roman obedience, but was an ardent Freemason and wrote in the tradition of deism.*

240 *n.*7: *There certainly was a fine portrait of* Veronica van Sommelsdyck *at* Culross Abbey House, *which at that time belonged to Boswell's great-uncle, the Earl of Dundonald. Culross was originally the property of the Bruces, Earls of Kincardine, and has become so again. After having been owned by the Cochranes, Earls of Dundonald, and by another Cochrane cousin of Boswell's, Sir Robert Preston of Valleyfield, it came into the possession of the father of the present Earl of Elgin and Kincardine by a series of bequests too complicated for detailing in a note of this sort. (Information from the Right Honourable the Countess of Elgin and Kincardine, who has sent me a photograph of the picture, now at Broomhall, Dunfermline, Fife.)*

266 *n.*9: *instead of* Patrick (later Sir Patrick) *read* James *remainder of the note as it stands.* Patrick (later Sir Patrick) *who appears on pp.* 268 *and* 277 *was James's son, assistant, and successor. In* 1764 *he was only nineteen years old (Information from Professor Warnock).*

273, 2d line from bottom of text: *for* Stainer *read* Stammer (Ekard August von Stammer, *Lord Grand Master of the Horse. Information from Professor Warnock.*)

319 *n.* (and elsewhere): *for* Kirkheisen *read* Kircheisen

327, l. 22: *owners of the first printing will substitute* English caprice to marry a foreigner at the point of death. *for* surprised . . . for her? (*This printer's error reported by Mrs. John S. Lamont. It is now corrected in the plates.*)

362, l. 16: *Dr. K. A. Bisset reminds me that in Scots usage a* hurl *is merely a brief occasional ride in any small wheeled vehicle, and does not imply high speed.*

ibid., n.9: *François became the servant of Mr. Wishart (letter of the Reverend Robert Brown, 11 September 1764: see above, the correction for p.* 39)*, and no doubt accompanied him to Scotland in that capacity.*

374 *n.1: Miss Solveig Tunold, the translator into Norwegian of Boswell's "Life of Johnson," adds that not only was the Ghost Hamlet's father, but the Ghost had always been right. Lord Auchinleck had opposed the marriage to Belle de Zuylen from the first.*

402, 1st col., Amerongen, N. (Mossel) van *should be* Amerongen, Catharina Johanna (Mossel) van *and the entry should follow* Amerongen, Anna

404, 2d col., l. 19: *insert* John, St.

407, 2d col., l. 21: *for* 174; *read* 172;

409, 1st col.: *the entry* Boswell, Margaret *should go after* Boswell, Lieut. John

412, 1st col.: *the references to the two Craufurds are jumbled. Only* 268, 277, 358 *are certainly to* Patrick. 50 *n.*8, 266, 270, 278, 358, 362 *are certainly or probably to* James

413, 1st col., l. 15: *insert* of *before* Grandtully,

414, 2d col.: *the entry* Gascoyne *should go after* Galloway

415, 2d col., l. 17: *for* 263 *n.*2, *read* 263 *n.*3,

ibid., l. 35: *for* 264 *n.*3 *read* 263 *n.*2

418, 1st col., between ll. 25 and 26: *add* James, St., 211

ibid., between ll. 33 and 34: *add* John, St., 106

419, 2d col., ll. 14 and 16: *for* Kirkheisen *read* Kircheisen

422, 2d col.: *for* Neutchâtel, Public Library of *read* Neuchâtel, Public Library of

423, 1st col., l. 22: *for* 263 *n.*2 *read* 263 *n.*3

ibid., 2d col., l. 12: *for* 150 *read* 150 *n.*

424, 2d col., l. 29: *for* 244; *read* 243;

ibid., l. 32: *for* 266 *n.*, *read* 366 *n.*,

427, 2d col., l. 15: *delete* 76,

ibid., ll. 17–18, letters to JB: *insert* 76,

428, 1st col., next to last line: *for* 117; *read* 118;

429, 1st col., l. 15: *for* n.2, *read* n.3,

ibid., 2d col., l. 1: *for* 352; *read* 52;

ibid., l. 2: *for* 256 *n.*, *read* 156 *n.*,

ibid., l. 8: *for* 263 *n.*2; *read* 263 *n.*3;

ibid., l. 27: *for* 263 *n.*2, *read* 263 *n.*3,

430 1st col., l. 28: *for* 263 *n.*2 *read* 263 *n.*3

ibid., 2d col., ll. 5 and 6 from the bottom: *for* 263 *n.*2 *read* 263 *n.*3

432, 1st col., l. 13: *for* 264 *n.*3; *read* 263 *n.*2;